PAPERS FROM THE 4th ICEHL

AMSTERDAM STUDIES IN THE THEORY AND HISTORY OF LINGUISTIC SCIENCE

General Editor
E.F. KONRAD KOERNER
(University of Ottawa)

Series IV – CURRENT ISSUES IN LINGUISTIC THEORY

Advisory Editorial Board

Henning Andersen (Copenhagen); Raimo Anttila (Los Angeles)
Thomas V. Gamkrelidze (Tbilisi); Hans-Heinrich Lieb (Berlin)
J. Peter Maher (Chicago); Ernst Pulgram (Ann Arbor, Mich.)
E. Wyn Roberts (Vancouver, B.C.); Danny Steinberg (Tokyo)

Volume 41

Roger Eaton, Olga Fischer, Willem Koopman and
Frederike van der Leek (eds.)

Papers from the
4th International Conference on English Historical Linguistics

PAPERS

from the

4th INTERNATIONAL CONFERENCE

on

ENGLISH HISTORICAL LINGUISTICS

Amsterdam, 10-13 April, 1985

Edited by

ROGER EATON
OLGA FISCHER
WILLEM KOOPMAN
FREDERIKE VAN DER LEEK

JOHN BENJAMINS PUBLISHING COMPANY
AMSTERDAM/PHILADELPHIA

1985

Library of Congress Cataloging in Publication Data

International Conference on English Historical Linguistics (4th: 1985: University of Amsterdam)
Papers from the 4th International Conference on English Historical Linguistics.

(Amsterdam studies in the theory and history of linguistic science. Series IV, Current issues in linguistic theory, ISSN 0304-0763; v. 41)
Includes bibliographies.
1. English language -- History -- Congresses. I. Eaton, Roger. II. Title. III. Series.
PE1075.I57   1985   420'.9   85-22908
ISBN 90-272-3531-7 (alk. paper)

© Copyright 1985 - John Benjamins B.V.
No part of this book may be reproduced in any form, by print, photoprint, microfilm, or any other means, without written permission from the publisher.

CONTENTS

PREFACE ... vii
LIST OF PARTICIPANTS ... xi
PROCEEDINGS OF THE 4th ICEHL ... 1
JEAN AITCHISON & RAMA KANT AGNIHOTRI ... 3
    'I deny that I'm incapable of working all night': Divergence of Negative Structures in British and Indian English
FRANCES O. AUSTIN ... 15
    Relative *Which* in Late 18th-Century Usage: The Clift Family Correspondence
JOAN C. BEAL ... 31
    Lengthening of *a* in Tyneside English
DAVID DENISON ... 45
    The Origins of Periphrastic *Do*: Ellegård and Visser Reconsidered
OSSI IHALAINEN ... 61
    Synchronic Variation and Linguistic Change: Evidence from British English Dialects
ANS VAN KEMENADE ... 73
    Old English Infinitival Complements and West-Germanic V-Raising
SAMUEL JAY KEYSER & WAYNE O'NEIL ... 85
    The Simplification of the Old English Strong Nominal Paradigms
WILLEM F. KOOPMAN ... 109
    Verb and Particle Combinations in Old and Middle English
LINNEA M. LAGERQUIST ... 123
    The Impersonal Verb in Context: Old English
ROGER LASS & SUSAN WRIGHT ... 137
    The South African Chain-Shift: Order out of Chaos?
DONKA MINKOVA ... 163
    Of Rhyme and Reason: Some Foot-Governed Quantity Changes in English

TERTTU NEVALAINEN 179
  Lexical Variation of Early Modern English Exclusive Adverbs: Style Switching or a Change in Progress?
RUTA NAGUCKA 195
  Some Remarks on Complementation in Old English
FRANS PLANK 205
  The Interpretation and Development of Form Alternations Conditioned across Word Boundaries: The Case of *Wife's*, *Wives* and *Wives'*
PATRICIA POUSSA 235
  A Note on the Voicing of Initial Fricatives in Middle English
MATTI RISSANEN 253
  Expression of Exclusiveness in Old English and the Development of the Adverb *Only*
M. L. SAMUELS 269
  The Great Scandinavian Belt
DIETER STEIN 283
  Discourse Markers in Early Modern English
ROBERT P. STOCKWELL 303
  Assessment of Alternative Explanations of the Middle English Phenomenon of High Vowel Lowering when Lengthened in the Open Syllable
THOMAS E. TOON 319
  Preliminaries to the Linguistic Analysis of Old English Glosses and Glossaries
LISA DEMENA TRAVIS 331
  The Role of INFL in Word Order Change

PREFACE

The Fourth International Conference on English Historical Linguistics (ICEHL) was held the week after Easter, from 10th to 13th April 1985 at the University of Amsterdam. Like its bigger sister the ICHL (International Conference on Historical Linguistics), the ICEHL was born in England in the seventies and has been growing ever since. It is held at two-yearly intervals alternately in England and on the continent of Europe. The first conference met in Durham in 1979; the next two were held in Odense (1981) and Sheffield (1983). The present conference was 'blessed' by weather which ensured that delegates' attendance was optimal; it progressed in a highly congenial atmosphere culminating in a festive luncheon cruise through the Amsterdam waterways on a steamed-up canal boat.

The number of participants has grown steadily ever since the first conference, and so has the number of papers offered. This time twice as many abstracts for papers were received as could be accommodated, even with the institution of parallel sessions. A quite rigorous selection, therefore, was necessary. This was not an easy task — and it was hard on some delegates — but we think it contributed to the high quality of the conference. For this, we also owe a debt of gratitude to the invited speakers: Jean Aitchison, William Labov, Frans Plank, M. L. Samuels and Thomas Toon. Here we also would like to include Roger Lass, who managed to come in spite of some considerable hurdles put in his way. These scholars also agreed to contribute to a workshop on 'Language Change and Explanation', which took place a few days before the conference. Not surprisingly perhaps, this topic became a point of focus for the conference itself; many of the papers included in this volume are concerned with finding an explanation for a given change, as well as providing an adequate description for it.

Not all the papers given at the conference are included in this volume, in part because of editorial selection. The papers published here are given in alphabetical order (the papers by Minkova and Nevalainen were not presented at the conference). Most studies — and this is only to be expected in connection with a conference on English Historical Linguistics — deal with some aspect of an earlier stage of (British) English, though present day varieties of English are also under investigation. The work of Labov and others has shown that the study of ongoing change can provide new insights into the nature of change. In this connection, Aitchison and Agnihotri's paper studies the difference in the development of negative constructions in Indian and British England; Beal is interested in a phonetic aspect of present-day Tyneside; Ihalainen deals with syntactic variation in present-day English dialects. Lass and Wright discuss certain phonological differences between South African and other types of English and provide a historical explanation for the South African development.

Many papers in this volume show that there is a growing interest in the question *why* a certain change has taken place, this especially in the field of phonology and morphology, where so much descriptive work has already been done by Luick, Jordan, Dobson and others, although Toon's paper on Old English glosses shows that not all data sources have been exhaustively studied. Minkova, Poussa and Stockwell each offer a new explanation for otherwise well-documented changes in the phonology of Middle English; Keyser and O'Neill propose a reinterpretation of the Old English strong noun system as a single class, and Plank offers a historical explanation for the fact that no voice alternation takes place in genitives.

Historical syntax has attracted less attention in the past than phonology and morphology, but this situation has changed considerably, partly as a consequence of the publication of Visser's monumental work and partly because of new insights developed in modern generative grammar. This explains the relatively large number of papers on syntax in this volume. Van Kemenade, Koopman and Travis all deal with questions related to word order change; Denison offers a new explanation for the origin of periphrastic *do*; Austin looks at variation in the early Modern English relative pronoun system, and Nagucka's paper is on verbal complementation in Old English.

Two papers on syntactic and morphological variation, Lagerquist and Stein, can be grouped together in that both explain variable forms in terms of a difference in discourse function. Finally, there is a paper by M.L. Samuels on the influence of the Scandinavian settlers on northern English dialects, and two papers on lexical variation, by Nevalainen and Rissanen, both dealing with the system of exclusive adverbs in various phases of the English language.

The organizers would like to express their gratitude to the students of the English Department at the University of Amsterdam for their freely given, enthusiastic help. They made sure there was enough coffee when and where it was needed; they took care of the nitty-gritty of the registration; they acted as living signposts in our labyrinthine university buildings and brightened up dull rooms with spring flowers. Without them the organizers would not have been able to listen to the conference papers themselves. We would also like to thank the technical and administrative staff of the English Department, especially Margaret Oomen and Ity Siesling for their assistance in typing up the abstracts and a number of these papers, and for doing all the correction work involved. Further, we must not forget to thank the contributors to this volume, who supplied the editors with camera-ready copies of their own papers. Thanks to them and to the publishers, Claire and John Benjamins, we have managed to bring out this volume within less than a year after the conference. Finally, we are grateful to the Ministry of Education and Science and the City of Amsterdam for a generous welcome reception given at the Amsterdam Historical Museum; to Cambridge University Press for a subsidy towards the conference (which the Organization received for providing time and space for a workshop on the new *History of the English Language*, to be published by C.U.P.) and to the Faculty of Arts of Amsterdam University for their financial help towards the organization of the conference and the publication of these papers.

Roger Eaton
Olga Fischer
Willem Koopman
Frederike van der Leek

Organizers of the
Fourth International Conference
on English Historical Linguistics

LIST OF PARTICIPANTS

A. Adamska-Salaciak
Institute of English
Adam Mickiewicz Univ.
Poznan
Poland

Sylvia Adamson
Faculty of English
9 West Road
Cambridge
England

H. Aertsen
Vrije Universiteit
Subfac. Engelse Taal- en
Letterkunde
Postbus 7161
1007 MC Amsterdam
The Netherlands

Karin Aijmer
English Department
Lund University
Helgonabacken 14
Lund
Sweden

Dr. J. Aitchison
Dept. of Lang. Studies
London School of Econ.
Houghton Street
Aldwych
London WC2A 2AE
England

Carine Alders
Univ. van Amsterdam
Spuistraat 210
1012 VT Amsterdam
The Netherlands

John Algeo
Dept. of English
University of Georgia
Athens, GA 30602
USA

John Anderson
Dept. of English Lang.
University of Edinburgh
David Hume Tower/
George Sq.
Edinburgh, EH8 9JX
Scotland

Dr. Frances Austin
Dept. of Engl. Lang. & Lit.
The University
P.O. Box 147
Liverpool L69 3BX
England

Doc.Dr.Hab. W. Awedyk
Institute of English
Ul.Marchlewskiego 124/126
61-874 Poznan
Poland

Prof. Ermanno Barisone
Università Di Genova
2, Piazza S. Sabina
16124 Genova
Italy

The Univ. of New Castle
Upon Tyne
School of Eng. Lang. & Lit.
The University
New Castle Upon
Tyne NE1 7RU
England

Prof. Michael Benskin
Britisk Institutt
Universitet 1 Oslo
P.O. Boks 1003 Blindern
0315 Oslo 3
Norway

Prof. N.F. Blake
Dept. of English Lang.
University of Sheffield
Sheffield S10 2TN
England

Priv. Doz. Dr. Hans Ulrich
Boas
Seminar für Engl. Phil.
Humboldtallee 13
D - 3400 Göttingen
West-Germany

LIST OF PARTICIPANTS

Peter Boonman
Univ. van Amsterdam
Spuistraat 210
1012 VT Amsterdam
The Netherlands

Alain Bossuyt
Kralenbeek 1772
1104 KJ Amsterdam
The Netherlands

Rob Brands
Univ. van Amsterdam
Spuistraat 210
1012 VT Amsterdam
The Netherlands

Rolf Bremmer
Erasmusplein 1
6500 HD Nijmegen
The Netherlands

Benno Bruggink
Univ. van Amsterdam
Spuistraat 210
1012 VT Amsterdam
The Netherlands

Ans Bulles
Blankenstraat 177 II
1018 RZ Amsterdam
The Netherlands

G.H.V. Bunt
Anglistisch Instituut
Grote Kruisstraat 2 I
9712 TS Groningen
The Netherlands

Dr. R.W. Burchfield
14, The Green
Sutton Courtenay
Oxfordshire OX14 4AE
England

Dr. Juliette De Caluwé-Dor
27/3 Rue Louis Fraigneux
B-4000-Liege
Belgium

Ms Penny Carter
Cambridge Univ. Press
The Edinburgh Building
Shaftesbury Road
Cambridge CB2 2RU
England

Mr. Philip Champ
22, Storey Avenue
Westfield Village
Lancaster LA1 5PA
England

Cecily Clark
13, Church Street
Chesterton
Cambridge CB4 ID7
England

Fran Colman
Dept. of English Lang.
University of Edinburgh
David Hume Tower/
George Sq.
Edinburgh, EH8 9JX
Scotland

Dr. M.A. Cooper
13, Leopold Street
Oxford OX4 1PS
England

Esther Daams
Univ. van Amsterdam
Spuistraat 210
1012 VT Amsterdam
The Netherlands

Mike Davenport
Engelsk Institut
Odense Universitet
Campusvej 55
5230 Odense M
Denmark

Dr. David Denison
Dept. of Engl. Lang. & Lit.
University of Manchester
Manchester M13 6PL
England

Prof. Dr. F.N.M. Diekstra
Inst. Engels-Amerikaans
Erasmusplein 1
6500 HD Nijmegen
The Netherlands

Ailie Donald
3 Gayfield Place
Edinburgh
England

Patricia Donegan
Dept. of English
Ohio State University
164 West 17th Avenue
Columbus, OH 43210-1370
USA

P.D. Dr. Dürmüller
English Seminar
University of Bern
CH-3012 Bern
Switzerland

R.D. Eaton
Univ. van Amsterdam
Spuistraat 210
1012 VT Amsterdam
The Netherlands

LIST OF PARTICIPANTS

Dr. C.J. Ewen
Vakgroep Engels
Rijks Universiteit Leiden
Postbus 9515
2300 RA Leiden
The Netherlands

Drs. O. Fischer
Univ. van Amsterdam
Spuistraat 210
1012 VT Amsterdam
The Netherlands

Prof. Dr. Jacek Fisiak
Institute of English
Ul.Marchlewskiego 124/126
61-874 Poznan
Poland

Prof. Thomas Frank
Piazza S. Dominico
Maggiore 9
80134 Napels
Italy

Prof. Dr. Udo Fries
Schüracherstr. 24
CH 8700 Küsnacht
Switzerland

Drs. Marinel Gerritsen
P.J. Meertens Instituut
Keizergracht 569-571
1017 DR Amsterdam
The Netherlands

Prof. Dr. J. Gerritsen
Troelstralaan 97
9722 JH Groningen
The Netherlands

Manfred Görlach
Universität zu Köln
Englisches Seminar
Albertus-Magnus-Platz
D-5000 Cologne 1
West Germany

Anita Graafland
Univ. van Amsterdam
Spuistraat 210
1012 VT Amsterdam
The Netherlands

Pieta Gijsen
Univ. van Amsterdam
Spuistraat 210
1012 VT Amsterdam
The Netherlands

Jan de Haan
Univ. van Amsterdam
Spuistraat 210
1012 VT Amsterdam
The Netherlands

Lecturer Erik Hansen
Dept. of English
Odense Universitet
Campusvej 55
5230 Odense M
Denmark

Prof. John Hewson
Dept. of Linguistics
Memorial University
St. John's
Newfoundland
Canada - A1B 3X9

Risto Hiltunen
Department of English
Turku University
Finland

Prof. Dr. R.M. Hogg
English Department
University of Manchester
Manchester M13 9PL
England

Prof. Ossi Ihalainen
Porthania 312
Dept. of English
University of Helsinki
Helsinki 10
Finland

A.R. James
Univ. van Amsterdam
Spuistraat 210
1012 VT Amsterdam
The Netherlands

Th. Johnson
Institute of English
Adam Mickiewicz Univ.
Poznan
Poland

Paul Jongsma
Univ. van Amsterdam
Spuistraat 210
1012 VT Amsterdam
The Netherlands

Ms. Leena Kahlas-Tarkka
Niemenmäentie 3K 81
SF-00350 Helsinki
Finland

Prof.Dr. Dieter Kastovsky
English Department
University of Vienna
Universitätstr. 7
1010 Vienna
Austria

LIST OF PARTICIPANTS

Ans van Kemenade
Dept. of English R.U.U.
Oudenoord 6
3513 ER Utrecht
The Netherlands

Samuel Keyser
Dept. of Ling. & Philos.
Room 20D-210 MIT
Cambridge MA 02139
USA

Matti Kilpiö
Aurorankatu 15 D 50
00100 Helsinki 10
Finland

Mr. John M. Kirk
Dept. of English
The Queen's University
of Belfast
Belfast BT7 1NN
Northern Ireland

Dr. Veronika Kniezsa
Budapest
Nemetvölgyi üt 53/c
Budapest 1124
Hungary

Dr. W.F. Koopman
Univ. van Amsterdam
Spuistraat 210
1012 VT Amsterdam
The Netherlands

Dr. Gillis Kristensson
Rönnbärsgränden 23
22356 Lund
Sweden

Ella Kruzinga
Univ. van Amsterdam
Spuistraat 210
1012 VT Amsterdam
The Netherlands

Ms Merja Kytö
Liisankatu 11 A 10
00170 Helsinki 17
Finland

Prof. Dr. W. Labov
University of Pennsylvania
Linguistics Laboratory
3732 Locust Walk/CW
Philadelphia PA 19104
USA

Linnea M. Lagerquist
63, Wroslyn Road
Freeland,
Oxford OX7 2HL
England

Roger Lass
Dept. of General Ling.
University of Cape Town
Rondebosch 7700
South-Africa

Drs. F. van der Leek
Univ. van Amsterdam
Spuistraat 210
1012 VT Amsterdam
The Netherlands

Bettelou Los
Univ. van Amsterdam
Spuistraat 210
1012 VT Amsterdam
The Netherlands

Dr. Angelika Lutz
Institut für Englische Phil.
Universität München
Schellingstrasse 3
8000 München
West Germany

Dr. A. A. MacDonald
Inst. Engels-Amerikaans
Katholieke Universiteit
Erasmusplein 1
6500 HD Nijmegen
The Netherlands

Mr. L.H. Malmberg
Dept. of English Language
& Medieval Literature
Durham University
Elvet Riverside
New Elvet
Durham DH1 3JT
England

Ms H. Mausch
Institute of English
Ul.Marchlewskiego 124/126
61-874 Poznan
Poland

Prof. Dr. Hans H. Meier
Randwycklaan 22
1181 BM Amstelveen
The Netherlands

Dr. Gunnel Melchers
Klyftvägen 7
S - 16135 Bromma
Sweden

LIST OF PARTICIPANTS

Prof. Paule Mertens-Fonck
37, Bd. Frère-Orban
B - 4000 Liege
Belgium

Dott. Mara Messina
Via Filippo Raga 29
80132 Napoli
Italy

Anneli Meurman-Solin
English Department
University of Helsinki
Hallituskatu 11-13
00100 Helsinki 10
Finland

D. Minkova
UCLA
Dept. of English
Los Angeles - CA 90024
USA

Alexandra Muskita
Univ. van Amsterdam
Spuistraat 210
1012 VT Amsterdam
The Netherlands

Prof. Ruta Nagucka
Inst. of English Philology
The Jagiellonian Univ.
Mickiewicza 9/11
30-120 Kraków
Poland

Ms Terttu Nevalainen
Kustaankatu 9 A 24
00500 Helsinki 50
Finland

Prof. Saara Nevanlinna
Merikatu 5 A 12
00140 Helsinki 14
Finland

Dr. Hans F. Nielsen
Engelsk Institut
Odense Universitet
Campusvej 55
5230 Odense M
Denmark

Dr. P. Nieuwint
Bronckhorststr. 25 II
1071 WN Amsterdam
The Netherlands

Ms Aune Österman
Hattel Malantie 8-10 C12
00710 Helsinki 71
Finland

Prof. Wayne O'Neil
Dept. of Ling. & Philos.
Room 20D-210 MIT
Cambridge MA 02139
USA

Prof. N.E. Osselton
Dept. of English Language
University of Newcastle
Newcastle upon
Tyne NE1 7RU
England

Monique Persijn
Univ. van Amsterdam
Spuistraat 210
1012 VT Amsterdam
The Netherlands

Prof. Dr. F. Plank
Sprachwissenschaft
Universität Konstanz
Postfach 5560
D-7750 Konstanz
West Germany

Patricia Poussa
University of Helsinki
Dept. of English Philology
Hallituskatu 11-13
00100 Helsinki 10
Finland

Prof. Matti Rissanen
Dept. of English
University of Helsinki
Hallituskatu 11-13
00100 Helsinki
Finland

Ian G. Roberts
Dept. of Linguistics
Unvi. of Southern Calif.
University Park
Los Angeles/
California 90089-1693
USA

Anita van Roy
Univ. van Amsterdam
Spuistraat 210
1012 VT Amsterdam
The Netherlands

Mvr. Drs. A.E. Rutten
Telefoonstraat 5
5038 DL Tilburg
The Netherlands

LIST OF PARTICIPANTS

De heer R. Ruyten
Graaf Engelbrechtstraat 51
4756 AP Kruisland (N.B.)
The Netherlands

Prof. Dr. M.L. Samuels
Dept. of English Language
The University
Glasgow Q12 8QQ
Scotland

Ms R.D. Smith
Vakgroep Engels
Rijks Universiteit Leiden
P.N. van Eijckhof 4
2300 RA Leiden
The Netherlands

Else Smits
Univ. van Amsterdam
Spuistraat 210
1012 VT Amsterdam
The Netherlands

Prof. Knud Sòrensen
Råhój Allé 12
8270 Hójbjerg
Denmark

David Stampe
Dept. of English
Ohio State University
164 West 17th Avenue
Columbus, OH 43210-1370
USA

Dr. Detlef Stark
Englisches Seminar
Universität Hannover
Im Moore 21
3000 Hannover 1
West Germany

Prof. Dr. Dieter Stein
Justus-Liebig-Universität
Giessen
Inst. für Anglistik und
Amerikanistik
Otto-Behaghel-Strasse 10
D-6300 Giessen
West Germany

Dr. Patrick V. Stiles
Grayre Institute
2, Bucclench Place
University of Edinburgh
Edinburgh EH8 9LW
England

Prof. Robert P. Stockwell
Dept. of Linguistics
UCLA
Los Angeles CA 90024
USA

Ms Menekse Suphi
28, Cameron Park
Edinburgh
Scotland

Berni Tebrunsvelt
Univ. van Amsterdam
Spuistraat 210
1012 VT Amsterdam
The Netherlands

Dr. Linda L. Thornburg
Dept. of Linguistics
California State University
Fresno
Frenso. CA 93740-0001
USA

I. Tieken-Boon van Ostade
Vakgroep Engels
P.N. van Eijckhof 4
2300 RA Leiden
The Netherlands

Prof.Dr. T.E. Toon
Dept. of English
The Univ. of Michigan
7607 Haven Hall
Ann Arbor
Michigan - 48109
USA

Renate Traas
Univ. van Amsterdam
Spuistraat 210
1012 VT Amsterdam
The Netherlands

Prof. Lisa Travis
Dept. of Linguistics
McGill University
1001 Sherbrooke West
Montreal Quebec H3A 1G5
Canada

Theo Vennemann
Inst. für Deutsche Phil.
Universität Muenchen
West-Germany

Drs. P. Verdonk
Univ. van Amsterdam
Spuistraat 210
1012 VT Amsterdam
The Netherlands

Pieter Vermeulen
Univ. van Amsterdam
Spuistraat 210
1012 VT Amsterdam
The Netherlands

Ms Katie Wales
English Department
Royal Holloway College
University of London
Egham Hill
Egham, Surrey
England

LIST OF PARTICIPANTS

Annemieke Witsel
Univ. van Amsterdam
Spuistraat 210
1012 VT Amsterdam
The Netherlands

Ms Susan Wright
Trinity Hall
Cambridge CB3 0DQ
England

W. van der Wurff
Univ. van Amsterdam
Spuistraat 210
1012 VT Amsterdam
The Netherlands

PROCEEDINGS OF THE 4th ICEHL

'I DENY THAT I'M INCAPABLE OF NOT WORKING ALL NIGHT': DIVERGENCE OF NEGATIVE STRUCTURES IN BRITISH AND INDIAN ENGLISH

JEAN AITCHISON
London School of Economics
and
RAMA KANT AGNIHOTRI
University of Delhi

1.0. *Introduction*. Syntactic change occurs more slowly than phonological change. It is therefore harder to study, and we know considerably less about it. In recent years, however, we have begun to understand some of the mechanisms involved. One insight is the realization that syntactic change normally involves a period of time in which two or more functionally similar structures coexist. The change comes about when one (or more) of the possibilities drops out of use (e.g. Fischer & van der Leek, 1981, 1983). In view of this insight, it seems likely that changes in progress could be identified by considering cases in which a language has several possible means of expressing a particular concept, and attempting to find out how these options are ranked. A useful way of dealing with this might be to make a contrastive study of different varieties of a language which appear to be developing independently. This would shed light not only on tendencies inherent in the language under study, but also on syntactic change in general. This paper therefore analyses one area of syntax in British and Indian English. In both varieties, the overall rules are similar, since the same range of structures is acceptable to both groups. However, within the possible options, the preferred structures show interesting divergences.

1.1. *British and Indian English*. There are a number of ways in which Indian English differs from British English, and these have received a considerable amount of attention (for recent work see Kachru, 1983; Sahgal, 1983). In fact, the syntactic divergences are not very numerous (Sahgal and Agnihotri, 1985). Yet in spite of this, Indian English syntax often appears odd to British speakers. These oddnesses could perhaps be summarized by the statement: 'It's probably all right, but I wouldn't say it like that myself'. This suggests that we are dealing with similar syntactic rules, but dissimilar preferences when it comes to choosing between the possible options in cases where more than one construction is permitted. It is of course important to distinguish between failure of acquisition (since for many Indians English is a second language in which they are never entirely at home) and genuine differences between the two varieties. Genuine differences can be identified in cases where a usage has become conventionalized among fluent speakers.

In a preliminary attempt to identify some of these differences, the first author noted down cases in which she judged Indian English to use an odd or stylistically clumsy way of expressing things, by British standards. These were particularly easy to identify in Indian newspapers. After several months of randomly noting down 'odd' structures, without any attempt to analyse them, it gradually became clear that a number of these odd structures were negatives, especially negatives in subordinate clauses. For example:
(a) 'But it is not unimaginable that the UCIL's MIC process would not have undergone the scrutiny (of whatever kind that exists) because ... UCIL ... sets standards for India'. (*The Hindu*, 8/1/85).
(b) 'Three all-India ski champions ... told this reporter that even Kashmir had not had enough snow for skiing'. (*The Statesman*, 20/2/84).
(c) 'Evidence that it is not so has come recently'. (*The Statesman*, 20/2/84).

A spot-check with several British informants suggested that they would preferentially have rephrased the sentences in a way which altered the negation. For example:
(a') 'But it seems possible that UCIL's MIC process would have failed to undergo the scrutiny (of whatever kind exists) because ... UCIL ... sets standards for India'.
(b') 'Three all-India ski champions informed this reporter that even Kashmir lacked sufficient snow for skiing'.
(c') 'Evidence demonstrating the falsity of this viewpoint has recently come to light'.

A pilot experiment was therefore carried out, which investigated these and similar structures. The results suggested that there might be interesting differences between negative preferences in British and Indian English, particularly in subordinate clauses. We therefore devised a fuller experiment comparing negative usage in subordinate clauses in British and Indian English. The aim of the experiment was firstly, to explore the extent to which British and Indian English differed in this area, secondly, to attempt to account for the differences.

2.0. *Negation in English.* Following Klima (1964), negation in English can be classified into three major types:
    (a) *Explicit negation*, in which an overt negative element is typically placed after the first verbal element: *Petronella was not happy.*
    (b) *Morphological negation*, in which the negative element is a prefix attached to a following stem: *Petronella was unhappy.*
    (c) *Implicit negation*, in which the negative element is no longer overt, but is integrated into another word: *Petronella denied the story.*

Fodor, Fodor and Garret (1975) have discussed a fourth possible category, which they name 'pure definitional negatives'. These are words such as *kill*, *bachelor*, or *sad*, which are not in themselves negative, but whose definition seems to require a negative as in 'cause become not alive' for *kill*, 'not married' for *bachelor*, and 'not happy' for *sad*. In fact, it is often extremely difficult to distinguish between implicit negatives and pure definitional negatives (e.g. how should one classify words such as *refuse*, *reject*, *lie*?) and for the purpose of this paper, the two have been conflated.

The negative types outlined above can also occur in subordinate clauses:
    (a) *I think that Martin isn't likely to arrive.*
    (b) *I think that Martin is unlikely to arrive.*
    (c) *I think that Martin will probably stay away.*
The main complication, as far as subordinate clauses are concerned, is that with certain main clause verbs the negative can be moved up into the higher clause, a process that is usually referred to as negative raising. For example:
    (d) *I don't think that Martin is likely to arrive.*
There has been some discussion in the literature as to which clause 'really' contains the negative (Stockwell, Schachter, and Partee, 1973: 253 ff., Horn, 1978) though most people take the view that the negative in a sentence such as (d) should be regarded as belonging to the VP in the subordinate clause.

From the point of view of negative function, it is clear that negatives usually negate expectations or beliefs which people hold (Wason, 1965). This paper, however, is concerned entirely with negative structure, which can be manipulated without reference to function, provided that the negated sentences are plausible.

3.0. *Eliciting negatives*. The experiment described below was an attempt to elicit negative structures in subordinate clauses from British and Indian speakers of English, and to obtain a ranking of the various structures elicited.

3.1. *Subjects*. The British subjects were 50 linguistically naive first year students from an English University who claimed that English was their first language. The Indian students were from colleges attached to the University of Delhi, most of whom spoke Hindi as a first language. Originally, 250 Indian students were involved, but for the purpose of the analysis the 50 whose English seemed most acceptable to both of the authors of this paper were selected for comparison with the English group, as we wanted fluent speakers rather than imperfect learners.

3.2. *Procedure*. Each student was given a questionnaire entitled 'Negatives - opposites' which contained the following instructions:
> This questionnaire deals with 12 sentences, each of which has two parts. The second part is written in capital letters. We would like you to rewrite each sentence in as many ways as you can so that the second part means the opposite of what it originally did. There are no right or wrong answers, and sometimes there are a number of possibilities. You should be able to think up several versions for each sentence. When you have done this, please rank your answers in order of preference. That is, please put (1) against the answer which sounds most natural to you and (2) by the one that is the next best, and so on. If two different versions sound equally good, please assign them the same rank. For example, consider the sentence below:
> John said that MARY HAD RECOVERED FROM HER ILLNESS.
> In order to make the part in capital letters mean the opposite, here are some of the ways in which you could rewrite the sentence:
> A. John said that Mary hadn't recovered from her illness.
> B. John said that Mary wasn't better yet.
> C. John said that Mary was still ill.
> D. John said that Mary was still unwell.
> E. John denied that Mary had recovered.
> If you think B is the most natural, put (1) against B. If A is the second best, put (2) against A, and so on. If, on the other hand, you think all five sound equally good, then put (1) against A, B, C, D, and E.

The twelve sentences, which contained three subordinate clause types (8 *that* or deleted *that* complement clauses, 2

wh-clauses, 2 *if*-clauses), were as follows:
  (1) We decided that PAM WAS TELLING THE TRUTH.
  (2) I think I'M CAPABLE OF WORKING ALL NIGHT.
  (3) She sang WHEN EVERYBODY WAS AWAKE.
  (4) I heard that THE MOUNTAINEERS REACHED THE SUMMIT.
  (5) Paul will be upset if MARY COMES TO THE PARTY.
  (6) We realized that ALEX MUST HAVE BEEN ASLEEP AT THE TIME.
  (7) I wonder why JOHN CAME.
  (8) Anne said that YOU SOLVED THE PROBLEM.
  (9) I would be surprised if BILL TURNED UP.
  (10) I am sure that THINGS WILL IMPROVE.
  (11) We think DAVID IS JOKING.
  (12) Stan decided that IT WAS POSSIBLE TO CATCH THE MORNING TRAIN.

3.3. *Data and analysis*. Our aim in this analysis was to find out first, if British and Indian English speakers used similar strategies for negating or making opposite the above sentences. We were interested both in possible strategies and in preferred strategies. Second, we wanted to discover whether British and Indian English speakers were consistent in their strategies (both possible and preferred) across different subordinate clause types.

We therefore classified each answer, for each student in accordance with the type of negation utilized: explicit within the subordinate clause, morphological, implicit, raised, or 'other' (i.e. responses which did not fit into any of the above categories). For example, the following were typical responses to sentence (2) *I think I'M CAPABLE OF WORKING ALL NIGHT*.
  (i) *I think I'm not capable of working all night* (explicit).
  (ii) *I think I'm incapable of working all night* (morphological).
  (iii) *I don't think I'm capable of working all night* (raising).
  (iv) *I think working all night is beyond my capability* (implicit).
  (v) *No way could I work all night* (other).
(The sentence quoted in the title of the paper, from an Indian subject, was the only case in which all negative types were included in a single response).
We then classified in the same way those sentences which were ranked '1' by the respondents, i.e. were their preferred choices.

3.4. *Results*. The total number of responses for the British subjects, was 2233, and for the Indians 2208. For both groups this is an average of just under four (3.7) responses per sentence. The responses are thus directly comparable, with no allowances needing to be made for differing number of responses. (Owing to shortage of space, the tables showing the overall distribution of responses among negative types, and the preferred responses, have not been included in this paper.)

3.4.1. *Explicit negation in subordinate clauses*.
Since many of the sentences in Indian newspapers that had seemed 'odd' to British speakers contained explicit negatives in subordinate clauses, the percentage of explicit negation in subordinate clauses was examined, and compared with other types of negation. If all twelve sentences are treated together, the results are remarkably uniform, as shown from Table 1:

TABLE I	OVERALL		FIRST CHOICES	
	BRIT	IND	BRIT	IND
EXPLICIT	47%	51%	50%	52%
REMAINDER	53%	49%	50%	48%

In brief, Table 1 suggests that there is virtually no difference between British and Indian English, whether one is dealing with overall responses, or preferred options, since the percentage of explicit negation comes out as approximately 50% everywhere. However, if one separates out the subordinate clauses which involve *that* (or deleted *that*) and compare them with the others (*wh* and *if* clauses), then there is an interesting difference between the two groups. This is shown on Table 2:

TABLE 2	OVERALL		FIRST CHOICES	
	BRIT	IND	BRIT	IND
EXPLICIT + THAT	51%	54%	41%	51%
EXPLICIT - THAT	53%	50%	67%	54%

The difference does not show up on overall responses, which are roughly similar, but on preferences. Here the Indian preferences are similar to their overall responses. For the British subjects, however, there was a considerable discrepancy between the overall responses and the first choices. When preferred options were considered, it turns out that the English appear to disfavour explicit negatives in *that* complement clauses, but favour them in other types of clauses. Indians, however, had no preference either way.

3.5. *Implicational scaling*.

In order to probe the question of preferred structures more deeply, the technique of implicational scaling was used. This enabled us to examine firstly, which individual items were most favoured for explicit negation, secondly, to what extent explicit negation in some items subsumed explicit negation in others.

The implicational tables (which have been omitted due to lack of space) showed those items for which each subject marked explicit negation as a first choice at least once (since the questionnaire allowed for multiple first choices) versus those for which no explicit negation occurred as a first choice. Scalability (i.e. the extent to which the actual data fitted an ideal implicational scale) was 83% for Indians, and 96% for the British. Guttman (1944) who developed the scale suggests that 85% or better can serve as efficient approximations to perfect scales. So the scalability obtained here was high, indicating that the scales are reliable and useful, particularly in relation to the British subjects, whose behaviour is shown to be stable and polarized. In brief, the tables showed that negative strategies were by no means random. Certain items were strongly favoured for explicit negation, others strongly disfavoured. Moreover, there were interesting implicational relationships in that for each subject, the presence or absence of an explicit negative in one item was likely to be a good predictor of its presence or absence in other items

Table 3 (which has been extracted from the implicational tables) shows those items for which explicit negation was favoured (on the left) versus those in which it was disfavoured (on the right). The percentage of subjects who marked explicit negation as a first choice for each item is listed underneath. For example, we noted that 100% of British subjects preferred explicit negation for item (7). These percentages show the more extreme behaviour of the British subjects, in that, compared with the Indians, a higher percentage favoured explicit negation in the items on the left, but disfavoured it in the items on the right.

TABLE 3	1	2	3	4	5	6	7	8	9	10	11	12
BRITISH	7	5	8	9	4	12	10	1	6	11	2	3
% TOTAL	100	94	94	78	74	58	48	36	28	22	10	0
INDIANS	7	8	4	9	5	10	6	11	2	12	1	3
% TOTAL	82	80	80	73	70	68	62	54	54	44	44	20

The implicational scales showed some striking parallels. For example, both Indian and British subjects considered item (7) *I wonder why Paul came* as the best candidate for explicit negation, and both consider item (3) *She sang when everybody was awake* as least suitable. However, there were also some interesting divergences. Among the British subjects, items (2), (3), (6) and (11) are strongly disfavoured for explicit negation, in that relatively few subjects put an explicit negative as a first choice. We therefore examined the behaviour of each group in relation to these items in some detail. Table 4 shows the percentages of different types of negation used (excluding the category 'Other'):

TABLE 4	EXPLICIT		MORPHOL		IMPLICIT		RAISED	
	B	I	B	I	B	I	B	I
(3)	0	14	14	14	78	63	6	7
(2)	10	49	10	28	0	0	72	23
(11)	18	47	0	0	47	33	35	20
(6)	25	46	4	0	67	46	5	9

As already noted, there was a high degree of agreement over item (3), where both British and Indian speakers preferred an implicit negative, with morphological negation coming in as a second choice. However, the picture changes when we examine items (2), (11), and (6). Items (2) and (11) have the verb *think* in the main clause. For these sentences, Indians often negated the subordinate clause explicitly, as in: *I think I'm not capable of working all night. We think David is not joking.* The British had raising as the preferred strategy for item (2): *I don't think I'm capable of working all night.* But raising and implicit negation were equally favoured for item (11): *We don't think David is joking* was as likely as *We think David is serious*.

In the case of item (6), the favoured British pattern was a lexical opposite: *We realized that Alex must have been awake at the time*. The Indians, however, favoured a lexical opposite the same percentage of time as they favoured explicit negation, as in *We realized that Alex must not have been asleep at the time*.

The interaction between different negative possibilities provided preliminary evidence for preferred strategies. We note that in (2), raising (72%) was strongly favoured by the British subjects over both morphological (10%) and explicit negation (10%) (there being no obvious implicit negative), whereas the Indians preferred explicit (49%) negation, followed by morphological negation (28%), with raising the least favoured strategy (23%). In (11) the British favoured implicit negation (47%) over raising (35%), and raising over explicit negation (18%) (there being no obvious morphological negative), whereas the Indians had the order explicit negation (47%), then implicit negation (33%), then raising. In (6),

where the main choice was between explicit and implicit
negation, the British preferred implicit (67%) over explicit
(25%), whereas the Indians were equally balanced over implicit and explicit (both 46%), even though they were likely to
know the obvious lexical opposite *asleep* > *awake*. We may
therefore propose a tentative ordering of strategies as
follows:

BRITISH	INDIAN
Implicit	Explicit
Raising	Implicit
Explicit	Morphological
Morphological	Raising

The British predisposition towards raising is shown
additionally by the reaction to sentence (9), where raising
scored a total of 24% as a first choice, even though it was
an inappropriate strategy for the item in question: *I would
be surprised if Bill turned up*. The raised negative/opposite
I wouldn't be surprised if Bill turned up does not mean the
same as the 'real' negative/opposite *I would be surprised if
Bill didn't turn up*. The obvious conclusion is that raising
simply 'sounded better'. (By comparison, 16% Indians
preferred raising in this sentence).

The Indian predilection for morphological negation is
further shown by item (12), where morphological negation
(possible) > impossible) was chosen (54%) in preference to
explicit negation (37%), whereas the British subjects
preferred explicit negation (53%) to morphological (45%).

4.0. *Discussion*. The results (which due to lack of
space we have only been able to report partially) suggest
that our hypothesis stands, that the negative structures
found in subordinate clauses in British and Indian English
are the same, but differ with regard to the frequency with
which they are used. Explicit, morphological, implicit
negation and raising are all found, but in different
proportions. Where these negative types interact, and
choices are possible, the British prefer implicit negation,
then raising. Explicit and morphological negation are used
mainly when the preferred alternatives are unavailable.
Indians, on the other hand, prefer explicit negation. Since
Indian English is based on British English, how did the
discrepancy arise?

It seems likely that there are a number of tendencies
working independently in British and Indian English, and that
these are gradually drawing the varieties further apart.
These are :

(a) *Leftward movement predisposition*. There is a tendency in British English to favour leftward movement of negative elements. This is seen not only in raising (which occurs with verbs of belief and opinion, volition, perception, probability, and judgment, Horn, 1978), but also in negative incorporation in main clauses. For example, *None of these pens work* is preferable to *All of these pens don't work* in British English, though the latter construction is frequently heard in Indian English. The motivation behind constructions of this type is controversial. Horn (1978), for example, argues for a pragmatic explanation for raising, suggesting among other factors, that raised negatives are weaker and so politer than negatives *in situ*. A psycholinguistic explanation might also be possible. Since explicit negatives are relatively difficult to comprehend (Clark & Chase, 1972; Fodor, Fodor & Garrett, 1975), it might be advantageous to signal the negative force as early as possible. But whatever the reason, this predilection for leftward-moving negatives is not shared by Indians.

(b) *Lexicalization tendency*. There is a tendency in British English to utilize implicit negatives (lexicalized opposites) whenever possible. McCawley (1978) has noted that if a lexical item exists in place of a periphrastic expression e.g. *pink* for 'pale red') the lexicalized expression is normally used, unless one wants to designate a non-central instance of the category. An additional factor may be that implicit negatives are easier to comprehend than explicit ones (Fodor, Fodor & Garrett, 1975), and so tend to be favoured. Furthermore, Indians may not be as aware as British speakers of the lexical resources of the language.

(c) *Interference from Hindi*. Negation in Hindi (the language of the majority of the Indian subjects) is simple, and involves most commonly placing the negative *nahī̃* 'not' before the verb which is normally in final position:
Bill hindustānī nahī̃ hai.
Bill - Indian - not - is.
This would perhaps effectively counteract a tendency towards the leftward movement of negatives in English and would favour explicit negation *in situ*. Furthermore, since negation in Hindi does not present very much variety, this would tend to encourage uniformity of construction over all types of clauses.

(d) *Regularization by second language speakers*. It has frequently been noted that Indian English tends to iron out exceptions found in British English (e.g. *-ing* occurs freely both with stative and non-stative verbs). This regularization may be due to the fact that it is a second language for its speakers, so there is likely to be a tendency to acquire more regular rules in order to ease the load on memory and streamline production processes. This would tend to promote uniformity among negative structures, particularly between different types of clauses.

(e) *Pedagogical practices*. There is a tendency among teachers of English in India to concentrate on the manipulation of explicit negation (i.e. inserting *not*) and also on morphological negation.

All the factors listed above seem to be moving British and Indian speakers in different directions, and there may be others which we have so far failed to identify. Are they random factors, or is there any overall generalization which can be captured? One possibility is that there may be a psycholinguistic motivation behind these multiple factors. It is possible that the British are moving English in the direction of ease of comprehension by means of implicit negation and leftward movement of the negative, whereas the Indians as second language speakers may be moving English in the direction of transparent and regular constructions which are simpler to produce, but harder to comprehend. Bever and Langendoen (1972) argued that there may be a clash between the needs of comprehension and the needs of production. It may be that native speakers move their language in the direction of parsing simplicity, but that second language speakers move a language towards production simplicity and a lowered memory load.

5.0. *Summary and conclusion*. The motivation behind this paper was to find out how the possibilities inherent in a language can be differentially utilized, and so shed light on the process of syntactic change in general. With this aim in mind, we have explored divergent preferences for negative structures in subordinate clauses in British and Indian English. Our results suggest that negation in British English may be becoming more varied, whereas negation in Indian English may be becoming more regular, and we have identified a number of factors which might be gradually drawing British and Indian English further apart. Overall, we suggested that parsing needs may influence British speakers to a greater extent than Indian speakers, who may be more affected by production needs and a desire to lighten the load on memory.

REFERENCES

Bever, T.G. & D.T. Langendoen. 1972. 'The Interaction of speech perception and grammatical structure in the evolution of language'. *Linguistic Change and Generative Theory* ed. by R.P. Stockwell & R.K.S. Macaulay, 32-95. Bloomington: Indiana UP.

Clark, H.H. & W.G. Chase. 1972. 'On the process of comparing sentences against pictures'. *Cognitive Psychology* 3. 472-517.

Fischer, O.C.M. & F.C. van der Leek. 1981. 'Optional vs radical reanalysis: mechanisms of syntactic change'. *Lingua* 55. 301-50.

Fischer, O.C.M. & F.C. van der Leek. 1983. 'The demise of the Old English impersonal construction'. *JL* 19. 337-368.

Fodor, J.D., J.A. Fodor & M.F. Garrett. 1975. 'The psychological unreality of semantic representations'. *Linguistic Inquiry* 6. 515-532.

Guttman, L. 1944. 'A basis for scaling quantitative data'. *American Sociological Review* 9. 139-50.

Horn, L.R. 1978. 'Remarks on negative-raising'. *Syntax and Semantics 9: Pragmatics* ed. by P. Cole, 129-220. New York: Academic Press.

Kachru, B.B. 1983. *The Indianization of English*. Delhi: Oxford University Press.

Klima, E.S. 1964. 'Negation in English'. *The Structure of Language: Readings in the Philosophy of Language* ed. by J.A Fodor & J.J. Katz, 246-323. Englewood Cliffs, NJ: Prentice Hall.

McCawley, J.D. 1978. 'Conversational implicature and the lexicon'. *Syntax and Semantics 9: Pragmatics* ed. by P. Cole, 245-259. New York: Academic Press.

Sahgal, A. 1983. *A Sociolinguistic Study of the English spoken by Delhi Elite*. Unpublished M.Phil.thesis, University of Delhi.

Sahgal, A. & R.K. Agnihotri. 1985. 'Syntax - the common bond. Acceptability of syntactic deviances in Indian English'. *English World-Wide* 6:1. 117-129.

Stockwell, R.P., P. Schachter & B. Hall Partee. 1973. *The Major Syntactic Structures of English*. New York: Holt, Rinehart & Winston.

Wason, P.C. 1965. 'The contexts of plausible denial'. *JVLVB* 4. 7-11.

RELATIVE *WHICH* IN LATE 18TH CENTURY USAGE: THE CLIFT FAMILY CORRESPONDENCE

FRANCES O. AUSTIN
University of Liverpool

The Clifts were a Cornish family of six brothers and sisters who lived in the second half of the 18th century and on into the early 19th century. They were from a strictly poor level of social background but because, as they grew older, the family was widely scattered, they wrote many letters to each other, some of them of considerable length. The members of the family exhibit varying degrees of literacy or illiteracy, which makes their language of particular interest for the linguist. By good fortune many of the letters have been preserved in various places and collections.

The language of the Clifts is frequently seen to be in a state of transition, from conservative or old-fashioned to non-standard usage. This is probably partly because of the period at which they were writing, but *more* probably it would be true of any writers of their social background at any time. It is also partly because the ages of the family span a period of eighteen years from the oldest to the youngest. In addition, because they vary in their literary competence, an older relatively literate writer may use the same construction as a younger but more *il*literate one, while a younger and reasonably literate member of the family will avoid that particular usage altogether. There are other complicating factors that will emerge.

Just a brief word about the family is necessary. The names and dates can be found in Appendix I. The letters cover the years 1792 to 1846 but about two thirds were written before 1801 (at least in bulk - the later letters tend to be shorter in many cases). In this paper, I am dealing solely with the letters written between 1792 and 1800, inclusive. Only three of the six writers write after 1800. It can be seen from the dates of the members of the family, that they were all brought up during the second half of the 18th century. Elizabeth, the eldest, was 43 at the turn of the century, and the youngest, William, was 25. Their formative years for acquiring language habits, therefore, were firmly in the late 18th century. Note, again, the wide range of ages, Elizabeth being 18 years old when William was born. The father was an unsuccessful miller, who, after owning his own mill for some years was forced to revert to being in the employ of others; he turned back to journeyman and eked out a living by cutting walking sticks and fishing rods from the hedgerows. Although poor, the family set great store by learning, especially a mastery of the 'three Rs', reading and writing in particular. The brothers almost certainly all attended school for some years at least. Robert is a puzzle. He is clearly the least literate of the family and at times the others write of him somewhat contemptuously. Perhaps he was less able or simply lazy at school. He seems to have run away to sea when he was about 21, in 1790. William records that after his father's death, when he was nine years old, his mother starved herself to pay the 3d a week for his schooling. But when she herself died two years later William had to leave school at the age of eleven. He also notes that the curriculum of the school, probably a 'writing school', was reading, writing and 'casting accounts'. The two sisters almost certainly did *not* have any formal education. They were probably taught to read and write after a fashion at home by their father, who was, from William's account, an unusually well-educated man for his station. Later, they were also very probably encouraged by the wife of the squire who seems to have kept a friendly eye on the family. At all events, read they could and write they did, Elizabeth at enormous if rather plodding, length, and Joanna with verve and gusto and a total disregard of all the principles of composition. The spelling of both of them, although it probably reflects their pronunciation to some extent, seems wildly haphazard, and they seem quite oblivious of the existence of punctuation. This obviously irritated their young brother, William. You can actually see where he has jabbed punctuation marks on to some of Elizabeth's letters, probably as he was reading them.

Of this family, only William, by a stroke of good fortune, rose above his early social background. He was apprenticed to the well known surgeon, John Hunter, the 'father' of modern surgery, in 1792, and he left his native

Bodmin in Cornwall for London when he was just 17. Eventually, he was to become the first Conservator of the Hunterian Museum (still housed in the Royal College of Surgeons in Lincoln's Inn Fields in London - the Royal College was actually built to house Hunter's famous Collection). He was also elected an FRS in 1823 and above all he was a 'character', known and respected by all the medical men and natural scientists of the early 19th century. He was, therefore, not only the youngest, but as he grew to manhood, he became more educated than the rest of the family, who remained in lowly employment all their lives. This fact is partly offset in the *very* early letters by the close relationship between him and Elizabeth, who became virtually a second mother to him when their own mother died. The effect of this on his language is sometimes very clear (as in the epistolary formulas he uses) and his usage frequently resembles hers more closely than might otherwise be expected.

The various factors I have mentioned very briefly here, as well as others, make this a particularly rewarding family for linguistic study. In taking the use of the relative *which*, I am examining only two points in detail. In 1765 William Ward said, 'The construction of the relative is a most difficult part of the syntax of all languages'. (Ward 1765: 139). Not only is it difficult but it has many related uses and this makes it impossible to look at all of them here, even in a relatively small corpus. The first use of *which* that I intend to examine is that with a human antecedent, where we now use *who*. The second is basically the alternative uses of *which* and *that* or *who* and *that*. The 18th century grammarians had much to say on both of these usages, and so they seem appropriate ones to examine.

First the use of *which* with a personal or human antecedent. The three oldest writers, Elizabeth, John and Thomas all occasionally use *which* with a personal antecedent. Thomas uses it twice in subject position and once in object position. His letters reveal no instances of *who* but they are relatively few in number and also short. Both Elizabeth and John use *who* more frequently than *which* but they do use *which* on occasions. Elizabeth uses it three times but *who* thirteen times, all in subject position. John has two examples of *which* and eight of *who*. Some examples are at the end in Appendix I. The only other writer to use *which* instead of *who* is William, in a letter of 1796, but there is only the one instance and this is doubtful. John also has one further instance of it later, used in object position in a letter of 1814.

The PrDE use of *who* in relative clauses with a personal antecedent has been common since the 17th century, although, of course, it can be found much earlier. Jespersen (1927: 119) notes that both Milton and Bunyan follow modern practice. *Which* occurred beside *who* until the beginning of the 18th century, when it gradually began to be limited to inanimate and non human antecedents. S.A. Leonard (1929: 237) says that *which* used of persons had virtually disappeared by the 18th century but was one of the features of the language that was 'exhumed .. for critical obloquy' by the 18th century grammarians. It was condemned by most grammarians, and, according to Leonard, they probably correctly represented the facts of usage at the time. William Ward actually used it in his *Essay on Grammar* in 1765, but may have been influenced by the fact that he was writing of its use earlier. He says, 'In all the English writers, which flourished above a hundred years ago, "which" is applied to both persons and things' (Ward 1765: 136). Noah Webster (1807: 18) also used it as late as 1807. James Beattie, writing in 1783, also supports the use of *which*, but he is writing specifically of the Lord's Prayer. In this, he says, the use of *who* is 'an extreme modern delicacy' and expresses his preference for the archaic form (Beattie 1783: 158, n).

There was some variation in the use however, for *which* appears to have survived longer in restrictive clauses (henceforth r clauses) than in non-restrictive (henceforth non-r clauses). This fact is not borne out from the instances in the Clift letters, where *which* occurs more frequently in non-r clauses. This may not be too surprising, as we shall see later that they use far more non-r clauses than r ones. Examples of the use of non-r clauses can be seen in Appendix I. Elizabeth uses it twice in non-r clauses and John once. All three of Thomas's uses are in non-r clauses.

Which in non-r clauses seems to have disappeared from standard and literary English during the early part of the 18th century. It occurs quite frequently in the letters of upper-class writers in the 17th and early 18th centuries. Lady Wentworth uses it in 1710, but it is not much found after that. Examples in non-r clauses recorded in the *OED* after 1710, occur in the mouths of illiterate speakers - naturally mainly from novels. Dickens uses this device very often to indicate the speech of a lower class character.

The appearance of *which* as a personal relative in non-r clauses in the Clift letters during the last decade of the 18th century confirms that it did persist longer in non-standard English than in polite society; but it should be noticed that only the three oldest writers use it. This seems to indicate that it was obsolescent even in this section of the community by the end of the 18th century.

Some of Elizabeth's uses have a distinctly biblical sound as can be seen in one of the examples. This is almost certainly the influence of the *Authorized Version of the Bible* or the liturgy. *Who* is rarely used as a relative pronoun in the *AV* and when it does occur it is usually found in non-r clauses (Jesperson 1927: 118-19). On the one occasion when Elizabeth uses *which* in a r clause it occurs in a similar passage, however. The conservative usage of the *AV* may well have been a factor contributing to the persistence of *which* in the language of the lower classes.

It is in a r clause that we find the one instance of *which* as a personal relative used by William. This may confirm the fact that it survived longer in r clauses generally. Here, however, there is some doubt as to the status of *which*. Lindley Murray (1795: 150-51) says,

> A term which only implies the idea of persons, and expresses them by some circumstance or epithet, will hardly authorize the use of it [*who*]: as, 'That faction in England *who* most powerfully opposed his arbitrary pretentions'.

This is not quite the same as William's use of a group of people. Just before this, however, Murray had written,

> The pronoun relative *who* is so much appropriated to persons, that there is generally harshness in the application of it, except to the proper names of persons, or the general terms, *man, woman,* &C.

Is *shoemakers* equivalent to *man* and *woman*? It seems Murray was not too sure himself:

> In some cases it may be doubtful whether this pronoun is properly applied or not: as, 'The number of substantial inhabitants with *whom* some cities abound.' For when a term directly and necessarily implies persons, it <u>may</u> in many cases claim the personal relative.
>   (My underlining)

So, perhaps, conversely it may *not* and William's *which* would be considered equally 'correct'. Lindley Murray's *Grammar* was published in 1795 and William's letter was written in 1796. To return to r clauses, Elizabeth, as we have seen, uses *which* once in a r clause and John also uses it once (not included in the count given in Appendix II).

Which as a personal relative in r clauses seems to have had a longer history than *which* in non-r clauses: the *OED* records examples up to the beginning of the 20th century. Poutsma (1916: 968) maintains, without qualification as to position (subject or oblique) that *which* as a personal relative was still current in literary English. He gives many examples from the 19th and early 20th centuries, almost all of which occur in r clauses.

William's use, therefore, can not be accounted particularly unusual, although many speakers of PrDE would undoubtedly prefer the relative *who* in this particular case. John's second use of personal *which* (both occur in the same letter apart from the later example) is in a non-r clause, but again seems somewhat different in type, since it introduces a list of names. This example (see Appendix I) sounds strange partly because of the apparent lack of concord between the following singular verb form *is* and the antecedent *servants*. Of course, one could say, in any case, that *servants* is a similar word to *shoemakers* and therefore open to the same linguistic interpretation as William's example. I think it is very likely that the construction would pass unnoticed in PrDE speech, especially *informal* speech, but many people would object to it as a written form.

A related use, or rather, avoidance of the use, of *who* is found in contact clauses. Two examples are given in Appendix I. All the instances occur with an introductory *there is*. Joanna and William use it as well as Elizabeth and John, although rarely. Quirk (1972: 865, n) says that the relative cannot be omitted if in subject position. Jesperson (1927: 144-46) says that in cases where the relative would have been the subject of the following clause, contact clauses are frequently found in sentences beginning with *there is*. He gives examples from writers of the 14th to the 20th centuries. The contact clauses of Elizabeth and John in the Appendix have a distinctly colloquial sound. Contrary to Jesperson's opinion, Sweet (1898: 77) states quite emphatically that the omission of the relative in subject position is already very rare in late 19th century spoken English. Perhaps he had not noticed the introductory *there is* exception. It would seem likely that instances such as these from the Clift letters are not unusual or certainly were not then. They might also be more common in dialect or non-standard English. Wright (1965: §§ 423, 280) reminds us that the relative was frequently omitted in dialect English in subject as well as in object position, although not everyone would accept

Wright unreservedly now. Certainly, the practice of omitting the relative in this position was much used formerly and not only in dialect and non-standard English. Kaesebier (1898: 29) notes that Pepys frequently leaves it out; and Uhrström (1907: 64-65) observes that it was often omitted in the early 18th century, giving examples from Richardson's novels.

Further instances of omission of this type occur in the Clift letters, some omitting *which* and some *who*:

> there is nothing I Can see or Desire in this world would give me at Least resemblance of its hapiness   JC

> there is / is some very creditable looking girls run and tumble   WC

> there is scarcely any person goes into it   WC

It will be noticed, however, that in present written English, even writing of an informal register, the examples quoted would almost certainly not be expanded to include a relative but would omit the introductory *there is*, thus obviating the need for a relative clause altogether:

> I believe noone knows how it is between them but themselves

In informal speech the construction written by the Clifts is still probably used occasionally even among educated speakers.

Secondly, we come to the use of *that* as a relative. This was the subject of much controversy among the 18th century grammarians, and generally, the usage was condemned. Probably the most famous or well-known argument against the use of *that* was made by Addison in a number of *The Spectator* in 1711 (No. 78), called 'The Humble Petition of Who and Which'. According to Leonard (1929: 64), both Lowth and Hornsey were tentative in their statements about it. Hornsey (1793: 24) says '*That* is perhaps better expressed with who and which'. Lowth (1762: 100) takes a slightly different approach, allowing *that* for things but not for persons. He writes, 'That is used indifferently of persons and things; but perhaps would be more properly confined to the latter'. James Buchanan in 1767 was much more dogmatic. 'That', he says (1767: 74), 'is often used, but inelegantly, for *who*, *whom* and *which*'. On the other hand, William Ward (1765: 136) takes the use of *that* as a matter of course: 'Either sort of objects with "the powers of speech and intelligence" or without may be represented by the relative "that".'

In the Clift letters, the two greatest users of *that* as a relative are Elizabeth and William. Here we see an instance of Elizabeth's and William's usage being similar. Even the fact that they write at greater length than any of the others, even John and Joanna, cannot account for the very large increase in the figures (See Table 2a.). William's frequent use of *that* is in line with his greater use of relative subordination, and of subordination altogether. This was almost certainly a result of his increasing education during his years in London. Even though all the letters come in his early years away from home, there is no doubt he made rapid advances during that time. His mastery of more complex syntax is readily observable over the eight years that these letters cover.

William uses *that* for *which* 19 times in all and 17 times for *who*, making a total of 36. What does *not* appear in the tables as they are presented here is the fact that in the course of the first eight years in London, his use of *that* for *who* and *which* declined, especially for *who*, which increases dramatically after his first year in London. The greatest use of *that* is, correspondingly, in 1792, his first year away from home. It reduces markedly in 1793 and 1794, almost disappears in 1795, then increases again slightly but very slightly in 1796. After that it virtually disappears again. William was, as we know, busy adopting the cultural and social life of his employers and their circle as far as he could, and this undoubtedly had an effect on his language. In today's terms he would be called an 'auto-didact', I suppose, and even a social climber. We do not know, unfortunately, if he either possessed or consulted any of the current grammars, but it seems more than likely, knowing his habits, that he did one or the other. It is extremely possible, therefore, that the decline in his usage of relative *that* was a result of the influence of the grammarians. Strangely, Lindley Murray is not against the use of *that*. He says (1795: 149),

> ... the pronoun *that* is frequently applied to persons as well as things; but after an adjective in the superlative degree, and after the pronominal adjective *same*, it is generally used in preference to *who* or *which* ...

However, Murray's grammar did not come out until 1795 and it is in the first year of his time in London, 1792, that William uses *that* most frequently. Over half the instances in his letters occur in the first two years he was in London. Elizabeth, the next most frequent user of relative *that*, particularly for *who* (her usage of *that* about equals her use of *who*) is more surprising, as one would expect

her to use subordination less often and generally she does,
preferring a more co-ordinate style. However, after William,
she is the next highest user of relative subordination
altogether, followed by John. One would expect John to be
nearer to William in use even though Elizabeth's corpus
is quite considerably larger. Her use of subordination with
the relative is greater than any other type of subordination she uses, except for reported clauses. This is partly
accounted for by her use of formulaic type phrases which
recur regularly in her letters:

> you are the only brother that takes account of me
>
> all them that desired to be remembered to you
>
> them that put their trust in the Lord

(and similar religiously derived phrases)

The totals for her letters are 10 uses of *that* for *which*
and 28 for *who*. Notice also 2 uses of personal *that* occur
with a preposition *to*, both of which could be substituted
by *who* or rather *whom*. These are included in Table 2a
under personal *that*. Oddly enough, Elizabeth also uses
the oblique form *whom*, which she usually spells *home* or
some way similar. The only other writers to use the oblique
form of *who*, and only once each, are John and William. It
seems again that Elizabeth and John, being the two oldest,
show the survival of the inflected form, whereas William's
use may be the result of Elizabeth's influence or of his
increased education. It is impossible to say which.

Of the other writers, only John and Joanna use *that*
to any extent worth mentioning and both use *which* and *who*
more. This is not, perhaps, what we might expect, especially in the case of Joanna, who was unlikely to be influenced
by grammars. If Elizabeth had not used *that* to such an
extent, one would suppose that *who* and *which* were more in
use at the time among the less self aware of lower class
strata of society. There seems no explanation for this.
Thomas and Robert scarcely use *that* at all as a relative
in any function, but generally the figures for their use
of the relative are so low that nothing of significance
can be deduced from them. The main reason for this is that
the amount of their writing is small compared with that of
the others, although Robert does use a number of unrelated
instances of *which*, one example being in Appendix I. This
seems to be a feature of his sentence structure and shows
a lack of command of basic syntax or rather illogical
thinking - probably both.

The only other case of *who* that perhaps deserves some

comment is the genitive *whose*. Here, Elizabeth does not use *whose* nor the alternative form, *of which*. Instances of *of which* which are genitives are not easy to identify with certainty. John uses *whose* once, so must have been familiar with the form or had it within his competence. William uses it twice in 1796, again possibly as a result of his growing control of the language. Whilst speaking of control, Joanna is interesting, particularly if one considers her rather wild use of prepositions with *which*. Her writing is flamboyant, probably learned from fellow servants, and seems to show an attempt to write at a level beyond her competence as far as syntax goes. Table 1 notes that of her 9 uses of *which*, four prepositions are redundant and in two other cases she repeats the preposition. Both of these involve the preposition *for*. Examples are in Appendix I.

To return to *that* as a relative, Leonard (1929) indicates that the grammarians, and Addison in particular, did not represent or understand the current trend accurately. People were using *that* as a relative in all walks of life and had been doing so ever since Anglo-Saxon times. *Who* and *which*, from the interrogative pronouns, developed later, basically in the ME period. It may seem that the grammarians had some influence on certain sections of the population, such as young men anxious to climb the social ladder as William was. The Clifts' use of *WH*-forms, however, is far greater than their use of *that*, with the exception of Elizabeth's use in restricted personal clauses. On the whole, such influence, if it existed, was not lasting, at least as far as *that* as a personal relative goes. To compare with present day usage I have taken Quirk's Survey of 1957 (over a quarter of a century ago now). More recent studies have been conducted but this was the only one that could be used for comparison. There are three sections to Quirk's experiment; 1) spontaneous conversation when the participants did not know they were being taped; 2) the same but the participants did know they were being taped; 3) informal discussion on a platform which was being broadcast. There is, therefore, an increase in the formality of each of the sections. The differences are not differentiated in the results in Quirk's tables. I have simplified Quirk's tables drastically. Certain points emerge from a comparison with the Clifts. They use far fewer clauses altogether. The greatest discrepancy occurs in *WH*-clauses: 524 and 54. (Table 2b). Stars mark where the Clifts usage is markedly less than Quirk's; daggers anywhere indicate where it shows an increase in usage even if slight. Contrary, it seems, to the findings in his own survey, in their grammar Quirk et al. (1972: 864) say,

> ... it is in the non-restrictive clauses that the most explicit forms of relative pronouns are typically used. In restrictive clauses, frequent use is made of the general pronoun *that* which is independent of the personal or nonpersonal character of the antecedent and also of the function of the pronoun in the relative clause.

The Clifts use slightly more *that* personal r clauses than Quirk shows. (Table 2b). Elizabeth's and William's usage accounts for the increase here. (Table 2a). The proportion of use of *WH*-clauses by the Clifts is greater than their usage of *that* clauses compared with Quirk overall (Table 2d). The proportion of r to non-r clauses used by the Clifts is slightly less than three r to four non-r (Table 2c). Here, the usage of Quirk's sample reverses this trend completely: he shows slightly fewer than five non-r to one r clause. Why do the Clifts use fewer r clauses generally? One reason for the increase of non-r clauses may lie in their rather loose way of writing, but one might expect this to compare reasonably with spoken English even of today. Another possible answer is that they could use many more contact clauses for relatives in object position. I did a count of 1792 (one of the largest years for correspondence) and the number of 'zero relatives' is really exceedingly small: 5 only for all the writers together for that year. This does not seem to be the answer. This also does not bear out Wright's theory that the relative is more frequently omitted in dialect. One could say that the Clifts use this type of subordination less altogether and that may be because of their social background or just a feature of their language. However, their usage is slightly greater for non-r non personal clauses for both *WH-* and *That*. Finally, I suppose, and rather unsatisfactorily, the evidence is inconclusive and is likely to remain so unless more writings of a similar kind can be found and analysed. Then, with a larger corpus on which to base deductions, more satisfactory statements could be made about the linguistic characteristics of this social stratum of the population at the time.

APPENDIX I

THE CLIFT FAMILY

    Elizabeth Clift (EC)   1757-1818
    John Clift (JnC)   1759-1819
    Thomas Clift (TC)   1762-1835 or 6
    Joanna Clift (JC)   1765-1846
    Robert Clift (RC)   1768/9-1799
    William Clift (WC)   1775-1849

EXAMPLES OF THE USE OF THE RELATIVE IN THE CLIFT FAMILY CORRESPONDENCE

1. *Which* as a personal relative

    i) In non-restrictive clauses

        I was at Mr. Barrons when Mr. Paynter wich is my Master Came ther   EC

        ... different parts of the Human Body Dissected by Dr. Hunter which I suppose was your Master   JnC

        I have a shop mate with me which I Call on at Bath and he Intends to Come with me to London   TC

        I hope and trust the Lord our God wich hath been with him and preseved him this far will be with him still   EC

        he hath discharged four of the Servts I find which is Mary Edwards house maid and a Laundry maid likewise my worthy friend the Coachman and Jas Netting   JnC

    ii) In restrictive clauses

        I do not think there are many Journeymen Shoemakers which can afford 15 Shillings   WC

        I hope the Lord will all waise be a freind to you for..he is a freind at all times to them wich Put thir trust in him   EC

        she was with the Children which she pays Schooling for - Examining their work   JnC

2. Avoidance of relative *who*

        I Be live there is no one knowes how it is be twen them but thir selves   EC

        I am bound to say there is not a Gentleman and Lady In Britain can show Greater Respect to any person than they do to me   JnC

3. Redundant use of *and*

> I have credit for as much Tea and Sugar, and Bread as I can use, and which is my principal living   WC

4. Redundant use of preposition

> this being the first opportunity of which I am happy to imbrace to inform you of my arival at Plymouth   JC

5. Repeated preposition

> I find Every thing did not answer his Expectation for which I was realy sory for   JC

6. Unrelated *which*

> I rote a letter to you last Febry But Never recd no answer which I would be Glad to No from you whether you recd it or Not   RC

Restrictive or non-restrictive?

> he sent his sister so much Cloths that was worth Fifty Pound just be fore he was home that was his wifes an Childs
>   EC

APPENDIX 2

RELATIVE PRONOUNS & THE CLIFT FAMILY CORRESPONDENCE 1792-1800

Table 1. Uses of *which*

	EC	JnC	TC	JC	RC	WC	Total
Personal	3	2	3			1	9
Non-Personal	20	8	3	4		45	80
Antecedent Sentence	17	23	1	8	6	19	74
Redundant *and*	1					11	12
Prep + *which*		6		9*		7	22
Unrelated *which*					4		4

> * 4 redundant and 2 repeated - i.e. before and after *which*

28　　　　　　　　　　　　FRANCES O. AUSTIN

```
nrnp = nonrestrictive nonpersonal
nr p = nonrestrictive personal
 rnp = restrictive nonpersonal
 r p = restrictive personal
```

Table 2a. WH-relatives compared with *That*

WH-	EC	JnC	TC	JC	RC	WC	Totals
nrnp	38	20	4	21	6	66	155
nr p	13(51)	8(28)	(4)	1(22)	1(7)	26(92)	49(204)
rnp	6	2				15	23
r p	2(8)	2(4)		1(1)		26(41)	31(54)
							258

That							
nrnp		2		2		1	5
nr p		1(3)		(2)		1(2)	2(7)
rnp	10	4	1	6		19	40
r p	28(38)	4(8)	1(2)	1(7)		17(36)	51(91)
							98

Table 2b. WH- and *That*: Quirk's Survey (1957) & the Clifts

WH-	Quirk	Clifts		Quirk	Clifts
nrnp	142	$^+$155	nr	173	$^+$204
nr p	31	59	r	524	*54
rnp	300	*23			
r p	224	*44			

That					
nrnp		$^+$5	nr	1	$^+$7
nr p	1	$^+$2	r	372	*91
rnp	337	*40			
r p	35	$^+$51			

Table 2c. Restrictive and nonrestrictive clauses

	Quirk	Clifts
nr	174	$^+$211
r	896	*145

Table 2d. WH- and *That* clauses

	Quirk	Clifts
WH-	697	*258
That	373	*98

REFERENCES

Beattie, James. 1783, repr. 1787. *The Theory of Language in Two Parts*.
Buchanan, James. 1767. *A Regular English Syntax*.
Hornsey, John. 1793. *A Short English Grammar in Two Parts*.
Jespersen, Otto. 1927, repr. 1961. *A Modern English Grammar on Historical Principles*. Vol. III. London: George Allen & Unwin Ltd.
Kaesebier, Kurt. 1898. *Beobachtungen über den Sprachgebrauch in Samuel Pepy's* (sic) *'Diary'*. Greifswald.
Leonard, S.A. 1929, repr. 1962. *The Doctrine of Correctness in English Usage 1700-1800*. New York: Russell & Russel Inc.
Lowth, Robert. 1762. *A Short Introduction to English Grammar*.
Murray, Lindley. 1795, 15th edition 1806. *English Grammar*.
Poutsma, H. 1916. *A Grammar of Late Modern English*. Vol. II. Groningen: P. Noordhoff.
Quirk, R. 1957. 'Relative Clauses in Educated Spoken English'. *English Studies*, 38, 97-109.
Quirk, R. et al. 1972. *A Grammar of Contemporary English*. London: Longman.
Sweet, Henry. 1898. *A New English Grammar*. Vol. II. Oxford: O.U.P.
Uhrström, Wilhelm. 1907. *Studies on the Language of Samuel Richardson*. Uppsala.
Ward, William. 1765. *An Essay on Grammar*.
Webster, Noah. 1807. *Letter to Dr. Ramsay*.
Wright, Joseph. 1905, repr. 1968. *An English Dialect Grammar*. Oxford: O.U.P.

'LENGTHENING OF a^1 IN TYNESIDE ENGLISH

JOAN C. BEAL
University of Newcastle upon Tyne

It is a truth universally acknowledged amongst English dialectologists that, north of a line running from Shropshire to the Wash, words such as *bath, fast, laugh, pass*, in which ME *a* is followed by a voiceless spirant will be pronounced with a short, open vowel [a], thus: [baθ],[fast],[laf],[pas]. That this particular isogloss is etched deeply into the consciousness of native speakers of English is apparent from the existence of a lay term for the Northern short [a], which is always described as 'flat': in the folk-linguistic view, flat caps and flat vowels belong together. Indeed, the distinction between [a] and [ɑ:] is more salient in differentiating Northern from Southern dialects than that between [ʊ] and [ʌ] in words like *cup, strut*, etc., for educated Northerners often neutralise the latter distinction by producing a schwa- like vowel in these words, but as Wells (1982:354) points out:

> Retention of a short vowel in BATH words extends much further up the social scale than does the retention of unsplit /ʊ/...... There are many educated northerners who would not be caught dead doing something so vulgar as to pronounce STRUT words with [ʊ], but who would feel it to be a denial of their identity as northerners to say BATH words with anything other than short [a].

The designation 'flat', when used by laypersons, also covers the long vowel used in northern dialects before /r/ and in words like *palm* and *calm* as well as in relatively recent borrowings like *banana* and *pyjamas*. In most of the North, this vowel has a mid to front quality more or less identical with that of short [a]: thus [pa:m], [pa:k], [bəna:nə]. This contrasts with the long back [ɑ:] of R.P. and many Southern dialects.

Given this conflation of scholarly evidence concerning the [a]/[ɑ] isogloss with the lay notion that flat caps and flat vowels belong together, it is surprising to find that in Tyneside and Northumberland, where the number of flat caps per head of population is perhaps greater than anywhere else in England, the vowels concerned are not always 'flat'. In fact, the realisation of /a/ in Tyneside speech differs from that of what Wells (1982:357) terms 'the middle north' in the following ways:

Firstly, a small number of words pronounced with short [a] elsewhere in the North are pronounced with a long vowel by speakers in Tyneside and Northumberland. These words are *master*, *plaster*, and *plasticine*. These words thus belong in the same lexical set as words with ME *a* before /r/, *palm*, *banana* etc. The second important difference between Tyneside and Northumberland and the middle north is that words in this lexical set are pronounced with a long back vowel, either similar to the [ɑ:] of R.P. or rounded to [ɒ:]. There is a long front [a:] in Tyneside and Northumberland dialects, but it is phonemically distinct from the [ɑ:] of *master*, *palm*, *park* etc. This front vowel is found in words in which R.P. has [ɔ:] developed from rounding of ME *a*. Thus Tyneside has [a:l], [wa:k], [ba:l], corresponding to R.P. [ɔ:l], [wɔ:k], [bɔ:l].

Fig. 1, below, illustrates part of the long vowel system of Tyneside, compared with the corresponding part of the R.P. system.

R.P.	/ae/	/ɑ:/	/ɔ:/	/ɜ:/
Tyneside	/ae/	/ɑ:/	/a:/	/ɔ:/
	pat, *dance*	*farm*, *master*, *plaster*, etc.	*all*, *wall*	*shirt*, *bird*

Fig. 1 (Adapted from Hughes and Trudgill 1979: 66)

Given the system outlined in Fig. 1, the presence of the long back /ɑ:/ in Tyneside English could perhaps be explained by the need to keep this phoneme phonetically distinct from /a:/. However, this does not explain the presence within the lexical set with /ɑ:/ of the words *master*, *plaster* and *plasticine*. My own interest in this matter arose from my shock as a 'middle northerner' on hearing my then fiancé (a Northumbrian) pronounce the word *master* thus: [mɑ:stə]. An argument ensued in which my accusations of 'selling out' to R.P. and talking 'posh'

were strenuously denied: I was assured that everybody in
his area (mid-Northumberland) pronounced the word in this
way. Most dialectologists, however, have failed to notice
this phenomenon, possibly because these words are not of
the agricultural type elicited in surveys like the Survey
of English Dialects (henceforth SED). Hughes and Trudgill
(1979: 65) do not include *master*, *plaster* or *plasticine*
in their word lists, and so only note that in Tyneside
speech 'words like *dance* and *daft* have /ae/' whilst 'words
like *farm* and *car* have /ɑ:/'. The specification of
linguistic variables for the Tyneside Linguistic Survey
(Pellowe et al. 1972: 8) lists *master* along with *path*,
grass, *have*, *after*, *alsation*, *pal* and *lather* as examples
of the localised Overall Unit[2] /ae/, whilst *father*,
barn, *farm*, *half*, *rather*, are given as examples of the
localised Overall Unit /ɑ/. Wells notes that:

> One or two of the BATH words are particularly susceptible
> to Broadening[3] as a result of their association with
> school and school-inspired standards of correctness. An
> instance is master often pronounced /ma:stə/ by northerners
> who would nevertheless pronounce plaster and disaster with
> short /a/. (1982: 354)

Now, it may well be the case that in the 'middle north'
master stands alone as the only word in which *a* is
lengthened before voiceless spirants (although Shorrocks
(1977) suggests that in Bolton even *path*, *grass* etc are
pronounced with a long vowel), but this is certainly not
true of Tyneside or Northumberland where both *plaster*
and (presumably by analogy with the former) *plasticine*
can be heard with the long vowel. The suggestion that
this is a lengthening of [a] under the influence of R.P.
speaking schoolmasters at first sight looks plausible, for
in folk-linguistic mythology, Universal Education is
blamed for the decline of traditional Northumbrian
dialect features such as the 'burr' or uvular fricative
[ʁ], as is evidenced in the dialect rhyme:

> They taaked the gud aad Tyneside burr
>   i' them aad fashund days
> For they had nee Eddication Boards to
>   teach them fancy ways.
>   (Geeson 1969: 32)

Nevertheless, for several reasons, I think it highly
unlikely that the long [ɑ:] of *master*, *plaster* and
plasticine in Tyneside and Northumbrian speech owes its
origin to R.P. Firstly, modified Tyneside speakers, such
as the presenters of the BBC 'Look North' programme,
when lengthening a short [a], tend to use a more fronted
sound than the [ɑ:] used in *master*, etc by more localised

speakers. Thus the name of the city, *Newcastle* is
pronounced [njəˈkasl] by localised speakers; [ˈnjuːkɑːsl]
by R.P. speakers; and [ˈnjuːkaːsl] by modified Tyneside
speakers.

Secondly, speakers of Tyneside and Northumbrian
varieties, when asked about their pronunciation of *master*
etc, perceive it as highly and specifically localised.
Driving southwards through Newcastle, you will come, just
before the Tyne Bridge, to a road sign which reads:
'Durham: The South'. This represents a perceptual
reality for Tynesiders and Northumbrians, who believe that
the South begins on the north bank of the River Wear (if
not the south bank of the River Tyne). When asked about
their pronunciation of *master* and *plaster*, two young
women from Morpeth, Northumberland asserted that: 'only
people from Sunderland say /mastə/ and /plastə/'.
Sunderland is, of course, the first major town south of
Newcastle. It stands on the River Wear and is the focus
of rivalry with Newcastle United in years when the two
teams happen to be in the same division of the football
league. Furthermore, Tyneside and Northumbrian speakers
will be amazed and insulted if accused of 'talking posh',
or, to use more technical terminology, of using a long [ɑː]
under the influence of R.P.

A third reason for my scepticism concerning the
supposed influence of R.P. is the collocation of the long
[ɑː] in *master* and *plaster* with the ending [a]. This
'strong' pronunciation of what in R.P. would be schwa is
highly localised, and is a feature which on Tyneside
enjoys a great deal of what Labov (1966: 108) would call
'covert prestige'. For instance, the names of young
skinheads, when painted on the walls of Tyneside buildings,
will often be spelt with final <a> rather than <er>.
Thus a boy whose surname is Dobson will be *Doppa* (the
glottalisation and subsequent devoicing of medial voiced
obstruents is another feature of Tyneside speech). Given
this evidence it is very unlikely that the pronunciation
of [ɑː] is produced under the influence of R.P.

Finally, *master* in nineteenth century Northumbrian
usage was by no means restricted to an educational context,
and may not have even have been very widely used in such
a context. The Northumbrian informants, in reply to the
SED questionnaire item: 'At school the class is taken by
the ......' all gave the response *teacher*, except for the
informant in Thropton who gave *domini*. Now, this may have
been an attempt at non-sexist usage on the part of the
informants, but it may also be the case that *master* simply

was not the word which first sprang to mind in an educational context. On the other hand SED informants in Northumberland do give *master* as a response to questions designed to elicit words for *husband* and *Mr.* Moreover, Heslop (1892) includes the names of two types of official in a colliery *master shifter* and *master waster*, indicating that the word was used in a context which, if anything, would be conducive to the spread of dialect rather than R.P. features (cf. Pahlsson 1972).

The above arguments do not absolutely rule out the possibility that influence from R.P. may have had a hand in the development of the long vowel in *master*, *plaster* and *plasticine*, but they do create sufficient doubt to make a search for an alternative explanation desirable. I should therefore like first to look at the origins of the words *master* and *plaster* themselves, and then at the history of *a* lengthening in R.P., before examining the history of these words in the Northumbrian dialect.

Master and *plaster* are, in fact, both distinct from other words in which ME short *a* precedes /st/, in that they each have hybrid origins, leading to variability of pronunciation even in ME.

Master occurs in OE as *maeȝister*, *maeȝester*, *maȝister*, all deriving from the Latin *magister*, but in ME the forms *meister*, *maister*, *maistre* are found, all deriving from the Old French *maistre* (Modern French *maître*). This leads to variation in ME and later in dialects of Modern English between forms with reflexes of ME *a* and *ai* respectively.

Plaster likewise occurs in OE in the form *plaster*, derived from the Popular Latin *plastrum*, which was a shortened form of *emplastrum*, meaning plaster in a medical sense. In ME, this word is reinforced by the Old French *plastre*, meaning builders' plaster. Forms spelt with ⟨ai⟩ occur from the fourteenth century onwards, probably, according to the OED, from an alternative Old French form with ⟨ai⟩. As with *master*, variability between forms with reflexes of ME *a* and *ai* occurs in ME and in dialects of Modern English.

It would appear, then, that from a very early stage these two words have variable pronunciations, and that any later pronunciation may be a reflex either of the variant with ME *a* or of that with ME *ai*. Dobson (1968) places *master* and *plaster* in a list of words which show early lengthening of ME *a*. Obviously, these occurrences of the long vowel, found in Hart for *master* and in

Bullokar and Robinson for *plaster*, are reflexes of the ME *a* variant: these early reports show that these words are particularly susceptible to lengthening. It could be that their hybrid origin rendered them unstable, but Dobson demonstrates that there are sound phonetic reasons for the early lengthening in these words. In fact, the lengthening of *a* in Early Modern English seems to have progressed by means of lexical diffusion, and in accordance with phonetic conditioning such as that described by Labov (1974) with regard to sound change in progress. Cooper, who, according to Dobson, gives us the earliest (1687) reliable evidence for *a* lengthening as a sound change in progress, indicates that *a* is pronounced long before /sC/; /rC/; /θ/: thus in *can*, *pass by*, *car*, *a* is short, but in *cast*, *past* (= passed), *carp*, *a* is pronounced long. (Sundby 1953: 34). Dobson goes on to draw up a list of environments favouring the lengthening of ME *a* in Early Modern English. These are, in descending order of powerfulness:

1. before /rC/
2. before /r/
3. before the voiceless spirants /f/, /s/, /θ/ especially (at least in the case of /s/) if part of a group of spirant + C
4. a group of consonants, especially if the second member of the group is a syllabic or non-syllabic /r/.

In addition to these, which have an even greater influence if combined, preceding consonants involving lip protrusion ie bilabial or labio-dental consonants, /r/ and /l/ assist with lengthening. Of these, the most powerful is /w/, but /r/ preceded by a bilabial consonant also has a very powerful effect on lengthening.

Dobson suggests that all these phonetic conditions involve the same general influence on the preceding or following *a*: these consonants all require the teeth to be held closer together, and, since the lengthened vowels involve narrower mouth openings than the unlengthened ones, the vowel is affected by assimilation to the mouth position required for the preceding or following consonants. Clusters have a more powerful influence than single consonants because they involve this narrow mouth opening being sustained for longer. For the same reason, spirants are more effective than stops in this respect. The part played by /r/ in this lengthening process is, according to Dobson (1968: 540) 'a special case', bringing about lengthening not only because of its 'quality as a continuant with narrow mouth opening' but also because of its lowering and retractive power, which is 'one of the most obvious features of Modern English phonology'. Moreover /r/ can have rounding power because of the lip protrusion involved in its articulation.

Dobson suggests that in Southern English, the lengthening of ME *a* proceeds in two stages:
1. raising and fronting of ME *a* to [ae] is inhibited in the environments listed above;
2. those occurrences of ME *a* not subjected to fronting and raising are subsequently lengthened.

In dialects in which ME *a* remains in all environments, ie Northern and Midland dialects, the lack of lengthening depends on the absence of fronting and raising. The long [a:] before /r/ in these dialects is, according to Dobson, a later development connected with the loss of post-vocalic /r/.

If we accept Dobson's account of the phonetic influences involved in the lengthening of ME *a*, it is tempting to regard the occurrence of long [ɑ:] in *master* and *plaster* in Tyneside and Northumbrian speech as the thin end of the wedge in a new process of lengthening, since, in both these words, the ME *a* is surrounded by consonants which have been shown to favour lengthening. Both have /st/ plus what would, prior to loss of post-vocalic /r/, have been a syllabic /r/ following the vowel, whilst *master* has a bilabial consonant preceding the vowel and *plaster* a bilabial consonant plus /l/. Given that these dialects already have long [ɑ:] before /rC/ and /r/, the two most powerful environments in Dobson's list, these two words, having such an impressive accumulation of favourable conditioning factors, would surely be 'next on the list'. However, the process cannot be exactly the same as that outlined by Dobson for Southern dialects since the first stage of the process, raising and fronting of ME *a* to [ae] clearly never occurred in any of the Northern dialects, all of which have the 'flat' [a]. Moreover, there is no sign of the long [ɑ:] in Tyneside and Northumbrian dialects being extended to words like *pastor*, which has the same number of favourable conditioning factors as *master*. The question which confronts us is, why (apart from the analogical lengthening in *plasticine*) should lengthening before spirants be confined to these two words?

The answer to this question lies in the hybrid origins of these words, which sets them apart from *pastor* etc. The pronunciation of these two words was, in dialects throughout the North of England in the nineteenth century, based on reflexes of ME *ai*. Wright (1898) records spellings with <ai> for *master* in Northumberland, Durham, the Lakelands, Cumberland, North Yorkshire, West Yorkshire and North Lincolnshire; and for *plaster* in Yorkshire. Although he gives no indication as to how *master* was pronounced in these dialects, Wright gives the pronunciation [ple:stə(r)] for *plaster*. Since Wright's notation does not distinguish between close and open *e*, the pronunciation indicated could be either [ple:stə] or [plɛ:stə], either of which could be derived from ME *ai*. More specific information is provided by Heslop (1892) who indicates that, in nineteenth century Northumbrian, as today, *master* had the same vowel as did certain words with reflexes of ME *a* before /r/, and that this vowel was distinct both from the short /a/ and from reflexes of ME *a* before /l/ or after /w/ (cf. figure 1, above). Heslop provides no systematic guide to the pronunciation of words in his glossary and in his introductory notes on pronunciation, he lists examples rather than exhaustive or definitive word lists for the sounds referred to. This means that, whilst we have some phonological information, we cannot really know the full extent of the lexical sets represented by Heslop's examples. Heslop writes as follows: (1892: xviii)

Of vowels the most characteristic are the following:-

1. The short A, like the sound of a in a la mode or the German Salz (salt). Salt, malt, fault, are pronounced thus, except in West Tyne.

2. The same sound prolonged produces the Northumberland aa (or aw as it is sometimes written) in waa (wall) blaa (blow) snaa (snow) etc which are thus spoken in South Northumberland and on Tyneside.

3. The long ai heard in chair, is heard throughout Northumberland in maister (master) gaird (guard) quairt (quart) etc.

If we accept that Heslop is here choosing examples which illustrate the peculiarities of Northumbrian speech, and that words other than those cited have the short [a] described under 1, above, then the phonemic distribution shown by Heslop is the same as that outlined in figure 1 above. Moreover, the phonetic description of vowels 1 and 2 is the same as that of present-day Tyneside and Northumbrian. However, Heslop's description of 3 as the vowel heard in *chair* suggests that this vowel, occurring in *master* and in words with ME *a* before /r/, has changed over the last century from [ɛ:] to [ɑ:]. It could be, then, that the long [ɑ:] of present day Tyneside and Northumbrian dialects is derived, not from a lengthening of [a], but from a backing of what in the nineteenth century appears to have been [e:] or [ɛ:]

In order to discover whether this could be the case, we need to look at descriptions of Northumbrian and/or Tyneside speech in the transitional period, ie the early twentieth century. Unfortunately, information from this period is thin on the ground and, as Orton points out, the vast amount of dialect literature from this period is written in conventional orthography and as such is 'comparatively useless for students of phonology' (1930: 17). Indeed, it is to Orton himself, and to his co-workers on the SED that we must turn for further inform-ation on this transitional period. Orton (1930) lists among the many diphthongs found in Northumbrian speech, [eØ] in *arm, bairn*. This diphthong is, later in the same dialect, given in the pronunciatin of *cart* [keØt] Orton, like Heslop, does not give us the full lexical distribution of this diphthong, but merely uses examples of words containing the sound to illustrate his point. Orton's list does at least suggest that, before /r/, reflexes of *ai* and *a* have merged. His evidence therefore corroborates that of Heslop in suggesting the existence in Northumbrian dialects, of a lexical set containing reflexes of ME or later *ai* (such as *master, bairn*,[4] *chair*) and of ME *a* before /r/ (such as *quart, cart*). The absence of post-vocalic /r/ in Orton's transcription of [keØt] suggests that the second element of this diphthong developed as a consequence of the loss of post-vocalic /r/, just as in R.P., the loss of post-vocalic /r/ in the eighteenth century led to the development of central vowels in words like *bird*.

The SED material for Northumberland, which was collected in the 1950's from informants who were aged 65 or over at the time, and who were therefore youths at the time when Heslop's glossary was compiled, shows a considerable amount of variation in the pronunciation of words with ME *a* before /r/ and with ME *ai*. Post-vocalic /r/, which in Northumbrian speech is realised as [ʁ], is present in all except the most westerly of locations, Allendale. Where /r/ is present, either fully pronounced or in the form of r-colouring, pronunciations for *arm* range from [ẹ:ʁəm] through [eəʁm] and [aeəʁʁ m] to [aʁm], the [e:]/[ẹ:] pronunciations on the whole coming from the northern and coastal areas. For *quart*, there are more pronunciations with [a:], but Lowick and Ellington on the coast, and Wark have [kweʊɾt.] *Farmer*, *harvest* and *barn* have [aː] throughout, whilst *bairn* has [beːʁə n,] [bɛ ɔʁ n,] [beəʁn,] [bɛəʁn,] and *chair* has [tʃeˑɔʁ], [tjɛɔʁ], [tʃiɔʁ]. *Master* appears sporadically as a response to questions designed to elicit words for *Mr* or for *husband*. Pronunciations recorded are [meəstɔʁ] and [meːstər].

Thus for members of the lexical set described by Heslop as having the same vowel as *chair*, and by Orton (1930) as having the diphthong [eØ], the SED gives a wide range of pronunciations, from [eː] to as far back as [aː]. The [aː] realisations do, however, only occur in words with orthographic ⟨a⟩, whilst those with orthographic ⟨ai⟩ vary from [eː] to [ɛː], with *chair* having a diphthong similar to that described by Orton, with a rounded second element. Such variability could represent a change in progress during the lifetimes of the SED informants: such a change would involve lowering and backing of [eː] to [ɛː] and possibly to [ae:] of words with ME *ai* and with *a* before /r/. For some of the SED informants, words with *a* before /r/ seem to have undergone a further development to [aː]. O'Connor's (1947) account of the speech of adolescent boys in the city of Newcastle, shows the further development to today's system (the youths of 1947 would, of course, be in their fifties now), with a back [ɑː] for *a* before orthographic ⟨r⟩, suggesting that, in the mid-twentieth century, a further backing of [aː] to [ɑː] occurred in this environment. *Master* and *plaster* are not included in O'Connor's transcription, but it would appear from the evidence of Heslop and the SED that *master* at least has been carried along with the development of ME *ai* words from [eː] to [ɛː]; and from Wright that *plaster* would at least share the same nineteenth century starting-point with [eː]. At some point, these two words have joined in with the further backing of *a* before /r/ to the present day pronunciation with [ɑː]

This analysis presents us with two problems: firstly, it involves the reversal of the merger of *ai* and *a* reported by Heslop and Orton, and the removal of *master* and *plaster* from the *ai* lexical set to that with *a*; secondly, the lowering and backing of [eː] to [ɑː] appears to be both phonetically wide-ranging and rapid, taking place between 1896 and 1947. The first of these problems is dealt with by Labov (1974) who shows that there is such a thing as a 'near-merger' in which sounds reported by native speakers to have merged or to be 'the same' may, in fact, be phonetically distinct and thus liable to later separation. The problem tackled by Labov is that of the merger reported in seventeenth century sources of ME *i*:

and *oi* as in the homophones *loin* and *line*. Here, as in the case of ME *ai* and *a* in Northumbrian, the later separation may have been assisted by the consistent orthographic distinction between the two. Thus, it is quite plausible that *ai* and *a* before /r/ though reported as 'the same' by Heslop and Orton, may have remained sufficiently distinct to reseparate, and that, at the point in time when the introduction of Universal Education would be enforcing the standard spellings of *master* and *plaster*, the orthographic similarity would have caused these to fall in with the *a* set.

With regard to the rapidity and extensiveness of the change, the dating of the evidence may not give us an accurate picture of the time-scale involved. Heslop and Orton were both engaged in the task of enumerating the peculiarities of the Northumbrian dialect and would therefore be likely to give the most rural and archaic forms in use at the time. The SED informants were likewise chosen as those most likely to use traditional forms. On the other hand, O'Connor's youths of 1947 are the mature men of today and, furthermore, represent an urban and so probably more advanced, dialect. The time-span involved, then, is probably more like 150 years, from the youth of the speakers whose language is described by Heslop in 1896, ie from the mid-nineteenth century, to the present day.

The extent and nature of the change, as well as its timing, can be explained with regard to the presence in all the words concerned of /r/, whether in the syllable following the vowel, as in *master* and *plaster*, or immediately after the vowel as in *arm*, *cart*. We have already noted (above, p. 35) Dobson's remarks concerning the uniquely powerful influence of /r/ on other phonemes in its vicinity. In some dialects, this influence continues to be exerted even when the /r/ is no longer pronounced, an example being the lowering of the vowel in R.P. *bird* /bɜ:d/. In Northumbrian and Tyneside dialects of English, the influence of /r/ continues into the present century, because the loss of post-vocalic /r/ is a much more recent phenomenon here than in R.P.. Indeed, Pahlsson (1972) shows that it is still in use amongst older speakers in rural areas. The Northumbrian /r/ is a uvular fricative [ʁ], which, as well as being produced at the back of the mouth, involves lip-rounding such that some Tyneside speakers now produce an /r/ which has lost its friction but retains lip-rounding and so is labialised. It is therefore to be expected that the Northumbrian [ʁ] will have even more backing and lip-rounding power than the [r] of R.P., and that developments associated with the loss of post-vocalic /r/ will be more recent than the parallel developments in R.P. In fact, the influence of Northumbrian [ʁ] on neighbouring vowels is a well-documented process, known as 'burr-modification'. Pahlsson (1972: 19) defines burr-modified vowels as 'vowels that have been retracted and lowered (in most cases) due to a following posterior /r/ eg /fɔ:st/; /wɔ:d/', and goes on to state that such modification may occur 'whether the /r/ is actually realised or not'. Geeson (1969: 32) also notes this phenomenon, stating that 'the peculiarity and difficulty of the sounding of the letter "r" lies in the modification of the preceding vowel'. Thus 'er' becomes 'ar' or 'or' as in very, pronounced 'varry' and Percy pronounced 'Porcy'. Now, if a following /r/ can, as Geeson suggests, cause the retraction of [e] to [a] in *very*, it is possible that the same process of burr-modification caused the retraction of [e:] to [ɑ:] in *arm*, *guard*, etc. *Master* and *plaster* do not have an /r/ immediately following the vowel, but we have already seen (p. 36 above) that in the lengthening of *a* in R.P., a following syllabic /r/ was almost as powerful as a post-vocalic /r/, and this could equally be the case here: the same phonetic forces which inhibited raising and fronting of *a* to [ae] and allowed for later lengthening in R.P., are in Northumbria causing the lowering and retraction of [e:] to [ɑ:] and, more recently, its rounding to [ɒ:]. The timing of the change from [e:] to [ɑ:] in *cart*, *master*, *plaster*, etc is also consistent with that of burr-modification: Orton (1930) implies that the modification in words like *bird* and *third* was an innovation at the time, for he is suspicious of the dialectal purity of the pronunciations [bɔ:d], [θɔ:d], which are, of course, precisely the pronunciations cited by Hughes & Trudgill (1979) as being typical of present-day Tyneside. Thus the burr-modification of [ɜ:] to [ɔ:] in *bird*, etc like that of [e:] to [ɑ:] in *master*, *plaster*, *cart*, etc is a feature of the twentieth century, depending as it does on the rapid and recent loss of post-vocalic /r/ in these dialects. (The SED records post-vocalic [ʁ] for all locations in Northumberland except the westerly Allendale, but some twenty years later, Pahlsson (1972) shows its disappearance from the language of all but the most elderly and rural speakers).

It would appear, then, that the long [ɑ:] in *master*, *plaster* in Tyneside and Northumbrian speech is due not, as Wells (1980) implies, to lengthening of *a* under the influence of R.P., but to an internal development within these dialects of the reflexes of ME *ai*. If R.P. has any part to play at all, it is in encouraging the loss of post-vocalic /r/ on which this internal development depends. However, the end result of burr-modification (if we can say that an end has been reached) is the development of pronunciations which distinguish Tyneside and Northumbrian from other dialects of English, North and South, as clearly as the burr itself did in previous centuries. The burr-modified vowels in [bɔːd][θɔːd] are recognised within and outside the region as characteristic of these dialects: the localised nature of the Northumbrian and Tyneside long back [ɑː] has hitherto not been recognised because, quite coincidentally, it happens to sound like R.P. and because laypersons and professional dialectologists alike are so confident about the power and influence of R.P. on provincial dialects that they always assume that any change in the direction of R.P.-like pronunciation is due to this influence.

NOTES

1. Philological symbols are italicized here as in Dobson (1968). However, a is used in place of ɑ, since the typewriter available did not include the latter.
2. The Overall Unit is 'an arbitrarily chosen abstract phonological symbol which encapsulates the complete lexical set in which it occurs'. (Pellowe et al. 1972, p2).
3. 'Broadening' in Wells' usage refers to the lengthening of *a*. Words in capitals exemplify the lexical sets used by Wells to distinguish the accents of English.
4. *Bairn* did not have *ai* in ME, but in those spellings in which it survives beyond ME, such as Scottish, spellings with <ai> are recorded from the sixteenth century onwards.

REFERENCES

Dobson, E.J. 1968. *English Pronunciation 1500-1700*. (2nd edition). Oxford: Oxford University Press.
Geeson, C.A. 1969. *Northumberland and Durham Word Book*. Newcastle: Harold Hill.
Heslop, O. 1892. *Northumberland Words*. London: English Dialect Society.
Hughes, A., Trudgill, P. 1979. *English Accents and Dialects*. London: Edward Arnold.
Labov, W. 1966. *The Social Stratification of English in New York City*. Washington D.C.: Center for Applied Linguistics.
Labov, W. 1974. 'On the Use of the Present to Explain the Past'. *Proceedings of the Eleventh International Congress of Linguists*. ed. L. Heilman, 825-51. Bologna: Il Mulino.
O'Connor, J.D. 1947. 'The Phonetic System of a Dialect of Newcastle-

upon-Tyne'. *Le Maître Phonetique.* 89: 6-8.
Orton, H. 1930. 'The Dialects of Northumberland'. *Transactions of the Yorkshire Dialect Society.* Part XXI. Vol V: 14-25.
Pahlsson, C. 1972. *The Northumbrian Burr.* Lund: CWK Gleerup.
Pellowe, J., Nixon, G., McNeany, V. 1972. *Defining the Dimension of a Linguistic Variety Space.* Unpublished draft prepared for Colloquium on Urban Speech Surveying in Newcastle-upon-Tyne.
Shorrocks, G. 1977. 'Long and Short "a" in a Lancashire Dialect'. *University of Lancaster Regional Bulletin.* 20: 5-6.
Sundby, B. 1953. *Christopher Cooper's English Teacher.* Lund: CWK Gleerup.
Wells, J.C. 1982. *Accents of English.* Cambridge: Cambridge University Press.
Wright, J. 1898. *English Dialect Dictionary.* London: Henry Fronde.

THE ORIGINS OF PERIPHRASTIC DO: ELLEGÅRD AND VISSER RECONSIDERED

DAVID DENISON
University of Manchester

0. *Introduction.* The origin of periphrastic DO becomes important in retrospect, because of the obvious importance of the construction in ModE. It is unsatisfactory that so much should be obscure or controversial about its first appearance, including the date, dialect, register, syntactic pre-history, and original function. That's my excuse for allowing periphrastic DO to rise again.[1]

The fifteenth century is pivotal, with abundant examples of DO + infinitive in apparent synonymy with a simple tensed verb—hence the term periphrasis. Before that time we have to explain how the verb DO developed into a periphrastic auxiliary and how its use spread. After that time we have to explain how the 'regulation' of periphrastic DO brought it into such close association with the 'NICE' properties (negation, inversion, code, emphasis) that it was virtually excluded from simple affirmatives and became a central structural element in the English verbal system, although that process may well have begun earlier. Here I shall concentrate on the period up to the fifteenth century.

Periphrastic DO was comprehensively treated by Ellegård (1953, henceforth 'E'). There have been other theories of origin before and since, and we ought to look in particular at the objections raised by Visser (1963-73, = 'V'), since he is E's only serious rival in the width (if not the quality) of his data collection. E is more accurate, but one of V's proposals can lead us to a better solution. I will date the arrival of true periphrastic DO rather later than most recent accounts have done.

1. *Ellegård's account.* For E, periphrastic DO derives from causative DO by the semantic re-analysis of an existing surface form.

1.1. For **causative** DO we may borrow V's convenient labels 'cdsi' and 'cdi', standing for 'causative DO (+ subject-of-the-infinitive) + infinitive'. Possible examples:

(1)   (1460) *Paston* 55.4   preyng you þat ye wole do them spede them in þat matier.
(2)   a1225(c1200) *Vices & V.(1)* 25.10   Ðis hali mihte ðe dieð ilieuen ðat ...
(3)   (1480) *Paston* 229.39   and wulleth that if the seid Thomas paie or do paie to the seid Margaret yerly xviij li. as is aboveseid, ...

E (54) and others have argued that the use in OE of an infinitive after DO, rather than the far more common þæt-clause, is probably due to Latin influence, though V (§1212) is less sure. Cdsi is found rarely in OE, commonly in some varieties of ME, especially eastern ones, and then becomes obsolete by the sixteenth century (V §2068). The chronological distribution of cdi is similar, except that it is very rare indeed in OE (E 17, 48; V §1212), and unambiguous examples are not common in ME.[2] A similar pattern with other verbs of causation is widespread in OE and ME, however (V §1195).

1.2. Some examples of DO with an infinitive are indeterminate between a causative (cdi) and a periphrastic reading—what Engblom calls **ambiguous** DO (1938: 71) and E **equivocal** DO (= V's 'edi' type), though at times E distinguishes between 'equivocal' and 'ambiguous' uses. I think the distinction matters. The meaning of the DO + verb syntagm is usually vague rather than ambiguous:

(4)   (1386) *RParl.FM* in *Bk.Lond.E.* 34.25   And in the nyght next after folwynge he did carye grete quantitee of Armure to the Guyldehalle

Equivocal DO is found from the thirteenth century onwards, at first in verse (E 55, V §1213).

1.3. E's argument runs as follows. Since most possible ME cdi's must strictly be classified as equivocal, there are many opportunities for 'permutation' of a DO + verb string, whereby without overall change of meaning the lexical verb could itself be interpreted causatively and DO taken as an empty auxiliary. One of the classic examples (E 28) is:

(5)   ?a1400(a1338) Mannyng *Chron.Pt.2* 97.22   Henry ... þe walles did doun felle, þe tours bette he doun.

Did felle can be interpreted either as *did* 'caused' + *felle* 'to fell/be felled' or as *did* 'past tense' + *felle* 'cause to fell/be felled'. The motivation for the semantic change (E does not consider the syntax) is not strictly linguistic at all: periphrastic DO is a convenience in rhyming verse, as it allows the lexical verb to appear as an infinitive in rhyming position and also offers a bit of metrical padding.

1.4. Unambiguous **periphrastic** DO (V's 'pdi') first occurs in thirteenth-century verse, e.g.:

(6)   c1300(?c1225) *Horn* 1057   His sclauyn he dude dun legge

Once the construction has come into use in south-western poetic texts, it spreads gradually to other areas and to prose. At this stage it is unemphatic and entirely synonymous with the simple verb.

1.5. *Objections to Ellegård*. E's theory requires a sufficient frequency of equivocal DO for the semantic change to be possible, but without too high a frequency of causative DO for it to be inhibited. Therefore he sets great store by the relative frequency of equivocal and causative DO in the different dialects, that is the ratio edi : (cdi+cdsi), though in fact he measures edi : cdsi, since clear cdi is rare enough not to affect the figures significantly (E 45). The south-western dialect is said to be one where the ratio is high: causative/equivocal DO is used there frequently in poetry without an expressed subject for the infinitive, but rarely *with* one, other causative verbs being used instead.

1.5.1. There are other problems. Firstly, as E admits (37, 55), clear cases of cdi are rare. When discussing imperative DO he even silently collapses cdi and edi (127). Secondly, equivocal and periphrastic DO appear more or less simultaneously. Therefore in the putative development cdi > edi > pdi, we have little evidence for the first stage, while the chronological support for the second stage is weaker than one would like. E appears to acknowledge the problems (55f., 62f., 118f.), but I cannot see that he solves them.

1.5.2. V disputes the possibility of causative origin (§1417). First he claims that there are few examples of equivocal DO before 1400, and that many of these may not have been equivocal at the time. Then he also dismisses as rare before 1400 what he sees as the most plausible cases of equivocal DO, those with a lexical verb like BUILD denoting a communal activity, where the subject is the instigator of the project. (He makes them look rarer birds than they are by classifying several as unambiguous causatives (§1212).) Numbers are therefore important in evaluating V's objection, particularly the ratio of equivocal to periphrastic DO, edi : pdi (not the ratio focussed on by E). On E's totals, if we confine attention to thirteenth-century western verse the ratio edi : pdi is 39 : 57. Thirteenth- and fourteenth-century examples, verse and prose, bring the ratio to 70 : 91 in the west or 295 : 107 in the country as a whole (E 44, table 1). V's citations increase the national totals to c315 : c147 (at least) (§§1213, 1418).[3] On these figures, E's argument looks tenable: there is an ample number of equivocal DO before 1400. Of the 70 edi's in the west, 11 involve a verb of communal activity like BUILD with instigator as subject, and a further 7 involve verbs like LERE, TEACH, CLEPE 'summon', SEND AFTER/FOR, which, when the subject is suitable, I find equally plausible candidates for E's proposed semantic change. It is a matter of subjective judgement whether this is too small a total to sustain the more specific hypothesis.

1.5.3. Turning specifically to E's argument, V asserts that 'the weak point in this theory is the assumption of the possibility for *fell* to mean "cause others to fell"'. Now I see no problem there, particularly in the light of the parallel *bette doun* in (5) and modern examples like:

(7)   Nixon bombed Cambodia.

Marchand actually found the semantic change causative > periphrastic a 'mental impossibility': '"Causing a thing to be done" is fundamentally different from "doing a thing"' (1939: 123). Yet GET or HAVE + past ptcp. can show the same equivocation in ModE between doing something oneself and having it done by another:

(8)   I will get/have the work finished on time.

I am not claiming that causative GET and HAVE developed into non-causatives: in the case of HAVE, at least, the chronology is wrong. What the modern comparison shows is that language can tolerate a vagueness of this kind.

1.5.4. The whole change is envisaged as taking place in poetic language. E argues that periphrastic DO was 'a peculiarity of the poetic diction, belonging to the paraphernalia of the verse-maker's craft' (146, though cf. 208). The implication is that but for the advent of rhyming verse there would have been no motivation for the semantic change which produced periphrastic DO. An arbitrary fact of cultural history seems a poor explanation for the appearance of what was to become a central feature of the English verbal system. That does not mean that E was necessarily wrong, but we would be happier to find specifically linguistic, structural factors.

1.5.5. Finally, the origin is essentially an accidental and isolated phenomenon, and no real explanation is given by E for the spread of DO to prose and ordinary speech.

2. *Visser's account*. V derives periphrastic DO from a cataphoric use of factitive DO. Such a development from loose parataxis towards tight syntax would have many parallels. The data are as follows.

2.1. DO can be used cataphorically, anticipating another, 'explanatory' verb:

(9)   (c970) *BenR* 71.15   gif he aðor dyde, oððe ofer-
       gimde, oððe forgeat, oððe tobræc ænig þing
(10) (c1000) *WHom* 7.1 Leofan men, doð swa eow mycel
       þearf is, understandað þæt ælc cristen man ...
(11) a1225(?a1200) *Trin.Hom.*(=*OEHoms* II) 179.34 Hire
       ne dide noðer. ne oc. ne smeart. þo þe hie bar
       ure louerd ihesu crist. ... Ac elch oðer wimman
       doð. akeð. and smerteð sore. þan hie beð mid
       childe bistonden.

Such examples occur from early OE onwards. In OE and ME the explanatory verb is in the same tense or non-finite part as DO (**anticipative DO + appositive verb**). Later the explanatory verb can be in the infinitive even when DO is not (**anticipative DO + infinitive**).

2.2. V's account is confusing. First he claims that OE factitive DO may take as its object a nominal, an imperative, or a finite verb form. He then claims that 'it is only natural to assume' that factitive DO in OE could take an infinitive as object too, except that the pattern 'had nothing to recommend itself because it expressed nothing more, or better, than' the simple verb. The next stage of the argument is not clearly stated but seems to be that this alleged potential for factitive DO + infinitive, latent at least from OE times, was finally exploited in ME when a useful purpose was found for it. V claims support from the fact that reduction of stress on non-adjacent anticipative DO and deletion of material intervening between DO and infinitive would yield periphrastic DO (§§1412-14a). Thus in (12), for example, the attested (a) would become (b):

(12)(a)   a1450 *Wor.Serm.* 23.54   we do rythe als þe childyr
           of Israel dede, gedder vs to-gedre
    (b)   we do gedder vs to-gedre

It is not clear whether he regards such a process as actually occurring or as merely theoretical support for his hypothesis. Why should it happen?

2.3. *Objections to Visser*. In V's OE material it is noticeable that when DO precedes non-contiguous imperatives or finite verbs, it always has a complement within its own clause, such as *swa*, a *swa*-clause, *oþer þæra*, or whatever. Particularly interesting are citations like:

(13) (c900) *CP* 397.19 Ægðer he dyde, ge he egesode ða ðe on unryht hæmdon, ge he liefde ðæm ðe hit forberan ne meahton.

(14) (c1000) *WPol* 200,§55 And we lærað, þæt preostas swa dælan folces ælmessan, þæt hig ægðer don, ge God gegladian ge folc to ælmessan gewænian.

The placing of *ægðer* suggests that it was perceived as the object of DO (thus E 133; cf. Mitchell 1985: §1545), and anticipative DO is rarely adjacent to the explanatory verb. So the premise that OE factitive DO could take a verbal 'object' other than a verbal noun is highly dubious. Fischer and van der Leek have commented on the paucity of evidence for the alleged nominal character of the OE and early ME infinitive (1981: 318-21).

2.3.1. The main problem with V's hypothesis is that it depends on the presence of anticipative DO + infinitive in OE and early ME, and yet all of his copious collection of examples can, and many should, be discounted (§1413). Thus he gives eight from late OE of the type

(15) (c1000) *WHom* 8c.125 ac utan don swa us þearf is, gelæstan hit georne

where the infinitive is most plausibly taken as dependent on *uton*, not *don* (cf. the similar (10) above, where *uton* is lacking and the lexical verb is not an infinitive). The remaining three OE examples are less clear-cut, but Bruce Mitchell has recently criticised V's analysis of them in detail (1985: §666). The ME ones are similarly suspect, in that they may as well be anticipative DO + appositive verb, or else causative. The first two are:

(16) a1225(?a1200) *Trin.Hom.*(=*OEHoms* II) 179.2 Swo don in þis woreld þe riche þe ben louerdinges struien þe wrecche men þe ben underlinges. and naðeles bi hem libben. and habbeð of here swinche hundes and haukes. and ...

(17) a1225(?a1200) *Lay.Brut*(Clg) 4990 heom heo ... brohten to þen kinge. | þat þe king heom sculden: don: oðer slan oðer hon.[4]

Similar doubts apply to the next sixteen, until we reach:

(18) ?c1450 *Knt.Tour-L.* 2.24 And so thei dede bothe deseiue ladies and gentilwomen, and bere forthe diuerse langages on hem

(19)   1463-77(a1450) *Yk.Pl.* 9.111 Woman, why dois þou þus? | To make vs more myscheue?[5]

And E (133) regards example (18) as unambiguously periphrastic, while (19) has a *to*-infinitive. Now it is entirely possible that some of V's earlier examples do in fact contain anticipative DO + infinitive, but it is noteworthy that no examples before the fifteenth century are certain and that many have *to*-infinitive rather than plain infinitive.[6] What may be a related construction, DO + *but* + infinitive (V §1414a), also fails to provide a secure example before the fifteenth century.

3. *Negatives and non-declaratives*. So far we have mainly considered simple affirmative declaratives, whereas it is in other clause types that periphrastic DO has come to serve an important function. To save space I must simply assert here that other clause types do not alter the picture. No separate explanation is needed for the *origin* of DO in questions and negatives (first appearance late fourteenth century), though periphrastic DO was relatively more common in interrogatives (and negatives) than in simple declaratives from the earliest period when all three types are recorded (E 161-2).[7] Imperative DO was probably more influenced by periphrastic DO than vice versa (cf. E 132, 148). And evidence is lacking for an original emphatic function of periphrastic DO (E 24, 147-8). It is legitimate, therefore, to base our discussion of the origins on simple affirmatives.

4. *A new(ish) proposal*. We have two principal candidates for the syntactic source of the periphrasis. Both have dubious, sporadic attestations which predate it, but whereas E's causative/equivocal DO is at least as old as periphrastic DO, V's anticipative DO + infinitive is not securely attested until some 200 years later. It is hard to find other grounds for discriminating between them. I had thought, for instance, that the early occurrence of the periphrasis with impersonal verbs and dummy *it* subjects could be used to argue against V's derivation, but then example (11) showed that anticipative DO could be followed by an impersonal explanatory verb.

Many writers have been led to the conclusion that both sources made a contribution. Even E (146-7) and V (§1417) acknowledge it, though V appears to deny it. Having argued that derivation from causative DO is unconvincing, he goes on to speculate that the distinction between causative DO without expressed NP (= cdi) and anticipative DO + infinitive is probably an artefact of modern linguistic analysis, and thereby apparently brings many of E's equivocal DO examples into the chain of development of periphrastic DO (whilst still denying the relevance of causative DO!). This is tantamount to arguing that the type cdi is a phantom, and that all cdi examples should be re-classified as equivocal, edi. Now there *are* grounds for the latter suggestion, given the rarity of unambiguous cdi (see §1.5.1 above). It is this I wish to build on, rather than the notion of a dual source, which although quite possible is unnecessary. We can accommodate the idea that cdi is a linguists' figment without bringing in the chronological uncertainties of anticipative DO.

4.1. The virtually simultaneous appearance of cdi, equivocal and periphrastic DO is very suggestive. It militates against V's account, which assigns separate origins to the periphrasis, but it doesn't really help E, since there is no time lag for the proposed semantic change. Suppose we re-classify the material without the cdi/edi/pdi split and simply say that a new construction, DO + infinitive, arose during the thirteenth century. (E calls it '*do x*', of course, precisely because his three semantic subtypes can be hard to distinguish.) Then, picking up V's hint, we suggest that its meaning was factitive, with purely contextual clues as to whether or not an intermediary actually performed the action. Thus we will no longer have to assume that an apparently non-causative thirteenth-century DO has the same status as the fifteenth-century (or modern) periphrasis.

4.2. I shall now outline a possible history of periphrastic DO. It makes use of familiar elements in (I think) a new way. It integrates DO better into wider syntactic developments and motivates some co-occurrence restrictions not usually accounted for. The chronological problems and arbitrary changes involved in both E's and V's accounts are removed.

4.3. *Syntactic origin*. Causative DO + NP + infinitive (cdsi) enters late OE probably as a Latinism, and since it clashes neither with OE syntax nor with the semantics of DO, it gradually enters more general use. Eventually it spawns a variant construction with subject of the infinitive unexpressed, a natural development given the examples particularly of HATEN and LETEN and perhaps also of French FAIRE.[8] This would be a two-clause structure, and for those who prefer EST terminology, the subject of the infinitive would be PRO, carrying the index *arb*:[9]

(20)   NP [DO [$_S$ PRO VP]]

(I am ignoring INFL and other niceties.)

4.3.1. *PRO and NP coreferential?* The contemporary (ME) interpretation of the pattern depends on the verb and the context: the majority are equivocal between direct agency and action through an intermediary, a distinction which the construction itself leaves unspecified. In some examples a causative reading (i.e. action through an intermediary) is ruled out lexically or pragmatically, and we have assumed with hindsight that it must be an empty DO periphrasis. In other cases (much fewer, and often in translated and legal texts), context rules out direct agency and we have classified the example as cdi, causative DO. Returning to my modern GET/HAVE + pa.ptcp. analogy, we could compare contextual interpretations of:

(21)   I got my car professionally resprayed. (by somebody else)
(22)   I got the wheelnuts unscrewed. (by somebody else *or* by myself)
(23)   I got my hand stuck in the door. (by myself)

4.4. *Semantics*. The construction is used to focus not on who did it but on what happened. Deciding on the exact meaning is speculative, though there is corroborative evidence for what follows. I surmise that the meaning might at first have been perfective or completive, something like 'achieve (the action of the infinitival VP)', but without agentive associations.

4.4.1. *Three observations on the meaning of the DO + infinitive construction.* I have explained its *syntactic* origin on the basis of an analogy with HATEN and LETEN, which already show infinitival complementation with and without overt embedded subject, but the semantics must be slightly different if those verbs disallow an interpretation where PRO is coreferential with the matrix subject.[10] This would follow if HATEN and LETEN in the structure with subject NP retained enough of the 'command' and 'permit' senses, respectively, to rule out coreference (cf. E 38), whereas DO 'bring about' would not suffer from the same restriction. Secondly, a development from a word meaning 'do' or 'done' to a perfective marker would be widely paralleled cross-linguistically, and could perhaps even be paralleled within ME for certain lexical uses of *done* (Jones 1972: 157). Thirdly, the eleventh to the thirteenth centuries witness the development of various new aspect- and Aktionsart-marking devices in parallel with the obsolescence of the OE prefixal system; see Samuels (1972: 160-65) for a long list. The DO + infinitive construction could be seen as an experimental form of Aktionsart marking, later altered in structure and function.

4.4.2. *Co-occurrence restrictions*. If I am right about the meaning of the construction, it would be incompatible with certain types of lexical verb. I have checked all the thirteenth- and fourteenth-century examples against the classification of Vendler (1967) as elaborated in Dowty (1979). Exact figures are inappropriate in view of all the uncertainties,[11] but the vast majority of infinitive clauses are 'accomplishments'—that is, telic—while a couple of dozen are 'achievements' (punctual), the other class which is compatible with perfectivity. Of the rest, under 20 or so look more like 'activities', and fewer than 10 look like 'states' (cf. Goossens 1984: 155-6). But set these against the 400+ examples which fit.

4.4.3. Now, incompatibility of DO with a stative infinitive would explain nicely the non-occurrence of DO followed by main verb HAVE, main verb BE,[12] the modals,[13] and perhaps perfect HAVE and BE. Absence of DO + progressive BE, if not accounted for by the relative rarity of the progressive, would follow from a restriction on DO + activity verb. E and V do not attempt to explain these facts. Absence of DO + passive BE is explained differently, by the fact that a passive infinitive would be without nominal arguments. DO itself has a full morphology, however, occurring in infinitive, past participle and imperative as well as finite forms, and this too is what we would expect.

4.5. *Re-analysis*. Over the late OE and ME periods several other causative verbs enter the syntactic subsystem in question, e.g. GAR, MAKE, CAUSE; there is much dialectal variation. Each of them occurs in both types of construction, with and without subject of the infinitive expressed. The subsystem expands and flourishes. But by the early ModE period the subjectless pattern has become obsolete for most verbs of commanding and causing, with exceptions for Scottish English and fixed idioms like *make believe*; see V §§1195-1249. The DO + NP + infinitive (cdsi) pattern also disappears. So DO + infinitive would have become entirely isolated.

4.5.1. However, instead of being lost, DO + infinitive begins to function within the modal verb subsystem which it resembles formally. It loses its vagueness as to agency and becomes, like the modals, an auxiliary verb. That is, it operates with a lexical verb to form a complex verbal group which has a single subject argument. (Whether you regard this as a one-clause structure depends on your analysis of ModE auxiliaries: for me it is.)[14] The perfective sense may already have been lost—witness the imperfective complements noted in §4.4.2—and the true DO periphrasis has now arrived. Its use can now be extended to all lexical verbs, but the earlier restriction on co-occurrence with modals, HAVE and BE remains intact, becoming grammaticised: the auxiliaries are beginning to form a highly structured and formally patterned subsystem. Along with the other infinitive-governing auxiliaries, namely the modals, DO loses its non-finite forms, or alternatively, loses the possibility of occurring anywhere but first in the verbal group. In Scottish English, DO follows the somewhat different development of modals there.

4.6. In the conventional accounts of periphrastic DO, three main phases are recognised: origin, spread, and regulation. I am proposing instead four phases, with two different kinds of regulation. Phase 1 (thirteenth century) is the appearance of DO + infinitive within the subsystem of causatives, dependent on the prior existence of the cdsi pattern. Phase 2 is the spread of the construction, overlapping (perhaps thirteenth to fifteenth centuries) with phase 3, a syntactic re-analysis in which DO leaves the subsystem of causative catenatives and becomes an auxiliary verb. This leads to a kind of morphological regulation of DO, as there are consequences for its defectiveness, its patterning within the verbal group, and its meaning. Phase 4 (mainly fifteenth and sixteenth centuries) is another period of regulation, when differential behaviour according to clause type is grammaticised, giving us the 'NICE' properties.

4.7. Now let me sketch some advantages of this way of organising the material.

4.7.1. First there is the virtually simultaneous appearance of what had been called cdi, equivocal and periphrastic DO, but which in early texts I regard as contextually determined tokens of the same type, DO + infinitive. Furthermore, the time of appearance, maybe a century after the naturalisation of cdsi and only two centuries after its first use outside literal translation (E 47-54), is explicable rather than accidental.

4.7.2. Then we have the virtual absence of DO followed by what are now auxiliary verbs. Periphrastic DO + HAVE is not used at all until the nineteenth century (V §§1466-76).[15] I have no examples of DO + perfect BE, nor of DO + modal.

Periphrastic DO + BE (progressive, passive, main verb) is hardly found except in modern Irish or Scottish English (V §§1415, 1438). There is a lone citation from More in V (p.1530), worth quoting at greater length than he does:

(24)   1532-3 St. Th. More, *Wks.*(Yale) 8.469.32   For
        ellys yf Tyndale sayd trew, that euery elect
        person wolde be reformed at the fyrste / it muste
        folow that who so euer dyd not when he were
        better taught, retourne and be reformed at the
        fyrste, were a fynall reprobate ...

Here we may have partial neutralisation of anticipative and periphrastic DO.[16] I suspect that V's immersion in the language of More, which shows very free use of anticipative DO at a time when periphrastic DO was flourishing, may have predisposed him to look for the origins of the latter construction in the former. V's line of argument and many of his examples are taken wholesale from Visser (1946-56: II.502-9), actually written before the war. His account and E's are essentially independent and coeval.

4.7.3. In my account the modal verbs have nothing to do with the origin of the DO + infinitive construction and only become relevant with the first phase of regulation. The only available evidence[17] comes, indirectly, from the DO *but* construction, in which E suggests that DO is quite different from the modals:

> The finite form of the explanatory verb was the rule before 1400 and often occurs later as well. This is remarkable, since the but-phrase is also used with modal auxiliaries, in which case the verb is always in the infinitive form ... [*Footnote and two examples omitted—DD.*] This difference of construction shows conclusively that *do* was not felt as an auxiliary in the 13th century (E 135-6).

Actually, the total number of examples of CAN *but*, WILL *but*, etc. is not large (cf. V §§973, 1414a, 1624), but the point is valid: DO in this construction is probably anticipative DO, and everything said above (§2.3.1) about the late introduction of anticipative DO + infinitive applies equally to DO *but*; the pull of CAN *but*, etc. does not seem to have had much early effect. Later, of course, the influence of the modals is seen in the loss/absence of non-finite periphrastic DO, my next point.

4.7.4. *Non-finite periphrastic DO?* Non-finite DO + infinitive is found up to the sixteenth century (V §§1414a, 2022, 2133). This account makes it unnecessary either to explain its existence or to prove every case to be non-periphrastic, for only when DO enters the auxiliary subsystem should we expect such patterns to die out.

4.8. *Periphrastic DO as tense marker?* I wish to make an observation which is independent of the hypothesis I have been advancing. One effect of using DO is that two or more infinitives can be coordinated without repeating the tense marking. It is interesting that many of V's examples of anticipative DO—often truncated in §1413—involve a coordination of lexical verbs, suggesting a functional/stylistic reason for its use. A number of fifteenth- and sixteenth-century examples of periphrastic DO are also followed by coordinated verbs (cf. Trnka 1930: 44, 50)—notice too how coordination seems to improve an otherwise impossible structure in the More example, (24) above. Here one can see at least a *functional* similarity between the anticipative and the periphrastic.

5. *Conclusions*. It should be obvious now how I would answer most of the implicit questions I started with. I regard a kind of periphrastic DO as coming into being in the thirteenth century or a little earlier, but not in OE. This DO + infinitive had a two-clause, causative structure and DO was not an auxiliary verb. Its origin had little to do with semantic change, with main verb or substitute or imperative DO, with (stressed) emphatic use, or with modal verbs. The construction probably contained the notion of perfectivity or the like in its meaning. Later there was a syntactic re-analysis into a one-clause structure, motivated by the analogy of the modals and the loss of parallel causative constructions, and probably involving the loss of perfective value. The spread and regulation of purely auxiliary periphrastic DO was led by the interrogative and (to some extent) negative forms.

5.1. As far as socio-dialectology is concerned, early usage might have been principally in formal or literary registers if the antecedent construction (cdsi) was originally Latinate, but the evidence for early prose use (or non-use) of DO + infinitive is conflicting. I have not dealt with early functions of DO apart from perfectivity: some may have been essentially colloquial. Thus the question of register remains open. The origin was independent of the introduction of rhyming verse, though metrical usefulness would have helped the spread of the construction. The two-clause construction probably developed in the east, as E has shown causative DO (cdsi) to have been far stronger there than in the west. Perhaps the re-analysis into a one-clause structure was connected with the spread to the west. Incidentally, DO + infinitive is not used in the late-twelfth-century, eastern *Ormulum* (with the dubious exception of 5612), and the select few who have waded through that text may find it difficult to imagine Orm passing up such a glorious device for metrical padding if it had been available to him. I don't make the point too seriously, but it does reinforce my belief that DO + infinitive came into use in the thirteenth century.

5.2. Finally, although I don't believe in a deterministic view of (language) history, I had found the coincidences and unmotivated changes in the conventional accounts rather puzzling. In the development I have sketched here there is still a lot to be filled in, in particular on the rise of the modals and the loss of subjectless infinitives after causative verbs, but they are facts, and within those larger givens, each stage in this partial history of periphrastic DO is not only plausible but one could almost say probable.

NOTES

1. This is a revised and shortened version of the paper written for the 4th ICEHL, omitting much citation of data and sections on substitute, emphatic and imperative DO, on 'Equi' constructions, and on generative treatments. I am grateful to Anthony Warner, M. L. Samuels and Richard Hogg for comments, not all of which I have managed to allow for. All OE and ME citations apart from *Orm.* and *Paston* are to be found in Engblom (1938), Ellegård (1953), and/or Visser (1963-73).
2. For (2) cf. *ibid.* 25.8 *hie iliefð ðat hie næure niseih*, suggesting that the personified virtue can be subject of ILEVE and thus weakening the evidence for causative use. (3) is in the possibly archaic legal jargon of an indenture of lease (cf. E 71).
3. The extra edi's are (references corrected): *Gen. & Ex.* 2629, *Guy* 1289, *Tristrem* 2194, Mannyng *HS* 6779, *KAlex.* 425.207, *Cursor* 7896, 8349, 11083, 11774, 13364, 14800, 17775, 24398, Mannyng *Chron.Pt.1* 3251, 3615, 4245, 4255 (not in V), *Chron.Pt.2* 245.12, *Curye* II 57.7 (not in V), II 59.5. For the pdi's I have simply counted V's citations, less the obviously erroneous ones, as V implies that he is citing all (apart from Mannyng?) he knows of for the thirteenth and fourteenth centuries (p.1500n.1).
4. In (16), *struien* and *libben* may be pres.t.: cf. *habbeð* in the next clause, not printed by V. Both *-en* and *-eð* are used for pres.pl. in this manuscript, though conceivably *libben* inf. (as 183.9) contrasts with *liuen* pres.pl. (as 179.2). In (17), *sculden* may be responsible for the infinitive, or the structure may be cdsi. MS. Otho has no metrical punctuation before *don*.
5. The earlier edition cited by V punctuates this sentence as a single interrogative clause.
6. Cf. also c1180 *Orm.* 13087 *& didenn alls he seȝȝde, | To lokenn whære he wass att inn*, again with *to*-infinitive. But this may well not be anticipative DO + infinitive at all but instead derived elliptically from SAY 'order' + NP + infinitive, which is extant at this time (V §2078 and cf. §1241).
7. Kroch, Myhill & Pintzuk (1982) have confirmed E's claim that the interrogative was crucial to the *spread* of the DO periphrasis.
8. Comrie, in a cross-linguistic account of causatives, writes: 'Thus, the overall generalization remains, that it is the

embedded subject that is the expendable and/or mobile constituent of the causative construction' (1976: 265). Admittedly he is most concerned with languages in which causative and embedded verb become fused, but the modern French FAIRE + infinitive construction qualifies for inclusion.

I accept E's assumption (39-40) that the DO to wit idioms are independent of cdsi, and I assume that rare, possible OE examples of cdi (E 48), mostly word-for-word glosses of Latin, do not demonstrate a living use of the DO + infinitive construction. Only the dating would be altered if we accepted them.

9. I interpret 'arb' literally, to mean that matrix subject and embedded subject *could* be coreferential even though not co-indexed. Published (R)EST accounts of *arb* disagree or are vague on this possibility, but the articles of that everchanging faith would take me too far afield. I am very grateful to John Payne for elucidation of, and references on, the syntax of embedded infinitives and the semantics of causatives.

10. Actually, the possibility of periphrastic use of HATAN and LÆTAN has been canvassed for OE, though Mitchell is unconvinced (1985: §§679f.). For ME too, V (p.1356n.) has cited the following example as 'proof' for LET: c1450 *Palladius* (BodAdd) II.18 *To wite if alle be well, thyself allone | Transversall thourgh the forowes everichone | Lette rush a rodde*. But since RUSH may be used of an inanimate NP transitively *or* intransitively at this time in the required sense, *rodde* is perhaps its subject.

11. For example, whether SIGNIFY is a state or achievement verb depends on the exact sense. FORCE and perhaps MOLESTE and SMERTE in Chaucer are better taken as nouns at *Bo.* 2.pr4.165, *TC* 4.880, and *TC* 4.1618, respectively.

12. Except in rare cases of agentive BE; cf. note 16 below.

13. Goossens (who is happy with V's evidence on the syntactic source of DO) has made a similar observation with respect to the non-occurrence of periphrastic DO + modal (1984: 155-6).

14. Comrie, not bound by the Procrustean analyses that EST demands, talks of *degrees* of reduction to simplex sentences in derived structure (1976: 302).

15. Cf. however (1340) *Ayenb.* 196.31 *þe holi man ... ne hedde none ssame of þe poure / ase doþ zome greate lhordes of þis wordle. þet wel doþ elmesse to poure / ac alneway his habeþ ine onworþ-nesse uor hare pourehede* (V §1476), where DO may be a substitute for HAVE (although it is also anticipative).

16. Incidentally, anticipative DO *can* stand for BE, though only if the subject is agentive: *What you must do is be absent that day* (Cruse 1973: 17); *What she did was be seen in that dress*. See Cruse (1973) for a more subtle characterisation of the kinds of sentence which are hyponyms of DO *something*. Some historical examples are cited by Goossens (1984: 155).

17. DO + infinitive is not found in coordination with other auxiliaries until the fifteenth century. Although from the earliest times DO resembles 'modals' in clauses with VP-deletion (*John*

spoke/could speak French but Mary didn't/couldn't), this **substitute DO** has to be kept distinct from DO + infinitive, for example because it occurs from early OE onwards and from the first can stand for a stative verb (cf. also note 15).

REFERENCES

Comrie, Bernard. 1976. 'The Syntax of Causative Constructions: Cross-language similarities and divergences'. *The Grammar of Causative Constructions* ed. by Masayoshi Shibatani, 261-312. (= Syntax and Semantics, 6.) New York, etc.: Academic Press.

Cruse, D. A. 1973. 'Some Thoughts on Agentivity'. *JL* 9. 11-23.

Dowty, David R. 1979. *Word Meaning and Montague Grammar: the semantics of verbs and times in generative semantics and in Montague's PTQ*. (= Synthese Language Library, 7.) Dordrecht: D. Reidel.

Ellegård, Alvar. 1953. *The Auxiliary 'Do': The establishment and regulation of its use in English*. (= Gothenburg Studies in English, 2.) Stockholm: Almqvist & Wiksell. [= E in text]

Engblom, Victor. 1938. *On the Origin and Early Development of the Auxiliary 'Do'*. (= Lund Studies in English, 6.) Lund: C. W. K. Gleerup.

Fischer, O. C. M. & F. C. van der Leek. 1981. 'Optional vs Radical Re-analysis: Mechanisms of syntactic change. Review of: David W. Lightfoot, *Principles of Diachronic Syntax*'. *Lingua* 55. 301-49.

Goossens, Louis. 1984. 'The Interplay of Syntax and Semantics in the Development of the English Modals'. *English Historical Linguistics: Studies in development* ed. by N.F. Blake & Charles Jones, 149-59. (= CECTAL Conference Papers Series, 3.) Sheffield: Department of English Language, University of Sheffield.

Jones, Charles. 1972. *An Introduction to Middle English*. New York, etc.: Holt, Rinehart & Winston.

Kroch, A., J. Myhill & S. Pintzuk. 1982. 'Understanding Do'. *PCLS* 18. 282-94.

Marchand, Hans. 1939. Review of Engblom (1938). *ES* 21. 121-5.

Mitchell, Bruce. 1985. *Old English Syntax*, 2 vols. Oxford: Clarendon Press.

Samuels, M. L. 1972. *Linguistic Evolution: With special reference to English*. (= Cambridge Studies in Linguistics, 5.) Cambridge: Cambridge U.P.

Trnka, B. 1930. *On the Syntax of the English Verb from Caxton to Dryden*. (= Travaux du Cercle Linguistique de Prague, 3.) Prague.

Vendler, Zeno. 1967. *Linguistics in Philosophy*. Ithaca, N.Y.: Cornell U.P.

Visser, F. Th. 1946-56. *A Syntax of the English Language of St. Thomas More*, 3 vols. (= Materials for the Study of the Old English Drama, n.s. 19, 24, 26.) Louvain: Librairie Universitaire.

──. 1963-73. *An Historical Syntax of the English Language*, 3 parts [4 vols]. Leiden: E. J. Brill. [= V in text]

SYNCHRONIC VARIATION AND LINGUISTIC CHANGE: EVIDENCE FROM BRITISH ENGLISH DIALECTS

OSSI IHALAINEN
University of Helsinki

This short paper discusses two areas of grammar that show a great deal of variation in British dialects. These are subject-verb agreement and pronouns. In particular, I shall be concerned with the alternation of standard and dialectal forms in these areas. I shall argue that in the cases that I discuss the alternation is not random but controlled by linguistic factors. I shall also argue that the study of synchronic dialectal variation suggests what sort of questions we should ask about historical data.

Dialectologists today will be working with highly mixed grammars, their informants using standard forms and older dialectal forms in a way that might seem quite random. Situations like the ones listed below are the rule rather than the exception:[1]

1.a. I'm under no obligation about this, be I? (EC T1:1)
  b. They'm gone up dear now. Oh, sky-high dear they be now. (FIVE SENTENCES LATER) They are gone up now. (CF T7:75)
  c. They'm gone. The ones that used to do my shoeing is gone. They'm all dead. ... All these big places, they're turned into flats. (BB T17:14)
  d. If you was lucky enough to find a (nest)... (THREE SENTENCES LATER) They were range birds and they could run anywhere on the farm. (SJ T1:6)

Dialectal and standard forms may occur very close to each other during a single interview. In fact, they may occur in one single sentence, as shown in sentence (1a). Some people feel that this kind of situation is unfortunate because the data gathered today are not 'pure', as the term goes. However, I should like to show that present-day dialects are worth studying even if one is mainly interested in the earlier stages of English.

I have recently argued on the basis of the distribution of invariant *be* (*I be tired* 'I am tired') in British English dialects that the implementation of standard verb forms is conditioned by 'prominence', which consists of stress, syntactic position and sentence modality.[2] Assuming that these dialects are in a state of change, with older dialectal forms being replaced by standard forms, or in some cases by new dialectal forms, analysis of the variation involved should contribute to our understanding of the nature of linguistic change. Here I shall look at subject-verb agreement with full verbs and with the past tense forms of the verb *to be*.

NOUN SUBJECTS VS PRONOMINAL SUBJECTS

In a number of British English dialects the -*s* ending is used throughout the present tense paradigm. These dialects typically have forms like the ones listed below:

2. a. They keep hens.
   b. They do keep hens.
   c. They keeps hens.

The tape-recordings from Somerset referred to above show that agreement is highly variable: a speaker who says *They uses em* or *They do use em* will also say *They use em*. However, it seems that pronominal subjects show agreement far more often than noun subjects.

The figures in the following table (based on the *Survey of English Dialects*) illustrate this trend in British English dialects in general. The sentences concerned are 'They go to church' (SED VIII.5.1), 'They keep hens' (SED IV.6.2), 'Burglars steal them' (SED VIII.7.2) and 'Bulls bellow' (SED III.10.7).

Frame	Standard	Non-standard
Bulls bellow	119	157
Burglars steal	216	96
They go to church	274	30
They keep hens	283	28

Table 1

The differences are too obvious to need statistical testing. What these figures very strongly suggest is that pronominal subjects show more standard agreement than noun subjects do, and that the difference is not accidental.

Subject-verb agreement with full verbs then suggests that pronouns show more standard agreement than nouns do; that is pronouns are innovative, nouns conservative. Fairly similar results can be obtained from the study of the past tense forms of the verb *to be*. Since the SED has no information about the past tense forms of *be* with noun subjects, I used my own tape-recorded material from Somerset to study this point.

The past tense forms of the verb *to be* show two distinct tendencies in Somerset: there are speakers who prefer *was* with all persons of the verb, and then there are speakers who prefer *were* with all persons of the verb.

Another preliminary observation is that, at a very early stage of developing standard agreement, the variation between standard and non-standard forms seems quite unpredictable. It is only at a rather advanced stage that a distributional pattern emerges and the contexts that favour standard forms stand out.

To determine whether noun and pronoun subjects differed with respects to agreement, interviews with three dialect speakers from Somerset were analysed. The speakers prefer *was* with all persons of the verb, but *were* does occasionally occur. The results can be seen from the following table:

subject	was	were
plural pronoun subjects	43	14
plural noun subjects	20	0

Table 2

The figure 20 (noun subjects) includes existential sentences like *There was three blacksmiths in the village*. In existential sentences *was* is used irrespective of the grammatical number of the subject, so that there are no sentences like *There were three blacksmiths in the village*. The value of X^2 for this table is 6.00; that is, the differences are significant beyond the .05 level of significance.

The present tense forms of *to be* also show a sensitivity to the noun/pronoun distinction. A singular form of the verb is frequently used with noun subjects, but not with pronominal subjects:

3.a. Horses is gone.
  b.*They is nice.
  c. They're nice.

To recapitulate the findings so far: there is a clear-cut distinction between noun subjects and pronominal subjects with respect to subject-verb agreement, pronouns showing standard agreement more frequently than nouns.

CASE STUDY: PLURAL *AM*

On the basis of the distribution of invariant *be* in conservative Southern and South-Western dialects (Ihalainen: forthcoming a), I have recently suggested that the contexts that retain old dialectal forms longest are the most prominent ones, and that new forms appear to enter the grammatical system through non-prominent contexts -- 'prominence' being understood as a combination of stress, syntactic position and sentence modality. The position that appears to be the most favourable to new forms is the so-called weak affirmative position. From here innovations spread to other contexts. The most conservative contexts are the strong contexts, strong negatives in particular. The contexts that proved to be relevant are listed below:

WEAK AFFIRMATIVE

They be witty, you know.

QUESTION

Be em nice?
When be going? 'When are you going?'

NEGATION

I ben't taking her down there.

STRONG AFFIRMATIVE

They BE there. (contradicts the statement 'They aren't there.')
He's older than what I be. (Cf. *He's older than I'm.)

STRONG NEGATIVE

Oh no, I ben't.

Weak affirmative positions are positions where verbs like *am* can freely contract; that is, contexts where one can say *I'm* instead of *I am*. In 'strong' contexts no such contraction is possible, so that in sentences like

He is older than I am only the first verb may contract (*He's older than I am*).

To illustrate the relevance of both syntactic context and the nature of the subject in explaining the spread of verb forms, I would like to look at the distribution of plural *am* in South-Western British dialects. The history of this development is not known, but the present distribution of plural *am* in Somerset is shown below:

    4.a. They'm nice.
       b. *They am nice.
       c. *Those boys'm clever.
       d. *Am em nice?
       e. *Yes, they am.
       f. *No, they amn't.

Am occurs in weak affirmative positions only, and even there only with pronominal subjects. One way of explaining the history of the present situation is this: at some point *am* entered the system in the weak affirmative position, but did not spread further. At least I am not aware of any Somerset varieties of English where plural *am* occurs in syntactic contexts other than the weak affirmative. We could characterize the present situation then as an instance of incomplete change.

In Surrey, however, in locality 34:2, *am* occurs in weak affirmatives, questions, and strong affirmatives. In this variety, then, the change seems to have been completed. However, there are also speakers in Surrey that show *are* in weak affirmatives but *am* elsewhere. This kind of situation obtains in locality 34:1. The evidence from these two localities (in one variety non-standard forms all the way through, in another variety standard forms in the weak affirmative position) very clearly shows how standard forms first establish themselves in weak affirmatives. Or to look at the situation from a different viewpoint, old forms first disappear from weak affirmatives. A remarkable instance of this kind of development is the history of periphrastic *do*. It would seem that it entered the grammatical system of English through weak affirmative positions and then spread to questions and negatives (Traugott: 1972, Ellegård: 1952). And then, around the time it became obligatory in negatives, it disappear from weak affirmatives.

I suggested above that the situation in Somerset, as outlined in (4) above, is an instance of incomplete change. It is possible, of course, that plural *am* was once found in all contexts, and has retreated since. However, had this been the case, *am* would have left relics in contexts other than the weak affirmative, because, as we have seen, these appear to be the most conservative contexts. Also, since pronouns seem to be the first to be affected by new forms, we should expect some non-standard *am* forms as relics with noun subjects if the change had covered the whole grammatical system.

Having illustrated the relevance of syntactic position and the nature of the subject in the development of agreement, I shall now go on to relative pronouns.

RELATIVE PRONOUNS: KEENAN AND COMRIE'S NOUN PHRASE ACCESSIBILITY HIERARCHY

Recently the spread of WH-relative pronouns has been closely studied by Suzanne Romaine (1982) and Nadine M. Van den Eynden (1984). Romaine discovered that WH-forms entered the language in the least accessible positions in terms of Keenan and Comrie's accessibility hierarchy. This hypothesis was confirmed by Van den Eynden with another set of data. Keenan and Comrie's accessibility hierarchy is given below:

SUBJECT>DIRECT OBJECT>INDIRECT OBJECT>OBLIQUE>GENITIVE>OCOMP
(Keenan and Comrie 1977)

Since there are quite a few modern dialects where WH-forms are non-indigenous, it would be very interesting to look at the variation between regional and standard pronouns in the light of Romaine's findings. Unfortunately, the SED data do not allow a very close analysis of different syntactic positions, as the *Survey* only has information about subjects and possessives. However, if the SED material behaves as Romaine's principle suggests, we should expect the possessive to show more standard forms than the subject.

It is perhaps worth pointing out that some British English dialects do not seem to have indigenous possessive relatives at all. Various periphrastic forms are used instead, or speakers simply avoid the whole construction. These possibilities are outlined below:

AVOIDANCE   : This is the man (as) had his horse stolen.
PRONOUN RETENTION : This is the man (as) his horse was stolen.
WHOSE   : This is the man whose horse was stolen.

The following table, based on SED IX.9.5. and IX.9.6, shows the number of standard and non-standard forms in subject and possessive position in British English dialects:

SYNTACTIC FUNCTION	STANDARD FORMS	NON-ST FORMS	TOTAL
subject	112	197	309
possessive	214	83	297

Table 3

These figures show that standard genitive pronouns are more frequent than standard subject pronouns. Assuming that standard forms are in the process of spreading over the whole grammatical system, this means that they enter the language in the less accessible of the two positions studied.

But the SED data also suggest that, other things being equal, the referential nature of the antecedent is a conditioning factor. Consider the sentences below. They are the two frames used to elicit pronouns in the SED.

    IX.9.5. 'The work in the garden is getting me down. You say: Well, get some help in. I know a man ___ will do it for you.'

    III.3.7. If I didn't know what a cowman is, you would tell me: He is the man ___ looks after the cows.'

The difference between these two is that while in the first sentence the antecedent is specific, the antecedent of the second pronoun is non-specific. While in the first sentence the speaker has a certain person in mind, in the second sentence no specific person is being referred to -- the sentence is a definition, a generalization.

Analysis of the SED material shows that, besides being regionally conditioned, the choice of the pronoun is sensitive to the specific/non-specific distinction, specific antecedents favouring standard forms.

The pronouns that figure in the SED material are *as*, *who*, *at*, *that*, *what*, and *zero*. There was one instance of *which*. This was not included in the analysis. The frequencies of each pronoun in the two contexts studied are given in the following table:

pronoun	specific	non-specific	total
as	109	127	236
who	100	13	113
at	24	52	76
that	13	58	71
zero	39	15	54
what	23	39	62

Table 4

With the exception of *as*, relative pronouns appear to be sensitive to the specific/non-specific distinction; however, it is the non-indigenous pronoun *who* that shows the greatest difference between the two contexts. The difference between *who* and the other pronouns with respect to sensitivity to the specific/non-specific distinction is too great to be accidental. (For example, the value of Chi^2 for the table of *who* and *zero* is 6.93.) These figures very strongly suggest, then, that not only is the specific/non-specific distinction relevant in predicting contexts where regional variation might occur, but it also controls the spread of WH-forms.

Although, Suzanne Romaine's study of relative clauses in Middle Scots does not cover the specific/non-specific distinction, as it is understood here, she does study the modification of antecedents by idefinite pronouns; but this turned out to be insignificant (Romaine: 1982:89-92, 143-144). Dialects, on the other hand, suggest that indefiniteness controls the distribution of relative pronouns. The evidence comes from the distribution of the pronoun *as* in those dialects where it is not a dominating pronoun. The pronoun *as* in the SED data shows a very clear-cut distributional pattern regionally: it is the dominating pronoun in the West Midlands. Only scattered instances were found in the South-West and none in Somerset.

However, a seven-hour sample of Somerset speech recorded in the seventies showed eight instances of *as*, all of them occurring in contexts not covered by the SED. Five of these eight instances found in the tape-recordings occurred with *all* as antecedent or modifier of the antecedent (the types *all as you had to do* and *all the work as you had to do*). This suggests that indefinite antecedents and indefinite pronouns in particular favour the conservative pronoun *as*. The same tendency is shown by the so-called incidental material occasionally recorded by the SED fieldworkers in addition to the actual responses elicited.

In the light of the evidence presented, then, there are two factors regulating the spread of WH-relative pronouns: syntactic position and the nature of the antecedent. WH-pronouns turned out to be more frequent in the less accessible position of the two syntactic positions studied. Specific antecedents were more favourable to WH-forms than nonspecific antecedents. Antecedents that are indefinite pronouns or are modified by indefinite pronouns seem particularly favourable to older dialectal pronouns.

It was argued above that the distribution of relative pronouns shows that standard forms do not enter dialects in the most accessible position, that is the subject position. Since personal pronouns in South-Western dialects are undergoing change as well, it might be instructive to look at the present situation from the viewpoint of the accessibility hierarchy. In South-Western British English instead of the third person pronoun *it* the masculine pronoun *he* is often found.[3] There is one restriction on the use of *he* though: the pronoun must refer to a 'thing'. The sentence below will illustrate the situation:

5.a. I don't want this knife. He's no good.
 b. I can't drink this tea. *He's too hot.
 c. He took the bottle and put'n in his pocket.
 d. *I don't drink tee because I don't like'n.

In a random sample of some 7000 words from the Somerset corpus referred to above, standard and non-standarded forms of the subject and object pronouns were counted in contexts where it was possible to use *he*. The frequencies are shown in the table below:

	he	it
subject	37	5
object	45	19

Table 5

Since it is somewhat difficult to see from these figures directly what is going on, I computed the Chi-square value for this table. The value is 4.58. The diffences involved are significant at the .05 level of significance.

To be a little more specific, what the table shows is that *it* is more frequent in object position than it might be expected to be, as is *he* in subject position. These figures suggest, then, that new forms spread over the grammatical system via the object position. Again, the standard form seems to be establishing itself in a less accessible noun position in the accessibility hierarchy.

To summarize the main findings: in addition to a previous observation that variation is controlled by stress, syntactic position and sentence modality (features called 'prominence' collectively), the evidence discussed also suggests that there is a difference between nouns and pronouns in the development of standard agreement. Noun specificity turned out to be a significant controller of standard and non-stantard relative pronouns. Evidence was also presented to show the significance of the accessibility hierarchy in explaining the distribution of new pronominal forms.

What I hope to have shown is that there is nothing mystical about mixed paradigms. The dialectal material that I have analysed so far, suggests that, with the exception of varieties where new forms are very rare, patterns emerge which can be described in terms of such well-known linguistic categories as noun, pronoun, subject, object, specific noun, and so on.

The implications of these observations for historical studies are obvious. Analysis of dialectal variation suggests distinctions that may not be so obvious from historical data, which are inevitably somewhat fragmentary. To illustrate how analysis of synchronic dialectal variation might suggest what sort of questions we should ask about historical material, I would like to take a brief look at auxiliaries. In South-Western dialects, there is a very clear-cut distinction between auxiliaries and full verbs. Auxiliaries do not show agreement, while main verbs do. Thus, we get oppositions like (6a) and (6b):

    6.a. I still dos a bit of gardening.
      b. He do start at Brue.

The same goes for *have*. This is in fact rather common in dialect: one finds it both in British and American dialects. This feature is so striking that one begins to wonder whether these auxiliaries and main verbs show similar inflectional contrasts at other points of history as well. And, of course, they do: In certain types of Early Modern

English both *eth* and *es* occur as the marker of the third person singular, auxiliaries favouring *eth* and full verbs *es*. The examples from *Arden of Feversham* listed below illustrate this trend:[4]

6.c. Ay, God he knows, and so doth Will end Shakebag... (1. 1328)
   d. Yet doth he keep in every corner trulls,... (1.471)
   e. The which I hear the wench keeps in her chest,... (1. 160)

In fact, there are no instances of *es* occuring with the auxiliary *do*, although *es* is very common with main verbs. The pattern that emerges from Greene's *Friar Bacon and Friar Bungay* is quite similar, as can be seen from the following table, where the third person singular forms of *to come* are given for comparison:

	has	hath	does	doth	comes	cometh
Arden of Feversham	1	36	1	15	24	0
Friar Bacon	0	45	0	17	9	0

Table 6

I am not saying we have made an earth-shaking discovery here. All I am saying is that modern dialectal material would lead us to look for inflectional differences between auxiliaries like *do* and full verbs in English material in general.

I set out to show how dialectal variation might suggest what sort of questions we should ask about historical data. It is commonplace to say that the present state of a language cannot be understood without reference to its history. But it is equally true that in order to understand earlier stages of a language it is essential to know what kind of variability is likely in that language today. Modern dialects have a great deal to offer in this respect.

NOTES

1. The data come from tape recorded interviews with fourteen elderly persons from rural Somerset in the 1970's. The total length of the sample is some 12 hours.

2. This work will be reported in detail in Ihalainen (forthcoming a) with additional data from the West Midlands. The effect of sentence modality on the alternation of standard and non-standard forms is perhaps most noticeable in the case of negation. In fact, there are speakers who have non-standard forms only in negative contexts. These speakers typically say things like *He is* but *He ain't*. But even speakers who have both positive and negative non-standard verb forms have more non-standard forms in negative contexts. Thus a random 7000-word sample from seven Somerset speakers showed 67 standard positive present tense forms of the verb *to be*, out of which only 5 were non-standard, whereas all the negatives forms (11 in all) were non-standard.

   The phenomenon that different sentence types may show different syntax is, of course, in no way restricted to non-standard language. For example consider the fact that the verb *need* behaves like an auxialiary in negatives (*He needn't do it*) but, in most circumstances, like a lexical verb in affirmatives (*He needs to do it*).
3. For a discussion of this and some other points of pronominal syntax in South-Western British English dialects, see Ihalainen (forthcoming b).
4. The texts used for these counts were the Ule machine-readable text of *Arden of Feversham* and the Lieser text of *Frier Bacon and Frier Bungay*, both distributed by the Oxford Archive of English Literature.

REFERENCES

Ihalainen, Ossi. Forthcoming a. 'On Linguistic Diffusion: Evidence from British English Dialects'. To appear in Szwedek and Kastovsky. Forthcoming b. *'He took the bottle and put'n in his pocket:* The Object Pronoun *it* in Present-Day Somerset'. To appear in Viereck.

Keenan, Edward L. and Bernard Comrie. 'Noun Phrase Accessibility and Universal Grammar'. 1977. *Linguistic Inquiry* 8. 63-99.

Orton, Harold et al. 1962-1971. *Survey of English Dialects*. Introduction and 4 Volumes. Leeds: K. Arnold.

Romaine, Suzanne. 1982. *Socio-Historical Linguistics: Its Status and Methodology*. Cambridge: Cambridge University Press.

Szwedek, Aleksandr and Dieter Kastovsky, eds. Forthcoming. *Linguistics Across Historical and Geographical Boundaries*. Moulton.

Van den Eynden, Nadine. 1984. *The Process of Relativization in Middle English: A Diachronic Approach Based on the Analysis of 12th – Late 14th Century Theological Prose*. Licentiate's Thesis. Katholieke Universiteit Leuven. Mimeographed.

Viereck, Wolfgang, ed. Forthcoming. *Focus on: England and Wales*. Varieties of English Around the World. General Series. Amsterdam: John Benjamins.

OLD ENGLISH INFINITIVAL COMPLEMENTS AND WEST-GERMANIC V-RAISING

ANS VAN KEMENADE
ZWO, State University of Utrecht

0. *Introduction.** In this paper I will discuss a number of complicated cases of Old English (OE) infinitival complementation that involve apparently unpredictable positions for both the finite and infinitival verb forms. It will be argued that we can get a better grasp of these structures if we view them as instances of Verb Raising. Verb Raising is a phenomenon that is well-attested in various forms in modern West Germanic (WGmc) languages. Evers (1975) gives an analysis of this phenomenon as it occurs in Modern Dutch (Du) and Modern Standard German (Gm). Den Besten and Edmondson (1983) have extended Evers' argument to other WGmc dialects such as West Flemish, Züritüütsch, and Alemannic. These two studies provide the observational framework for the OE infinitives to be discussed in this paper. Thus, we will see that a number of very complicated and so far badly understood infinitive patterns in OE fall in nicely with existing patterns in other WGmc languages. At the same time this extends the empirical base for the study of V-raising phenomena in WGmc languages.

The paper is set up as follows: in section 1, some of the core cases of modal + infinitive constructions will be presented. In section 2, the phenomenon of V-raising will be discussed as it occurs in modern WGmc. languages. In section 3, we will see how OE infinitivals fit into the general WGmc picture, and what kinds of evidence can be adduced for this. Section 4 is the concluding section.

Before embarking on the discussion of OE infinitivals, I make two preliminary assumptions. I will not argue for these here, although I consider them to be well-founded. The first is that OE is an SOV language underlyingly. Arguments for this can be found in Canale (1978); Koopman

(1984). The second is that 'verb second' patterns in main clauses are the result of a process of Verb Second, as discussed in van Kemenade (1984). Verb second patterns in embedded clauses will be largely the result of V-raising as discussed in this paper.

1. *Some Old English data.* The cases of infinitivals I discuss here appear mainly in the complement domains of modals, causatives, and perception verbs. I restrict the argument here to modals[1]. It is presupposed that modals are main verbs. This is argued convincingly by Allen (1974). Some core examples are the following (where *v* stands for *finite verb,* V for *infinitival verb,* X for *complements intervening between the verbs, or preceding or following them*).

(1) a. *þaet hie gemong him mid sibbe sittan mosten* (Vv)
    that they among themselves in peace settle must
    'that they must settle among themselves in peace' (Oros, 52, 33)

  b. *ðaet he Saul ne dorste ofslean* (vV)
    that he Saul not dared murder
    'that he didn't dare murder Saul' (CP, 199, 2)

  c. *þaet he mehte his feorh generian* (vXV)
    that he could his life save
    'so that he might save his life' (Oros 48, 18)

  d. *þaet hie ne mehten þa gefarenan to eorþan bringan*
                                                    (vXXV)
    that they not could the dead to earth bring
    'so that they could not bury the dead' (Oros 49, 23)

The examples in (1a) and (1b) represent patterns that are standard in Gm and Du respectively. This is illustrated in (2)

(2) a. Gm *dass er Saul nicht ermorden wollte* (Vv)
    that he Saul not murder wanted
    'that he didn't want to murder Saul'

  b. Du *dat hij Saul niet wilde vermoorden* (vV)
    that he Saul not wanted murder

Observe that (1c) and (1d) could easily be analysed as instances of S extraposition. However, the examples in (3) show that this is probably incorrect.

(3) a. *þaet he þaes gewinnes mehte mare gefremman* (XvXV)
    that he the victory could better achieve
    'so that he could achieve victory more easily' (Oros, 47, 14)

(3) b. *þaet hie mid nanum dinge ne mehten gesemede*
       weorþan   (XvXV)
   that they with no   thing not could   reconciled become
   'that there was no way for them to be reconciled'(Oros,39,13)

   c. *þaet mon ealcne ceap mehte be twiefaldan bet*
      geceapian   (XvXV)
   that people every purchase could by twofold   better buy
   'so that people could buy every commodity twice as cheap'
   (Oros,130,22)

   d. *and het þaet þider sceolde to him cumen* (XvXV)
   and ordered that to there should to him come ...
   'and ordered to come to him there...' (Vesp.Hom. 88, 32)

In these examples, material that properly belongs to the
embedded clause, spreads over positions on both sides of
the matrix verb. This shows that the material that is extraposed over the matrix V is not necessarily the whole embedded sentence, but can be only part of that sentence.
Before we proceed to analyse this, we will first discuss
the phenomenon of V-raising in WGmc languages.

   2. *Verb Raising.* Following Evers (1975), we assume
that Verb Raising is a phenomenon that unifies two clauses
(a matrix clause and an infinitival complement clause).
The mechanics of V-raising in languages like Dutch and German can be illustrated with the sentences in (4a) for which
the structure (4b) is assumed.

(4) a. *dat Jan het boekje wilde hebben*   (Du)
       dass der Johann das Buchlein haben wollte (Gm)
       'that John wanted to have the booklet'
   b.   S̄
          ┌──────┴──────┐
        COMP   S
        dat   ┌─────┴─────┐
        dass   NP   VP
                 Jan   ┌───┴───┐
                 Joh.   S   V   ──→   V
                      ┌───┴──┐ wilde   ┌──┴──┐
                     NP   VP wollte   V   V
                     PRO ┌──┴──┐   wilde hebben
                          NP   V   haben wollte
                        boekje hebben
                        buchl. haben

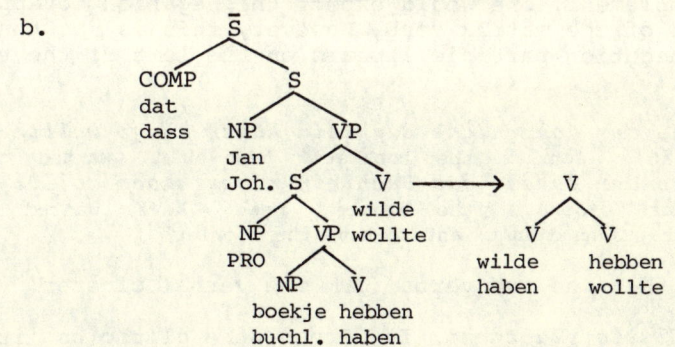

The structure (4b) to the left of the arrow indicates that
the structure is base-generated with a matrix modal verb,
and an embedded sentential complement S. This sentential
complement is broken up in the course of the derivation

and the verbs are joined into a verbal cluster, as in (4b)
on the right of the arrow. In Du the infinitival verb form
is adjoined to the right of the matrix verb; in Gm to the
left of the matrix verb. This process is generally triggered by modals, causatives and perception verbs². In this
paper I do not wish to go into the motivations for this
restructuring. One aspect that is probably relevant is that
complements of the relevant verbs do not constitute independent *tense* and *agreement* domains and therefore share in
the *tense* and *agreement* properties of the matrix clause
(cf. Evers (1982)). There are various criteria by which one
can show that there is a process of clause union. The main
argument for assuming a structure with a base-generated
sentential complement is to do with subcategorization; an
object of the embedded infinitival verb receives a semantic
role from that verb in a structural configuration. On the
other hand, there are various ways of showing that the derived structure is the one in (4b) on the right of the arrow. These have to do with negation, gapping, nominalisation, emphatic conjunction, word order variation, and
clitic placement. I will not review all of these here,
because most of them are particularly difficult to check
in a dead language like OE. The ones that are of potential
interest for OE are those to do with negation and clitic
placement. An argument of general interest is the one to do
with word order variation. Therefore I will restrict the
discussion to the latter three arguments.

2.1. *Negation*. According to Evers (1975);(1982), simple
object-verb sentences in Du and Gm have the negation
before the finite verb. If one were to assume that the
surface structure of a V-raising sentence is one with a
clausal complement, one would expect the negation to appear
on the left of the matrix verb. However, this is not the
case; the negation particle appears on the left of the verbal cluster:

(5)a.**das der Johann das Buchlein haben nicht wollte*
    that   John   the booklet have not wanted
  b. *das der Johann das Buchlein nicht haben wollte*
    that   John   the booklet not   have   wanted
    'that John didn't want to have the booklet'

This shows that the two verbs form one verbal cluster.

2.2. *Clitic placement*. In German, the clitic *es* 'it',
when the object of the infinitival verb, can appear to the
left of the matrix subject. This is illustrated in (6)

(6)a. *weil die Leute es Cecilia ins Arabische übersetzen
              lehren*
   because the people it Cecilia   into Arabic   translate
                                                    teach
   'because the people teach Cecilia to translate it into Ar.'
   b. *weil es die Leute Cecilia ins Arabische übersetzen
              lehren*

If the infinitival of which the clitic is an object, is in a sentential domain, it would be incomprehensible why the clitic can appear to the left of the matrix subject, since clitics never leave their sentential domain. Therefore we must conclude that this sentential domain is nonexistent in the derived structure.

2.3. *Word order variations.* In Gm there are some word order variations within verbal clusters resulting from V-raising. These cannot be plausibly described if we assume that in the derived structure there are embedded S-complements. An example is given in (7).

(7) *weil er die Kinder hat singen hören können* -
   because he the children has sing   hear   can
   'because he was able to hear the children sing'

In a structure where the sequence of verbs in (7) represents multiple embedding of S complements, one would have to assume that the verb form *hat* is lowered. However, if one assumes that the derived structure is one with a verbal cluster, it can be a simple permutation of *hat* to the left of the verbal cluster. These are three types of evidence that show that V-raising represents a process of clause union. Further arguments and discussion can be found in Evers (1975); (1982).

In WGmc languages other than Du and Gm, there are several variant forms of V-raising. Den Besten and Edmondson (1983) show that in W-Flemish and Züritüütsch, V-raising can raise a projection of the infinitival verb. Thus, the Dutch sentence in (4) above can take the following shape in W-Flemish:

(8)a. *dat Jan wilde het boekje hebben*
      that John wanted the booklet have
      'that John wanted to have the booklet'

(8) b.

```
         VP                              V
      ╱     ╲                         ╱    ╲
     S       V          ─→          V      VP
   ╱   ╲    wilde               wilde    ╱   ╲
  NP   VP                               NP    V
  PRO ╱ ╲                            boekje hebben
     NP  V
  boekje hebben
```

While again, it would be possible to analyse such sentences as instances of S extraposition, this is not likely, since van Riemsdijk and Haegeman (1984) have shown that incorporation of complements under V-raising results in systematic semantic differences in West-Flemish and Züritüütsch. There are also dialects where V-raising can incorporate two constituents. This is the case in Alemannic, as den Besten and Edmondson (1983) show. This completes our brief sketch of V-raising in WGmc. In the next section we will see how OE infinitival complements of modals fit into this picture.

3. *Old English infinitivals as V-raising structures.*
Against the background of the discussion of V-raising in section 2 I would want to suggest that all the examples of OE discussed in section 1 are instances of V-raising. On such a hypothesis, OE would have a process of V-raising of a comparatively free kind. There is a process of clause union; infinitival verb forms in the complement domain of modals form a verbal cluster with the matrix verb. In doing so they can incorporate one or two constituents (cf. examples (1c) and (1d)). The patterns in (1) do not exhaust the possibilities. The output of this comparatively free process of V-raising is further complicated by an - independently needed - rule of object extraposition as discussed in Stockwell (1977). This process can extrapose NP, PP, or S̄ over the VP-final finite verb, or verbal cluster. One example of this is (9).

(9) *þaet hie ofer þaet ne dorsten nohte gretan þa*
    that they after that not dared   not at all attack the
    halgan stowe (XvXVX)
    holy   place
    'that they didn't dare at all attack the holy place after that'
                              (GD,4,43,4)

Our hypothesis is then, that OE has a comparatively free process of V-raising that interacts with a process of object extraposition. This means that there is a process of clause union going on. The next question is whether there is evidence for such a process of clause union. In section 2. we have discussed two types of evidence in German and Dutch, which may possibly work the same way in OE, i.e.

evidence from negation and clitic placement. Unfortunately, the negation argument does not extend to OE. The negation particle *ne* in OE does not appear on the left of the verbal cluster, but on the left of the finite verb, as in (10).

(10) *þaet nan haeþen cyning aer gedon ne dorste* (Vnegv)
 that no heathen king before do not dared
 'that no heathen king had dared before' (Oros,45,12)

However, this is not necessarily counterevidence to our hypothesis, because it can be shown that the negation particle forms one constituent with the finite verb. This is evident from the many cases where it is cliticized onto the finite verb, as in (11).

(11) *and þone haeðenan wogere forþi habban* nolde
 and the heathen suitor therefore have not-wanted
 'and therefore would not accept the heathen suitor'(ASL,II,353)

We will see in the next subsection that the clitic placement argument does extend to OE. There are two further kinds of evidence for clause union in OE, which will be discussed in turn.

3.1. *Clitic placement*. As observed in van Kemenade (1984), OE has a form of cliticization whereby personal pronouns and locative pronouns ending in -*r*, can appear on the immediate left of their case-marking head (V or P), or move to other clitic positions in the sentence. There is such a clitic position in the left periphery of VP, and on $COMP^3$. For more detailed discussion I refer the reader to van Kemenade (1984). The positions are schematized in (12).

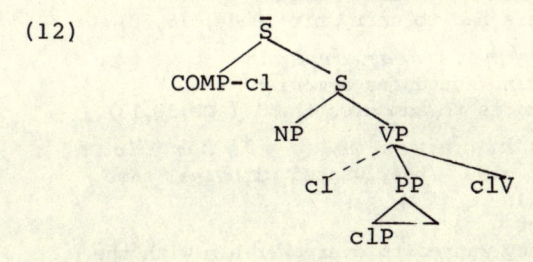

(12)
```
           S̄
          / \
      COMP-cl  S
              / \
             NP  VP
              \  /|\
              cI PP clV
                 /\
                clP
```

A number of examples of the positioning of these clitics are given in (13).

(13)a. *ða ðing þe he sylf him teahte* (on V)
 the things that he self them taught
 'the things that he himself taught them' (AHTh,pref,77)

(13) b. *ond se cyng* [$_{VP}$ *him eac wel feoh sealde*] (on VP)
and the king   him also well property gave
'and the king in addition gave him much property' (Parker 893)

c. *þe wende þaet him ne mihte nan werod wiþstandan*
                                              (on COMP)
who thought that him not could no   army   withstand
'who thought that no army could withstand him' (ASL,XXVI,28)

d. ... *and him to cwaed* (on P)
       and him to said
    ... 'and said to him' (AHTh,I,1,75)

e. *þa wendon hi* [$_{VP}$ *me heora baec to*] (on VP)
then turned they   me their back to
'then they turned their backs to me' (Boeth,II,8,12)

f. ... *ofdraedd ðaet him Godes yrre on becuman sceolde*
                                              (on COMP)
   afraid   that him God's anger on come would
   'afraid that God's anger would descend on him' (AHP,32,19)

There seem to be two conditions on the movement of such clitics. The first is that clitics only move to a position that c-commands the source position. The second is that the source position and the derived position are always clausemates, i.e. they belong to the same S-domain. Given this latter condition, it is striking that in our hypothesized V-raising constructions, clitic objects of the infinitival verb form can appear on clitic positions in the matrix sentence. (13f) above is an example of this, and some further examples are given in (14).

(14) a. *þaet hine his yldran beran sceoldon*
        that him his elders carry should
        'so that his elders had to carry him' (Bede,615,20)

b. *forðon hi nan mon ne dear dreagan*
   because them no man not dares admonish
   'because no man dares to admonish them' (CP,30,13)

c. *and wiste þaet hiene mon wolde mid þam ilcan*
   and knew that him they wanted with the same
   wrence beþridian
   strategy overpower
   'and knew that they wanted to overpower him with the
     same strategy' (Oros,155,2)

d. *þeh hie aet þam aerran gefeohte him ne mehten*
   though they at the former fight them not could
   to cuman
   to come
   'though at the former fight they could not come to them'
                                         (Oros,47,19)

The examples in (14) show, then, that an argument of clitic placement similar to that in Gm, holds in OE, and shows that OE, too, has a process of clause union. There are two further arguments in OE; one is to do with the functioning of the process of object extraposition; the other is to do with preposition stranding. These will now be discussed in turn.

3.2. *Extraposition*. Recall the extraposition process briefly discussed above, by which object material of a verb, NP, PP or S̄, can be extraposed over the VP-final verb or verbal cluster. This was exemplified above in (9), which is repeated here for convenience as (15).

(15) *þaet hie ofer that ne dorston nohte gretan þa*
    that they after that not dared not at all attack the
halgan stowe (XvXVX)
holy place
'that they didn't dare at all attack the holy place after that'
(GD,4,43,4)

In a structure such as (15), there is no telling from which underlying position the extraposition has taken place. However, the fact that extraposition takes place in this way, can be construed as evidence for clause union. Let us suppose that (16) is the D-structure of (15)

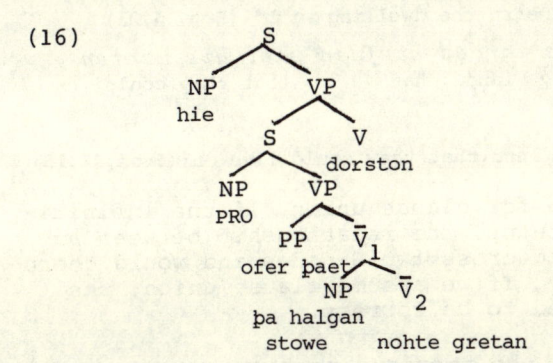

(16)
```
            S
           / \
         NP   VP
         hie  / \
             S   V
            / \  dorston
           NP  VP
           PRO / \
              PP  V̄₁
           ofer þaet / \
                    NP  V̄₂
                  þa halgan
                    stowe   nohte gretan
```

Let us further suppose that extraposition is adjunction to VP, as Stowell (1981) does. Then if the NP *þa halgan stowe* is extraposed in the structure (16), it would be adjoined to the embedded VP. Verb-projection raising of $\bar{V}_1$ or $\bar{V}_2$ would not move along the NP, and we would have to assume that for some reason the NP extraposes again, and the matrix VP would not be an obvious landing site. If, on the other hand, we assume that V-raising breaks up the sentential status of the embedded S, and unifies the clauses into one, extraposition results straightforwardly in adjunction to the matrix VP. This shows that again, clause union makes the right predictions.

3.3. *Preposition stranding*. Further evidence for clause union comes from preposition stranding constructions. One type of relative clause in OE, the þe-relative, allows preposition stranding[4]., as in (17)

(17) & het forbaernan þaet gewrit þe hit on awriten waes
and ordered burn the writ that it on written was
'and ordered to burn the writ that it was written on'(Oros, 131,22)

I will not discuss here how this construction should be analysed; for some contradicting opinions, see Allen (1980) and Jan Vat (1978). The one point on which there is agreement in the literature, is that such constructions are subject to Subjacency; i.e. the relation between þe and the stranded preposition cannot cross more than one S-node, unless there is a possibility to make intermediate links. Given these assumptions, it is quite striking that in V-raising constructions, stranding of a preposition in a PP that is an object of the embedded infinitival, is possible, both in Vv and vXV constructions:

(18)a....þe we þa eardunge mid geearnian sceolon
that we the dwelling with earn must
'that we must earn the dwelling with' (Ben, 4,23)

b. ..., hwaer hie landes haefden þaet hie mehten an gewician
where they land had that they could on live
'where they had land that they could live on'(Oros,46,15)

Again, this is evidence for clause union. If the infinitival complement had S-status, the relationship between þe and the stranded P would cross two S-nodes and would therefore violate Subjacency. If we assume clause union, the structures are predicted to be correct.

4. *Conclusions*. In the previous sections we have seen that there is clear evidence in OE for the V-raising status of modal + infinitive constructions, since there are three clear ways of showing that they are clause-union constructions. We have seen that the variant forms of V-raising in WGmc dialects cooccur in OE under a comparatively free process of V-raising that interacts with the process of object extraposition. This accounts in a systematic way for the wide array of word order patterns found in such constructions, and reveals some interesting aspects of OE

syntax. One final remark can be made about the hypothesis that OE has SOV order undelyingly. We have seen in the previous sections that verbs in OE cluster at the end of the sentence. To my mind this provides striking support for the SOV hypothesis, since it would be rather incomprehensible for verbs to cluster there if that position were not the basic position for the verb.

NOTES

*   I am grateful to Fred Weerman for drawing my attention to the potential relevance of V-raising literature for vXV constructions in OE. Research for this paper was supported by the Foundation for Linguistic Research, which is funded by the Netherlands Organization for the Advancement of Pure Research, Z.W.O.
1. Causatives and perception verbs show a number of variant uses and properties, discussion of which would take us far beyond the scope of this paper. I take it, however, that the essentials of the argument presented in this paper, carry over to causatives and perception verbs.
2. Cf. note 1.
3. The clitic patterns on COMP are grossly simplified here, since it is not our purpose here to present an analysis of clitic patterns. More details can be found in van Kemenade (1984).
4. In fact, preposition-stranding occurs in OE in more types of relatives, notably all those relatives that do not have an overt relative pronoun. The þe relative is a representatitive case. For a wealth of data on P-stranding in relatives, see Allen (1977).

REFERENCES

Data sources/abbreviations

Bede	= *Bede's Ecclesiastical History*, ed. Miller, London 1890.
CP	= *King Alfred's West Saxon Version of Gregory's Pastoral Care*, ed. Sweet. EETS 45 and 50.
GD	= *Gregory's Dialogues*. Reference from Microfiche Concordance.
Oros.	= *The Old English Orosius*, ed. Bately, EETS SS 6.
AHP	= *Homilies of Ælfric*, ed. Pope, EETS 259, 260.
AHTh	= *The Homilies of the Anglo-Saxon Church*, ed. Thorpe, London 1842.
ASL	*Ælfric's Saints' Lives*, ed. Skeat, EETS 96, 82, 94, 114.
Vesp.Hom.	= *Early English Homilies*, ed. Warner, EETS OS 152.
Parker	= *Two of the Saxon Chronicles Parallel*, ed. Earle & Plummer, Oxford 1892.
Benet	= *Die Angelsächsischen Prosabearbeitungen der Benediktinerregel*, ed. Schröer, Darmstadt 1964.

Allen, Cynthia. 1974. 'Old English modals'. In *Papers in the History and Structure of English*, ed. by Jane Grimshaw. UMOP 1, pp. 99-106.
Allen, Cynthia. 1977. *Topics in English Diachronic Syntax*, unpublished PhD dissertation UMass/Amherst.
Allen, Cynthia. 1980. 'Movement and deletion in Old English'. *LI 11.2*, pp. 261-325.
Den Besten, Hans and J. Edmondson. 1983. 'The verbal complex in continental West Germanic'. In *On the Formal Syntax of the West-Germania*, ed. by W. Abraham. Amsterdam: Benjamins, pp. 11-61.
Canale, William. 1978. *Word Order Change in Old English*, unpublished PhD dissertation McGill University.
Evers, Arnold. 1975. *The Transformational Cycle in Dutch and German*, IULC.
Evers, Arnold. 1982. 'Twee functionele principes voor de regel 'verschuif het werkwoord'. In *Glot*, pp. 11-31.
Kemenade, Ans van. 1984. 'V2 and Clitics in Old English'. In *Linguistics in the Netherlands 1984*, ed. by H. Bennis and W.U.S. van Lessen Kloeke. Dordrecht, pp. 101-110.
Koopman, Willem, 1984. 'Some thoughts on Old English word order'. In *Papers of the Fifth Philological Symposium*, ed. by Erik Kooper. Utrecht, pp. 2-21.
Riemsdijk, Henk van and L. Haegeman. 1984. 'V-projection raising, scope and the typology of verb movement rules', unpublished paper, Tilburg University.
Stockwell, Robert. 1977. 'Motivations for Exbraciation in Old English'. In *Mechanisms of Syntactic Change*, ed. by C. Li. Texas, pp. 291-317.
Stowell, Tim, 1981. *Origins of Phrase Structure*. Unpublished MIT diss.
Vat, Jan 1978. 'On footnote 2; Evidence for the pronominal status of Old English *þaer*'. In *LI 9*, pp. 695-716.

THE SIMPLIFICATION OF THE
OLD ENGLISH STRONG NOMINAL PARADIGMS

SAMUEL JAY KEYSER AND WAYNE O'NEIL
Massachusetts Institute of Technology

0. *Introduction.* In Keyser and O'Neil (1985) extensive support is provided for the notion that the status of rules upon entry into a language is optional and that such rules, if they persist in the language, become obligatory. It is also shown that the change from optional to obligatory status can result in significant simplifications. These simplifications come about in order to deal with complications which the obligatory rule introduces into the grammar. In the material that follows, based largely on Keyser and O'Neil (1985: Chapter 3), we explore this same view in terms of changes which took place in a large number of Old English nominal paradigms. We hypothesize that certain phonological rules entered the language as optional rules and, becoming obligatory, introduced stem allomorphy, which, in its turn, set the stage for reanalysis.

First, we present the strong nominal paradigms according to their historical categories as given in the philological literature. We then present a synchronic categorization of Old English nouns which is much simpler in character than the traditional handbook accounts. Taking these as end points in our discussion, we account for the evolution of Old English nominals from the prehistoric picture given in the handbooks to the synchronic picture given below.

2. *The Data as Represented in Old English Handbooks.* Old English nominal paradigms are divided into two major classes, depending upon whether the nouns originally (i.e. in Indo-European) ended in a consonant or in a vowel. The vocalic classes, which are displayed below, are subdivided according to the particular vowel which followed the stem in Germanic. The classes, finally, are also displayed in terms of gender, a morphological category, and in heavy and light syllable pairs, a phonological category. This last characteristic is somewhat obscured by the historical

change and reorganization of paradigms to be discussed below. The paradigms which we discuss are drawn from the West Saxon dialect of Old English.

(1) a-stem masculine nouns

Singular

Nom.	wer	'man'	staan	'stone'
Acc.	wer		staan	
Gen.	weres		staanes	
Dat.	were		staane	

Plural

Nom.	weras		staanas
Acc.	weras		staanas
Gen.	wera		staana
Dat.	werum		staanum

(2) a-stem neuter nouns

scip	'ship'	word	'word'
scip		word	
scipes		wordes	
scipe		worde	
scipu		word	
scipu		word	
scipa		worda	
scipum		wordum	

(3) ja-stem masculine nouns

here	'army'	bridd	'bird'	ende	'end'
here		bridd		ende	
herge		briddes		endes	
herge		bridde		ende	
hergas		briddas		endas	
hergas		briddas		endas	
herga		bridda		enda	
hergum		briddum		endum	

(4) ja-stem neuter nouns

cynn	'race'	wiite	'punishment'
cynn		wiite	
cynnes		wiites	
cynne		wiite	

```
            cynn                wiitu
            cynn                wiitu
            cynna               wiita
            cynnum              wiitum

(5)   wa-stem masculine nouns

            bearu    'grove'    þeaw    'custom'
            bearu               þeaw
            bearwes             þeawes
            bearwes             þeawe

            bearwas             þeawas
            bearwas             þeawas
            bearwa              þeawa
            bearwum             þeawum

(6)   wa-stem neuter nouns

            searu    'device'   deaw    'dew'
            searu               deaw
            searwes             deawes
            searwe              deawe

            searu               deaw
            searu               deaw
            searwa              deawa
            searwum             deawum

(7)   o-stem feminine nouns

            lufu     'love'     laar    'learning'
            lufe                laare
            lufe                laare
            lufe                laare

            lufa                laara
            lufa                laara
            lufa                laara
            lufum               laarum

(8)   jo-stem feminine nouns

            synn     'sin'      gierd   'rod'
            synne               gierde
            synne               gierde
            synne               gierde
```

	synna	gierda	
	synna	gierda	
	synna	gierda	
	synnum	gierdum	

(9) wo-stem feminine nouns

sinu	'sinew'	lææs	'pasture'
sinwe		lææswe	
sinwe		lææswe	
sinwe		lææswe	
sinwa		lææswa	
sinwa		lææswa	
sinwa		lææswa	
sinwum		lææswum	

(10) i-stem masculine nouns

wine	'friend'	giest	'guest'
wine		giest	
wines		giestes	
wine		gieste	
wine,-as		giestas	
wine,-as		giestas	
wina,-iga		giesta	
winum		giestum	

(11) i-stem feminine nouns

cween	'queen'
cweene, cween	
cweene	
cweene	
cweena	
cweena	
cweena	
cweenum	

(12) i-stem neuter nouns

clyne	'lump'	gecynd	'race'
clyne		gecynd	
clynes		gecyndes	
clyne		gecynde	

```
       clyne             gecynd
       clyne             gecynd
       clyna             gecynda
       clynum            gecyndum
```

(13) u-stem masculine nouns

```
       sunu     'son'    feld     'field'
       sunu              feld
       suna              felda
       suna              felda

       suna              felda
       suna              felda
       suna              felda
       sunum             feldum
```

(14) u-stem feminine nouns

```
       duru     'door'   hand     'hand'
       duru              hand
       dura              handa
       dura              handa

       dura              handa
       dura              handa
       dura              handa
       durum             handum
```

3. *The Data Represented Synchronically.* While the nominal classes illustrated in (1)-(14) recapitulate the traditional strong noun class divisions in Old English, a somewhat different perspective arises when these nouns are viewed in terms of their inflectional endings, their genders and their underlying phonological shape. Thus the a-, ja-, and wa- stem masculine nouns all take the same endings; similarly with the a-, ja-, and wa- stem neuter nouns and the feminine o-, jo-, and wo- stems. Leaving to one side for the moment the various genders of the i-stem and u-stem nouns, we represent the classes of nouns in (1)-(9) in terms of their endings as follows:

(15) a. a-, ja-, wa-stem nouns

   masculine (=1,3,6)   neuter (=2,4,6)

                Singular

Nom.	∅	∅
Acc.	∅	∅
Gen.	es	
Dat.	e	

	Plural	
Nom.	as	u ~ ∅
Acc.	as	u ~ ∅
Gen.	a	
Dat.	um	

(15) b. o-, jo-, wo-stem nouns
         feminine (=7,8,9)

	Singular
Nom.	u~∅
Acc.	e
Gen.	e
Dat.	e

	Plural
Nom.	a
Acc.	a
Gen.	a
Dat.	um

Thus, instead of nine separate noun classes, we may view Old English as exhibiting three major noun classes, defined by the endings listed above in (15a-b).

At this point let us return to the i-stem nouns listed in (10)-(12). These are listed in handbooks traditionally as separate noun classes to be mastered by the student and, presumably, by the Old English language learner. But this complication disappears when in fact one considers their inflectional endings.

Consider, for example, the strong i-stem masculine noun *giest*. The endings of this form, apparent by inspection of (10), are exactly those we see in the masculine column of (15a). That is, surface considerations alone would lead one to identify *giest* not with a new nominal declension but rather with (15a), that already designated for a-, ja-, and wa-stem masculine nouns. Similarly, the strong i-stem neuter noun *gecynd* exhibits the endings in (15a). Once again, there is no obvious (or inflectional) reason to assign *gecynd*, whatever its historical origin, to a noun class different from that for *word*.

Finally, the i-stem feminine noun *cween* possesses endings identical to those in (15b). Once again there is no reason from the point of view of the inflectional endings to identify *cween* as belonging to a nominal class other than the o-, jo-, wo-stems listed in (7)-(9) above.[1]

Let us suppose, then, that in Old English nominals are classified in accordance with the endings they take. Thus, it is possible to view many of the nouns reviewed thus far as comprising a single class subdivided into masculine, feminine and neuter subclasses, with some inflectional differences between the three genders. The division is illustrated below.

(16) Strong Noun Class I

Singular

	Masculine	Neuter	Feminine
Nom.	[	∅]	u~∅
Acc.	[	∅]	e
Gen.	[	es]	e
Dat.	[	e	]

Plural

	Masculine	Neuter	Feminine
Nom.	as	u~∅	a
Acc.	as	u~∅	a
Gen.	[	a	]
Dat.	[	um	]

where bracketed endings are shared by as many genders as indicated.

In order for us to claim that Old English was characterized by this single major noun class, we make two minimal assumptions. The first is that Old English exhibits both monosyllabic stems (for example, *staan*) and bisyllabic stems (for example, *wiite* and *heafud*). The second is that Old English phonology contains two rules that are centrally involved in nominal derivations.[2] These are (17) High Vowel Deletion, and (18) Prevocalic Deletion:

(17) High Vowel Deletion

$$V \longrightarrow \emptyset \ / \ F \ [\underset{|}{\overset{R}{\rule{0pt}{0pt}}} \underline{\hspace{1cm}}]$$
$$\underset{[+high]}{|}$$

(18) Prevocalic Deletion

$$\begin{matrix} V \\ | \\ [-\text{high}] \\ [-\text{stress}] \end{matrix} \longrightarrow \emptyset\ /\ \underline{\quad}\ \begin{matrix} \text{morpheme} \\ | \\ V] \end{matrix}$$

In order to best illustrate the application and order of these rules, we give sample derivations of selected nominative/accusative plural forms of the following nouns: *scip* and *word*, both of which are monosyllabic neuter nouns and *wiite* and *wine*, both of which are bisyllabic, the first a neuter and the second a masculine stem. The derivations appear in (19):

(19)

[scip u]	[word u]	[wiite u]	[wine as]	
-	∅	-	-	by (17)
-	-	∅	∅	by (18)
scipu	word	wiitu	winas	output

The derivation of *wiitu* provides the argument for ordering the rules as in (19). Were the order reversed, Prevocalic Deletion would delete the stem final -*e* yielding the string [wiit u], which would then undergo High Vowel Deletion to yield an incorrect surface from **wiit*.

4. *The Relationship between Historical and Synchronic Paradigms*. If, in fact, Old English is best represented by the strong noun class illustrated in (16), then why should it be the case that without exception all Old English handbooks represent the noun classes as in (1) through (14)? In our view this is because Old English philologists have tacitly adhered to the following procedure. First, they have limited themselves to presenting nominal classes only if there is at least one form of that class which is actually attested.[3] This is a necessary move. After all, it is very unlikely that in the entire Anglo-Saxon corpus one will find all forms of a particular nominal paradigm, say, *scip* or *ende*. Therefore, it is necessary to find some means to supply the forms which history has not preserved. The method selected by philologists is the comparative one. They determine, given a particular defective paradigm, what its class must be in terms of what its class is in other Germanic languages and on the basis of this information they fill in the missing forms. Thus, the paradigms in (1) through (14) are to a certain extent misleading since they do not in all cases actually occur historically.

Let us compare our approach with the historical one. Unlike the traditional approach, we exclude comparative evidence, being concerned with devising an account of Old English which takes into consideration only synchronic evidence. The resultant difference in approaches is not over the facts but rather in the way in which these facts are organized. Thus, the historical approach proliferates nominal classes whereas the synchronic approach restricts them. This does not mean that the historical account is wrong. Rather, it suggests that the historical account represents a stage of the language which predates recorded Old English.[4] We take this to be the case. In the sections that follow we provide a descriptive account of the changes which led from the paradigms given in (1) through (14) to the single paradigm given in (16). For certain of these changes we are able to present the underlying principles according to which the changes took place. The emphasis in the following sections is, of course, on these principles.

4.1 *Reanalysis of Stems without Surface Allomorphy*. We look first at simple cases that offer no problems with respect to renalysis because these cases lack stem allomorphy. In the nouns discussed in this section High Vowel Deletion has operated to minimize the inflectional differences between i/u-stems, on the one hand, and the a/o-stems on the other. This, however, is not in itself sufficient reason to explain why these i/u stems lost their identity as separate paradigms and fell together with the a/o-stem paradigms. Perhaps there is some general principle of paradigm reduction at work which favors such collapse. Thus, a grammar with fewer paradigms may be more highly valued than one which contains a great number.

4.1.1 *Giest, Cween and Gecynd*. The synchronic evidence gives no indication that nouns of the type *giest* 'guest' and *gecynd* 'race' are in any way different from ordinary a-stem nouns. Therefore, we propose that these nouns were treated as belonging to the same paradigm in attested Old English. There is evidence that at least the feminine forms of the i-stem declension retained their separate character in early Old English. Thus in the early texts, we do find *cween* 'queen' beside *cweene*. The former is the older i-stem feminine accusative singular. However, in later texts this minimal evidence of a separate i-stem paradigm has been lost and these forms are indistinguishable from the o-stem nouns such as *laar*.

4.1.2 *Feld, Duru and Hand.* These nouns formed a separate u-stem type as exemplified in the idealized paradigms given in (13) and (14) above. However, Campbell (1959: Section 614) notes that no nouns of the type *feld, duru* and *hand* are free from the influence of the *staan, lufu* and *laar* types. In fact, in recorded Old English there were traces only of the original historical u-stem endings. In general, these nouns were reformed according to the *staan, lufu* and *laar* models.[5]

4.2 *Reanalysis of Stems with Surface Allomorphy.* We turn now to a number of noun types, in fact, the vast majority of strong nouns in Old English, whose reanalysis is by no means straightforward. That is to say, the operation of phonological rules like High Vowel Deletion and Gemination operate to provide competing stem types throughout a given paradigm in a variety of cases. The task confronting us is to explain why in any given paradigm, one stem type is chosen over another.

4.2.1 *Ende and Wiite.* Consider the ja-stem noun *ende*. What is the status of the final *-e*? It is not an inflectional ending synchronically, as comparison with other ja-stem nouns indicates; for example, *bridd*. Historically it derives from an underlying *-i*, a stem extension after which inflectional endings are added. Thus, a prehistoric string for the form [[end]i as] would give rise to a prehistoric surface form *endas* by High Vowel Deletion. However, such an analysis ought also to give **end* in the nominative/accusative singular form from underlying [end]i]. In fact High Vowel Deletion fails in this case. Rather, the earliest recorded nominative/accusative singular form of this type is bisyllabic; that is, *endi*.[6]

Traditional philologists account for this unexpected form by making use of the assumption that the final syllable of the form '...had an intonation similar to the old IE abnormal intonation' (Campbell 1959: Section 355.3). This abnormal intonation is supposed to protect the extension vowel *i* from undergoing High Vowel Deletion in just these instances.

We, too, have a special explanation for this form. Rather than invoking 'abnormal intonation', we assume that reanalysis is responsible for the failure of High Vowel Deletion to operate here. Given an underlying string for the nominative/accusative singular and plural forms as follows: [[end]iØ] (singular) and [[end]i as] (plural), reanalysis incorporates the *i* into the stem yielding [[endi]∅] and [[endi]as]. The effect of this reanalysis is to exclude the nominative/accusative singular forms from the domain of High Vowel Deletion while including the nominative/accusative plural forms. In the former case, the principle of Strict Cyclicity prevents the stem final -*i* from deleting on the second cycle in the singular forms since the nominative/accusative singular morpheme is not instantiated by phonologically realized material. Consequently, the string is not derived and hence High Vowel Deletion may not apply. In the plural forms, on the other hand, the string is derived by virtue of the concatenation of the stem morpheme with the nominative/accusative plural morpheme. Both morphemes are realized phonologically.[7]

There is reason to prefer this analysis over the traditional one since the traditional analysis is considerably less general, restricting 'abnormal intonation' to the nominative/accusative singular forms only. This restriction is ad hoc. Reanalysis treats the entire paradigm in a uniform fashion, yielding an underlying bisyllabic stem where previously the stem had been monosyllabic.

This analysis extends without complication to neuter nouns of this class; for example, *wiite*. Prehistorically, the nominative/accusative plural underlying string would be [[wiit]iu]. High Vowel Deletion would apply to this form yielding a correct surface form *wiitu*. In the nominative/accusative singular, however, an underlying [wiit]i∅] ought to yield a surface **wiit* (cf. **end* above). This form is never attested historically. Rather, the attested form is *wiiti*, later *wiite* by Lowering (see footnote 6 above). Clearly, reanalysis of [[wiit]i∅] to [[wiit i]∅] will account for the failure of High Vowel Deletion to apply in the nominative/accusative singular forms.

There is, however, a problem with the reanalysis of *wiite* and *ende* and that is to explain why these types were not reanalyzed according to the monosyllabic pattern. We will be better able to answer this question after considering another type of noun, to which we now turn.

4.2.2 *Cynn and Bridd*. The expected nominative/accusative singular form in Old English for the noun *cynn* 'race' is **cyne* and not the actually occurring form *cynn*.[8] To account for this disparity traditional philologists assume that the nominative/accusative singular *cynn* '...must be regarded as analogical forms from the other cases.' (cf. Campbell 1959: Section 576). While this is certainly the case, it merely provides a name for a problem which remains to be solved. In particular, the question that is avoided is why *cynn* is chosen over *cyne* in the reanalysis of this noun. This, however, is a question with much wider significance because one can ask precisely the same thing about a number of similar cases in Old English in which paradigms exhibiting stem allomorphy at one point are reanalyzed without stem allomorphy at a later stage. For example, we have already seen that in the reanalysis of *wiite*, the stem form *wiite* is chosen over other allomorphs. We will discuss these and a number of similar cases in what follows. In our discussion we assume a principle which we call the Structural Hierarchy Principle. This principle is stated in (20):

(20) Structural Hierarchy Principle

Whenever a paradigm contains more than one stem type on the structural hierarchy, reanalysis is based on the least marked type available.

The structural hierarchy referred to in (20) is based upon rime structure and orders rime structures as follows:

(21) The Structural Hierarchy

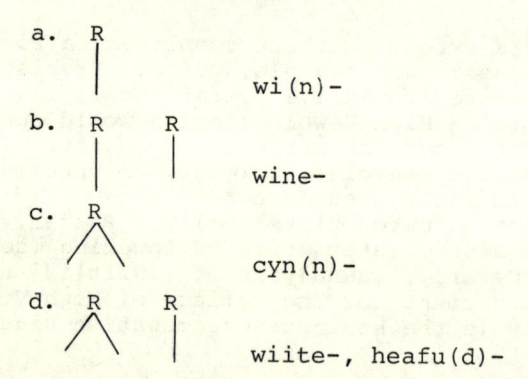

a. R
   |
                    wi(n)-

b. R   R
   | |
        wine-

c. R
   /\
                    cyn(n)-

d. R   R
   /\ |
        wiite-, heafu(d)-

In order to understand how this hierarchy works we must consider two separate questions. The first question is: What constitutes a potential candidate for a stem in a given paradigm? The second question is: What determines the relative position on the structural hierarchy shown in (21)?

We begin by examining the first question. We assume that a possible candidate for a stem must meet one of the following two criteria:

A potential candidate for a stem is:

i. any sequence which occurs without an inflectional ending, or

ii. any sequence remaining after the inflectional ending has been removed,

where the final consonant is always assumed to be extrametrical. According to these criteria, there are two possible stem candidates for *wine*; namely, *wine* itself or else *wi(n)-*, the sequence which remains after the syllable containing an inflectional ending has been removed; for example, *wi(n)-es* or *wi(n)-as*.[9] In *cyne* the stem types are either *cyne-* or *cyn(n)-*. In *wiite* the stem types available are *wiite* and *wii(t)-es*. With respect to *heafud*, the stem types are either *heafu(d)-* or *heaf(d)-* because of oblique cases such as *heaf(d)-e* or *heaf(d)-es*.

Given these stem types, we now turn to the second question; namely: What determines a syllable's position on the structural hierarchy. Here we make two observations. The first is that we assume that the farther down one goes on the hierarchy listed in (21), the less marked is the corresponding syllable sequence. More generally, we claim that the structural hierarchy can be derived from what we take to be universal tendencies:

i. Stressed syllables with branching rimes are less marked than stressed syllables with non-branching rimes.

ii. Bisyllabic stems are less marked than monosyllabic stems.

From the first principle we derive the fact that in the structural hierarchy in (21) all sequences with initial branching rimes appear farther down than all sequences without branching rimes. In Old English it is the initial syllable of a word that is stressed. Hence we assume that the ordering of (21c and d) after (21a and b) results from the fact that branching rimes are preferred in stressed syllables. The second principle focusses attention on the number of rimes in each sequence. In particular, this principle places (21b) lower on the hierarchy than (21a). That is, all other things being equal, two rimes are less marked than one. Similarly, among the sequences which contain branching rimes, (21d) is lower, i.e. less marked than (21c) for the same reason that (21b) is less marked than (21a); namely, a bisyllabic stem is preferred over a monosyllabic one.

We are now ready to see how the Structural Hierarchy Principle selects a stem from candidate stems in a given paradigm. Let us consider first *wine*. As we have seen, the competing stems are *wine* and *wi(n)-*. The former contains two non-branching rimes in a row whereas the latter contains only a single non-branching rime. According to the Structural Hierarchy Principle, the latter is higher on the hierarchy (it corresponds to (21a)) and is therefore more highly marked than the former, which corresponds to (21b). Hence the Structural Hierarchy Principle selects the stem *wine* as the appropriate stem for the paradigm. Consider next the stem alternants *wiite* beside *wii(t)-*. The latter contains a rime sequence of the (21c) type, whereas the former sequence corresponds to (21d). The Structural Hierarchy Principle selects (21d) over (21c). As we have already seen, this is the correct result. Now consider the stem types available in the *ende* paradigm. These are *en(d)-* and *ende*. Here, too, the Structural Hierarchy Principle selects the less marked of the two, i.e. *ende*.

When we turn to *cyne*, we find the following two stems available in prehistoric Old English: *cyni* and *cyn(n)-*. The paradigm for this stage appears as (22):

(22) cyni ∅   'race'
     cyni ∅
     cynn es
     cynn e

     cynn u
     cynn u
     cynn a
     cynn um

The stem *cyni* corresponds to (21b) and the stem *cyn(n)-* corresponds to (21c). The Structural Hierarchy Principle correctly chooses the latter if we make an additional assumption; namely, that the universal tendencies given in (i) and (ii) are themselves ordered. That is, whenever both principles compete with respect to a given pair of alternants, (i) prevails.

The same argument holds for the masculine ja-stem noun *bridd* (see (3) above). In this paradigm the stem type **bridi* is replaced throughout by the stem type *brid(d)-*, once again in according with Principle (20).

Finally, let us consider *heafud*. The paradigm provides us with two potential alternants; namely, *heafu(d)-* itself and *heaf(d)-*. These correspond to (21d) and (21c), respectively. The Structural Hierarchy Principle correctly chooses the former over the latter.[10]

There is another representative of this type of noun illustrated in (3) above which requires some comment; namely, *here*. This form without a geminated consonant arises because *r* did not undergo gemination in Old English. However, the stem final *-i* was desyllabified before vowel initial inflections as the oblique cases in (3) show.[11]

If we apply Principle (20) to the prehistoric precursor of the *here* paradigm in (3), we are led to adopt *her(g)-* over *here-* as the stem, since this form of the stem is less marked than *here-*. Note, however, that in the nominative/accusative singular forms the underlying /y/ surfaces as *i*, later *e* by the rule of Lowering (see footnote 6).[12]

4.2.3 *Excursus on Freme*. At this point let us consider a problem posed by some interesting data drawn from Middle Kentish. (See Keyser and O'Neil (1985: Chapter 2) for background discussion.) In the Post-Middle Kentish period a slight bit of evidence suggests that the final modification of the *freme* paradigm appeared to be moving in the direction of selecting *frem* over *freme* as a new stem form. We now see that this selection follows from Principle (20) and, in fact, recapitulates the selection of *cynn* over *cyni*.

However, earlier in the history of *freme* type verbs, reanalysis appears to have proceeded in contradiction to (20). In particular, the paradigm offers two possible candidates for stem reanalysis; one of type (21b); that is, *freme*, and two of type (21c), that is *frem(m)*. (20) would select the latter. However, Middle Kentish selected the former. We account for this by the observation that the selection of any stem other than *freme* would complicate the derivation of forms of this conjugation.

Let us see how this argument works. Recall that we select stem candidates by examining surface forms and eliminating inflectional endings. This process gives us three stems from the Middle Kentish paradigm; namely, *fre(m)-*, *frem(m)-* and *freme* from, for example, *frem-st*, *fremm-e* and *frem-de*, respectively. Suppose that according to (20), *fre(m)-* were to be selected. In this case the derivations would require a number of otherwise unmotivated rules; for example, the insertion of an imperative ending -*e*, as well as the insertion of an epenthetic -*e* throughout the past tense. Suppose (20) were to select *frem(m)*-. Then the resultant derivations would require a further set of unmotivated rules; for example, a rule which would replace the final consonant of *frem(m)*- with an -*e* in the imperative singular and throughout the past tense, as well as a rule which would degeminate all forms containing nonsyllabic endings, as in the 2nd person singular *fremst* (from *fremmst*). If *freme*- is selected, no unmotivated rules are required for the derivation of the forms. Moreover, the historical development from Old Kentish to Middle Kentish proceeds in a straightforward way.

Consequently, we must suppose that Principle (20) is subject to the same evaluation metric that governs all other changes in phonology. Notice, then, that the situation in the development of the weak verbs in Middle Kentish differs from that of the reorganization of the nominal paradigms in Old English in that in the latter case Principle (20) operated freely since its choice of stems was not constrained by resultant complications of the phonological rules.

4.2.4 *Gierd and Synn*. Prehistorically, we would expect to find nominative singular forms *gierdu* and *synnu* deriving from underlying strings of the form [[gierdi]u] and [[synni]u] by High Vowel Deletion. There is, in fact, one possible extant form of this type; namely, the word *ætgæœru* 'spear' from the Epinal and Corpus glossaries. However, there are no other traces of this type in the entire Anglo-Saxon corpus. As long as High Vowel Deletion was an optional rule, there would be overwhelming surface evidence for the bisyllabic stem *gierdi* and *synni*. Thus, there would be surface forms like *gierdiu* and *synniu* beside *gierdu* and *synnu*. However, once High Vowel Deletion became obligatory, surface evidence for the bisyllabic stems *gierdi* and *synni* is reduced to the fact that the inflectional nominative singular -*u* in the form [[gierdi]u] and [[synni]u] fails to delete because it is protected by the stem final -*i* which does delete.

There is a question which arises at this point; namely, why do *gierd* and *synn* rather than *gierdi* and *synni* survive as basic stems since (20) predicts the opposite? The answer must be that (20) is a Principle which operates on surface rather than underlying forms. That is, it cannot use the evidence offered indirectly by such forms as *gierdu* and *synnu*.

4.2.5 *Wine and Clyne*. We have discussed i-stem nouns with heavy syllable structure in section 4.1.1 above. Here we turn to i-stem nouns with light syllable structure. When we examine these types, we find strong evidence for the independent status of the masculine/ neuter types as a separate paradigm.[13]

Let us first consider masculine nouns of this type, exemplified by *wine*. Historically, we know that it was analyzed as [[win]i] with the final -*i* being an inflectional ending. By the time we come to attested Old English, however, it is clear that this -*i* has been reanalyzed as part of an underlying bisyllabic stem. There are a number of compounds containing *wine* as first element which attest to the bisyllabic status of the stem; for example, *wine-scipe* 'friendship', *wine-leas* 'friendless'. The earlier separate i-stem paradigm is reflected in the nominative/accusative singular forms *wine* and the nominative/accusative plural forms *wine* and the genitive plural form *winiga*. However, in light of early attested forms such as nominative/accusative plural *winas* and genitive plural *wina*, it is clear that a shift has taken place. But note that the nominative/accusative singular *wine* is consistently maintained. The resultant paradigm with endings appears as:

(23)
stem	ending
wine	∅
wine	∅
wine	es
wine	e
wine	as
wine	as
wine	a
wine	um

Simple inspection of the paradigm in (23) indicates the need for a phonological rule which has the effect of deleting the stem final vowel just in case that vowel occurs before a vowel initial desinence. We have already formulated the rule in (18) above. The effect of this rule is to delete the stem final -*e* everywhere in the paradigm in (23) except in the nominative/accusative singular forms.

We take this renalaysis of *wine* to mark the entry of (18) into the language. Recall that in the derivation of *wiite* and *ende*, the rule of High Vowel Deletion carried out the required deletion of the stem final vowel under the assumption that it was an underlying -*i*. However, High Vowel Deletion does not allow us to derive the correct forms in paradigms such as that illustrated in (23) since the stem final vowel of *wine* is not in a High Vowel Deletion site. Prevocalic Deletion does correctly delete the stem final vowels in both the *wiite* and *wine* types without recourse to High Vowel Deletion. Moreover, it allows us to take the stem final vowel of the surface form, that is -*e*, as the underlying vowel, giving us a simpler derivation for the forms in these paradigms.

There is another possible account of these data. Suppose that the nominative/accusative singular ending -*e* is retained in Old English and is added to a monosyllabic stem *wi(n)*-. We reject this hypothesis since it fails to account for the compounding facts just mentioned. Moreover Principle (20) gives us this result automatically since -*e* is not a possible nominative/accusative singular inflection for masculine nouns. Thus, *wine* will be selected as one stem and *wi(n)*- as another on the basis of such forms as *winas*. Since *wine* is less marked than *wi(n)*- on the Structural Hierarchy, it will be chosen as the appropriate stem form.

The neuters of this type, for example, *clyne*, are reanalyzed in the same fashion as *wine* is. Furthermore, there is available for them the same sort of evidence from compounding. For example, Old English compounds with nouns of the *clyne*- type are attested; for example, *spere-leas* 'without a point'; *spere-niiþ* 'spear strife'.

4.2.6. *Bearu and Searu*. (5) and (6) above present paradigms for *bearu* and *searu*.[14] We assume that these noun stems, like earlier *here*, end in a glide, in this case /w/, and that Old English, as suggested above in the discussion of *here*, contains a rule of glide vocalization that vocalizes glides in word final position. Hence, an underlying *bearw* surfaces as *bearu* in the nominative/accusative singular and an underlying *searw* surfaces as *searu* in the nominative/accusative singular and plural. In all other cases the glide surfaces as a glide because it is not in word final position. This account assumes that glide vocalization must follow High Vowel Deletion since the latter rule feeds the former in the derivation of neuter plural forms; for example, [[searw]u] would undergo High Vowel Deletion to delete the final -*u*, leaving the *w* in stem final position where it vocalizes to *u* yielding *searu*. (The reverse order would yield an incorrect surface form *searw.)

We see, then, that the surface paradigms of *bearu* and *searu* provide two candidates for stems. In the former case the candidate stems are *bearu-* and *bear(w)-* and in the latter *searu-* and *sear(w)-*. Principle (20) predicts that in each case the glide final stems will be selected since their syllabic structures are lower on the Structural Hierarchy.

There is independent evidence in favor of this analysis. Consider forms like *bearwum* and *searwum*, dative plural forms of their respective nouns. In prehistoric Old English the /w/ which appears before a /u/ typically deletes so that a sequence /-wu-/ simplifies to /-u-/. However, in recorded Old English we do not find the expected **bearum* and **searum*. Rather we find the forms with /w/ cited above. This is a natural consequence of the theory presented here, which states that early Old English reorganization of the nominal class takes place in accordance with Principle (20). Thus, this principle explains why the /w/ has been restored and why the historically expected **bearum* and **searum* do not occur.

5. *Some Problematic Cases.*

5.1 *Sunu.* Nouns of the *sunu* type maintained separate paradigmatic status through the entire Old English period. This is not a problem with respect to Principle (20) since that principle selects between stem allomorphs. In the case of *sunu* the paradigm exhibits no stem allomorphy. However, *sunu* does present a problem since the heavy counterpart of *sunu*, i.e. *feld*, was reanalyzed as a masculine a-stem, leaving *sunu* unpaired. This should have led to reanalysis of *sunu* as a masculine a-stem as well. And, indeed, some members of the *sunu* type exhibit a certain amount of shift away from their historical status as u-stems. Thus we find oblique cases which indicate this. Campbell (1959: Section 614) cites *spite*, a dative singular of *spitu* 'spit', where we would expect to find *spita*.

However, the overwhelming force of evidence is that words of the *sunu* class retained their independent status. Hence, they appeared to have lagged behind other Old English nouns in the process of the reorganization of the nominal classes. We have no explanation for their behavior.[15]

5.2 *Dene.* As noted above, feminine i-stems of the type *dene* were assimilated to the ordinary o-stem paradigm prehistorically. Were this not the case, one would expect a feminine nominal paradigm for *dene* indistinguishable from *wine*. However, there is no synchronic evidence for a feminine counterpart to *wine*. To account for this gap we suggest that a further principle may have operated in the reanalysis of the Old English nominal paradigms; namely, a principle of gender conservation whereby reanalysis from one paradigm to another must preserve gender. Hence *dene*, albeit phonologically identical to *wine* on the surface, was constrained from falling into the latter model because the genders of the two differed, being feminine and masculine respectively. The reanalysis of *dene* that actually occurred preserved its gender, although changing its paradigmatic membership. Hence *dene* becomes *denu* and is inflected according to the pattern exhibited by *lufu*.[16]

There is evidence from compound formation which indicates that reanalysis did take place. Reanalysis implies a shift from a bisyllabic to a monosyllabic stem. On the usual assumption that the first elements of Old English compounds contain stem forms, one would expect to find compounds whose first element contains the monosyllabic *den-* and not the bisyllabic stem *dene-*. This is, in fact, the case. Thus, we find compounds of the form *den-sæœte* 'dwellers in valleys'; *den-bera* 'swine pastures'. In this respect these compounds are formed just as they are for ordinary o-stem nouns of the *lufu* type; for example, *luf-taacen* 'love token'.

5.3 *Here*. The analysis of *wine* given above allows us to better understand a problem raised earlier; namely, that in the oblique cases *here* lost its stem final /y/ glide.

We noted above that the subsequent history of *here* shows that the stem *her(g)-* apparently gave way at a later stage to the stem *here-*. We can account for this reanalysis by assuming that forms like *herges* were subject to an attested Old English phonological rule which inserted an epenthetic vowel between /r/ and a following glide. Thus, the paradigm would have shown a stem allomorph of the form *heri(g)-* beside *here-*. Forms with the epenthetic vowel are, in fact, attested. Thus, Dahl (1938: 89-90) cites *herige*, *-herigas*, etc. Notice that the Structural Hierarchy Principle cannot choose between these stem alternants. In this case we might expect a subsequent stage of Old English to yield two possible dialects, one in which *heri(g)-* is selected as the stem model and one in which *here-* is selected. We have already seen that paradigms built on the former stem did occur. The data also show that the latter occurred as well. Thus, we find *here, heres, heras, herum*, etc.[17]

5.4 *Sinu*. We turn finally to the type represented by the feminine noun *sinu* 'sinew'. This noun seems to have been partly reanalyzed according to the *lufu* model, although a significant number of forms from all stages of Old English show a /w/ in the oblique cases; for example, the dative singular *sinwe* exists beside *sine*. Let us consider the interaction of the forms of this paradigm with Principle (20). Recall that prehistoric Old English was characterized by a rule which deletes /w/ before inflectional /u/. Hence, in the *sinu* paradigm, we would find the following range of forms: *sinu* (nominative singular), *sinwe* (all remaining singular forms), *sinwa* (nominative/accusative plural and genitive) and *sinum* (dative plural). Principle (20) indicates that the more complex of the two, namely *sinw-*, should serve as the model for reanalysis. However, the range of forms just mentioned indicates that both surface stems were used in the reanalysis of this type. Hence, Principle (20) provides the wrong prediction in this case. However, there are only two nouns of the *sinu* type in Old English; namely, *sceadu* 'shade' and *sinu* itself. These are, to our knowledge, the only exceptions to the Structural Hierarchy Principle in Old English.

6. *Conclusion*. We have shown that the reduction in the large number of nominal paradigms of prehistoric Old English to a single paradigm in recorded Old English is primarily the result of the fact that High Vowel Deletion and Gemination, on becoming obligatory, introduced surface allomorphy and obscured the relationships among the forms of the paradigms.

As a result of the operation of the Structural Hierarchy Principle, the paradigms were reanalyzed in a way which severely limited the scope of High Vowel Deletion and eliminated Gemination altogether from nominal derivations.

NOTES

1. To a large extent the u-stems given in (13) and (14) above can also be assimilated to the major noun classes. There are, however, some difficulties with this assimilation to which we return in sections 4.1.2 and 5.1.

2. There are a number of other phonological rules which play a secondary role in the derivations to follow. These include a rule of lowering and a rule of glide vocalization. We discuss these latter rules at appropriate points in the discussion.
3. Thus note that in (11) above there is only one type of i-stem feminine noun given; namely, *cween* 'queen' and there is no light stemmed partner with wich it is paired. This gap is a result of the fact that the light stemmed partner was reanalyzed before recorded Old English.
4. In this sense it seems clear that most Old English handbooks are misleading since, under the guise of representing a description of attested Old English, they actually provide a description of a prehistoric stage of the language.
5. The masculine u-stem *sunu* is dealt with separately in section 5.1.
6. Note that in standard Old English only *ende* is recorded beside the earlier form *endi*. To account for this we assume a rule of lowering which operates to lower a word final unstressed i to e in forms like this. We assume this rule without formulation here. However, the rule figures prominently in Keyser (1975) and O'Neil (1976).
7. For discussion of the Strict Cyclicity Condition see Keyser and O'Neil (1985: Chapter 2).
8. There are, however, a few attested examples of the earlier stem *cyne to be found in Old English. Thus, Campbell (1959: Section 579.3) says, 'In a few nouns a formative element has retained the phonological nom. and acc. sg. in -*e* (<-*i*) without gemination...' Such forms as *cynedom* 'royalty' and *cynegerd* 'a scepter' and proper names such as *Cynewulf* illustrate the earlier bisyllabic stem under the reasonable assumption that the first elements of Old English compounds contain stem forms, that is forms which are uninflected. In this regard we assume that they are like *animal-hospital* and not *animals-hospital*.
9. In these two alternants and in several of those that follow the extrametrical consonant appears in parentheses and the inflectional endings are separated from the stem alternant by a hyphen.
10. For details of this nominal type and others like it see Keyser and O'Neil (1985: Chapter 7).
11. The *g* in this paradigm does not represent the velar consonant but rather the palatal glide [*y*].
12. This stem underwent further modification in later Old English. In particular it lost its stem final glide throughout the paradigm so that forms like genitive singular *heres* are recorded. We return to a discussion of this development below.
13. The feminine i-stem is excluded from this status by the fact that it was assimilated very early on to the ordinary o-stem paradigm. We return to this matter below.
14. Arguments for a monophthongal interpretation of the digraphs in these and similar forms are given in Keyser and O'Neil (1985: Chapter 7, Section 2).

15. That some other factor may be operating with respect to nouns of this type is suggested by the behavior of *sunu* type stems in compounds. Recall that the first member of a compound constitutes the stem form. Thus, one finds compounds such as *friþ-leas* 'peaceless' and *friþ-burh* 'town with which one is at peace' based upon the u-stem *friþ-*. However, one also finds bisyllabic first elements for the same compounds; for example, *friþu-leas* and *friþu-burh*. Hence there appears to be some question as to whether the basic stem for nouns of this type is monosyllabic or bisyllabic. It is not clear to us what the basis for this variability might be.

16. In the data we have examined in the paper something like this principle appears to have been adhered to. However, we make no claims for its universality since there are a number of cases from other languages, for example, Slavic, in which gender has not inhibited nouns from moving from one paradigmatic type to another.

17. It seems likely that a subsequent phonological rule very likely deleted /y/ after the epenthetic /i/, reducing the stem alternants to *here-* and *heri-*. Lowering would yield *here-* in the latter stem, thereby erasing any differences between the two stems and causing the *herige-* to disappear from the language. The reason why we think this is likely is that exactly the same change occurred in the weak verb system (see Keyser and O'Neil (1985: Chapter 6).

REFERENCES

Campbell, A. 1959. *Old English Grammar*. Oxford, England: Oxford University Press.

Dahl, I. 1938. *Substantival Inflexion in Early Old English: Vocalic Stems*. Lund, Sweden: C.W.K. Gleerup.

Keyser, S.J. 1975. 'Metathesis and Old English Phonology'. *Linguistic Inquiry* 6.377-411.

Keyser, S.J. and W. O'Neil. 1985. *Rule Generalization and Optionality in Language Change*. Dordrecht, Holland: Foris Publications.

Kiparsky, P. and W. O'Neil. 1976. 'The Phonology of Old English Inflections'. *Linguistic Inquiry* 7.527-557.

VERB AND PARTICLE COMBINATIONS IN OLD AND MIDDLE ENGLISH

WILLEM F. KOOPMAN
University of Amsterdam

0. *Introduction.* There are in Old and Middle English combinations of verb and particle. They can be seen as the precursors of the Modern English Phrasal Verbs, although their syntactic properties are quite different. In many respects they resemble the separable verbs of Dutch and German, though there are substantial differences.

In this paper I will claim that the distribution of verb and particle in Old English can be accounted for in a natural way if we assume a verb movement rule in root as well as embedded clauses. I will argue for a leftward particle movement rule, which in Middle English, due to the change in basic word order from SOV to SVO, becomes a rightward particle movement rule. Other ways of accounting for the particle distribution have serious shortcomings.

1. Let us start by looking at the position of particle and verb relative to each other. I will assume that the base-generated word order of Old English is SOV (see Canale 1978), and that in root clauses a V-second rule moves the verb from its structural position. (see van Kemenade 1984 for a discussion). I will also assume that particle and verb are generated together.[1] There are then two possibilities for the structure of the node:

(1)   a.   V   b.   V
               part V   V part

To establish what the order of verb and particle is we must look at cases where they occur in their base-generated position, i.e. clause finally. That position is found in some embedded clauses. Almost without exception such clauses show the order of (1a) with the particle immediately preceding the verb:

(2) ðonne we ðara gyltendra scylda mid arfæsððes ingeðonces
    when we of the guilty the sins with pious thought's
    'when we cut away the sins of the guilty with the
    lare aweg aceorfað (CP 167.6)
    instruction away cut
    instruction of pious thought'
(3) se þa gebundenan of þissum carcerne ut alædde (BlHom 241.1)
    who the bound ones of this prison   out brought
    'who brought out of the prison those who lay bound there'

There are only very few examples with the particle following the verb:[3]

(4) oððet twegen cyngas innan Normandige mid heoran folcan
    until the two kings in Normandy   with their armies
    'until the two kings joined battle with their armies
    coman togædere (ChrE 248.20 (1119))
    came together
    in Normandy'

It seems reasonable to assume that the particle precedes the verb in base position and that the few cases with the particle following are derived from it, perhaps by a stylistic rule.

    1.1. With a base order SOV, and a V-second rule in root clauses, we still need further rules to account for the position of the particle:

(5) ac he teah forð þa his ealdan wrenceas (ChrE 135.10 (1003))
    but he brought forth then his old tricks
    'but then he produced his old tricks'
(6) þa ahof Paulus up his heafod (BlHom 187.35)
    then raised Paul up his head
    'then Paul raised his head'
(7) ne hebbe ge ... up eowre hornas (CP 425.22)
    not raise you ... up your horns
    'do not exalt your horns'

These are all root sentences with (obligatory) V-second, but the particle is followed by the object. There are two possible ways to account for these word orders:
    (i) The particle remains in its base position, but the object is moved:

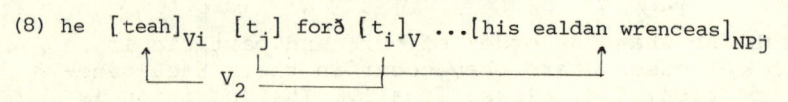

(8) he [teah]$_{Vi}$ [t$_j$] forð [t$_i$]$_V$ ...[his ealdan wrenceas]$_{NPj}$
        |_____ V$_2$ _____|

    (ii) The particle is moved:

(9) he [teah]$_{Vi}$ [forð]$_{partj}$ ... his ealdan wrenceas [t$_j$]$_{part}$[t$_i$]$_V$

    ↑_____V$_2$_____|_____|

I will consider both possibilities, as there is motivation for both movement rules.

    1.1.1. Movement of the Object, or Object Extraposition, can be motivated independently. Clear cases occur when with verbs that take two objects one precedes the verb and the other follows. Basing ourselves on SOV as base-generated order we must assume that the object that follows the verb is extraposed, as in the following embedded clause:

(10) siððan he his cnihtas gelæred hæfde ðone cræft ðæs
     when he his disciples taught had the art of
     'when he had taught his disciples the art of teaching'
     lareowdomes   (CP 385.3)
     teaching

Object Extraposition is obligatory with clausal objects:

(11) þæt hie him gefultumadon þæt hie wiþ þone here
     that they them helped that they with the host
     'to help them fight against the host'
     gefuhton (ChrA 68.32 (868))
     fought

The fact that clausal objects always follow the verb may have more to do with restrictions on embedding rather than with Extraposition.

    Some evidence for Object Extraposition can be found, but the number of clear examples are few. Many examples can be accounted for by the V-second rule in root clauses. I will argue that we do not need Object Extraposition to account for the position of particle and verb.

    1.1.2. There is motivation for a particle movement rule too. In many sentences the particle does not appear in its base-generated position. In embedded clauses the verb frequently appears clause finally, but the particle does not always precede the verb immediately:

(12) and þærrihte wearþ þæt fæt upp to heofenum abroden   (ÆLS
     and straightaway was the vessel up to heaven pulled   226.94)
     'and straightaway the vessel was pulled up to heaven'
(13) þe nu up on þysne heofon from eow astag (BlHom 123.22)
     who now up to this heaven from you went
     'who has now gone up from you to heaven'

(14) þonne hi ðe forð mid him to ðam ecan forwyrde
    when they you forth with them to the eternal damnation
    'when they led you with them to eternal damnation'
    gelædon   (ÆCHom i 516.18)
    led

Examples such as (12), (13), and (14) make it clear that a particle movement rule to the left is necessary even if we assume that Object Extraposition can account for some cases, such as (6). It seems to me more reasonable to assume that there is a particle movement rule rather than that as soon as there is an object following the verb (as in (6)) it is due to Object Extraposition and not to Particle Movement. I will, therefore, assume that a particle movement rule to the left is motivated and has operated when the particle is not in its base-generated position.

1.2. This leftward particle movement rule would move the particle within the VP only. The arguments I have for this statement are the following. As far as I am aware, there is no example where the particle appears before the subject (see Denison 1981 , Mitchell 1978, 1985), as in Modern English *Out he went*. Secondly with pronominal objects we never find (apart from cases where the object is contrasted with something else, or where there is clear Latin influence) the surface order: V - particle - Pronominal Object, but always: V - Pronominal Object - particle. As has been argued by van Kemenade (1983) pronoun objects are clitics and can cliticize on to the VP on the left. By restricting the particle movement to the VP we can account for the position of pronominal objects in a natural way. The clitic position ensures that the particle stays to the right of the pronominal object.

Apparent counterexamples to this rule which restricts particle movement to the VP are:

(15) and aweg gelædde micelne dæl þæs folces to his rice (ÆCHom ii
    and away led a great part of his people to his kingdom   18.21)
    'and led away a grat part of his people to his kingdom'
(16) þæt heo onweg adyde þa gemynd þara treowleasra
    that they away did the record of the faithless
    'that they would strike out the record of the faithless
    cyninga (Bede 154.10)
    kings
    kings'

Between particle and verb no other element can intervene. This suggests a close link between particle and verb. I will claim that this

order is due to an optional reanalysis rule which ensures
that particle and verb are seen as one node for the
V-second rule, and moved together. I will discuss V movement in embedded clauses later.

1.3. Let us now have a closer look at embedded clauses.
Apart from the order SOV, there are also many examples
with surface word order SVO:

(17) siþþan he onfeng bisc̃ dome (ChrA 46.5 (745))
    'after he received the bishopric'
(18) þæt hi sceoldon oncnawan heora Scyppend (ÆCHom i 96.12)
    'that they might acknowledge their creator'

There are two ways in which we can account for this order:
(i) The verb has been moved:

(19) buton ða lareowas [screadian]$_{Vi}$ ... ða leahtras þurh
    unless the teachers prune   the sins   by
    'unless teachers prune away sins by their teaching'
    heora lare aweg [t$_i$]$_V$ (ÆCHom ii 74.15)
    their teaching away

(ii) The verb has not been moved, but other elements
have:

(20) buton ða lareowas [t$_i$]$_{NP}$ [t$_j$]$_{PP}$ [t$_k$]$_{part}$ screadian ...
    [ða leahtras]$_{NPi}$[þurh heora lare]$_{PPj}$[aweg]$_{part\ k}$

In (20) an NP, a PP, and a particle, 3 elements in all,
have been moved to the right of the verb. (Exbraciation,
see Stockwell 1977). This raises at least two important
questions: (a) Which element is moved first?, and (b)
Are the traces properly governed? I will not attempt to
discuss these questions here.[4] Important for my argument
is that a particle movement rule to the right is needed
if we assume that the verb has not been moved from its
base-generated position.

2. Above I have argued for a particle movement rule
to the left and for a particle movement rule to the right.
A movement rule which goes both ways is unprecedented
and poses great theoretical problems. It would be much
to be preferred if we were left with just one rule (or
perhaps with no rule at all). I will discuss below the
alternatives for the particle movement rules.

2.1. *Leftward particle movement*. The examples given
so far illustrate some of the positions of the particle
within the VP. In (5) the particle precedes the object,

in (12) it is separated from the verb by a PP, in (13) and (14) there are two PP's in between. Further positions are illustrated below:

(21) þa ahof Paulus up his heafod (BlHom 187.35)
then raised Paul up his head
'then Paul raised his head'
(22) þæt ða tanas up æpla bæron (Sat 479)[5]
so that the branches up apples bore
'so that the branches bore apples'

It seems that within the VP the particle can have any position. If we are looking for an alternative to a particle movement rule to the left we would have to predict the position of the particle in some way or other. If we assume that the order of elements in the VP is base-generated, there is no way out of having a particle movement rule. If on the other hand the order of the elements within the VP is not base-generated, but can be predicted by some principle of grammar, a movement rule would be superfluous.

Let us assume that we only specify that the VP is head final, i.e. that the verb is in final position. The order of elements is not specified. Case assignment is not structural, but lexical through subcategorization. The particle forms part of the subcategorization frame of the verb. Such an approach would predict that the order of the complements of the verb is free, i.e. those items which occur in the subcategorization frame of the verb can appear in any order in the VP, with the only restriction that the verb is in final position. Is there any support for such an approach?

We can then expect that verbs taking double objects (dative and accusative) have them in any order. Indeed there are examples which seem to support this:[6]

(23) ðæt hi mid ðære licettunge [oðrum mannum]$_{Oi}$ [yfle bisne]$_{Od}$
that they with the dissimulation for other men bad example
'that with the dissimulation they do not set a bad example
ne astellen (CP 449.22)
not set
to others'
(24) God sylf forbyt [ælcne að]$_{Od}$ [cristenum mannum]$_{Oi}$ (ÆCHom i 482.15)
God himself forbids every oath Christian men
"God himself forbids Christians every oath'

Mitchell (1985: 3940) writes:'when both the direct and indirect objects are nouns, their relative position varies.'

Brown (1970) also found both orders. However, when one looks at verbs with the double object construction[7], it seems that the order of (23) with the indirect object preceding the direct object is far more frequent than the order of (24) with the direct object preceding the indirect object. A free order in the VP would predict that there are plenty of examples of both orders, not that there are substantially more of one construction. Other complementation types similarly do not show the expected variation. Verbs which are accompanied by an object and a prepositional phrase almost always have the prepositional phrase after the object:

(25) ic ræhte mine hond to eow   (CP 247.21)
     I offered my hand to you
     'I offered you my hand'

Verbs with an object and object complement too have them in this order (judging from the examples quoted by Visser 1963:550 ff).[8] All this suggests that there is as yet insufficient support for the assumption that the order within the VP is free. We must therefore conclude that a leftward particle movement rule is necessary to account for the distribution of the particle within the VP.

2.2. *Rightward particle movement*. Above I have argued that a rightward particle movement rule is inevitable if we assume that the verb in embedded clauses has not been moved. Let us therefore explore the possibility of verb movement in embedded clauses. From (18) and (19) it is clear that movement cannot be to COMP, but instead to a position to the right of the subject. I will claim that this position is INFL.

In a V-second language such as Dutch there is no V movement in embedded clauses. The usual explanation is that in root clauses the verb moves to COMP.[9] Movement of V to COMP is not possible in embedded clauses because COMP is filled with lexical material. In Old English the situation is different in that the verb is not always in final position in embedded clauses:

(26) þæt se ylca arwyrða wer hof upp glæsene leohtfatu in þam
     'that the same venerable man lifted up glass lamps in the
     gebedhuse   (GD 49.20)
     chapel'
(27) gif þu offrast ðine lac to Godes weofode   (ÆCHom i 54.17)
     'if you offer your sacrifice to God's altar'

Let us assume that in embedded clauses there is movement

of V to INFL (optionally). This would mean that the underlying order of Old English is:

(28) (COMP) S INFL O V[10]

In root clauses there can be further movement of V + INFL to COMP, giving the surface order V - S. This order is not found when the subject introduces the clause. Here is an example from Dutch:

(29) Jan koopt morgen een auto
 John buys tomorrow a car
 'John will buy a car tomorrow'

These constructions prove somewhat difficult for the usual V-second analysis. If V moves to COMP, then the subject in (29) cannot be in its structural subject position, but must be in a pre-COMP position, i.e. in the TOPIC position. This is motivated for Dutch on the basis of sentences where we can assume topicalization of the subject:

(30) Jan (die) heeft hem ontmoet
 John (that) has him met
 'John met him'

This so-called d-word analysis (see Koopman 1984) is not without its problems. The d-word is not always lexicalized and thus it accounts for the two possibilities of (30).[11]

There is no trace of a d-word construction in Old English, and I feel that it cannot be used for arguing for a subject in TOPIC position. The d-word would never be lexicalized and that would be *ad hoc*. I assume therefore that sentences in Old English corresponding to (29) do not have a COMP. They show the base order S INFL O V, with V movement to INFL.

Motivation for the position of INFL comes from topicalization. In Dutch topicalization combined with V-second accounts for the order TOPIC V S:

(31) Die auto moet je kopen
 that car must you buy
 'You must buy that car'

Topicalization in Old English has a different effect:

(32) þa medomnesse ðære strengio se salmscop ongeat (CP 85.22)
 'the excellence of the strength the psalmist acknowledged'
(33) ðas ilcan geornfulnesse ðara hierda sanctus Paulus
 'this same zeal of the shepherds St.Paul aroused'
 aweahte (CP 137.25)

In (32) and (33) the subject precedes the verb. This is

frequent in Old English:[12]

(34) be ðæm æðelum ðæs gæstes Petrus cwæð (CP 85.17)
of the nobility of the spirit Peter spoke
'of spiritual nobility Peter spoke'
(35) be þinre hese seo sunne bringð leohtne dæg (Solil 9.14)
'on your command the sun brings forth a bright day'

Root clauses because of the V-second constraint show
V movement. As can be seen from (35) movement is to INFL.
Further movement of V + INFL to COMP can take place optionally. When it does we get the characteristic V - S
order of many root sentences in Old English. This analysis predicts that we can find cases of topicalization
where movement of V + INFL to COMP results in the word
order TOPIC - V - S. These do indeed occur in Old English:

(36) ac eall ðiss aredað se reccere suiðe ryhte (CP 169.3)
but all this arranges the rule very rightly
'but all this the rule arranges very rightly'
(37) þæt deð God to tacne eallum monkynne (Or 38.35)
that does God as a sign for all mankind
'that God does as a sign for all mankind'

We could argue that (35) is derived through Object Extraposition and that there is no V movement at all. Object
Extraposition would then be obligatory. Such an approach,
however, for root clauses runs into difficulties. Without
V-movement we would have to assume all kinds of (obligatory) extrapositions to account for the surface word
order: not only objects, but also PP's and adverbials
as well. I think that that is highly unlikely. That V
movement must be assumed is clear from (38) where the
finite part of the verb is moved to second constituent
position, but the non-finite part remains in its base-generated clause final position:

(38) ac we sculon swiðe smealice ðissa ægðer underðencean (CP 49.
but we ought very closely of these both consider   23)
'but we ought to consider both cases very closely'

I conclude that there is evidence for the position of
INFL to the right of the subject, and that the underlying order of Old English is (28). V movement to INFL is
obligatory in root clauses, with further optional movement to COMP, when present. In this way the different
word orders in topicalized sentences can be accounted for.
In embedded clauses V movement to INFL is optional. Further movement to COMP cannot take place because there is
lexical material in the COMP.

We have thus found a valid alternative for a particle

movement rule to the right. It is unnecessary when we assume that V movement to INFL takes place in root and (optionally) in embedded clauses. I conclude that we need only a particle movement rule to the left.

3. *Middle English*. It is generally assumed (Canale 1978) that the underlying word order changed from SOV to SVO in early Middle English. Above I have argued that V movement in embedded clauses is optional. There is an increase in the number of sentences with this optional rule in late Old English (Bean 1983).Generalization to an obligatory rule could have taken place and could have led to reanalysis of the surface patterns. If the verb is now no longer found in clause final position, its surface position could be taken for its base-generated position. As a consequence the number of sentences with verb final position would quickly decrease. The Middle English material bears this out.[13] Reanalysis would have the following consequences:

3.1. *A*. The verb is now in VP initial position, with possibly only a clitic position to its left. The normal order will then be with the particle following the verb. This is supported by the evidence from Middle English. By about 1200 the pattern where the particle follows the verb has clearly been firmly established.[14] Denison (1981: 137) says: 'pre-verbal particle positions appear to be in a clear minority even as early as the mid-twelfth century'. He found (1981:172-174) that in the *Ormulum* only a few percent of the particles precede the verb. Among the factors associated with pre-verbal position is the initial placement of a particle. The pattern *Out he went*, not recorded in Old English, is found in Middle English.[15]

(39) awei he warp his gode breond   (Lay. Brut A 2535)
     'away he cast his good sword'

A second factor is a tendency to behave like a compound verb.[16] When the particle immediately precedes the verb there would be a tendency to reanalyse it as a verbal prefix.

3.2. *B*. A particle movement rule to the right would be another consequence of the reanalysis. In Old English there are no surface patterns with V - particle - Pronominal Object, due to the clitic status of the pronominal object. This constraint is incorporated in the movement rule, and must be the ultimate source for the ungrammaticality of Modern English *He blew up it*.

In Old English there can be various elements between

the verb and the particle, due to V movement and/or particle movement. An object can intervene, (a) prepositional phrase(s), and (an) adverbial(s). We find exactly the same possibilities in Middle English:

(40) me schal holden scheld ine vihte up a buuen ðe
'people must hold the shield in the fight up above the
heaued   (Ancr.Riwle 132.16)
head'
(41) 7 feol of fearlac adun on hire rihthalue   (St.Marg. 32.3)
'and fell from fear down on her side'
(42) þat hit urne enddelong hire leofliche lich adun to
'so that it ran along her lovely body down to her heels'
hire healen (St.Jul. 31.4)

Later the movement possibilities of the particle will be further restricted. In Modern English only on Object can regularly come in between verb and particle. Only a very restricted set of adverbs can exceptionally come between verb and particle.[17]

4. *Conclusion*. In this paper I have argued for a particle movement rule to the left to account for the position of the particle within the VP. A reanalysis rule accounts for those cases where particle and verb are moved together. Evidence for a V movement rule in embedded clauses is presented and it is argued that the underlying order in Old English is (COMP) S INFL O V. V movement in root and (optionally) in embedded clauses is to INFL, with further movement to COMP optional in root clauses. It is only in this way that the syntactic behaviour of verb and particle in Old English can adequately be described. The change in word order in Middle English also causes a change in the underlying order of particle and verb, so that it becomes verb - particle. A particle movement rule to the right becomes necessary then.

NOTES

1. See Koster (1975). According to Denison (1981:148 ff) the first idiomatic combinations occur in the Peterborough Chronicle.
2. The short titles of Old English texts are those proposed by Bruce Mitchell *et al* (1975).
3. Hiltunen (1983) found only 4 in his large corpus. The others are: CP 277.23, ÆCHom ii 160.21 , and BlHom 9.32.
4. Proper government of the traces may pose serious problems.
5. There are very few examples of (22). See Mitchell (1978),(1985), and Denison (1981).
6. Because my material is limited the conclusion is somewhat tentative.

7. Because of the clitic behaviour of pronominal objects I have only looked at cases where both objects are nominal.
8. Brown (1970) records one example (CP 277.16) where the object complement precedes the object, as against 27 with the object preceding the complement.
9. See den Besten (1977) and Koopman (1984).
10. I follow Travis (1984:139 ff) in assuming that in embedded clauses with V in final position INFL can remain empty, provided it is properly governed by COMP.
11. For a not always convincing refutation of this analysis see Travis (1984).
12. See Bacquet (1962:697 ff).
13. Hiltunen (1983) in his corpus found no examples with the verb in final position. It should be borne in mind, however, that he only looked at sentences with a particle.
14. Hiltunen (1983:114, table 18) records only a few cases with the particle preceding the verb. In a few texts he found examples in some number: *Vices and Virtues, The Life of St.Chad,* and *The History of the Holy Rood Tree.*These are either copies of Old English Texts or heavily influenced by them.
15. See also Denison (1981:142) and de la Cruz (1976:27). I do not have an explanation why this pattern becomes possible in Middle English. One suspects that it has to do with the change in word order, but how exactly is not clear.
16. Denison (1981:180) adds: 'possibly under foreign influence' See also Visser (1963:599 ff).
17. See e.g. the introduction in Cowie & Mackin (1975).

REFERENCES

Bacquet,P. 1962. *La structure de la phrase verbale à l'époque Alfredienne*. Paris, Les Belles Lettres.

Bean, M.C. 1983. *The development of Word Order Patterns in Old English*. London & Canberra, Totowa, Croom Helm, Barnes & Noble.

Besten, H. den 1977. 'The Interaction of Root Transformations and Lexical Deletive Rules'. Unpublished ms., Amsterdam.

Brown, W.H. jr. 1970. *A Syntax of king Alfred's* Pastoral Care. The Hague & Paris, Mouton.

Canale, W. 1978. *Word Order Change in Old English: Base Reanalysis in Generative Grammar*. Ph.D.Dissertation, McGill University.

Cowie, A.P. & R. Mackin. 1975. *Oxford Dictionary of Current Idiomatic English*. London, Oxford University Press.

Cruz, J.M. de la 1976. 'Context-Sensitivity in Old and Middle English' *SAP* 8. 3-43.

Denison, D. 1981. *Aspects of the History of English Group-Verbs, with Particular Attention to the Syntax of the Ormulum*. Ph.D. Dissertation, Oxford University.

Hiltunen, R. 1983. *The Decline of the Prefixes and the Beginnings of the English Phrasal Verb*. Turku, Turun Yliopisto.

Kemenade, A. van 1984. 'Verb Second and Clitics in Old English'. *Linguistics in the Netherlands 1984* ed. by H.Bennis & W.U.S van Lessen Kloeke, 101-109. Dordrecht & Cinnaminson, Foris.
Koopman, H. 1984. *The Syntax of Verbs. From Verb Movement in the Kru Languages to Universal Grammar*. Dordrecht & Cinnaminson, Foris.
Koster, J. 1975. 'Dutch as an SOV Language'. *LA* 1. 111-136.
Mitchell, B. 1978. 'Prepositions, Adverbs, Prepositional Adverbs, Postpositions, Separable Prefixes, or Inseparable Prefixes, in Old English?" *NM* 79. 240-257.
Mitchell, B. 1985. *Old English Syntax*. Oxford, Clarendon Press.
Mitchell, B., Ball. C., Cameron, C. 1975. "Short Titles of Old English Texts". *ASE* 4. 207-221.
Stockwell, R.P. 1977. 'Motivations for Exbraciation in Old English'. *Mechanisms of Syntactic Change* ed. by C.Li, 291-316. Austin, University of Texas Press.
Travis, L. 1984. *Parameters and Effects of Word Order Variation*. Ph.D. Dissertation, MIT
Visser, F.Th. 1963. *An Historical Syntax of the English Language*. Part I. Leiden, Brill.

THE IMPERSONAL VERB IN CONTEXT: OLD ENGLISH
LINNEA M. LAGERQUIST
University of California, Los Angeles

A problem which seems perennially popular in linguistics is the evolution of so-called 'impersonal' verbs from Old English (OE) to Modern English (NE), as exemplified in (1, 2).

(1a) *þam   licode   þaes
     they-DAT please-PAST-SG that-GEN
     'that pleased them / it pleased them about that'

(1b) they liked that

(2a) *hine   hyngred
     he-ACC   hunger-SG
     'he is hungry'

(2b) he hungers

Accounts of this development have sprouted forth in all corners, with Government-and-Binding and Relational Grammar at present proving especially fertile seedbeds. The later studies differ (sometimes wildly) from the earlier, in at least vocabulary and method, but share with their precursors a tacit or explicit reliance on grammatical relations as primitive within sentential syntax.

Even from the beginning (Jespersen 1894, van der Gaaf 1904; cf. also the nineteenth-century bibliographical entries in Visser 1963), the development of impersonalia[1] has been considered in terms of subjecthood. The traditional point of view takes nominal morphology as criterial: thus constructions having in OE a non-nominative argument - a non-subject - in preverbal position became reinterpreted at some point of late Middle English as being SVO. Wahlén (1925) asserts that he, not van der Gaaf, is first to *define* impersonal constructions as subjectless; Jespersen (1931-40) claims to adhere to the Wahlénian definition, but his notorious reconstruction of the reanalysis takes as starting point a structure in which a host of later researches have found case and verbal concord that are consistent with *peran* 'pears' being a subject (3: parenthesized material and emphasis supplied).

(3) þam cynge   licod*on*   peran
    (NP-DAT-SG   V-PAST-*PL* NP-(NOM)-*PL*)

    the king   liceden   peares
    (NP-SG   V-PAST-PL   NP-PL)

    the king   liked   pears
    (NP-SG   V-PAST   NP-PL)

    he   liked   pears
    (NOM V-PAST   NP-PL)

Among the reasons traditionally given for the reanalysis are the decline of unambiguous case morphology (Jespersen 1894, van der Gaaf 1904, Marchand 1951); the semantics of the verbs involved, which are *verba sentiendi* (Fay 1917), denoting states of involuntary affectedness (Curme 1931:8-9), or 'expressions denoting different aspects of the course of events', among others (Wahlen 1925:70); and the inherent or increasing psychological preeminence of human experiencers (Jespersen 1931:II_2; see also McCawley 1976, Tripp 1978).

With the ascendance in linguistics of the notion of autonomous syntax, accounts referring to the role of semantic, pragmatic and psychological factors in synchrony and diachrony have correspondingly declined in favor. Thus Lightfoot (1979, 1981) repudiates any but purely structural motivations for syntactic change. In discussing impersonalia, however, he arrives at essentially the traditional conclusion: the object-initial pattern inherited from OE got reanalyzed in ME as subject-initial. According to Lightfoot, the canonization of SVO base order and the erosion of case morphology conspired to make OVS constructions excessively 'opaque' to the language learner in ME. Lightfoot's original account includes rules of NP Postposing and NP Preposing that both operate on the SVO base, as in Fig. 1, to yield surface OVS.

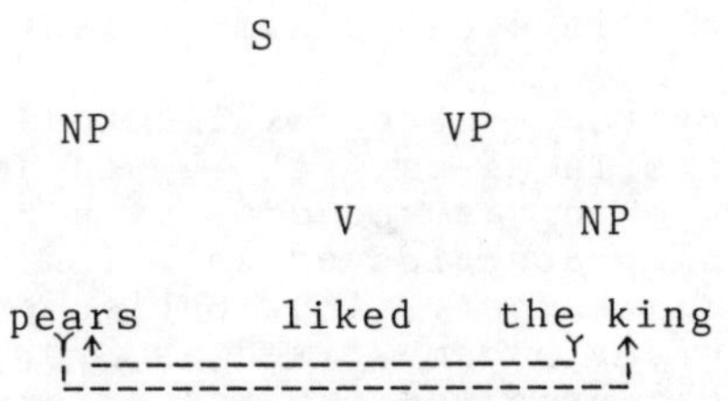

```
                    S
         NP                  VP
                       V           NP
       pears        liked       the king
        ↑↑_____↑↑
        ↑_____↑
```

Fig. 1
Lightfoot's NP Preposing/Postposing
(after Fischer & van der Leek 1983:340)

This maneuver violates the Trace Erasure Principle (Dresher & Hornstein 1979), for the slot into which the object is preposed is already occupied by the *t* left behind by the postposed subject. Lightfoot (1981) therefore drops one of the movement rules and adduces the Trace Erasure Principle as the explanation for the opacity of OVS.

Under neither version can Lightfoot account for preposed experiencers of ME that fail to evolve into subjects, nor for the non-abruptness of the subjectivalization that does occur (Lagerquist 1980:28-31, 41; Fischer & van der Leek 1983:352-4).

Underlying the traditional explanations is the assumption of a fairly close correspondence between morphology and grammatical relations (and, for that matter, logical relations). A more recent approach is that there is no necessary connection between subjecthood and nominative case (cf. Anderson 1976). Thus what appears to be OVS on grounds of case morphology is actually to be seen as SVO based on structure and behavior. The most extreme analysis in these terms is A. Harris' 'On the loss of a rule of syntax' (1980). In Relational Grammar, an experiencer argument, whatever its final grammatical relation, is assumed to be a basic subject - 'initial 1' (one), in RG argot - which may be demoted by Inversion from subject status in favor of the basic object, or initial 2; coding rules then assign non-nominative case to the erstwhile subject and lack of concord with that argument to the verb. Harris claims that over time the coding rules of ME gradually came to apply before Inversion, with the result that the demoted experiencer finally appeared with subject marking and verb concord after all. It is not clear, Harris' title aside, that she has decided whether or not Inversion is in fact *lost*: 'since Inversion was an optional rule with most of the predicates that conditioned it, even in Old English, it is remarkable that in the process of loss the rule did not simply cease to apply.' (167-8).

A more orthodox (and better explicated) position is that preposed objects in ME may retain non-nominative case-marking while functioning as subjects with respect to such behavior and control properties as deletion under co-reference and verb agreement. Thus Butler proposes that, once English word order became fixed as SVO, then the 'transformation' that preposed impersonal experiencer objects 'became in effect a subjectivizing transformation' (1977:166). He cites data such as *Me seem my head doth swim* [1571], in which the NP has subject position and verb agreement but not subject-like case marking, in support of the principle of Keenan's (1976) Coding Hierarchy but as counterevidence to Keenan's ordering of verb agreement after casemarking in the hierarchy.

Butler has little to say about what might cause the experiencer object to be preposed, but Seefranz-Montag (1982) claims that it is in fact topicalized. She is neither the first to say this nor even the first to suggest a typological correlation between subjectivalization of experiencers and the shift from SOV word order through TVX to SVO (cf. Kossuth 1978). Hers is, however, the first detailed account to bring together the typological correlations within and without Indo-European.

These accounts presuppose a reanalysis that takes as input all data meeting the structural description OVS; correspondingly, they entail that, after the point in time at which the postulated reanalysis took place, instances of subjectlessness should no longer be possible. Lightfoot (1979:229-39) is of course most explicit about this 'catastrophe'. As I have suggested elsewhere, however, and as Elmer (1981) meticulously documents, non-nominative initial experiencers persist with some but not all verbs well into NE; furthermore, some but not all impersonal verbs occur with nominative personal subjects from earliest OE. Fischer & van der Leek 1983 provide a formal account of this variation within a Government-and-Binding framework, which allows them to distinguish case assigned lexically from case assigned on the basis of (surface) grammatical relations to NPs not already bearing lexical case.

The OE impersonal verb, according to Fischer & van der Leek, might have a lexical entry like that in Fig. 2.

$$\begin{bmatrix} \text{NP} \quad \text{NP} \quad \underline{\quad} \quad (\bar{S}) \\ \text{NP: DATIVE; } \theta\text{-role: experiencer} \\ \left\{ \begin{array}{l} \text{NP: GENITIVE} \\ \bar{S} \end{array} \right\} \quad \theta\text{-role: cause} \end{bmatrix}$$

Fig. 2
OE Impersonal Verb Lexical Entry
(Fischer & van der Leek 1983:357)

Such a verb could optionally fail to assign one of the lexical cases specified in its lexical entry; then the argument left unmarked would move into subject position and receive structural case (Nominative). Fischer & van der Leek thus allow an OE impersonal verb to take a nominative causer or a nominative experiencer. They have specified 'no fixed order' (362) for experiencers and causers in OE or ME; if, they suggest, one order should turn out to predominate, their theory may require a minor amount of additional machinery. As morphological case distinctions collapsed through ME, case specifications disappeared from lexical entries, leaving only the structural cases Nominative (assigned to the subject) and Objective (assignable to no more than one argument per clause: thus in a two-argument clause of NE one NP has to be Nominative). The reanalysis, then, was not so much syntactic as lexical: the NE lexical entry now specifies, not case, but whether the θ-role 'experiencer' is assigned to the subject, as is the case for *like*, or elsewhere, as for *please*. According to Fischer & van der Leek, no one verb in NE (except the highly restricted *ail*, 364-5) should be able to alternate between experiencer or causer as subject. This prediction, however, is not entirely correct: *delight* and *grieve* are among the exceptions.

All these descriptions, formal and non-formal, have in common the acceptance of grammatical relations as axiomatic, requiring neither further analysis nor elaboration in order to function as sufficient explanations for word order and morphology (and even semantic roles, although to a lesser extent). Throughout the literature, word order typology consistently appears as a sort of linguistic juggernaut; in the history of English, SVO is depicted as relentlessly advancing until the last initial experiencer object in ME was forced into morphological subjection. But if the SVO generalization was that irresistible, how is it that morphological objects in ME kept successfully infiltrating the 'subject' position? The answer may well involve some kind of topicalization, but it is no clearer from von Seefranz-Montag's account than from anyone else's that the T in TVX is 'topical' in any sense other than simply having undergone leftward movement.

Now am I asserting that the received tradition in linguistics and the impersonalia is worthless? By no means, as St. Paul saith. The assumption in general linguistics of grammatical relations as primitive has proven quite fruitful – perhaps even necessary given the prior postulation of autonomous components and in light of the exasperating realization that the the only property common to all subjects in all languages seems to be subjecthood itself (Keenan 1976:306). Certainly without some such simplifying assumptions, attempts to describe languages and to develop linguistic theories – and to see where a theory falters – would be seriously crippled. Indeed, without the notion 'subject' linguists would be hard pressed to characterize phenomena ranging from Equi-NP deletion to ergativity.

Closer to home, the whole issue of impersonalia might never even have been expressed without some recourse to grammatical relations. The researcher who identifies subjectlessness and the one who discusses non-nominative subjects may disagree as to which approach is best, but both obviously must have some idea *a priori* as to what is a subject, and each may concede that the other's position sheds considerable light on some aspect of impersonalia. It is hard to see why a language purportedly accusative should choose as it were to group some of its experiencers together with transitive objects (e.g., *hine hyngred*) unless they are on some level not like subjects. Conversely, it is difficult to justify a language arbitrarily according its non-nominative experiencers the position and behavior normally enjoyed by (full) subjects unless the former are felt to have something in common with the latter. The fact that some verbs seem to accept variable patterns of experiencer case or position again points to the relevance of both points of view.

There is – let me stress this point – no shortage of incisive insight in the current work on impersonalia. What bothers me, though, is that the understanding of subjecthood on which so many of us have relied may be an assumption not only simplifying but simplistic. A growing body of literature suggests that we must now consider more than case and constituency. Keenan's Promotion to Subject Hierarchy (1976:324) includes, along with the coding and control properties for which it is most often cited, semantic properties such as agency (cf. also van Oosten 1977, Hopper & Thompson 1980, Morley 1983) and selectional restrictions. Plank (1979) notes the relevance of social and 'ethno-psychological' factors, and Foster (1979) provides an illuminating case study of the connection between subjecthood and inferred responsibility in Ozark English. Studies from assorted backgrounds attest to the importance in connected text of a set of properties variously characterized as 'givenness', 'aboutness', 'thematicity' or 'focus' to the selection of both subject and topic (Chafe 1976, Firbas 1966, García 1979, Sidner 1983, Zubin 1979, MacWhinney 1977, Ehrich & Koster 1983). In addition, empathy or viewpoint seems to figure prominently (DeLancey 1980, Fillmore 1968, 1977, Kuno 1976).

In short, subjecthood is not a simple phenomenon. But how should the study of impersonalia now proceed? One possibility is to continue to refer to subjecthood while critically examining its intricacies. Linda Thornburg (this conference) has taken such an approach, with commendable resourcefulness and (to my mind) daring. For tackling subjecthood directly strikes me as the heroic way, not only because subjecthood remains intractably complex, but also because the terminology can exert a kind of Sapir-Whorfian seductiveness. Once one has labeled a set of arguments 'non-nominative subject', however provisionally, one may find it difficult to pay attention to the other respects in which each argument may or may not be a subject, to the other arguments, and even to the verbs involved. There is a related temptation to read into another's use of a term one's own pet presuppositions. The danger may be not only synchronic. Covington (1984:70, 137), for one, observes that the term *subiectum* as used throughout the Middle Ages meant 'logical subject'; there was a separate word, *suppositio*, for 'grammatical subject'. I do not wish to claim that the inclusive sense of 'subject' is irrelevant before AD 1575, but it is surely the better part of valor in discussing the English of AElfric or Wyclif to exercise caution in adducing 'subjectivalization' or 'topicalization' as mechanisms of change.

There is an alternative: to avoid using 'subject' and 'object' as classificative primitives, focusing instead on the data and the various properties suggested in the literature as contributing to subjecthood. This approach is relatively unheroic as compared to the first but, as I hope to show, it has its own appeal.

Now what data should we consider? The answer is not as obvious as it may seem. Fischer & van der Leek (1983) extended their research from impersonal constructions (in all attested orders) to impersonal verbs in personal constructions; Elmer (1981) included constructions that can be described as derived, whether by passivization or adjectivalization or nominalization. I would like to add semantically related non-impersonal verbs to the list. This addition is justifiable on the Jakobsonian principle (1962:304) that language is organized in terms of the systems of oppositions into which its constituent units enter (cf. also Stein, this volume): thus it seems reasonable to compare *verba sentiendi* that occur only in the frame [NP$_{Nom}$ __] with those that occur in the frames [NP$_{Nom/Dat}$ __] or [NP$_{Dat}$ __]. *Verba sentiendi* are an important part of Old English - in the classes 'fear', 'anger', 'need', 'think', 'like/loathe' and 'happen/undergo' alone, Dodd gives 103 non-derived verbs, comprising not less than 10.7% of Wulfstan's verbal vocabulary.

We should, moreover, pay attention to the contexts in which our data occur. To be sure, the morphological and structural facts can be ascertained from clauses in isolation (e.g., verbal concord, ordering of arguments, and whether the arguments, if any, are nominal, pronominal, 'dummy' or clausal - not that non-nominal arguments have received the scrutiny they deserve), as can such selectional restrictions as humanness or animacy. The adequate analysis of other properties, however, seems to require context. For instance, in isolated clauses from AElfric's homilies *hit* 'it' with impersonal verbs of occurrence looks like a dummy argument. In context, however, the presence of *hit* in a clause may indicate that the action described proceeds logically or causally from what has gone before (4).

(4) þa   saede he him þis bigspel;
    then said he them this parable

    Sum   saedere ferde to sawenne his saed.
    some seeder went to sow   his seed

    and *hit gelamp* ða ða he seow
    and it happened then when he sowed

    þaet sum   dael þaes saedes befeoll on ðam wege
    that some part of the seed fell   on the way

    '... then he told them this parable. A certain
    sower went to sow his seed and it happened as he
    sowed that part of the seed fell in the path...'
    [Aelf. Hom.(Godden) VI:4-6]

In contrast, *gelimpan* introducing a new, unrelated situation does not seem to take *hit* in Aelfric's usage (5).

(5) AEfter ðisum   *gelamp*   þaet micel manncwealm
     after   this-DAT happened that great man-death

     becom ofer ðaere romaniscan leode
     came over the   roman   people

     'After this it happened that a great plague
     came upon the Roman people...'   [AElf.Hom.
     (Godden) IX:89-90]

Because of the dative case, 'this' must be construed with
'after', not 'happened'. What 'this' refers back to is the
ordination of Gregory as Pope. Far from blaming the plague
on this election, AElfric reports the plague's end as one
of the miracles qualifying Gregory for sainthood. Wulfstan's usage is perhaps less straightforward: the English
portion of his homily II (Bethurum) begins, *Leofan men, hit
geweard hwilum*... 'Dear men, it happened once...' But the
generalization may not be lost, for what follows is a
recasting of the gospel for the day, which in the usual
order of service would just have been read in Latin.

Now what properties are of interest? Here is a list,
not even remotely exhaustive, of some of the relevant areas
and some ways in which they might be approached:
topicality (e.g., how many times an argument is mentioned
before or after an impersonal clause); probable empathy
focus (e.g., protagonist, narrator); agency and responsibility, both potential and actual (e.g., human or adult or
upper class vs. non-human, or child or lower class, and
also free vs. captive); and affectedness (no affect vs.
positive or negative effect). The extent to which different verbs select animate vs. nominal vs. clausal arguments, and the orders and casemarking combinations
attested, should also be explored, as should the effect of
metaphorical interpretation on the syntax of physical
impersonal verbs such as *hyngrian*.

At present I have little more to offer than this
outline of a research program. Let me conclude, however,
with some data from Wulfstan's homilies that indicate the
promise of the program.

One of Wulfstan's longest homilies (217 lines, or over
370 clauses by my count) is a highly moralized history of
the world beginning with Creation and ending with the
imminence of the Last Judgment. Not surprisingly, Satan
figures in it quite heavily. Here is how he is introduced
(6).

(6) Ða   weard þaer   an   þaera   engla
    there was   there   one of-the   angels

    swa scinende... þaet se waes Lucifer genemned.
    so shining   that he was Lucifer named

    Ða   þuhte him þaet he mihte beon
    then seemed him that he might be

    þaes   efengelica ðe   hine gescop 7 geworhte;
    of-him   co-equal   that him shaped & made

    and sona swa he þurh   ofermodignysse
    and soon as he through   pride

    þaet geðohte, þa   hreas he of   heofonum...
    that thought then fell   he from heaven

    'There was there one of the angels so shining...
    that he was called Lucifer. Then it occurred to
    him that he could aspire to be the equal of the
    One who shaped and made him; and as soon as he
    through pride thought that, then he fell from
    heaven...' [Wulf.(Bethurum)VI.27-31]

The implication of *þyncan* is that Lucifer has not yet gone
wrong: in Wulfstan's theology, being aware of temptation is
not a sin. Once Lucifer actually actively entertains the
idea of making himself God's equal, however, he seemingly
loses not only heaven but also most of Wulfstan's sympathy
as reflected by impersonal syntax. In just one of the
remaining 175 lines is Lucifer a non-nominative experiencer; when the poor devil discovers that God has created
mere humans to inherit the heaven he himself has just
forfeited, Wulfstan writes (7),

    (7) þa   waes him þaet on myclan andan
        then was him that on great envy
        'then that was a great vexation to him' [VI.42-3]

Otherwise, Lucifer is very active - too active, in fact,
and not at all to be pitied.
    Finally, Wulfstan seems to be pretty consistent in his
usage of three constructions relating to the notion *þearf*
'necessity' or 'benefit'. Briefly, Wulfstan uses *us is
þearf* 'us-ACC is need-NOM' when something is beneficial or
necessary to our salvation to which we, being properly
catechized, will naturally assent (8).

(8) Leofan men, utan ... don swa *us þearf is*
    dear men let-us   do as us need is

    lufian God over ealle oðre þing ...
    love   God above all   other things

    'Dear men, let us do as is beneficial to us,
    love God above all other things ...'
    [Wulf.(Bethurum)II.69-70]

The experiencer is *always* first person plural.
   The predicate *agan þearfe* 'have need-ACC' is used of people (nominative) who really should understand that something is in their interest. The speaker in (9) is Jesus, whose slow-witted disciples have just asked him another irrelevant question.

(9) Ða   andwyrde he heom ond cwaeð
    then answered he them and said

    þaet *hy   ðearfe ahtan* þaet hi
    that they need   had   that they

    waere wurdan ...
    wary were

    'Then he answered them and said that they had need to take care...' (lest anyone mislead them)
    [II.37-38]

The nominative argument may be a pronoun or a full noun (*folc* 'people' *ah eac myccle þearfe*, VI.16), but it seems not to be 'we'. There is a sense here of people who perhaps should know better having to be reminded of their responsibility, in light of which it is interesting that *agan* is related to both 'own' and 'ought'.
   Lastly, there is *beþurfan*. Dodd (1908:243) translates this verb as 'need, have reason to'; 'be entitled to' is also plausible. Like *agan þearfe*, it takes a nominative experiencer (10).

(10) ... hy   nabbað þa lare ...
         they not-had the lore

     þe   *hy   beðorfton*
     that they   needed

     '... they didn't get the teaching ... that they needed' [VI.13-14]

The context here is a discussion of the horrible fate awaiting a priest whose flock is lost to perdition because he has neglected their education. His is the responsibility; whether his people would have made good use of the teaching is irrelevant. The correlation between *beþurfan* and absence of responsibility is not always so clear (cf. VI.110-12), but taken together these three constructions suggest a role for both responsibility and empathy or perhaps even solidarity in the grammar of impersonalia.

NOTES

1. There is at least an eighty-year tradition of complaints about the terms 'impersonal', 'impersonal verb', and 'impersonal construction'. The objection to the first is that it is too psychological (Fischer & van der Leek 1983:343-4); I will not discuss this further. The objection to the other two has to do with the difference between (a) verbs that can sometimes take nominative experiencers as well as non-nominative and (b) constructions in which no nominative-marked argument is present. I will follow Fischer & van der Leek in referring to the former as 'impersonal verbs' and the latter as 'impersonal constructions'; to refer to impersonal verbs and constructions taken together, I will adopt Wahlén's (1925) term 'impersonalia'.

REFERENCES

Anderson, Stephen R. 1976. 'On the Notion of Subject in Ergative Languages.' In Li (ed.) 1976, 1-23.

Bethurum, Dorothy, ed. 1957. *The Homilies of Wulfstan*. Oxford: Clarendon.

Butler, Milton Chadwick. 1977. 'Reanalysis of Object as Subject in Middle English Impersonal Constructions.' *Glossa* 11.155-70.

Chafe, Wallace L. 1976. 'Givenness, Contrastiveness, Definiteness, Subjects, Topics and Point of View.' In Li (ed.) 1976, 25-55.

Covington, Michael A. 1984. *Syntactic Theory in the Middle Ages. Modistic Models of Sentence Structure.* (= *Cambridge Studies in Linguistics,* 39.) Cambridge: Cambridge University Press.

DeLancey, Scott. 1980. 'Parameters of Empathy.' *JLingRes* 1: 3.41-49.

Dodd, L.H. 1980. *A Glossary of Wulfstan's Homilies.* (= *Yale Studies in English*, 35.) New York: H. Holt. Rept. 1974 as Part III of *Word-indices of Old English Non-poetic Texts* (Hamden, CT: Archon).

Dresher, Elan & Norbert Hornstein. 1979. 'Trace Theory and NP Movement Rules.' *LIn* 10.65-82.

Elmer, Willy. 1981. *Diachronic Grammar: The History of Old and Middle English Subjectless Constructions.* (= Linguistische Arbeiten, 97.) Tübingen: Niemeyer.
Ehrich, Veronika & Charlotte Koster. 1983. 'Discourse Organization and Sentence Form: The Structure of Room Descriptions in Dutch.' *Discourse Processes* 6.169-95.
Fay, Edwin W. 1917. 'Syntax and Etymology. The Impersonals of Emotion.' *CQ* 11.88-93.
Fillmore, Charles J. 1968. 'The Case for Case.' *Universals in Linguistic Theory*, ed. by Emmon Bach & Robert A. Harms, 1-88. New York: Holt, Rinehart & Winston.
Fillmore, Charles J. 1977. 'The case for case reopened.' *Grammatical Relations* (= SynS, 8), ed. by Peter Cole & J.L. Morgan, 59-81. New York: Academic Press.
Firbas, Jan. 1966. 'On Defining the Theme in Functional Sentence Analysis.' *Travaux Linguistiques de Prague* 1.267-80.
Fischer, Olga C.M. & Frederike C. van der Leek. 1983. 'The Demise of the Old English Impersonal Construction.' *JL* 19.337-68.
Foster, Joseph F. 1979. 'Agents, Accessories and Owners: the Cultural Base and the Rise of Ergative Structures, with Particular Reference to Ozark English.' Plank (ed.) 1979, 489-510.
Gaaf, W. van der. 1904. *The Transition from the Impersonal to the Personal Construction in Middle English.* (= Anglistische Forschungen, 14.) Heidelberg: Winter.
García, Erica C. 1979. 'Discourse without Syntax.' *Discourse and Syntax*, ed. by Talmy Givón (= SynS, 12), 23-49. New York: Academic Press.
Godden, Malcolm (ed.) 1979. *Ælfric's Catholic Homilies. The Second Series. Text.* (= EETS, ss. 5.) London: Oxford U. Press.
Harris, Alice C. 1980. 'On the Loss of a Rule of Syntax.' *Papers from the 4th International Conference on Historical Linguistics* (= Current Issues in Linguistics, 14), ed. by Elizabeth Closs Traugott et al., 165-71. Amsterdam: Benjamins.
Hopper, Paul J. & Sandra A. Thompson. 1980. 'Transitivity in Grammar and Discourse.' *Lg* 56.251-99.
Jakobson, Roman. 1962. 'Zur Struktur des Phonems.' *Selected Writings, I: Phonological Studies*, 280-310. The Hague: Mouton.
Jespersen, Otto. 1894. *Progress in Language.* London: Allen & Unwin.
Jespersen, Otto. 1931-40. *A Modern English Grammar on Historical Principles.* Heidelberg: Winter.
Keenan, Edward L. 1976. 'Towards a Universal Definition of "Subject".' Li (ed.) 1976, 303-333.
Kossuth, Karen C. 1978. 'Icelandic Word Order: In Support of Drift as a Diachronic Principle Specific to Language Families.' *BLS* 4.446-57.
Kuno, Susumo. 1976. 'Subject, Theme, and the Speaker's Empathy - a Reexamination of Relativization Phenomena.' Li (ed.) 1976, 417-444.
Lagerquist, Linnea M. 1980. *Constraints on Abductive Reanalysis: English 'Impersonals'.* Unpub. UCLA MA thesis.
Li, Charles N., ed. 1976. *Subject and Topic.* New York: Academic Press.

Lightfoot, David W. 1979. *Principles of Diachronic Syntax*.
(= *Cambridge Studies in Linguistics*, 23.) Cambridge: Cambridge University Press.

Lightfoot, David W. 1981. 'The History of Noun Phrase Movement.' *The Logical Problem of Language Acquisition*, ed. by C.L. Baker & John J. McCarthy, 86-119. Cambridge, MA: MIT Press.

McCawley, Noriko A. 1976. 'From OE/ME "Impersonal" to "Personal" Constructions: What is a "Subjectless" S?' *Papers from the Parasession on Diachronic Syntax*, ed. by Sanford B. Steever et al., 192-204. Chicago: CLS.

MacWhinney, Brian. 1977. 'Starting Points.' *Lg* 53.152-68.

Marchand, Hans. 1951. 'The Syntactical Change from Inflectional to Word Order System and some Effects of this Change on the Relation "Verb/Object" in English.' *Anglia* 70.70-89.

Morley, G.D. 1983. 'Agentivity: A Componential Functional Approach.' *Lingua* 60.177-82.

Oosten, Jeanne van. 1977. 'Subjects and Agenthood in English.' *CLS* 13.459-71.

Plank, Frans. 1979. "Ergativity, Syntactic Typology and Universal Grammar: Some Past and Present Viewpoints.' *Ergativity: Towards a Theory of Grammatical Relations*, ed. by Frans Plank, 3-36. New York: Academic Press.

Seefranz-Montag, Ariane von. 1982. *Syntaktische Funktionen und Wortstellungsveränderung. Die Entwicklung 'subjektloser' Konstruktionen in einigen Sprachen*. U. Munich dissertation. Published 1983. Munich: Wilhelm Fink Verlag.

Sidner, Candace L. 1983. 'Focusing and Discourse.' *Discourse Processes* 6.107-130.

Stein, Dieter. 1985. 'Discourse Structure and Variant Forms in Early Modern English.' In this volume.

Thornburg, Linda. 1985. 'Syntactic Reanalysis in Early English.' Paper presented at the 4 ICEHL.

Tripp, R.P. 1978. 'The Psychology of Impersonal Constructions.' *Glossa* 12.177-189.

Visser, F.Th. 1963. *An Historical Syntax of the English Language*. Vol. I. Leiden: E.J. Brill.

Wahlén, Nils. 1925. *The Old English Impersonalia. Part I. Impersonal Expressions Containing Verbs of Material Import in the Active Voice*. Göteborg: Elanders Boktryckeri Actiebolag.

Zubin, David A. 1979. 'Discourse Function of Morphology: The Focus System in German.' *Discourse and Syntax*, ed. by Talmy Givón (= *SynS*, 12), 469-504. New York: Academic Press.

THE SOUTH AFRICAN CHAIN SHIFT:
ORDER OUT OF CHAOS?*

ROGER LASS & SUSAN WRIGHT
University of Cape Town

1. *The Problem.* The further back we go in the history of English, the more positive we seem to be about phonology and phonetics; perhaps partly because the hard data is thin enough to be convincing. But historians - especially of phonology - seem not nearly as interested in more recent times: with not too many exceptions, the 19th century is not seen as a very exciting field. This paper is an attempt at correcting the balance: reconstructing a fragment of the recent phonological history of one extraterritorial variety of English, using contemporary comparative evidence, fairly standard argument-strategies, and some original source materials.

One of the clearest diagnostics of South African English[1] (SAE) in general is the quality of the historical short front vowels: the *bat*, *bet*, *bit* (ME /a e i/) classes. To set it in context, SAE is typologically a post-18th-century Southern English dialect (or dialect-cluster). That is, it comes out on the southern side of all the major isophones: [ʌ]-type vowels in the *cut* (ME /u/) class; a contrast between a short front nucleus in the *cat* class and a long back(er) one in *pass* (ME /a/ isolative and lengthened before /f θ s ns/); a contrast between the *pull* and *pool* classes (ME /u/ after labials and ME /o:/); and a vowel of at least [æ]-height in *cat*. The fact that SAE is generally non-rhotic identifies it only as post-1700 non-Scots, non-Irish, non-western.

Compared with other southern dialect types, the nuclei in the SAE *bat*, *bet* classes are considerably raised, and that of *bit* extremely centralized - even fully central. A comparison of characteristic values for a standard Western Cape variety of SAE and RP gives:

(1)   SAE   RP
    bit   ï ~ ə̈   ɪ
    bet   e ~ ë   ɛ
    bat   ɛ̞   æ

Represented in terms of a rough auditory localization in the 'vowel space', the relations between the two sets are approximately as follows (SAE in caps, RP in lower-case):

(2)   BET   bit   BIT
      bet
      BAT
      bat

That is: SAE, with respect to RP and similar dialects, is 'one up' for the lower two heights, and 'one back' for the highest.

A note on our transcriptions is perhaps in order. If [ɪ] = (roughly)[ë], then [ï] is a further centralized [ë], but not yet fully central. There is in fact an alternation in many SAE varieties (see § 5 below) between [ï] and a fully central half-close nucleus. We will represent the latter as [ə̈] (*not* [ə] 'schwa' - the poor man's central vowel), i.e. the 'unofficial' Cardinal Vowel No. 19 (Abercrombie 1967: 161). The symbol [ï] has already been used for SAE by Wells (1982: § 8.3.2), and it might as well be accepted generally as the conventional symbol for the SAE reflex of ME /i/, with [ə̈] used when fine allophonic detail is in question. Since [ï] is not a standard symbol, an imitation-label may be helpful: the auditory quality we intend is pretty much that of Afrikaans *i* in *sit*, *is* (a point we return to below), or the Trager-Smith [ɨ] in some U.S. *just*, *twenty*, *finish* (Trager & Smith 1951: §§ 1.1, 1.33), or the more centralized varieties of RP /ɪ/ before syllable-final /l/ (*milk*, *children*).

There seem to be two contradictory approaches to explicating the history behind these correspondences:
(i) 'Atomistic'. Each of the 'aberrant' (i.e. non-RP, specifically SAE) qualities has an independent source: either contact with another language, or independent borrowing or selection out of the inventory of types available in, say, the English of the 1820 Settlers.[2] A typical (partial) account of this sort is Lanham & Macdonald (1979: 46): see § 2 below.
(ii) 'Systemic'/'Endogenous'. *All* the typically SAE qualities are systematically related, as the result of a

single process: an indigenous raising-and-centralizing chain shift of the short front vowels. Similarities to other vowel types (e.g. of the *bit* nucleus to that in Afrikaans *sit*) are convergent rather than derivative. A sketch of this view appears in Jeffery (1982).

Our title suggests that we like alternative (ii); and we will in fact argue for a modified version of it. In § 2 below we look at some of the methodological problems in (i); in §§ 3-4 we consider the chain-shift argument, and the historical evidence for it; in § 5 we look at the complex phonology of the [ï]-vowel, and its bearing on the chain shift scenario; and in § 6 we suggest an overall characterization and relative chronology of the main events

2. *The 'Atomistic' Alternative*. Of 'raised e' and 'raised æ ' Lanham & Macdonald (1979: 46) say only 'Origin is unknown'. Of [ï] (which they rather oddly call 'low schwa' - conflating as we will see two different values) they say bluntly: 'It originates in Afrikaans which phonemically opposes /i/:/ə/ in stressed syllables'.[3] The comment on the first two is honestly (if unnecessarily) agnostic; the categorical claim about [ï] is quite another matter. Since L & M cite no specific evidence for the borrowing of [ï] from Afrikaans, their claim must rest on some tacit inference, which the reader is presumably supposed to be able to reconstruct - at least in enough detail so he can agree with it.

This is a reasonable suspicion, since the kind of claim being made is familiar to anyone who reads accounts of language history involving a contact situation. It is in fact so common, so plausible, and so invalid that it deserves a 'rational reconstruction'; since the process of unpacking it reveals some interesting problems. The underlying argument probably goes like this:
(i) [ï] -allophones of the reflex of stressed ME /i/ are characteristically South African;[4]
(ii) Afrikaans has distinctive /ï/ in stressed syllables, from the same etymological source (West Germanic */i/), and in cognates easily recognizeable to English speakers (*sit* 'sit', *is* 'is', *vis* 'fish' /sït, ïs, fïs/;
(iii) Afrikaans and English have been in extensive contact for a long time, and there has been considerable full or partial bilingualism on the part of English speakers;
(iv) Situations of type (iii) are conducive to borrowing;

(v) Borrowing at other levels from Afrikaans into SAE is well-attested; both lexical (*veld*, *koppie*, *bakkie* 'basin, pickup-truck', *ag* 'oh') and phrasal or idiomatic (*I'm busy X-ing* as an alternative progressive from *ek is besig om to X*);
(vi) Therefore SAE [ɪ̈] is from Afrikaans /ɪ̈/ (L & M's /ə/).

If this is the reasoning behind their claim (and it's hard to see what else could be), then the claim is untenable because the reasoning is faulty. It's not that - in the abstract - SAE [ɪ̈] *couldn't* be from Afrikaans: it's simply that in the absence of hard evidence to show that it in fact was, the argument has no force.

We can illustrate this with a parallel (specious) argument that also looks good initially, and also involves putative borrowing. In Afrikaans, canonical surface verb position is second in main clauses, final in subordinate clauses (typically for West Germanic dialects other than English). Thus *Hy was hier* 'he was here' vs. *Hy het gesê, dat hy hier was* 'he said that he was here'. But in casual registers, deletion of the complementizer *dat* allows a verb second subordinate clause: *Hy het gesê, hy was hier*. I.e. in the absence of an overt subordinator, the complex is treated like two paratactically associated main clauses.

Given the argument schematized above, it would be easy to 'show' that the Afrikaans verb-second subordinate clause is a borrowing from English; indeed, this would seem obvious, since Afrikaans is a split-order language, and English is basic verb-second for (non-topicalized) declarative main clauses. But unfortunately the same verb-second option that we get in Akrikaans is available in cognate languages with split word-orders: Dutch, German and Frisian. Therefore the Afrikaans verb-second subordinate clause could equally well be a survival of an archaic continental West Germanic feature, and have nothing to do with English. Or again, it could be a perfectly natural convergent development: if there's no subordination-marker, a paratactic interpretation of a clause-sequence is a fairly obvious kind of 'reanalysis'.

The moral is that any contact-argument, no matter how obvious and 'simple' it looks at first, has to be evaluated against at least two other perfectly respectable source-types:
(a) Genetic convergence: an ancestral feature has survived in two cognate dialects;

(b) Non-problematic simple convergence: independent development of a feature that is likely to develop in any case - with or without contact or common ancestry. (For some methodological discussion of convergence arguments in general and their evaluation, see Lass, 1984a.)

Ancestry arguments are irrelevant in the case of [ɪ̈], since Modern Dutch and other Germanic evidence suggests that this quality is an innovation. And there is a good (if complex and somewhat indirect) type (b) argument available, which on both historical and methodological grounds supports a system-internal (non-contact) origin for [ɪ̈].

But before we look at this, it's worth mentioning one further difficulty with the Afrikaans source: the oddity of this particular type of borrowing. If we look at the rest of the short vowel systems of SAE and Afrikaans, we find that there are in fact no other qualities actually shared by the two. With the exception of Afr /ɛ/ (which is opener than SAE /e/ and closer than even the closest *bat* vowels), the inventories are disjoint. Typical qualities for an SAE system of the type shown in (1) and standard Afrikaans would be:

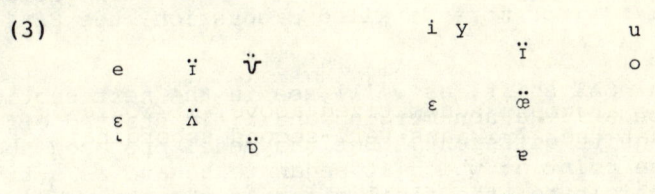

(3)

			SAE				Afrikaans	
e	ɪ̈	ʊ̈		i y		ɪ̈		u
								o
ɛ	ʌ̈			ɛ		œ̈		
ɛ̣	ɒ̈					ɐ		

Afrikaans-only qualities occur in borrowings into English, of course: *bakkie* with [ɐ], [o] in some speakers' versions of names with Afr /o/ like *Welkom* ['vɛ̈ɫkom] (where [ɛ̈] is the normal allophone of /e/ before [ɫ]), etc. But the kind of borrowing presupposed by Lanham & Macdonald's account is not like this: it is borrowing of a single quality, in a lexical set which is by and large (interestingly or suspiciously) cognate to the Afrikaans set. This seems at least implausible.

3. *The Chain Shift Alternative: Preliminaries*. A set of relations like those in (1) and (2) looks like *prima facie* evidence for a chain shift. The inference is a classic type going back at least to Grimm (1819). Taking a set of 'static' correspondences between presumed Proto-IE and early Germanic values for the obstruent system, Grimm extrapolated a *Lautverschiebung* as a process. The extra-

polation took - and still takes - the form (in the absence of genuine processual data) of establishing a geometry of change on the basis of 'diagrammatic' relations between two systems. In our rather simple case, the geometry is virtually inherent in the representation in (2).

This geometric correspondence, plus the anti-borrowing arguments in § 2, can be taken as suggesting a chain shift of some sort. And given the cross-linguistic frequency of vocalic chain shifts, especially in Germanic, we can add some empirical support to an essentially methodological argument: that the chain analysis is both simple and at least weakly explanatory - in the sense that it affords a unitary framework that predicts the kinds of relations we actually get between the attested nuclei. *If* (say) /æ/ raised; and *if* there was a general condition on the system disallowing merger;[5] *then* sufficient raising of /æ/ could trigger raising of /ɛ/, which could in turn trigger some kind of displacement of /ɪ/. And this, given the nature of English short vowel systems, would most likely be either raising or centralization. In English, centralization can be seen as the most likely option: a raising toward [i] would, in a non-merging shift, impinge on the short allophones of /i:/. (For more detailed discussion, see §§ 4-5 below.)

The actual SAE shift, as we'll see in the next section, was only secondarily a non-merging chain; it started off as something quite different. But the model proposed above applies to the point at which it began to behave as a true chain. To anticipate, the final shape of the chain is roughly the 'horizontal inverse' of the shift of long back vowels in Norwegian or non-low back vowels in French, or the 'vertical inverse' of the shift of short front vowels in Border Scots:

(4)

```
ʉ: ← u:           y ← u           i
    ↑                 ↑            ↓
    o:                o            e
    ↑                              ↓
    a:                             a → ɑ

 Norwegian        French      Border Scots
```

(On the Norwegian and other North Germanic shifts, see Lass 1976:78ff; on Border Scots Lass 1976: 120ff.)

It remains for us to come up with some evidence that this - or something like it - was what happened. The historical record suggests two things: (a) that the SAE developments represent at first an intensification of processes that had been going on in the ancestral dialects at least since the 17th century, and were current in the source communities that supplied the bulk of the 1820 Settlers; and (b) that the mechanism involved is more complex and elusive than that animating the usual 'Labovian' covarying chain shift (e.g. the types discussed in Labov et al. 1972). The SAE shift seems not to be a unitary process from the beginning, but to have emerged out of a set of quite disparate changes - including perhaps its own opposite. We will clarify this in the next section.

4. *Convergence and Stabilization: The Testimony of Jeremiah Goldswain*. The eventual chain shift originates in the raising of /æ/ and the lowering of /ɛ/ (as well as some changes affecting /ɪ/) in the speech of the 1820 Settlers in the Eastern Cape. In this section we discuss the evidence for this rather counter-intuitive origin, and its relation to earlier developments.

Our main evidence is provided by the *Chronicle* of Jeremiah Goldswain, one of the original settlers. A sawyer from Great Marlow, Buckinghamshire, Goldswain arrived in the Eastern Cape early in 1820, at the age of 19, having been brought out as an indentured labourer in a party of other working class families from the Home Counties. Goldswain left an enormous diary (528 foolscap pages), which is of great interest, as his spelling is naïve and highly personal.[6] The diary was begun in October 1819, before he embarked at London, and ends in December 1858. It is full of misspellings, some of which are consistent and systematic enough to indicate his pronunciation - especially in connection with independent evidence from the same period.

Casson (1955: 9), in a study of Goldswain's dialect, remarks that he
> sometimes wrote as he spoke; so far as his speech can be reconstructed from his spelling, it must be regarded as a class dialect, a form of Modified Standard, rather than a Regional Dialect as the term is commonly understood.

This seems an accurate characterization. Goldswain's sociolect is very likely to be representative of the majority of the 1820 Settlers. Like him, they were mainly working class, trained as shoemakers, wheelwrights, carpenters and stonemasons, or were unskilled labourers and farm workers. They came mostly from the Home Counties and the London Metropolitan area.

Evidence for the raising of /æ/ is provided by Goldswain's spellings of forms like *contrector* 'contractor', *atrected* 'attracted', *lementation* 'lamentation', *thenked* 'thanked', *thetch* 'thatch'. Such a raising is independently attested: A.J. Ellis (1889: 226f), commenting on notes of writers on pronunciation in the London area around the beginning of the 19th century, confirms raising of /æ/ to a quality he transcribes as [E] in items like *cab*, *hand*, *bank* and *Strand*; this raising is attested as early as the 1780s (cf. Jesperson 1909: § 8.6.2), and is condemned as a vulgarism by Batchelor (1809).[7] It seems clear that some raising of the front open vowel in the *bat* class was widespread in London and South-eastern English around the time of the Settlers' emigration, and that Goldswain's spellings are not idiosyncratic.

What ought to be a front half-open quality in *bet* is often represented by Goldswain with *a* instead of the expected *e*, which suggests a lowering. (We are concerned here with lowering in environments other than before /r/, which are common throughout the history of English, and have frequently stabilized: e.g. in *heart*, *clerk*, *parson*, etc.) Casson suggests that Goldswain is attempting to represent a quality close to [æ], but the subsequent history makes it unlikely that it ever lowered even this far. Some examples are: *amadick* 'emetic', *Madenhad* 'Maidenhead', *inclamence* 'inclemence', *hadge* 'hedge', *to gather* 'together', *sant* 'sent', *plashur* 'pleasure', *shipract* 'shipwrecked'.

Lowering of /ɛ/ (except before /r/ and sometimes /l/) is not well attested in the earlier literature; it seems (unlike raising of /æ/ and lowering of /ɪ/: see below) not to have been widely stigmatized as a vulgarism by the orthoepists. But it is quite consistent in Goldswain: there are more instances of this than there are of raised /æ/, and the environments in which the *a*-spellings appear are much more extensive: *e*-spellings of /æ/ are rare outside of high tongue-body environments (before and after velars and palatals).

Casson (11) interprets the converging spellings for /æ/ and /ɛ/ as the reflex of a phonetic convergence. He suggests that Goldswain pronounced the two vowels very similarly, raising /æ/ towards /ɛ/ and slightly lowering /ɛ/ towards /æ/: thus spelling *hadge* with *a* and *thenkful* with *e*. This is reasonable: if the orthographic system provides two graphs for two distinct qualities, and the writer is uncertain, because of an ongoing or recent change which graph ought to be used for a quality 'intermediate' between the original ones, the result is likely to be inverse spelling in both directions - i.e. near-random choice.

The apparent confusion in apportioning lexical sets to graphically delimited areas of the vowel space is extended in what looks like a raising of /ɛ/ to /ɪ/ - not consistent but quite common. *Get* is frequently spelled *git*, and before /t/ we also find *liter* 'letter', *kittle* 'kettle'. Other *i*-spellings occur before nasals: *agin* 'again', *expinces* 'expenses', *interd* 'entered', *rinched* 'wrenched', *wint* 'went', *aminetes* 'amenities', *trimbled* 'trembled'. Casson (12) comments that this development of historical /ɛ/ is a 'well-known feature of the modern Bucks dialect'.

And in fact it is - sporadically - quite an ancient process, especially before dentals, palatals, and velars. Predental raisings of ME /e/ occur as early as the 13th century, judging by spellings like *briþren* 'brethren', *brist* 'breast', *stynch* 'stench'(Jordan 1934: § 34 and Lass 1976: 179f). And there is more extensive attestation later, during the ENE period (Lass 1976: 182, cf. Wyld 1936: 222f). In the late 17th century it is condemned as a vulgarism; the anonymous author of *The Writing Scholar's Companion* (1695), for instance, lists *git* for 'get', *hild* for 'held' in his chapter on 'words vulgarly spoken and grosly mistaken in writing' (=Ekwall 1911: 86f). (The reflexes of the ME and ENE raisings are widely spread throughout modern English, especially in the north. In the modern standard we still have *string*, *wing*, *mingle*, *English cringe* with OE or ON /e/, and *silly*, *sick* with shortenings of OE /æ:/ or /e:/ depending on dialect origin and /eo:/ respectively.)

As we might expect now, Goldswain also shows an apparently opposite movement: lowering of /ɪ/ to /ɛ/, in forms like *presner* 'prisoner', *deferent* 'different', *convenced* 'convinced', *Bretsh* 'British', *sleped* 'slipped'. A tendency to lower /i/ was prevalent from the 15th century onward, especially in the East Midlands; forms seem to have entered London English early, and 'gained an increasing currency, first, probably, among the lower orders of the population' (Wyld 1936: 227). Spellings of *e* for ME /i/ are common in the 17th century, even in the writings of educated people: Wyld (229) cites examples from the *Wentworth Papers* and the writings of Lady Mary Wortley Montague.

Another feature which may be relevant - since we are concerned among other things with the status and instability of [ï] in SAE - is Goldswain's occasional use of *u*-spellings for what ought to be his /ɪ/: *buld* 'build', *bult* 'built', *busket* 'biscuit', *contunerd* 'continued', *contrubeted* 'contributed'. The first three might just be due to a faulty memory of an unmotivated orthographic *u*; but there could be another interpretation, which would suggest two phenomena of interest. *Buld*, *bult* might well be attempts to spell a retracted allophone of /ɪ/ before [ɫ]: and very retracted vowels here are a criterial feature of much SAE, e.g. [stV̈ɫ] 'still', [mV̈ɫk] 'milk'; and the others might be early examples of shifted [ɪ].

Wyld (1936: 229f) comments on *u*-spellings for 'bishop' as early as the 15th century, and takes them as reflecting rounding of /i/ to [y], and then retraction of this [y] along with other short /y/ (OE, as in *cudgel*, *crutch* < *cycgel*, *crycc*, and Anglo-Norman as in *judge*, *study*, *justice*). Wyld claims that *bishop* is the only such form; but *The Writing Scholar's Companion* (*loc.cit.*) includes among its 'grosly mistaken' forms not only *bushop* for 'bishop', but *tunder* for 'tinder', *wull* for 'will', *dud* for 'did', *wuth* for 'with', and *whuther* for 'whither'.

These are difficult to interpret. Except for *bishop* (OE *biscop*), all of them show OE /y/ (*tinder* < *tynder*), /y:/ (*did* < *dȳde*), or other vowels after /(h)w/, where even in Old English there are instances of rounding. If the *u*-spellings in *The Writing Scholar's Companion* represent [ʏ] or [ʌ] pronunciations (reasonable values for ME /u/ at the time), they may be south-western 'provincialisms', i.e. reflexes of late ME /u/ from retained OE /y/; or of course they may be attempts to spell some 'schwa-like' quality, the result of sporadic early centralization of /ɪ/. (It's interesting that /w/ is one of the favouring environments for [ï]-quality ME /i/ reflexes in the dialect of one of the authors (RL): he has what Trager & Smith would call /ɨ/ in *willies*, *with*, *will*, *winner*, *whip*, *whisper*, *William*. Cf. Lass 1981: 533f.)

It looks then as if Goldswain's spelling represents an intensification of an ongoing process of shifting vowel qualities within what we will call *convergence zones* in the vowel space of 16th-18th-century southern English. What we can draw from Goldswain is indeed a form of 'modified standard' as Casson calls it. Except for the extensive lowering of /ɪ/, the picture is not dissimilar to what the orthoepists of the 17th and 18th centuries describe, what is shown by informal spellings, and what is reported for the London area by Ellis and others.

More graphically, Goldswain's vowel space may be said to show two major convergence zones, in which the vowel qualities appear to be shifting and unstable:

(5)

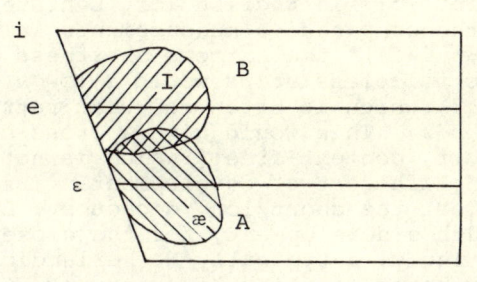

```
    i
       ┌──────────────────────────┐
       │ ╱╱╱╱╱                    │
       │╱ I ╱ B                   │
    e  │╲╱╱╱                      │
       ├──╲╱──────────────────────┤
       │ ╲╱╲                      │
    ε  │╱╱╲╱                      │
       │╱æ╱ A                     │
       └──────────────────────────┘
```

Hypothetically, the areas of convergence in (5) manifest themselves in Goldswain's spelling as follows: *contrector* 'contractor': /æ/ » /ɛ/ (where '»' = 'converges on'); *amadick* 'emetic': /ɛ/ » /æ/; both in Zone A. Zone B represents manifestations of 'expenses' as *expinces*: /ɛ/ » /ɪ/; 'prisoner' as *presner*: /ɪ/ » /ɛ/; and even perhaps 'build' as *buld*: /ɪ/ » /ï/ or /ɪ/ » /ə/. (The latter is not strictly a 'convergence', since there is no phonemic norm there to converge on; but a movement out of the convergence zone into a 'free zone': see below.)

The range of convergence or confusion suggested by Goldswain's spelling presents the precondition for a chain shift along the front periphery of the vowel space, and then centrally: we take it that this unstable set of norms, with /ɪ/ moving out into a free zone, is the beginning of the SAE-defining chain shift. Specifically, the raised position of the open front /æ/, and its proximity to /ɛ/, appear to trigger the stabilizing of the vowel-quality in the *bet* class. It is perhaps wise to use the term 'stabilize' rather than 'shift' because of the initial diversity of the realizations of this vowel. Accordingly, the 'safe' zone for the *bet* class is half-close - with a present range of realizations reaching centralized Cardinal 2 quality in speakers of more advanced SAE varieties.

The mechanism of the shift towards a central position for the *bit* vowel is more complicated and controversial. Why didn't the chain simply proceed upwards, toward [i]? We know that the same general pattern that occurs in SAE has also occurred, in more recent times, in New Zealand English (Bauer 1979); centralization is an attested and perhaps preferred strategy in this kind of shift in English. At least we know of no dialects with raising of all three relevant classes.

One motivation for choosing centralization goes as follows: since /i:/ is *ceteris paribus* shorter than any other long vowel except /u:/ in English (cf. Lehiste 1970: 18f in general, and the comparative measurements in Gussenhoven & Broeders 1976: 64ff), the extreme shortness of /i:/ allophones say before voiceless stops would allow a near merger of /i:/ in *beat* (which is often somewhat retracted) with a raised /ɪ/ in *bit*. This would give a cross-class merger (long with short, context-free), which is not a characteristically English sort of development. (Except in Scots, which has lost the short/long dichotomy: Lass 1976: ch. 1). But such a development, for the close vowels at least, is, interestingly, a typically Netherlandic one. Thus in Dutch and Afrikaans, earlier /i:/ and /u:/ from vowel-shift of /e:/ and /u:/ (as well as /y:/ from various sources) have joined the short series in most environments, and are now long only before /r/ and in foot-initial open syllables: e.g. canonical short values for historical /i:/ and /u:/ in Afrikaans *lief* 'dear', *goed* 'good'; original length retained in German *liebe*, *gut*. (Though there has in SAE been a short-lived movement toward [i] of some allophones of /ï/: see § 5 below.)

All these remarks apply, of course, only to English dialects that in fact retain three short front heights. Many East Midland and southeastern dialects show early merger of /æ/ and /ɑ/ with /e/, and have /ɛ/ in what for other dialects would be the ME /a/ and /e/ classes. *The Survey of English Dialects* shows this pattern in fourteen areas (Surrey 34.2-5, Kent 35.1, 4, 7, Sussex 40.1, Norfolk 21.9, 10, 13, Essex 29.7, 12, 15, and Middlesex 30.2). None of these dialects appears to have anything other than [ɪ] for ME /i/. (For data, see Orton & Tilling 1969, Orton & Wakelyn 1967, s.v. IV.5.3 *rat*, IV.7.8 *pheasants*.)

5. *The status of* [ï]. We now turn to the status of the centralized *bit* vowel in present-day SAE, and its bearing on our analysis of the origin of the SAE short front vowel pattern.

Lanham & Macdonald (1979: 46) describe the centralized vowel ('low schwa') as resulting from 'a polarization of the allophones of /i/'. They claim that these allophones are now in strict complementary distribution; specifically that

> the more central allophones of British English /i/ (e.g. without an adjacent velar consonant, as in *build, sit, did*

are, as the most advanced variant, low schwa, widely
separated in phonological space from fronted allophones
(e.g. *kiss*, *ring*, *big*).

They say that the fronted allophone is higher and more
'tense' (whatever that means) in SAE than in 'British
English' (usually = RP). On the basis of this claimed
separation of allophones, they posit a polarization: the
Afrikaans [ï]-quality has in their view been borrowed for
the non-fronted allophones, and the latter have been freed
to move up and forward.

Wells (1982: § 8.3.2) presents a rather different analysis. He says that SAE shows 'the *kit* split':

> Historical /ɪ/, the *kit* vowel, has undergone a phonemic
> split... The difference between the two resulting sound
> types is clearly heard if a word such as *sing* [sɪŋ~siŋ]
> is compared with one such as *limb* [lïm ~ ləm].
> Description of this phenomenon is complicated by the fact
> that both the vowel qualities used and the conditioning
> environments are variable.

His conclusion is that [ï] and [ə] are to be taken as allophones of one phoneme /ə/, and [i] and [ɪ] of another, /ɪ/.
But within each group the complementation is clear enough
to assign allophonic status in the usual way.

One problem with these two conflicting analyses is that
neither is supported (at least in published sources) by
large amounts of data - especially data from clearly localized speakers. Both Lanham & Macdonald and Wells talk of
'types' of accents, of 'broad' and 'conservative' (Wells)
or 'Conservative', 'Respectable' and 'Extreme' accent types
(Lanham & Macdonald); but there seem to be no available
descriptions of a large number of lexical items from particular idiolects or dialect-types, to enable such judgements to be tested in a reasonably clear way.

Another problem - for us anyhow - is that neither of
these descriptions seemed to us, at the beginning of this
investigation, to match very closely with our own experience of SAE, or with the kinds of transcriptions our
students were coming up with in detailed transcription-
tasks. Our initial view was that both the phonetic descriptions and phonological analyses were at least under-
discriminating. We therefore decided to look in detail at
the distribution of ME /i/ reflexes in a large number of
lexical items for individual speakers. Such an examination
could produce useful evidence on the points of contention:
e.g. the status of the [ï] and [ə] vowels, their relation

to the [i] quality which is so important a part of both Wells' and Lanham's analysis, and possible support for our claim that the centralized nuclei form part of the tail of a chain shift. We were also interested in seeing exactly how deeply entrenched the centralized qualities are in SAE, and whether there is any evidence for a continuation of the general centralizing trend.

We chose two speakers of SAE, of quite different varieties, and elicited citation-form pronunciations of 204 lexical items containing ME /i/ or a non-ME vowel that has fallen in with it in post-ME times - all items that in RP or any extraterritorial dialect except New Zealand English would have /ɪ/. The large number of items was designed to give us a wide spread of lexical types (hypocoristics like *Tim*, *Tish*, 'ordinary' core lexis, relatively inelegant items like *piss*, *shit*), and a full spread of phonetic environments - enough so that if there were any examples of possible lexical diffusion of a change we would stand a good chance of uncovering them.

The items were presented to our informants on flash-cards, with some delay or distraction after each item. This is particularly important: the informants never saw the whole list, nor did they ever see any two items at the same time. We were interested in avoiding any possible contiguity effects - especially since in an (*ex hypothesi*) relatively recent change, there is always the possibility of minimal pairs produced by incomplete diffusion. (For the word-list, see Appendix A.)

Our first speaker, B, is middle class female, and was born, educated, married and still lives in Bergvliet, an affluent middle class suburb of Cape Town. She would in Lanham's taxonomy be a speaker of 'Respectable SAE' - i.e. of a local (Western Cape) but fully standard variety.

B has two main variants of the *bit* vowel. The fronter is [ï]; the other is a lower, fully central [ə]. The distribution is largely phonetically predictable (but see below). At first glance, [ï] seems to occur after the velars /k g/, and /h/; [ə̣] in all other environments. It is worth noting that while she has both 'high schwa' [ï] and 'low schwa' [ə̣], she shows no sign whatever of 'polarization': the front allophone [i], so basic to Lanham & Macdonald's scenario, does not occur at all, even in high tongue-body environments. Instead she has the centralized [ï] there, after /h/, and initially. Thus [ï] is in fact the frontest allophone. In environments *preceding* velars

(/k g ŋ/) B has a fully central [ə], sometimes even retracted to [ÿ]. (The very back realizations may be due to the fact that her velars are generally quite retracted; though whether this is an idiosyncratic or a general feature is unclear.) Typical forms here are *big* [bÿg], *pick* [pʰÿk], *sting* [stÿŋ].

Actually it's not entirely true that [ï] is B's frontest allophone. She has, interestingly, a fronter [ɪ] in two highly restricted environments: (a) in proper names like *Lynn*, *Tim*, *Tish* (note that both grave segments like /m/, which in Wells' analysis predict [ə], and palato-alveolars, which ought to predict [i], occur here); (b) in disyllabic words in /-ŋgl/, e.g. *single*, *tingle*, *mingle*. The historically older [ɪ] remains only in one restricted lexical class, and one very specific phonetic environment.

Very retracted nuclei also occur before dark [ɫ], as back as [ÿ]: [sɏɫ] *sill*, [mɏ̈k] *milk*, also *dill*. If a velar or /h/ precedes and [ɫ] follows, the vowel has a slight onglide from [ï] through to [ÿ], as in *skill* [skᶦɏɫ] also *hill*, *kill*. Fully central and even backer realizations also occur after /w/, e.g. in *whist*, *which*, *whizz*, *wing*, *wince*, *with* (there is no /w/:/ʍ/ contrast); this quality covers the range [ə ~ ÿ]. We also find it after /f v/, and - somewhat inconsistently - after /ɹ l/. (The fact that the *following* environment makes no difference, and that even high and fronted tongue-body segments like /t/ take the backer vowel here suggests that gravity, rather than any articulatory feature, is involved; this is borne out by the implication of /f v/.)

One other instance of a backer quality where we might otherwise expect a fronter one leads to a minimal pair: *him* [həm] vs. *hymn* [hïm]. (On the significance of this pair see § 6.)

In general, the observations on where backer qualities occur tally with the idea that centralization has been intensifying over time, and that [ə] is a further development of [ï]. Obviously the precise qualities depend largely on phonetic environment; but the overall picture B presents (which we consider representative of at least one well-defined regional and class variety of SAE) is of the general entrenchment of a 'basic' quality for this class no fronter than [ï]. Rather than 'polarization', we find minutely varying phonetic quality, conditioned in principle by phonetic environment - unless interfered with by lexical idiosyncrasy (probably the result of historical diffusion: see § 6).

Let's assume that B's allophonic picture is representative of the general distribution of qualities for this class in SAE. We now turn to the status of the high front [ɪ], and consider its relation to the chain shift. Our second speaker, J, displays this quality. He is a twenty-five year old native English-speaking male, born in the white working class southern suburbs of Johannesburg; in the Lanham taxonomy his dialect would be 'Extreme SAE'.

J's most frequent value is [ï]. But he has, adjacent to the velars /k g ŋ/, following /h/, and word-initially, a closer and fronter [ɪ̈] - much fronter and closer than the 'fronted' variant of B. Thus *thing* [θɪ̈ŋ], *Kitsch* [kʰɪ̈tʃ], *gift*, *kiss*, *king* in velar environments, *hit* [hɪ̈t], *hymn*, *him* [hɪ̈m], *his*, *hitch* after /h/, *ink* [ɪ̈ŋk], *id*, *imp* word-initially. In all other environments he has either [ï], or a lowered and retracted vowel akin to B's [ə]. Interestingly, he doesn't show consistency after /w/ as B does: the influence of a velar, for instance, appears to override that of /w/ in *wick*, *wig*, *wing*, all of which have [ɪ̈]. The same thing shows up when the vowel occurs between a velar or /h/ and [ɫ]: here, rather than [ÿ], we get the original [ɪ̈] quality, with a slight offglide, from high front to a prevelar approximation: *skill* [skɪ̈ʸɫ], *hill* [hɪ̈ʸɫ], *kill*.

There are however some environments where [i] ought to be predictable, where a more central vowel occurs, approaching [ə]. This occurs in *big* [bəg], *flick*, *rick*. It's not entirely clear what this means, though it is probably connected with what seems to be an essential marginality or recessiveness of [i]: see below. But it does seem to indicate that J might have a tendency to produce something central or centralized except in the most tightly constraining environments.

J's distributions of [ɪ̈] and [ï ~ ə] suggest that centralized-to-central qualities cluster as a categorical norm, whereas [ɪ̈] is a special, wholly context-sensitive development. We can argue from this that whereas [ï] is part of the chain, [i] isn't. And there is some other evidence - if not very clearly focussed - that suggests this.

The use of [i] in ME /i/ words is characteristic of both 'Extreme SAE' and Afrikaans English (the English of first-language Afrikaans speakers). This should not however be taken as evidence that [i] is an Afrikaans borrowing. To begin with, [i] occurs in certain environments in these two types of English where it doesn't occur in Afrikaans (or most other varieties of English, for that matter): e.g. before /ŋ/ and /g/. More tellingly, while Afrikaans speakers have [ï] for historical short /i/ in Afrikaans, they have [i] in (cognate) English words when they speak English: Afrikaans [fïs] but English [fiʃ] *fish*, etc.

So [i] appears to be a native English allophone, originally the product of assimilation to high tongue-body position, and later partly diffused to nonhigh environments (e.g. before non-palatalized coronals and labials). Judging from the sharing of this development between Extreme SAE and Afrikaans English, it seems reasonable to date it back to the extensive English-Afrikaans contact that began on the Rand with the discovery of gold and diamonds in the 1870s. The primary contact here was between Afrikaans and English speaking working class - the two sociolects where the feature now occurs. (It seems generally clear that many of the more stigmatized features of Extreme SAE are perceived as 'Afrikaans' - whether they actually are or not: e.g. non-aspiration of /p t k/, a lowered and centralized onset in the *mate* class (e.g. [më̝ɪt]), and retention of prepausal and preconsonantal /r/.)

The systematically marginal status of [i] in J's speech is further suggested by the fact that it often fails to occur in places that ought to predict it. Aside from the examples with [ə̝] mentioned above, which may be the leading edge of a further centralization, J shows 'basic' [ï] in newer or more colloquial items: e.g. *Bic* 'pen, razor' [bïk], *flick* 'movie' as distinct from other senses. And words of obvious Afrikaans origin get the [ï] they would have at source: *dit* [dït] 'it', or the placename element *-sig/zicht* 'view' as in *Bothasig* [bvətəsïχ], *Oranjezicht* [əɹɛnjəzïχ].

It seems likely then, that by the time extensive urban migration began in the 1870s, the centralized [ï] - or at least the tendency toward centralization - was already well established. It was during this period that many of the descendants of the 1820 Settlers began to move to the Rand in search of work, and it is this group that formed the basis of the new white English-speaking working class in the Transvaal. Extreme SAE has, as a diagnostic feature, Lanham & Macdonald's 'low schwa' (our [ə̝]), pretty much regardless of where in South Africa it comes from; so it's reasonable to assume that Cape English, which has this vowel in at least some environments even in its 'respectable' varieties, provides the basis for the extreme type.

The results of our analysis suggest the following conclusions:

(i) The status of [ï] in SAE overall (assuming projectability from our speakers, i.e. that our 'judgement sample' is a good one) is that of a categorical norm for ME /i/ and post-ME categories that fall in with it. The quite general occurrence of the lower central [ə̞]-quality suggests that this nucleus hasn't yet stabilized completely but is continuing to centralize and lower, at least in certain contexts (e.g. quite consistently before dark [ɫ] and after labials, less so after /ɹ l/. It is of course possible (even likely) that the contextually determined lower and backer values will eventually diffuse to 'inappropriate' environments as some of our data suggests is already happening.

(ii) The [i]-allophone: this seems to be isolated from (and indeed to have nothing to do with) the shift proper. It is restricted to Extreme SAE and Afrikaans English, and in these varieties mainly to highly specific contexts. The fact that it fails to occur in newer forms suggests that whereas [ï] and [ə̞] are part of a continuing shift, [i] is a sort of relic which persists partly because of its assimilatory source, but has stopped diffusing.

(iii) SAE does not provide clear evidence for the 'polarization' of ME /i/ argued for by Wells and Lanham & Macdonald. Instead, speakers of the 'Respectable' type have minute variation: the 'fronted' allophone being [ï] or at most [ɪ], and the general or categorical value [ï] ~ [ə̞], governed mainly by phonetic environment, and to a small extent lexically. Speakers of Extreme SAE do not exhibit polarization either, but have a categorical centralized-to-central norm, and another value, the high front [i], in inconsistent and possibly receding contexts.

6. *Retrospect: The State of the Shift*. The material in §§ 4-5 suggests the following about the SAE chain shift:

(i) While the ultimate *effect* is that of a typical raising chain, the mechanism (assuming Goldswain's testimony to be as useful as we think it is) is atypical. Instead of covariation prompted by a directional 'impulse' (i.e. either a push- or drag-chain), we have what could be called a *secondary* or *stabilizing chain*. That is, the chain effect is partly an artefact, due to a set of nuclei 'spacing themselves out' as if by a kind of mutual repulsion, rather than either the high or low ends of the continuum acting as a starting point. The controllers are still (a) a no-merger condition and (b) the shape of the vowel space; but the impulse is holistic, not local or directional.

(ii) The data in § 5 concerned only the reflex of ME /i/, because of its complex phonology. In the speech of our two informants, as well as others we've observed, the behaviour of the ME /e a/ reflex sets is quite different. While there is extensive allophonic variation (e.g. marked lengthening of the *bat* vowel before voiced stops and nasals, centralization and lowering of both *bat* and *bet* classes before syllable-final /l/), there is no instability or variation in the norms themselves: the values for ME /a e/ are categorically fixed. In particular, there are no minimal pairs like B's *him*: *hymn*, and no examples of (context-free) 'original' values. A speaker with [e] in *bet* has it in the whole set, and the same for [ɛ̞] in *bat*.

(iii) On the general grounds that phonetic changes proceed from unstable/variable to stable/categorical (see Lass 1981: 534ff), the shifts involving the *bit* vowel are the most recent. In B's case, in particular, they show a pattern diagnostic of the last stages of a change. That is, the presence of marginal minimal pairs assignable to failure of an allophonic rule: the result, in all probability, of lexical diffusion that has as it were, not diffused. If we visualize the typical trajectory of a sound change in time as a sinusoid (cf. Chen 1972), then pairs like B's *him*: *hymn* represent the tail-off of the exponential or 'log' phase of the curve (see Lass 1984b: § 13.4 for discussion). Such residues are the garbage left behind - at least in the early stages - by the asymptotic nature of change-curves. Curves that complete - i.e. 'Neogrammarian' changes - normally require much more time than has been available for our shift. 'Exceptionlessness' develops by patch-up operations on the irregular detritus left by the tail-off of the curve. (Assuming a mid-to-late 19th century date for the large-scale centralization of ME /i/, the elapsed time is, on the appropriate 'geological' scale, rather small: cf. the datings of similar messy changes in Lass 1981: 535-7.)

(iv) The overall shape of the shift now seems clear: raising of ME /e a/ stabilizes first, and /i/, having a largely 'free' zone to move in, continues to develop, with no danger of merger. The available space is free of any possibilities of 'collision': the nearest short nucleus is the reflex of ME /u/ (*but*, *come*), which is characteristically in the range [ɐ̈~ɜ], and never appears to raise above half-open.

(v) The high front reflexes in J's dialect can be seen as representing a supervening and largely irrelevant development (whatever its source or motivation). While the /ɪ/ >[ɪ̈]/[ə] change was contextually determined in its earlier stages, its results are now essentially categorical, with traces of lexical and phonetic conditioning for both B and J. But the shift to [i] is in the main phonetically conditioned still - with a few lexical interferences. And it shows no strong evidence of productivity: it is, as we suggested, more or less a relic.

The whole shift and development of [i] can be visualized this way:

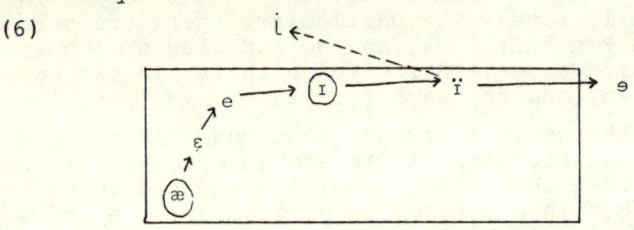

(6)

The boxed area represents the range of categorical inputs and outputs; values outside are either continuations of the original shift (⟶) or a supervening development (--→). Circled values have - in both Respectable and Extreme varieties - vanished.

One problematical area that still needs detailed investigation is the distribution of /ï/-allophones in the more 'conservative' dialect-types, i.e. those whose overall phonetic norms approximate more closely to RP or some general southern English type. Impressionistically, speakers of this kind of SAE show less raised reflexes of ME /e a/ (often no higher than in a conservative RP), and an allophonic range for /ï/ encompassing both unshifted [ɪ] (especially after /h/) and centralized [ï] in many (most?) other environments. This is a matter for further research: this paper is a preliminary report, based on what seem to us two highly characteristic 'indigenous' (i.e. not British focussed) dialect-types.[8]

NOTES

* This is an expanded version of the conference paper. We are grateful to the Human Sciences Research Council and the University of Cape Town's Bremner Travel Fund for grants that enabled one of the authors to attend. We are also grateful to L.W. Lanham and Menán du Plessis for comments on an earlier draft; to each other, for temperament-free collaboration; and especially to our informants without whose patient cooperation in an exceedingly tedious task we wouldn't have had any data to work with. All mistakes and misinterpretations are our own work.

1. The term SAE here covers all perceptibly 'local' varieties, i.e. those that couldn't be mistaken for anything southern English. The diagnostics hold for all dialects, in type if not necessarily in degree. See the discussion of phonetic detail in § 4 for a more differentiated picture.
2. The English first took over the Cape in 1806, but South Africa was not 'colonized' at that point: most English speakers in the early days were (potentially transient) military and government personnel, not settlers. But in 1819 the British government decided to establish a genuine colony; partly because of the depressed economic situation at home, and more importantly, because they wanted an established settlement as a buffer between the British army and the Xhosa along the Great Fish River in the Eastern Cape, as well as a potential source of bodies for 'commandos' or informal militias. The government offered land-grants and assisted passage under a kind of modified indentured-labourer scheme, and in 1820 about 5 000 settlers, mainly working class people from the south of England, left for the Cape. These speakers formed the nucleus for the emerging SAE: the next group of English speakers (mainly upper and middle class) came to Natal in the 1840s and 50s, and there was no other major influx until the discovery of gold and diamonds on the Rand in the 1870s.
3. They also have a system-internal explication of its spread in terms of 'polarization of the allophones of /i/', which is probably untenable: see § 5 below.
4. Actually they're not - at least not exclusively. See Bauer (1979) on New Zealand English, and the comment in § 4 below.
5. On 'no collapse' shifts see the discussion in Lass (1976: ch. 2) with reference to the English, Norwegian, Swedish and German long vowel shifts.
6. The only detailed study of Goldswain that we know of is Casson (1955); for biographical details and a description of the MS see Long (1946/9: vol 1). For a text-sample see Appendix B.
7. See Wyld (1936: 199). Wyld gives 'Bachelor 1809', and the name doesn't appear in his index or source-list; we presume that this should be Batchelor (1809). Wyld cites him as saying: 'Refinement should be kept within very moderate bounds with respect to this letter, as the real exchange of *a* for *e* is the result of ignorance or affectation, by means of which certain words will cease to be distinguished in pronunciation'. Among Batchelor's examples are *had > head*, *lad > led*, *man > men*. Wyld suggests (200) that the source of the raising is 'a desire for bogus elegance', and says that 'we may still hear *head* instead of *had* from a few would-be vulgarians, as well as from certain sections of Cockney speakers'. (There is something to this: hyper-refined ('refayned') speech of the 'Morningside' and 'Kelvinside' types in Scotland shows this same association of closer (and often fronter) qualities with 'poshness' or gentility.)

8. A two-speaker sample - for the statistically minded - may seem not a sample but a pair of arbitrary idiolects. If however the investigators using it can be assumed to be competent observers, with a knowledge of the speech-community, this is really not a problem. In this case both of the investigators are trained phoneticians, and one, (SW) is a native-speaker of what is in effect a dialect of SAE (Zimbabwean English), and has lived and taught in South Africa. A trained phonetician's judgement of what is 'typical' is, in the context of an essentially qualitative investigation, simply a way of avoiding tedious pseudo-procedures (Abercrombie 1963) involving unnecessary sampling. Since our judgements, and those of other qualified people, converge on these speakers as typical, we think they can be taken as - corrigibly - evidential. We also do not apologize for using words in isolation as primary evidence: in terms of 'psychological reality', 'canonicalness' or whatever, these are surely the primary input to *any* phonological study, synchronic or diachronic (cf. Lass 1984b: 294ff). Even if yesterday's allegro speech is today's lento (Dressler 1975), if we're investigating the systematic integration of a change-output, it's the categorical (lento) forms that are our first concern.

APPENDIX A: THE WORD-LIST

till	*wick*	lick	stiff	drift	prim
rib	lid	*bic*	Liz	sizzle	piss
priss	bill	mill	rid	silk	bitch
kiss	kin	pink	fib	vista	Syd
kip	rip	*milk*	gist	*Lynn*	nit
Tish	hid	bid	*hitch*	cig	sin
fist	ditch	*sill*	*gift*	mid	hiss
hint	hip	wrist	zip	*shingle*	nipple
king	fifth	kit	stipple	blink	*kitsch*
pip	plinth	*him*	miss	*ink*	rich
Vince	ship	prig	zing	*wince*	strip
kill	riff	rim	list	*whizz*	bib
thin	chip	brisk	lib	dish	nil
win	gypsy	slit	*wig*	river	shit
cling	sit	*wing*	*hill*	with	rig
wick	dif	dick	sic	ring	skim
slid	*his*	skid	dinky	wit	single
dizzy	*dit*	kick	kissed	in	fig
mist	whip	*skill*	pig	kin	*Oranjezicht*
nib	dim	dig	tick	sing	*pick*
hymn	mini	jig	*rick*	tin	*big*
ming	titch	bridge	slim	trip	*id*
skip	shin	brick	still	it	string
lip	Lil	tit	nifty	shrimp	flint
rill	itch	*fish*	writ	kid	lift
wither	click	skif	sister	cliff	thrift
sip	thing	miffed	disc	hint	*hit*

pitch	sink	sift	*which*	tizz	*tingle*
dip	tip	stick	hip	did	*Bothasig*
Tim	fling	*whist*	*flick*	bring	sniff
brim	*imp*	will	whiff	frisk	skit
tiff	bliss	ill	ching	if	*dill*
whim	bit	din	whither	flit	ridge
stitch	blimp	print	fin	shrill	pimple

(Items in italics are mentioned in text)

APPENDIX B: EXTRACTS FROM GOLDSWAIN'S *Chronicle*

(1820) Soon after this land was seen and not long after we came in site of Simon's Bay and as the ship was standing into the Bay it fell a dad calm and they had to toe in the Veasle up to the ankaige Ground: by this time it was dark. The next morning som of ous went erley on dack to see if we could disern aney of they sheep climen up the hills with thare Large tales as we had been told by old Solders and Salers that had been to the Cape of Good hope that they had seen the sheep climen up they hills with thear tailes maid fast to a little truck with two weals for they stated that the hills that they Sheep had to feed uppond ware so steep that all thear fat run into the Sheeps tale but thay ware noware to be seen but in corce of the day we say one thear tales waight about 5 lbs.

(1846) At last we saw that the day was braking and we begun to move for we was to cold to indulge our selves after daybrake not having too much bead cloce. We had three days rashons to carrey: our coffe Kittle: our kanteen for water or git not one drop for twentey four hours. The old Field Cornet gave orders to saddle up and eager we ware to do so: by this time it surfishently lite anuf for us to find the Drift. We cossed it and maid the best of our way to Trompetters Drift ware thear was a strong post and sum furage for our horses as the had not more then halfhours Grazen for the last 35 hours. Before we reached the post it comenced raining and contunerd more or less until the next day leven oClock.

(1843) About this time Mrs Goldswain was confined with her tenth Child. It was a son but bornd a criple in both harms and legs. . . We cept on untill the nineteenth day wen my poor wife caled me to her and told me her fears that the Child was not so well as she wold wish and what to do we did not know as thear was no Doctor nier than Grahams Town 28 miles. We concluded that if the Child did not git beter by the morn we wold send for the Docter but to our great grief we saw about nine oClock at night we saw that the Child was tuck for death. We sarched his little boadey and found that inflammation had taken place in the bouels: in two hours the Child died. The Mother tuck it so much to hart that I saw that if sum thing was not don to rase her spreats that it wold not be long before she followed the Child.

REFERENCES

Abercrombie, D. 1963. 'Pseudo-procedures in linguistics'. *Zeitschrift für Phonetik, Sprachwissenschaft und Kommunikationsforschung 16*. (Repr. in *Studies in Phonetics and Linguistics*, 114 - 19. Oxford: Oxford University Press, 1963.)
_____ 1967. *Elements of General Phonetics*. Chicago: Aldine.
Batchelor, T. 1809. *An Orthoepical Analysis of the English Language*. London: Didier & Tebbett.
Bauer, L. 1979. 'The second Great Vowel Shift?'. *JIPA* 9. 57 - 66.
Casson, L. 1955. *The Dialect of Jeremiah Goldswain, Albany Settler*. UCT Lecture Series, No 7.
Dressler, W.U. 1975. 'Methodisches zur Allegro-Regeln'. Dressler & Mareš 1975. 219 - 34.
_____ & F.V. Mareš, eds. 1975. *Phonologica 1972. Akten der zweiten Internationalen Phonologie-Tagung, Wien, 5-8 September 1972*. München: Wilhelm Fink Verlag.
Ekwall, E. 1911. *The Writing Scholar's Companion (1695)*. Halle: Niemeyer.
Ellis, A.J. 1889. *Early English Pronunciation*. Part V. London: Trübner & Co.
Goyvaerts, D. 1981. *Phonology in the 1980s*. Ghent: E. Story-Scientia
Grimm, J. 1819. *Deutsche Grammatik*. vol 1. Reprinted 1893. Gütersloh: Bertelmann.
Gussenhoven, C. & A. Broeders, 1976. *The Pronunciation of English. A Course for Dutch Learners*. Groningen: Wolters-Noordhoff-Longman.
Jefferey, C. 1982. Review of Lanham & Macdonald (1979). *Folia Linguistica Historica* 3. 251 - 63.
Jespersen, O. 1909. *A Modern English Grammar on Historical Principles. I, Sounds and Spellings*. Copenhagen: Munksgaard.
Jordan, R. 1934. *Handbuch der mittelenglischen Grammatik. I. Teil: Lautlehre*. Rev. Ch. Mathes. Heidelberg: Winter.
Labov, W., M. Yeager & R. Steiner. 1972. *A Quantitative Study of Sound Change in Progress*. 2 vols. Philadelphia: U.S. Regional Survey.
Lanham, L.W. & C.A. Macdonald. 1979. *The Standard in South African English and its Social History*. Heidelberg: Julius Groos Verlag.
Lass, R. 1976. *English Phonology and Phonological Theory: Synchronic and Diachronic Studies*. Cambridge: Cambridge University Press.
_____ 1981. 'Undigested history and synchronic "structure"'. Goyvaerts, ed. 1981: 526 - 44.
_____ 1984a. 'Survival, convergence, innovation: a problem in diachronic theory'. *Stellenbosch Papers in Linguistics* 12: 17 - 36.
_____ 1984b. *Phonology: an Introduction to Basic Concepts*. Cambridge: Cambridge University Press.
Lehiste, I. 1970. *Suprasegmentals*. Cambridge, MA: MIT Press.
Long, U. 1946-9. ed, *The Chronicle of Jeremiah Goldswain, Albany Settler of 1820*. 2 vols. Cape Town: Van Riebeeck Society Publications.

Orton, H. & M. Wakelyn. 1967. *Survey of English Dialects. B, Basic Material: the Southern Counties*. Leeds: Arnold.
────────── & P.M. Tilling. 1969. *Survey of English Dialects. B: Basic Material: the East Midland Counties and East Anglia*. Leeds: Arnold.
Trager, G.L. & H.L. Smith. 1951. *An Outline of English Structure*. Studies in Linguistics, Occasional Papers, 3.
Wells, J.C. 1982. *Accents of English*. 3 vols. Cambridge: Cambridge University Press.
Wyld, H.C. 1936. *A History of Modern Colloquial English*. Oxford: Blackwell.

OF RHYME AND REASON:
SOME FOOT-GOVERNED QUANTITY CHANGES IN ENGLISH

DONKA MINKOVA
University of California, Los Angeles

'In the first half of the 13th century -- in the North already in the 12th century -- *a, e, o* in open accented syllables of disyllabic words were lengthened to /aː/, /ɛː/, /ɔː/...' (Jordan 1934/74:47). With slight variations, this is the way in which textbooks legalize the process whereby OE *talu, æcer, mete, beofor, þrotu* become ME *tāle, ācre, mēte, bēver,* and *þrōte*. A new study of the relevant data (Minkova 1982) revealed a regularity which should be central to any description of the process: it takes place with overwhelming consistency only in those OE disyllabic words in which the final syllable is subject to loss in ME. The lengthening is sensitive to the presence of a short stressed vowel in an open syllable and transition from a disyllabic to a monosyllabic word structure as a consequence of schwa loss. This conclusion was prompted by a survey of *all* OE eligible forms, as defined above, which have survived beyond ME and which are entries in the OED. The results of the survey are unambiguous: only 16% of the 225 words which preserved their disyllabic structure in MnE do undergo lengthening (Minkova 1982:41).

My proposal for a reformulation of the environment for MEOSL has met some criticism to which I shall respond in the first part of this paper. Since the 1982 paper was a factual report and a call for a narrower definition of the conditions for the change, with very little pretence of offering a theoretical interpretation of the new facts, I will also speculate here about an alternative explanatory strategy. Two studies take my 1982 factual and statistical evidence into account, one criticizing the approach, and ignoring the results (Danchev 1983), the other accepting the results and proposing an explanation of the phenomenon within a non-linear phonological framework (Lass 1984b).

Danchev (1983) argues against the 'purely internal solution [of MEOSL] in terms of phonetic-phonological and/or morphological considerations' (p.59). His alternative is an explanation in terms of interlanguage developments, shifting the emphasis of the investigation 'from the purely linguistic to the communicative aspects of language change' (p.64). While I disagree with Danchev's implicit suggestion that it displaces and invalidates existing internal hypotheses, I, too, think that a broader view enriches our understanding of the process. I shall review Danchev's objections to previous analyses and then show that the interlanguage hypothesis is both compatible with and implicit in them.

The first score on which he finds internal solutions unsatisfactory is the 'prevailingly paradigmatic nature of the evidence' (p.60). In a sense this is true, insofar as there is no study, and no evidence of, the lengthening process in connected speech. Occasional spellings indicative of cliticization and apocope or syncope are all we can glean from the texts, and these tell us very little. Danchev concedes this point, but leaves out two other aspects of the change which further weaken his objection. First, traditionally, the dating and accounts of the lengthening rest on evidence from poetic texts, both rhyme evidence and scansion in general -- the first spelling evidence, the doubling of letters, does not appear until after 1300. Versification is not a source of information which we can characterize as 'words entirely in isolation' (p. 60). Poetic data is the closest we can hope to come to speech phenomena in a diachronic study, with due regard for the intervening conventions of verse composition. A second, more general, argument is that we are looking at a process of lengthening, a phonemic shift from one category of vowels to another. This suggests a phonological, prosodic, or morphological analysis. Of these, the prosodic approach, even in its incipient form in Minkova (1982), draws on syntagmatic and not paradigmatic information; the effect of the lengthening is both syntagmatic (prosodically) and paradigmatic (within the phonemic system of ME).

Danchev finds the approach of earlier scholars in the field (with the exception of Malsch and Fulcher 1975) lacking in theoretical rigor because it violates the familiar linguistic doctrine that 'words with functional and derivational endings behave differently and should therefore be treated accordingly' (p.61). This is a sound but not obligatory principle. Malsch and Fulcher's attempt at applying it was a mere nostrum, because they have to analyze words such as OE *seofon*, *wæter*, *weþer*, etc. as morphologically complex. The postulation of derivational morphemes in these words is very dubious, and even if it were correct, the same analysis should hold for *beaver*, *haven*, *hazel*, *raven*, *weasel*, where lengthening should have been blocked, too. An alternative analysis which refers to prosodic rather than to morphemic constituent structure, accommodates the data and saves the embarrassment of having to draw a fine and possibly arbitrary line between a syllable and an opaque derivational morpheme.(1)

My treatment, which relies heavily on the chronological ordering and compatibility between schwa loss and MEOSL, has been criticized as being in 'disagreement with an explicitly stated and solidly established body of scholarly opinion' (Danchev 1983:61). No one can be sure about the date of schwa loss, and as to dating MEOSL in relation to it, I have given the chronological issue special attention already (1982:43-7). To my mind, one very convincing piece of evidence is the unquestioned geographical parallelism of the two changes: both of them start in the North. Again, I think that a non-linear analysis that gives due weight to the status of the final syllable will clear up any doubts concerning the chronological straightforwardness of the claim simply by avoiding the post-hoc identification prevalent in the current textbook descriptions. That is, an assumed temporal sequence, lengthening prior to schwa loss, is taken as determining a causal relation: under that assumption, the lengthening must be 'caused' by the open syllable environment, a fallacy which is obviously behind one of Danchev's central claims.

Assuming that the 'open syllable' environment is the crucial condition for MEOSL, Danchev goes on to claim that the sound change 'does not seem to require much explaining' ... because 'it is something like a partial (or 'near') universal' (p.63). While open syllable lengthening is frequent, it is by no means universal (and even then an attempt at explanation would not be out of place). One reason why MEOSL has generated so much controversy is that the mere 'open syllable' environment does not make the right predictions; if we restrict ourselves to it, the facts do not square with the rule. On a slightly broader, Germanic, scale, the wrinkles in this 'natural phenomenon' theory become more visible: whereas vowel lengthening in open syllables may not be a strange quirk of English, the same environment can cause other types of quantitative adjustments (cf. MHG *gesniten*, *hamer*, MnHG *geschnitten*, *Hammer*, or it may have no effect whatever: cf. the preservation of short vowels in open syllables in Swiss German: e.g., *lesä*, *grabä*, etc. (Schirmunski 1976:285).

The interlanguage hypothesis put forward by Danchev as

an alternative explanation of why MEOSL occurred is not incompatible with the 'internal' solutions proposed in Lass (1984b) and in this paper; each reinforces the plausibility of the other, in fact. If we proceed from the assumption that inflectional impoverishment is a feature of creoles, then we can logically relate MEOSL to the process of creolization through the loss of {-e} -- a hypothesis borne out by real data and not resting on marginal and elusive language contact evidence.(2)

Features from the typology of interlanguage phonology can all be accommodated within an internal prosodic solution: features such as 'more distinctive syllabification', 'enhanced syllable perception', and 'lengthening of the vowel in the communicatively prominent syllable'. These generalizations (Danchev 1983:72) and the inference that 'An explanation in terms of interlanguage developments ... would imply that an originally disyllabic word structure was *not* a prerequisite for the lengthening' (p. 71) will be given a different interpretation in a foot-based metrical account of the process. As it stands, Danchev's rejection of the disyllabic condition is unacceptable and the evidence quoted as prompting it is flawed. The monosyllabic words of French origin, e.g., *lake, face, peak*, do not constitute counterexamples to the disyllabic requirement.(3) And even if we disagree with Bliss (1952/53:#45) that these were subject to OSL in Anglo-Norman, we still have a good explanation for them within the proposal made below. The lengthening of /i/ and /u/ in certain dialects after the loss of /-ə/ is no puzzle either. It does not require a special hypothesis to account for it. Also, by abandoning the disyllabic condition for the lengthening we would allow it to affect words of originally more than two syllables. This never happens: and if it did, it would intersect the trisyllabic shortening rule: *holy* vs. *holiday, south* vs. *southern*, OE ǣrende 'errand'.(4)

The interlanguage hypothesis may be an illuminating way of looking at language change within the context of bilingualism, but for the purpose of 'explaining' MEOSL it shrinks either to a rewording of Jespersen's familiar view of the Scandinavian influence on the loss of inflections in ME, or to a slightly altered version of Erdmann's (1972:234) description of MEOSL as a process preserving linguistic information.(5)

Another suggestion for the explanation of MEOSL has been put forward by Lass (1984b). His non-linear analysis in terms of internal syllable structure makes a good deal of sense and covers the data. My justification for attemp-

ting an alternative metrical analysis is theoretical: both
syllable-based and foot-based accounts of phonological
processes have much to offer. The domain of the syllable
has been shown to be relevant for a number of low-level
segmental rules of English; the hierarchically larger
foot-domain has attracted attention too, though not in the
specific historical context that it will be projected onto
in this paper. If the foot provides a satisfactory account
of otherwise murky quantitative changes, and if the account is simpler than a syllable-based one, then we can
perhaps accept it as a preferable analysis.

In my 1982 paper I treated OSL as a kind of rhythmic
weight compensation, whereby the stressed syllable ac-
quires an additional mora of length, where every segment
counts as moric, and the medial consonant(s) must be ambi-
syllabic. The interpretation was strictly linear; and
lengthening was seen in terms of the stressed syllable
becoming heavy, a process preserving the perceptual isochrony of the foot.(6) The hierarchical metrical approach
of Lass (1984a,b) improves on the linear treatment in that
suprasegmental 'structure' can reveal weak and strong
points in the hierarchical placement of constituents,
which in turn can trigger or block the operation of segmental rules. The principle of isochrony remains fundamental, however, to the adjustment process.

In (1)A and (1)B are relevant MEOSL data:

(1) A. bale   'bale'   B. baruh   'barrow'
        bod(en)   'bode'   bodig   'body'
        game   'game'   gamen   'gammon'
        mane   'mane'   maner   'manner'
        schame   'shame'   schamel   'shamble'
        rat(en)   'rate'   rædic   'radish'
        tale   'tale'   talent   'talent' etc.

The first columns in (1)AB give the pre-OSL forms; no need
to unscramble words of OE and AN origin -- they behave in
the same way with respect to the change. Here is a graphic
structural syllabification of e.g. *tale* and *talent* (7):

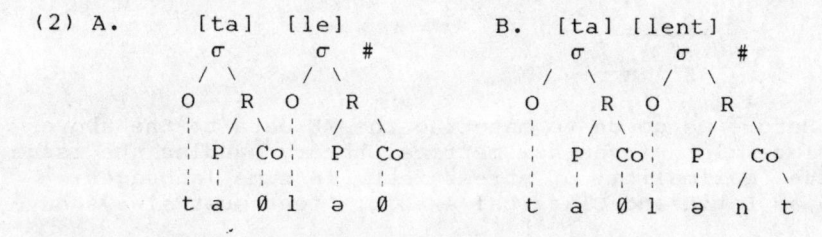

```
(2) A.     [ta]   [le]              B.   [ta]   [lent]
            σ      σ     #                σ      σ      #
           / \    / \                    / \    / \
          O   R  O   R                  O   R  O   R
          ¦  /\  ¦  / \                 ¦  /\  ¦  / \
          ¦ P Co ¦ P  Co                ¦ P Co ¦ P   Co
          ¦ ¦ ¦  ¦ ¦   ¦                ¦ ¦ ¦  ¦ ¦  / \
          t a Ø  l ə   Ø                t a Ø  l ə n   t
```

In a syllabic metrical representation, words of type (1)A will look like (2)A above and words of type (1)B like (2)B. Such graphs are a detailed hierarchical representation of syllabic structure, where each syllable is split into its *onset* and *rhyme* constituents, and the metrically important rhyme (8) is parsed into a *peak* and a *coda*. Structurally, the first syllables of *tale* and *talent* are identical; the second syllables differ in their rhyme structure, with (2)B exhibiting a branching rhyme which is more complex. Such words preserve their disyllabic structure, historically; (2)A is a geometrical restatement of the conditions for schwa loss in ME: a word-final syllable whose rhyme contains no branching nodes is the relevant condition for deletion. Rhyme branching in the second syllable of (2)B is a blocking device for deletion.

If we organize the same material into metrical feet, projecting rhymes only and labelling the constituents according to their relative strength and metrical prominence, the graphs will look like (3)A and B:

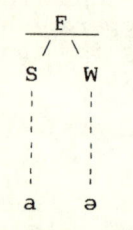

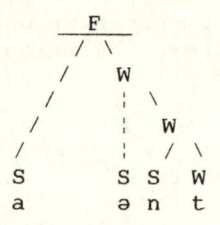

(3) A. [ta] [le]   B. [ta] [lent]

```
        F                         F
       / \                       / \
      S   W                     /   W
      :   :                    /   : \
      :   :                   /    :  W
      :   :                  /     : / \
      :   :                 S      S S  W
      a   ə                 a      ə n  t
```

The S's and W's in the graphs above are joined into feet -- the horizontal lines separate the foot level. The term 'foot' is defined as a 'category dominating structure, such that any occurrence of the category must contain one and only one 'stressed' syllable' (Prince 1980:522). There is no reason not to assume a basic foot template for ME like the one for MnE, namely:

(4)   S (L_1)

```
        F
       / \
      S   W
```

Before we go on to matching the ME data to the above template, let us see how metrical theory handles the issue of the 'maximality' of stress feet. In some languages, such as Latin and Classical Arabic, 'feet must always have the maximum size compatible with the foot template' (Hayes 1981:146-7). In others, maximality plays no role. English represents an 'intermediate' position; i.e., 'its feet are maximal, but more costly entries with non-maximal feet are permitted' (p.147).(9) However, Hayes has found that '[English] words in which the feet are maximal ... greatly outnumber those that are not. For example, in counting the words on the front page of a newspaper, I found that 84% of the metrical feet were in fact maximal ...' (p.146).

Where does this put monosyllabic feet? It has always been the case in English that monosyllabic feet (although only 16% of the total number of feet) are possible and acceptable. What is the justification for regarding them as different, somehow unequal in the stable metrical frame of the English foot, i.e., [S W (W)]?

First, there is the very general and intuitively powerful argument that 'F is intrinsically stronger than a naked syllable' (Prince 1980:523). Then, specifically for English, the difficulty of treating these more 'costly' monosyllabic entries (a non-branching, therefore prosodically light stress foot assigned to a lexical monosyllable) has prompted a formal analysis which systematically assigns a zero right-hand node to such structures (Giegerich 1981, 1985:12-13). Giegerich's monosyllabic lexical foot looks like (5):

(5)   σ   ∅
           ‾‾‾‾‾‾‾
              F
            /   \
           S   W

The usefulness of this stratagem for metrical theory in general is not at issue here -- what is interesting is the motivation behind the proposal, and the surface phonetic facts of English that it handles better.

In theoretical terms, if we construct our theory around the notion of relative prominence and if we define constituents relationally in terms of degrees of prominence, a non-branching monosyllabic foot is in some sense 'incomplete'. This incompleteness surfaces as 'pre-pausal lengthening' (... *he must have*, but *we will*), cliticization (*cuppa tea*, *bread'n butter* -- see discussion in Giegerich 1981, 1985). Giegerich (1985:12) refers to Nakatani and Shaffer (1978) who 'have observed that monosyllabic lexical items are distinguished from the syllables, stressed or unstressed, of polysyllabic words in terms of greater duration' (p. 12); this is O'Connor's (1973:198) statement that 'we say the word *manager* in not much more time than *man* and therefore the syllable /mæn/ is very different in length in the two cases'.

I shall conclude, then, that a monosyllabic foot is, indeed, defective. What are the remedies the language has to choose from to put the foot back on its feet? The most persuasive answer comes from the principle of phonological isochrony in stress-timed languages such as English.

> From the assumption that feet ... are in some way isochronous, it follows that adjacent stressed syllables are separated by pauses: the 'ideal foot' for stress-timed performance contains one or two unstressed syllables, following a stressed one; if a foot contains less material than that, *this material gets stretched* [emphasis DM] in order to reach normal duration (Classe 1939;Jespersen 1962;Ladefoged 1975).
> Giegerich 1985:185

Within a monosyllabic foot, the options for achieving durational parity are limited: reduplication is not productive in English, prosodic weight is insensitive to the composition of the syllable onset (8); the rhyme remains as the only constituent which can be modified in line with the requirements of the principle of isochrony.

This is the situation in Modern English. What was the situation in ME? All words of type (1)A are subject to two changes: ME schwa deletion and MEOSL -- in that order -- a claim with strong theoretical and significant empirical support. (None of the words in group (1)B -- or very few of them -- undergo either change, predictably, so we have nothing further to say about them.) Schwa loss converts a foot of type (3)A into a non-branching structure.

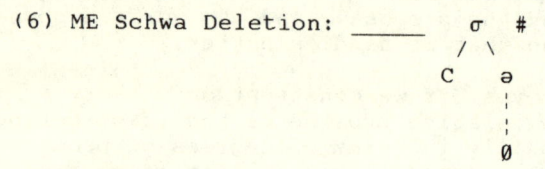

(6) ME Schwa Deletion:
```
              σ   #
             / \
            C   ə
                :
                ∅
```

In rhyme projection terms, the loss erases the structure in the right branch of the foot in (3)A and leaves:

(7)
```
      F
     / \
    S
    V
```

OF RHYME AND REASON   171

The S node in this foot is unattached; the metrical
frame is a bare [S]. Moreover, the post-schwa-loss foot
involves no branching on either the peak or the coda node.
The consonantal onset of the 'lost' syllable is attached
to the strong syllable, but in the vast majority of cases
(10) this is not the end of the story. The consonantal
coda of the new foot is unimportant in that the structure
of the language does not allow gemination, so the coda
cannot make up for the lost prosodic weight. The next
event is lengthening: i.e., MEOSL. The change occurs on
the peak in the following way:

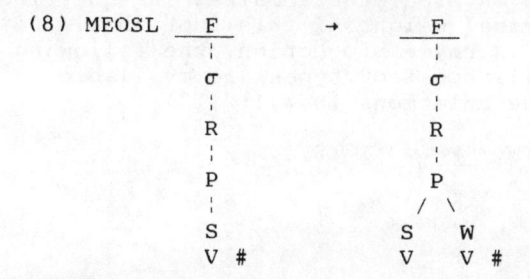

```
(8) MEOSL    F            →        F
             |                     |
             σ                     σ
             |                     |
             R                     R
             |                     |
             P                     P
             |                    / \
             S                   S   W
             V #                 V   V #
```

The metrical representation above shows that once the
balance of the pre-OSL foot has been tampered with by
schwa loss, an adjustment is effected on the peak node.
The 'imperfect' foot structure calls for a change down the
ranks; foot-structure becomes relevant to lower-level
phonological processes. In this case the 'orders' for
change percolate down to the peak level, where 'strengthening' takes the shape of branching. Peak branching gives
the foot some of its original prominence back, or at least
makes it more salient than a foot in which the peak is
non-branching. This is a frequent phenomenon across languages, and has been described extensively in the metrical
phonology literature of the last 7-8 years.(11)

A reasonable inference from the situation just outlined would be that a peak configuration (12) of the pre-
MEOSL type in (8) would be branded as somehow lacking in
metrical salience and should therefore be banned from
lexical representations of English at some stage. This
would be incorrect, since lexical monosyllables of the
-VC# type are not exceptional in the language. What I want
to argue is that within this group, certain predictions
can be made on the basis of the rhyme configuration: it
can be shown that lengthening is more likely to occur on
rhymes whose constituents don't branch: i.e., prosodic
strengthening is favored on the peak or on the coda. Although the actual quantitative processes take place only

within the domain of the rhyme, neither the rhyme alone, nor its higher node, the syllable, would be sufficient for an adequate description of the process: the foot and only one particular type of foot -- the monosyllabic lexical foot -- provides the proper domain for the quantitative changes. While lengthenings within the monosyllabic foot can be regarded as predictable, the predictions will not apply to the same rhyme or syllabic configurations within a different type of foot.

Claiming that some lengthening within the monosyllabic foot should be regarded as predictable raises the question of what the target metrical weight of this foot should be in the representation. In rhyme projection, the following combinations for monosyllabic foot types are available (omitting the prominence relations [S W]): (13)

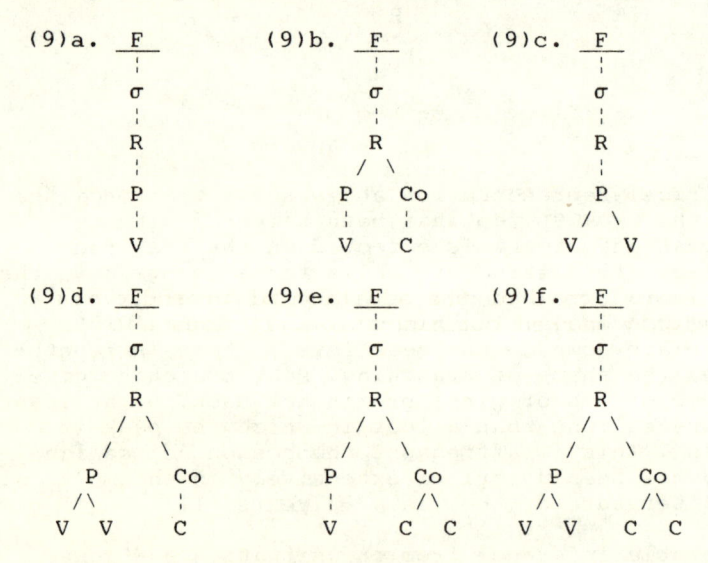

```
(9)a.   F          (9)b.   F            (9)c.   F
        |                  |                    |
        σ                  σ                    σ
        |                  |                    |
        R                  R                    R
        |                 / \                   |
        P                P   Co                 P
        |                |   |                 / \
        V                V   C                V   V

(9)d.   F          (9)e.   F            (9)f.   F
        |                  |                    |
        σ                  σ                    σ
        |                  |                    |
        R                  R                    R
       / \                / \                  / \
      /   \              /   \                /   \
     P     Co           P     Co             P     Co
    /\     |            |    / \            / \   / \
   V  V    C            V   C   C          V   V C   C
```

An expansion of the representations in (9)e and (9)f is also possible, but this is of no consequence to the argument. What may be an interesting idea emerging from the geometry above is the possibility of looking at the different types of trees as representing various degrees of acceptability or stability of the corresponding feet.

(9)a will be at the bottom of the scale -- it translates as -V#, and simply does not exist in English. The structure was eliminated with the WGmc lengthening in lexical monosyllables: OE þū, mē, nū.

All other configurations are allowed in English, but (9)b deserves special attention. It is the only representation in which branching occurs on the rhyme level alone; historically it is the configuration which seems to be most conducive to quantitative adjustments. Absence of branching within either the peak or the coda, i.e., a 'naked' syllable constituting a whole foot, can be regarded as significant in the following instances:

1. WG final -*u* and -*i* (-*e*) are retained in OE after short syllables and disappear after long syllables (Campbell 1959:144), hence the following OE paradigmatic variations:
 --Nom. Acc. Pl. of neuter *a*-stems: *scipu*, *hofu*, but *word*, *dēor*.
 --Fem. *ō*-stems: *faru*, *lufu* but *rōd*, *wund*.
 --Masc., Fem. *u*-stems: *sunu* but *feld*; *duru* but *hand*.
 --Nom. Sg. *i*-stems: *wine*, *mete* but *giest*, *dǣl*.
 --Nom Pl. of cons. stems: *hnyte*, *stude*, but *fēt*, *cælf*.
 --Imper. Cl.I weak verbs: *freme*, *nere* but *dēm*, *hīer*.

2. The LOE 'tendency to lengthen vowels before a single consonant in words like *wēl* 'well', *wēr* 'man', *bēt* 'better', etc. (Minkoff 1967:61).

3. MEOSL. This of course is the most significant quantitative change which the proposed analysis will explain. It is the clearest case of the addition of prosodic weight to avoid a highly marked configuration. It does not achieve the original prosodic weight -- schwa loss has destroyed that beyond repair -- but at least the monosyllabic foot resulting from it is 'stretched' in what may be an attempt at 'preservation/resolution/compensation' triggered by schwa loss.

The foot-based analysis also makes correct prediction for words of the *have*, *were*, *are* type. Being non-major-class words, they will not normally constitute feet in isolation and will therefore be ineligible for the readjustments following schwa loss.

Defining MEOSL as a process within the foot domain, not as an open syllable change, has another advantage: it explains why the change affected only words of originally disyllabic structure. Though schwa was lost in words of three and more syllables, the resulting structures were well-balanced [S W (W)] metrical frames: there was no significant change in the category of foot type.

Words like *āmen*, *ācorn*, *prōvost* (with short first

vowels in OE) are covered by the foot-domain account: the lengthening is required by their two-foot structure (as the foot is defined in Selkirk 1980): since the first foot contains (in OE) a non-branching rhyme of type (9)a, the situation is remedied by vowel lengthening.

4. While most nouns in ME rapidly develop analogical -*es* plurals, some former neuter monosyllables, but only with *long* stems, resist and appear without an inflectional ending in the 12th and 13th centuries: *word, thing, ger, hors, swyn, shep, der, neet* (Mossé 1952/68:51). The short monosyllabic stems were earlier in acquiring the syllabic -*es* plural, as this hypothesis predicts. A similar phenomenon is the perseverance of the inflectional -*e* in monosyllabic -VC(C) adjectives in ME, both weak and strong, while in adjectives of more than one syllable where schwa loss would not interfere with the overall well-formedness of the foot, the morphological loss of {-*e*} occurs much earlier (Mossé 1952/68: 64).

5. Even if it is not the case, as Bliss maintains, that *cage, page, rage, boot, coat, gout, gown* etc. were lengthened in AN, they fit here naturally.

6. Similarly, EMnE lengthening of /æ/ and /ɔ/, in some varieties of English, before /f,θ,s/. It is significant that when the codas with these spirants are branching, there is generally no lengthening (e.g. /-ft/), but when the cluster is 'unitary' (-sp, -st, -sk) there is: *pass, staff, path, ask, rasp*. Furthermore, the contrast between *pass* and *passenger, class* and *classical* (Barber 1976:312) strongly supports the view that the complexity of the foot in the second of each pair blocks a quantitative change which would be suggested by a purely segmental or syllabic environment.

7. Finally, there are some mostly unrelated and ungeneralizable examples from EMnE which would look regular from this point of view. Wyld (1920/53:401) quotes the following spellings and rhymes from EMnE: *forgoot* (1627), *to geet* (1638) (cf. Shakespeare's rhyme *get-heat*), *I toucke* (1639), *weet* (1640) (cf. Milton's rhyme *wet-great* and *eat-wet*), *feel* 'fell' (1641).

The MnE situation with regard to stressed lexical monosyllables is mixed. Support for the line of reasoning above can be gleaned from phonetic studies of durational (peak) changes in such words as (in the environment of a final lenis consonant) *bid, food, bad* (Gimson 1972:94-5). On the other hand, there are predictable objections, based on cases of shortening which run against the hypothesis formulated here. The strongest counter-case is EMnE shortening of long vowels in monosyllables ending in a single consonant: *bread, sweat, blóod, flood, dead, gone, shook, book*. One might speculate that powerful segmental rules (referring to /-t,-d,-k/) can override the not-so-rigorous foot construction constraint. 'The lexical incidence of this shortening ... varied in different places, with the consequence that in the north of England and in Ireland ... pronunciations such as /lu:k/ *look*, /bu:k/ *book* are still encountered' (Wells 1982:197).(14)

The hierarachy of prosodic salience which I have proposed and defended is not a new idea in English historical phonology. Many scholars have tried to define the 'ideal' prosodic unit in some way. Luick (1898) regarded quantitative changes in the history of English as uniformly directed towards a 'Normalisierung' of the stressed syllable. In a different theory, Jones (1980) argued in favor of a 'canonical' disyllabic shape. Lass (1984a,b) has proposed a syllable-based metrical analysis of MEOSL and other phenomena. Of these, Lass' approach and mine have most in common -- they are both crucially non-segmental and non-linear. At some point they both look at rhyme configuration; both lead to indeterminacy with respect to the status of the -VC syllable/foot.

Prince has argued (1980:558) that the idea of 'foot domain' is intrinsically more contentful than that of 'resyllabification rule', since foot structure is predetermined by the stress system, while resyllabification, of itself, could be just about anything, and that 'Foot, not syllable, is the principal determinant of English phonology'. It seems intuitively right that *pass, class* belong in a different prosodic category from *passenger, classify*; *word* and *scipu* are also different prosodic entities. A foot-based approach will put *tal-Ø* and *talent* in two separate compartments and then, if necessary, worry over the specific relations within each group. In its pristine simplicity foot-assignment seems to me preferable, as an explanatory strategy, to the syllable-resolution treatment in Lass. His works well for quantitative verse, but it also faces the necessity of postulating and justifying ambisyllabicity and the assignment of 'moricness' to consonants, an undesirable situation which I can avoid: a 'bad' rhyme in a monosyllabic foot is a good rhyme and reason for some quantitative adjustments in English.(15)

NOTES

1. The relevant observation in this regard is that, as is largely the case in MnE, inflectional affixes are neutral with respect to stress location and can therefore be considered irrelevant to stress-related quantitative processes. In the analysis I propose, inflectional and derivational can still be handled as two different groups. The stipulation is that if [-ə] is the entire phonetic material of which an inflection consists, then the stem will undergo the change. Other inflectional endings will not prevent lengthening, because of paradigmatic analogy. (This is different from the putative lengthenings in the plural, e.g., *staff - staves*, or the failure of lengthening in *coper - coperes*, etc., cf. Jordan (1934/74:47-8)/

    The results with respect to derivational affixes can vary according to their phonological composition: i.e., lengthening will occur regularly only when the affix is{-e}. Since the only case of a derivational suffix in ME with nothing but [-ə] in its makeup is the adverbial {-e} (*softe, hearde*, etc), speculation along these lines is futile: the relevant examples have long stems anyway.

    For the record: Malsch and Fulcher's strongest group would be *balloc, bannuc, hafoc, hassoc, mattoc, munuc, parroc, seoloc, weoloc*, all of which contain the OE/ME diminutive suffix *-uc/-oc* and none of which ever undergo lengthening.

2. For a survey of the creolization hypothesis cf. Poussa 1982.

3. The quantity of the vowel in *lake* is attributed to OE *lacu* which would naturally undergo OSL and produce ME *lāk*. (O)F *lac* is assimilated by the native form (Onions:512). *Face, mace, place, trace*, etc. are covered by Bliss (1952/53:#45) who describes them as instances of open syllable lengthening in AN, the conditions for which are similar to the conditions for MEOSL. The last example Danchev quotes in this connection, *peak*, does not belong to this group at all; it is a 16th c. borrowing (Onions:660).

4. Since the process is stress-related, trisyllabic forms with a prefix would naturally behave like disyllables, e.g., *behave, beneath, bequeath*. The same would apply to the stressed vowel in the second element of (unobscured) compounds, e.g., *nightingale*. In monomorphemic words, the short stressed vowel stays short, e.g., OE *letania, planete, saltere*, MnE *littany, planet, psalter*.

5. Although Danchev does not recognize it, Erdmann's (1972:234) view that MEOSL 'renders syntagmatic information paradigmatic', i.e., the lengthened vowel (a paradigmataic change) contains the same information as the sequence -VCə# (seen as a syntagmatic unit), is easily translatable into 'an enhanced syllable perception', making 'the root syllable perceptually more salient, with accompanying lengthening of the vowel in the communicatively prominent syllable' (Danchev 1983:72).

6. I use Abercrombie's (1964:217) definition of the foot. Selkirk's

(1980:565) differs in ways that do not affect this analysis.
7. I have syllabified in accord with the Maximal Syllable Onset Principle (Selkirk 1982:359). The possibility of ambisyllabicity, or its alternative, resyllabification (*ibid.* 365), is ignored because my analysis focuses on the structural properties of the *monosyllabic* foot.(Selkirk, it should be noted, does not see resyllabification as equivalent to ambisyllabicity.)
8. Rhyme structure determines prosodic weight: the onset composition is irrelevant in this respect (Hayes 1981:12).
9. This argument views the effects of metrical organization as a diagnostic of weight, which in turn can be realized in terms of phonemic length.
10. There is a small number of words in which ME -VCə emerges as -VC in MnE: e.g. MnE *beck, drop, fret, get, knock, lap, rot, tar, wag*. Such words pose a problem for any existing analysis. They constitute 4.9% of the relevant forms.
11. Branching 'is the central, unmarked criterion of prominence; the cases of prominence that are not definable as branching are marked, subsidiary phenomena, treated by analogy with the branching cases' (Hayes 1981:45).
12. 'Peak-Projection' might be a convenient term for the representations in (8), clearer than '[+syl] Projection' suggested by Hayes (1981:41-3), where rhyme projection is 'a universal domain for prosodic rules', with some language-specific rules affecting the [+syl] Projection as well.
13. A non-branching coda does not affect prosodic weight in the same way as a non-branching peak. (9)c,(9)d are better than (9)b.
14. 'The north of England remained unaffected by Pre-Fricative Lengthening, hence typical northern [baθ], [klaθ] (Wells 1982:205). 'The vowels /ɪ ɛ ʊ ʌ/, while normally monophthongal, tend to have centring-diphthong allophones when prosodically salient and when in the environment of a following final voiced consonant, thus *He's wearing a* `*bib* [bɪəb]! ... `*bed* [bɛəd], `*good* [gʊəd], `*rub* [rʌəb]' (485).
15. I am grateful for comments and suggestions on an earlier version of this paper from Robert Stockwell, Roger Lass, and Heinz Giegerich.

REFERENCES

Abercrombie, David. 1964. 'Syllable Quantity and Enclitics in English.' *In Honour of Daniel Jones* 216-23. London: Longmans.
Barber, Charles. 1976. *Early Modern English*. London: Andre Deutsch.
Bliss, A.J. 1952/53. 'Vowel Quantity in Middle English Borrowings from Anglo-Norman'. *Archivum Linguisticum* 4.121-47, 5.22-47.
Campbell, Alistair. 1959. *Old English Grammar*. Oxford: University Press.

Danchev, Andrei. 1983. 'The Middle English Lengthening in Open Syllables and the Interlanguage Hypothesis'. *University of Sofia English Papers*, II, 59-82.
Erdmann, Peter. 1972. *Tiefenphonologische Lautgeschichte der englischen Vokale*. Frankfurt: Athenaeum.
Giegerich, Heinz. 1981. 'Zero Syllables in Metrical Theory'. *Phonologica* 1980: 153-60.
-------. 1985. *Metrical Phonology and Phonological Structure: German and English*. Cambridge: University Press.
Gimson, A.C. 1972. *An Introduction to the Pronunciation of English*. 2nd Ed. London: Edward Arnold.
Hayes, Bruce. 1981. *A Metrical Theory of Stress Rules*. IULC.
Jones, Charles. 1980. 'Segment Gemination and Syllable Shape: A Dependency Approach'. FLH I/2.251-75.
Jordan, Richard. 1934/74. *Handbook of Middle English Grammar: Phonology*. Translated and revised Eugene J. Crook. The Hague: Mouton.
Lass, Roger. 1984a. 'Quantity, Resolution and Syllable Geometry'. FLH IV/2.151-80.
-------. 1984b. 'Minkova *noch einmal*: MEOSL and the Resolved Foot'. MS.
Luick, Karl. 1898. 'Die Quantitätsveränderungen im Laufe der englischen Sprachentwicklung'. Anglia XX.335-63.
Malsch, D.L. and R. Fulcher. 1975. 'Tensing and Syllabification in Middle English'. *Language* 51.2.303-14.
Minkoff, Marco. 1967. *English Historical Grammar*. 2nd Ed. Sofia: Naouka i Izkoustvo.
Minkova, Donka. 1982. 'The Environment for Open Syllable Lengthening in Middle English'. FLH III/1.29-58.
Mossé, F. 1952/68. *Handbook of Middle English*, trans. James A. Walker. Baltimore: Johns Hopkins Univ. Press.
O'Connor, J.D. 1973. *Phonetics*. London: Penguin.
Onions, C.T.(ed.). 1966. *The Oxford Dictionary of English Etymology*. Oxford: University Press.
Poussa, Patricia. 1982. 'The Evolution of Early Standard English: the Creolization Hypothesis'. *Studia Anglica Posnaniensia* XIV:60-87.
Prince, Alan. 1980. 'A Metrical Theory for Estonian Quantity'. LI 11.3.511-62.
Schirmunski, V. 1976. *Obscee i germanskoe yazikoznanie* [General and Germanic Linguistics]. Leningrad: Naouka.
Selkirk, Elizabeth. 1980. 'Prosodic Categories in English Word Stress'. LI 11.3.563-605.
-------. 1982. 'The Syllable'. *The Structure of Phonological Representations*, ed. H. van der Hulst and Norval Smith, 337-84.
Wells, J.C. 1982. *Accents of English*. Cambridge: University Press.
Wyld, H.G. 1920. *A History of Modern Colloquial English*. Oxford: Blackwell.

LEXICAL VARIATION OF EModE EXCLUSIVE ADVERBS: STYLE SWITCHING OR A CHANGE IN PROGRESS?

TERTTU NEVALAINEN
University of Helsinki

0. *Introduction*. This paper addresses the question of how lexical variation could be systematically observed and described over a longer period of time. A quantitative approach seems on the whole appropriate, even if it presents a number of well-known empirical problems. Thus, with the exception of high frequency items, a lexical study usually needs a large basic corpus. Secondly, while a diachronic perspective implies chronological segmentation, there are few (if any) non-arbitrary periods, which could serve as ideal sampling intervals in any given case. Moreover, as they multiply the material to be studied, periods also create the problem of stylistic compatibility of the data. The grounds for stylistic variation may be situational or literary or both.[1] Stylistic incompatibility is usually described in terms of style switching, i.e. as 'intrasystemic changes affecting different sets of register variants according to situation' (Samuels 1972: 119). Needless to say, these changes are relevant if we are dealing with style-conditioned lexical variation.

In many historical studies stylistic compatibility is taken for granted, or these pretheoretical matters are relegated to the sphere of philological skill (Lightfoot 1979: 5-6). While not questioning linguistic generalizations or philological skill, this paper nevertheless calls attention to questions of style switching which may affect diachronic analyses of lexical variation. The study is based on a stylistically stratified corpus that is sampled from three successive periods of Early Modern English (EModE; 1500-1700). It will be tentatively proposed that certain stylistic aspects of the diachronic data might be assessed on the basis of some recent research into the intrasystemic differences between written and spoken language. In other words, written language will be viewed only as a relatively autonomous system of communication (cf. Kay 1977).

1. *Exclusive adverbs*. The following discussion of lexical variation is part of a more extensive study in EModE exclusive adverbials. While the Old English class of exclusives had three morphologically related items, *an(e)*, *þæt an* and *for an* (Rissanen 1967, 1985), the number of exclusive adverbs had quadrupled by the end of the EModE period. Besides the by now marginal *one*, the developing EModE standard language includes the following items: *only*, *but*, *alone*, *alonely*, *purely*, *barely*, *simply*, *merely*, *solely*, *singly*, *exclusively* and *just*.[2] This set of lexemes consists of syntactically and semantically defined synonyms of 'only' (cf. definition in Quirk et al. 1972: 431). EModE speakers could of course avail themselves of a large number of lexical and syntactic paraphrases to produce the same quantifier reading at the expression level.[3] At the same time, even the exclusive adverbs are not always freely interchangeable in EModE. Some of them are already archaic and fall into disuse during this period (*alonely*), while others are only entering into the exclusive adverbial function towards the end of the 17th century (*exclusively* and *just*).

There are, however, some explicit instances of distributional overlap in the present corpus, although they are by no means common. The examples in (1) come from John Chamberlain's correspondence. Chamberlain uses *only* in his letter to Carleton of April 2, 1606, but changes it into *but* in his letter to Winwood with the same piece of news three days later.

(1a) To which he aunswered that from Catesbie he had yt *only* in generall termes, and from Tesmond sub sigillo confessionis, and that ... (Chamberlain 1939 (1606):220)

(1b) But for the late hellish conspiracie he was proved to be privie to yt both from Catesbie and Tesmond or Greenway a Jesuite, to which he aunswered that from Catesbie he had yt *but* in generall termes, and from Tesmond sub sigillo confessionis: (Chamberlain 1939 (1606):224)

In (2) we have three direct quotes of John Thompson's words in a House of Commons debate in 1691. The versions in (2a) and (2b) are reported by two different parliamentary diarists, Luttrell and Grey, respectively, and (2c) by Grey who quotes Mr. Hampden's speech later on during the same debate. Although none of them may contain Thompson's exact words, they nevertheless indicate that *only*, *merely* and *but* could be used interchangeably in this context.

(2a) But as to those designed (as pretended) for a descent, I look upon it *only* as a colour. (Luttrell 1972 (1691): 30)

(2b) We have the Skeleton, though not the Body, of the Forces.
I look upon this War with France to be *merely* a Colour.
Pray put the thing Head by Head. (Grey 1763 (1691): 177)

(2c) But when 'tis said "The Matter of the War with France is
but a Colour." - Do you think France will use you well that
you may put yourselves into his hands? (Grey 1763 (1691):178)

2. *Quantitative analysis*. The present material can be roughly divided into carefully edited, non-fictional prose, and texts more closely related to spoken discourse. The non-fictional prose corpus comprises educational writings from 1531 to 1570 (A) and *The Augustan Prose Sample* from 1675 to 1725 (C). The Tudor texts consist of about 200.000 running words and the Augustan ones of some 80.000.[4] These non-fictional texts are used as comparative material because they were all written for publication and for educated readerships. Table 1 shows the distributions of exclusive adverbs in this material; all the adverbs introduced above are taken into account except the correlative *not only - but also*.

TEXT TYPE	*ONLY*	*BUT*	OTHERS	*N*(100%)
A) Educational Prose	69%	30%	1%	441
C) Augustan Prose	58%	26%	16%	166

TABLE 1. Distribution of exclusives in non-fictional prose.

Table 1 suggests that *only* is the dominant exclusive during the EModE period. The frequency of *but* remains quite stable, whereas the total of the other exclusives increases in the data from the end of the period. The differences of distribution are statistically highly significant.[5] They would seem to support the lexicographical evidence for the increased lexical variety of exclusives in EModE.

The present main corpus consists of some 1.5 million running words and it is composed of four text types from three consecutive periods: A) 1500-1560, B) 1570-1630 and C) 1640-1700. The four text types of letters, sermons, plays and parliamentary diaries represent either the domain of private writing or the spoken idiom or both. The speech related material covers both recorded speech (parliamentary diaries) and writings for oral delivery (sermons and plays). The texts were selected on the basis of extralinguistic factors except for sermons, which were distinguished on the evidence of literary scholarship. The guiding principle was to keep the text types as constant as possible and only to vary the time of writing. Because of the size of the corpus (c. 110.000 words/text type/period), a fairly rough measure of homogeneity had to be applied in text selection.

Each text type was polarized stylistically and the more colloquial ends were matched for the three periods. Hence, private letters were selected instead of official ones; private House of Commons diaries instead of the official parliamentary journals; plain and colloquial sermons instead of ornate ones, and comic plays instead of tragedies. Some allowances had to be made for the first period, however. The fact that only verse comedies were written during the first half of the 16th century sets the period A plays in contrast to the prose plays of the two latter periods. Similarly, since no private parliamentary diaries exist from the first period, a collection of published parliamentary debates had to be used instead. These double variables will, of course, have to be taken into account in the interpretation of the first period data. A more detailed account of the materials and their selection criteria is given in Nevalainen (1983).

	PERIOD	*ONLY*	*BUT*	OTHERS	*N*(100%)
A)	1500-1560	41%	50%	9%	610
B)	1570-1630	37%	57%	6%	785
C)	1640-1700	54%	40%	6%	774

TABLE 2. Distribution of exclusives in the main corpus.

Table 2 shows the distributions of exclusives in the main corpus. It appears from these composite figures that, in fact, *but* prevails over *only* in the first two periods and is still much more frequent in C than the comparative material would suggest. On the other hand, the group of other exclusives seems to have maintained an even distribution in the main corpus. Since they are not nearly as frequent as *only* and *but*, we shall for the most part of what follows concentrate on these two quantitative prototypes of EModE exclusives.[6]

Comparing Tables 1 and 2 raises at least two questions. First, does the high frequency of *but* perhaps correlate with particular text types in the main corpus or, ultimately, is it related to some pragmatic and semantic distinctions that are reflected in the text type selection? Secondly, if this is the case, does the convergence of the main corpus data and the comparative material in C indicate that *but* is slowly beginning to lose ground as an exclusive?[5] We can study the first question by comparing the distributions of *only* and *but* in the four main text types and the comparative material. Table 3 shows, besides the frequencies of *only* and *but*, the *only/but* ratios broken down by text type. The figures represent the frequency of *only* divided by that of *but* in a given subcorpus. If *only* is more frequent than *but*, the *only/but* ratio is greater than 1; if *but* is the more frequent of the two, the figure remains between 1 and 0.

	TEXT TYPE	*N* of INST.	*N* of INST.	RATIO of
A)	1500-1560	ONLY	BUT	ONLY/BUT
	Parliam. records	42	17	2.47
	Educ. prose (*)	303	132	2.30 (*)
	Letters	84	86	0.98
	Sermons	70	76	0.92
	Plays	52	127	0.41
B)	1570-1630	ONLY	BUT	ONLY/BUT
	Parliam. diaries	114	106	1.08
	Letters	74	98	0.76
	Plays	57	127	0.45
	Sermons	43	120	0.36
C)	1640-1700	ONLY	BUT	ONLY/BUT
	Aug. prose (*)	97	43	2.26 (*)
	Parliam. diaries	118	70	1.69
	Sermons	98	68	1.44
	Plays	110	86	1.28
	Letters	89	87	1.02
	TOTALS:	1351	1243	$\bar{x}$ = 1.09

TABLE 3. Only/but ratios in the main corpus and the comparative material (*) (cf. period difference above).

Table 3 indicates that, throughout the EModE period, the non-fictional prose and parliamentary texts favour *only*. *But* prevails in comedies, sermons and letters in the first two periods but is outnumbered by *only* in these text types as well in the third. The verse plays in A do not markedly differ from the prose ones in B. In the light of this, it would seem that the relative frequency of *but* in A and B texts has perhaps more to do with colloquial use of language than speech *per se*: *only* consistently prevails in parliamentary texts, although they represent recorded speech.[7] On the other hand, there is still a significant difference between the private Commons diaries in B and the notes taken by the Clerk of the Parliaments for official use. The *only/but* ratio remains as low as 1.08 in the three private Commons diaries in B but reaches 3.02 (N = 193) in Elsing's notes for the Lords Journal 1621-1626 (Nevalainen 1983: 118).

On the basis of the distributional data we may answer the question about the possible colloquialness of *but* tentatively in the affirmative. There still remains the issue of internal homogeneity of the different text types. In other words, we would like to know whether the selected four text types are stylistically compatible in the three periods studied. This is important if we wish to interpret the adverb distributions in C diachronically as the first signs of *but* being in the process of becoming recessive.

3. *Spoken and written language*. The present main corpus consists of texts that are related to colloquial and/or spoken contexts of language use. Hence it does not seem impossible to seek to evaluate the data on the basis of what we know about the linguistic differences between spoken and written language in Present-day English (PE; cf. the bibliography in Tannen 1984). Usually these differences are not strictly medium specific but rather emerge in quantitative comparisons. PE research has produced indices of contrast which reflect the impact of medium (and situation) on the linguistic organization of the message. Maximum differentiation results from parallel influence of medium and situational style, viz. between spontaneous conversation and planned, carefully edited writing.

The background for the present account is furnished by the work of Traugott (1981), Tannen (1982), Chafe (1982) and Redeker (1984). On the basis of quantitative evidence Chafe suggests that typical written language differs from typical spoken language in that it is more integrated and detached, whereas speech is typically more fragmented and involved. Structural integration, i.e. syntactic complexity, is the product of the slow process of (re)writing, and detachment results from the separation of the writer from his audience in space and time. Chafe describes this variation in terms of sets of linguistic features that represent the poles of two intersecting continua, integration *v*. fragmentation and detachment *v*. involvement. Their main features are presented in Table 4.

In quantitative studies these features have been coded and counted for various texts in order to determine their involvement *v*. detachment and fragmentation *v*. integration scores. Typical speech is expected to show high values for involvement and fragmentation and low values for detachment and integration. The reverse would be expected of a typical sample of writing. Redeker (1984) found that, expect for detachment, the scales showed excellent discrimination between strictly matched spoken and written productions.

SPEECH	WRITING
INVOLVEMENT:	*DETACHMENT*:
First person references	Passives
Speaker's mental processes	Nominalizations
Monitoring information flow	
Direct quotes	Indirect quotes
Historical present	Past perfect
Emphatic particles	Literary expressions
Vagueness and hedges	
FRAGMENTATION:	*INTEGRATION*:
Independent clauses	Nominalizations
Coordinating conjunctions	Past & present participles
	Attributive adjectives
	Conjoined phrases
	Series of asyndetic phrases
	Sequences of prep. phrases
	Complement clauses
	Relative clauses

TABLE 4. Features of typical spoken and written language (Chafe 1982, Redeker 1984).

However, in her study of spoken and written narratives, Beaman (1984) concluded that the two media may also represent different types of structural complexity. In other words, the integration *v*. fragmentation distinction may turn out to be a shallow one.

On the other hand, Tannen (1982) draws two conclusions with respect to oral and literate strategies. One is that oral discourse features are also to be found in written discourse. Secondly, it is the involvement features expected in speech that written fiction typically combines with the syntactic integration features expected in writing. Chafe also points out that his numerical comparisons are from maximally differentiated samples of speech and writing. At the same time, 'there are other styles of speaking which are more in the direction of writing, and other styles of writing which are more like speech'(Chafe 1982: 49).

Assuming that, in principle, similar dimensions of contrast also apply to stylistically stratified diachronic data, we may have something to build a linguistic 'colloquiality measure' on. Nevertheless, since all the EModE data are written, they can only display varying degrees of planning.

Hence one would expect the fragmentation *v.* integration continuum to be telescoped considerably. If some longer stretches of continuous texts were to be analysed, the features of fragmentation and integration would presumably still covary with text types. One problem of this lexical study is, however, the amount of text to be analysed. In plays, for instance, style switching may be connected with speaker role, and in personal letters with the subject matter. Partly because of this and partly because of the length of the texts, it was decided that only the immediate cotexts of the adverbs would be taken into account in the present survey.

4. *Involvement index*. In order to eliminate sentence length variation, binary features are used as discriminants in this study. They are selected from the involvement *v.* detachment continuum and include first person references and non-past tense forms from the involvement end, and passive voice from the detachment end of the continuum. In Redeker's study (1984: 50-51), the passive voice turned out to be the best discriminant of the otherwise few detachment features. The non-past tense here also covers the historical present and direct quotes of involved speech as opposed to the past perfect and indirect quotes typical of detached writing (cf. Ochs 1979: 70). First person reference often covaries with the speaker's mental process and monitoring features and hence seems to be a good candidate for an involvement discriminant. Traugott (1981) also suggests that indicators of proximal deixis (first person pronouns and present tense) typically imply colloquiality as opposed to casualness (second person and future) and formality (third person and past) in narrative discourse.

There are, however, certain things to be pointed out before proceeding to quantification of the selected features. These features, like any others, also covary with other aspects of communication both synchronically and diachronically. Voice, for instance, may reflect demands of the situational context, e.g. the speaker's politeness strategy, or it may distinguish certain informative text types regardless of medium differences (cf. Quirk et al. 1972: 808, Granger 1983: 279-288). In some text types one would be likely to find clashing features, e.g. first person pronouns co-occurring with past tense forms in diaries and autobiographies. The topic of communication may hence affect the choice of person and tense. An extreme form of this would perhaps occur in the kinds of 17th century nonfiction where the use of *I* had developed a symbolic value. A writer like Donne or Burton could generalize his *I* into a cosmic personality symbolic of all men (Webber 1968: 3-14).

On the other hand, we should also ask whether these three PE distinctions were structurally available to EModE speakers. One would assume that, if they were, they would not deviate much from their present-day notional distinctions. Whereas the pronoun and tense dichotomies seem to be well-established, the EModE passive calls for a comment.[8] Although the opposition between active and passive exists in Old English, it is not until the EModE period that certain passive constructions, notably indirect passives and prepositional passives, gain momentum (Visser 1973: 2120-2146). It is also argued that the prepositional passive ('he was laughed at') was particularly common in colloquial writings in EModE (Visser 1973: 2125). While this cannot be contested, it appears to be rather infrequent in the main corpus adverbial cotexts. There are no more than eight occurrences, most of them in the third period parliamentary diaries. The indirect passive ('he was given a book') occurs twice in B texts and three times in C. Rare as these passives are, they nevertheless indicate some slight discrepancy in the structural resources between the first half of the 16th century and the latter half of the 17th.

As pointed out above, the present indices of involvement are based on the immediate cotexts of the exclusive adverb occurrences. *But* and *only* are scored separately. One point is allotted to each clause with an exclusive that has a non-past finite verb. One point is equally gained by an occurrence of an exclusive when the sentence in which it occurs contains one or more references to the speaker-writer (*I, me, we, us*). Finally, if the clause containing the exclusive is in the passive, a point is subtracted from its feature score. In other words, this procedure interprets the features of involvement and detachment as complementary. On this continuum, maximum involvement would yield a score of +2, and maximum detachment a score of -1. Maximum scores of these 'here and now' features are illustrated by the examples in (3), and the lowest ones, with past passive constructions and no first person pronouns, by the examples in (4).

(3a) A: I knocke your costarde if ye offer to strike me.
B: Strikest thou in deede? and I offer *but* in iest?
(Udall 1939 (c. 1550): 43)

(3b) I am in so greate /haste/ ... that I have *only* time to put that up and tell you, wch will be ye best acc^t you can have (I suppose), of that action, when I return thence. (Lyttelton 1672; Thompson, ed., 1878: 86)

(4a) Harry Savile is banished ye Court upon this acc^t: ...
For this he wase *only* put out /of/ company for that time,
and the next morning all ye blame wase layd on ye wine
and he pardoned. (Hatton 1676; Thompson, ed., 1878: 130)

(4b) ... and that, whereas there was due to his Majesty Two
Parts of Three of the Recusants Estates, his Majesty
out of Grace commanded there should be taken *but* a Third
Part: (Nicholas 1766 (1620/21) : 91-92)

Table 5 presents the involvement indices of the immediate adverbial cotexts. The relative frequencies of the features (i.e. text type averages multiplied by 100) are arranged by text type according to the feature totals of *but*. In the first period texts, for instance, letters have the highest score of involvement features and parliamentary texts the lowest. By and large, the parliamentary records contain more passives and fewer references to the speaker or writer in the adverbial cotexts than the other texts.

TEXT TYPE	COTEXTUAL INVOLVEMENT INDICES			
A) 1500-1560	*ONLY* (%)		*BUT* (%)	
Private letters	136		143	
Comic plays	133		140	
Plain/colloquial sermons	96		100	
Educational prose (*)	80	(*)	92	(*)
Parliamentary records	62		82	
B) 1570-1630	*ONLY* (%)		*BUT* (%)	
Private letters	130		145	
Comic plays	133		142	
Plain/colloquial sermons	128		137	
Parliamentary diaries	82		93	
C) 1640-1700	*ONLY* (%)		*BUT* (%)	
Comic plays	137		137	
Plain/colloquial sermons	116		131	
Augustan Prose (*)	87	(*)	119	(*)
Private letters	65		99	
Parliamentary diaries	80		77	

TABLE 5. Relative feature indices for the scale of involvement in the immediate cotexts of *but* and *only* in the main corpus and the comparative material (*).

The involvement indices in Table 5 are not intended to represent any causal relations. They only indicate the mean co-occurrences of the two exclusives and certain linguistic features that recent research has found typical of spoken language. Nevertheless, the following observations seem warranted. First, involvement features are slightly more frequent in the immediate cotexts of *but* than in those of *only* in all the text types. The only exception is the parliamentary subcorpus in C, and even there the difference in favour of *only* is almost negligible. In general *but* is rarely met in passive sentences. Solely in the parliamentary texts does it co-occur with the passive in some 12-14% of the cases; in all other text types the figure remains below 10%. In PE the passive voice has been found to be more frequent in planned than in unplanned discourse (Ochs 1979: 69-70), which may be a relevant distinction here as well. Many of the parliamentary diaries are presumably based on shorthand notes which were later written up in final form.

The second observation pertaining to Table 5 is that the text types of the three periods seem to form similar feature hierarchies. Letters and plays show the highest involvement scores, parliamentary texts the lowest. Only the letters from the third period are exceptional in this respect. Especially the cotexts of *only* deviate from the rest of the correspondence data. This may be due to the number of less personal news letters in C, i.e. the topic factor mentioned above.

In absolute terms, the texts of the second period (B) yield the highest involvement scores. As the absolute counts of the B and C texts were checked for statistical significance, however, their respective differences did not reach the 1% level of statistical significance in plays, sermons and parliamentary diaries. That is to say, as far as these involvement features are concerned, the cotexts of *only*, for instance, suggest no significant difference between the Restoration comedies in C and what are mostly citizen comedies in B. Nevertheless, the peak frequencies of *but* in B would of course tally both with the hypothesis of its colloquialness and its lexical dominance. On the other hand, the third period letters show that the choice of *but* need not covary with a high involvement score. In this case, besides the frequency of news letters, individual variation may contribute to style switching (cf. Samuels 1972: 120). The subcorpus consists of some twenty writers's letters, and some of the writers are more numerously represented than others.

5. *Discussion*. Tentative as the involvement indices are, they nonetheless indicate a certain measure of diachronic compatibility in the data. Using this type of linguistic evidence to supplement extralinguistic criteria of text type selection we can hope to be in a better position to give a diachronic account of style conditioned lexical variation. However, since *but* and *only* are at no point in EModE either absolute style markers or stereotypes in the Labovian sense (Labov 1972: 314), lexical variation alone cannot tell us much about the process of their diachronic change. The first signs of the decline of *but* in C raise a general question: how will a quantitative prototype lose its central position in the lexicon? Whereas *only* has maintained its position in PE, *but* has all but disappeared from the standard language. As opposed to the 1360 instances of the exclusive *only*, there are no more than 26 adverbial occurrences of *but* in the one-million-word Brown University corpus of written American English (Francis & Kučera 1982).

To account for the change in systemic terms, we are left with four alternatives: the adverbial functions of *but* may have been taken over by (a) *only*, the other quantitative prototype, (b) other members of the exclusive class, (c) some would-be exclusive(s) or (d) any of its possible lexical paraphrases. Any combination of the four is of course possible. Evidence for both (a) and (c) does exist in the present EModE data as both *only* and *just* are in partial distributional overlap with *but*. A few more steps can then be taken towards the actual process of lexical change by comparing these lexical items' syntactic and semantic contexts of use, i.e. their individual word grammars. Overlapping contexts are particularly interesting.

Grammatical analysis becomes even more relevant if lexical evolution is not perfectly linear. The present data suggest that *but* reached its peak frequency around the middle of the EModE period in the more colloquial texts. In his study of the various functions of *but*, which includes some later data, Joly (1982: 158) dates the beginning of the decline of the exclusive to the 18th century. Interestingly, however, he also reports on its brief revival in his 19th century prose texts. It would be illuminating to study the word grammars of the various 19th century exclusive adverbs to see how their respective relations have changed since EModE. We would expect grammatical redistributions to have taken place within the class of exclusives. Otherwise it would be difficult to account for the standard system in contemporary English.

If we go beyond the single main functions, like adverbial modification, of lexical items, we may also gain new insights into their diachrony. Thus, it is noteworthy that *but* still seems to be speech-oriented as a conjunction in Present-day standard English. The written Brown University corpus has some 4.9 occurrences of *but* per thousand words, whereas the corresponding figure is 8.8 for the London-Lund corpus of spoken British English.[9] Chafe's results (1982: 39) show even a more remarkable difference between the two media: 9.8 occurrences per thousand words in speech and 4.1 in writing. According to lexicographical evidence (*MED*), some of the speech-oriented functions of the conjunction *but* go back to Middle English, as indeed does the rise of the exclusive *but*.

6. *Conclusion*. Summarizing some of the empirical issues connected with lexical diachrony, we may conclude that a corpus of some 1.8 million running words is not sufficient to account for the entire class of EModE exclusive adverbs in quantitative terms. Hence the present investigation has only dealt with *but* and *only*, the quantitative prototypes of the class. Together they constitute more than 90% of the adverbial instances of the present data. Stylistic stratification of the data indicates that *but* is mostly favoured in the more colloquial text types, especially comic plays, private letters and plain sermons. *Only* prevails in the speech-based parliamentary texts as well as in the comparative samples of non-fictional prose. If simplified involvement indices are used as a measure of diachronic compatibility of the text types, only few significant instances of style switching can be detected. The text types tend to form similar hierarchical patterns in the three periods of EModE studied. Hence we may with more confidence interpret the statistically significant changes in adverbial frequencies as first signs of a slow process of lexical redistribution.

NOTES

1. Cf. Rydén (1979: 20, fn. 9): 'Ideally we need texts from various stages dealing with the same topic in the same tone, representing the same setting and written by authors with the same background, linguistic and non-linguistic.' The term *style* is here used to refer to both situational and literary styles, although the main criteria for selecting the data are situational; see Nevalainen (1983) for further details.
2. The class of exclusives was initially based on lexicographical evidence provided by *The Oxford English Dictionary* and *Middle English Dictionary*.

3. Cf. Romaine (1984) for further discussion of the problems of variational equivalence in grammar.
4. *The Augustan Prose Sample*, compiled by Louis Milić, is available from Oxford Text Archive, Oxford University Computing Service. For the breakdowns of the educational subcorpus in A, see Nevalainen (1983: 117).
5. References to statistical significance are based on X^2 tests (p < 0.01). The distributional differences between A and C in Table 1 are highly significant (X^2 = 48.64, df 2, p < 0.001), and so are the differences between B and C in Table 2 (X^2 = 48.47, df 2, p < 0.001), and those between C in Table 1 and C in Table 2 (X^2 = 23.49, df 2, p < 0.001).
6. For a discussion of prototype definitions and applications to lexical and grammatical problems, see e.g. Karlsson (1982).
7. Private parliamentary diaries are of course not verbatim records, nor were the official Journals at the time. To what extent note-taking language forms a register apart remains an open question. See, however, the discussion in Ferguson (1982: 58-60) and his references.
8. To be more exact, the non-past includes the present, present perfect and future tenses in the present dichotomy. Only passive constructions with *be* + past participle are counted as passives here; this excludes the few occurrences of constructions like 'the bill is reading' and 'the breach is punishable in the Star Chamber' which also have passive interpretations.
9. The Brown University corpus contains only printed materials. The London-Lund corpus of educated spoken British English forms part of the Survey of English Usage materials at University College London. Both are obtainable in computer-readable form from the International Computer Archive of Modern English (ICAME) in Bergen.

REFERENCES

Beaman, Karen. 1984. 'Coordination and Subordination Revisited: Syntactic Complexity in Spoken and Written Narrative Discourse'. *Coherence in Spoken and Written Discourse* ed. by Deborah Tannen, 45-80. Norwood, New Jersey: Ablex.

Chafe, Wallace, 1982. 'Integration and Involvement in Speaking, Writing, and Oral Literature'. *Spoken and Written Language: Exploring Orality and Literacy* ed. by Deborah Tannen, 35-53. Norwood, New Jersey: Ablex.

Chamberlain, John. 1939. *The Letters of John Chamberlain* ed. by Norman Egbert McClure (= *Memoirs of the American Philosophical Society*, XII, Part 1.) Philadelphia: The American Philosophical Society.

Ferguson, Charles. 1982. 'Simplified Registers and Linguistic Theory'. *Exceptional Language and Linguistics* ed. by Loraine Obler & Lise Menn, 49-66. New York & London: Academic Press.

Francis, W. Nelson & Henry Kučera. 1982. *Frequency Analysis of English Usage: Lexicon and Grammar*. Boston: Houghton Mifflin.

Granger, Sylviane. 1983. *The be + Past Participle Construction in Spoken English, With Special Emphasis on the Passive*. Amsterdam, New York & Oxford: North-Holland.

Grey, Anchitell. 1763. *Debates of the House of Commons, from the Year 1667 to the Year 1694*. Vol. 10. London: Printed for D. Henry, R. Cave & J. Emonson.

Joly, André. 1982. 'But, signe de l'exception et de la restriction dans l'histoire de l'anglais'. *Modèles linguistiques* 4.151-175.

Karlsson, Fred. 1982. 'Prototypes as Models for Linguistic Structure'. *Papers from the Seventh Scandinavian Conference of Linguistics*, Vol. 2, ed. by Fred Karlsson (= *Publications of the University of Helsinki Department of General Linguistics*, 10.) 583-604. Helsinki: University of Helsinki, Department of General Linguistics.

Kay, Paul. 1977. 'Language Evolution and Speech Style'. *Sociocultural Dimensions of Language Change* ed. by Ben B. Blount & Mary Sanches, 21-33. New York, San Francisco & London: Academic Press.

Labov, William, 1972. *Sociolinguistic Patterns*. Philadelphia: University of Pennsylvania Press.

Lightfoot, David. 1979. *Principles of Diachronic Syntax*. Cambridge: Cambridge University Press.

Luttrell, Narcissus. 1972. *The Parliamentary Diary of Narcissus Luttrell 1691-1693* ed. by Henry Horwitz. Oxford: Clarendon Press.

Nevalainen, Terttu. 1983. 'A Corpus of Colloquial Early Modern English for a Syntactic-Lexical Study: Evidence for Consistency and Variation'. *Papers from the Second Scandinavian Symposium on Syntactic Variation* ed. by Sven Jacobson (= *Stockholm Studies in English*, LVII.) 109-122. Stockholm: Almqvist & Wiksell.

Nicholas, Sir Edward. 1766. *Proceedings and Debates of the House of Commons in 1620 and 1621, Collected by a Member of That House* ed. by T. Tyrrwhitt. Vol. 1. Oxford: Clarendon Press.

Ochs, Elinor. 1979. 'Planned and Unplanned Discourse'. *Syntax and Semantics*, Vol. 12: *Discourse and Syntax* ed. by Talmy Givón, 51-80. New York: Academic Press.

Quirk, Randolph, Sidney Greenbaum, Geoffrey Leech & Jan Svartvik. 1972. *A Grammar of Contemporary English*. London: Longmans.

Redeker, Gisela. 1984. 'On Differences Between Spoken and Written Language'. *Discourse Processes* 7.43-55.

Rissanen, Matti. 1967. *The uses of One in Old and Early Middle English* (= *Mémoires de la Société Néophilologique de Helsinki*, XXXI.) Helsinki: Société Néophilologique.

Rissanen, Matti. 1985. 'Expression of Exclusiveness in Old English and the Development of the Adverb *Only*'. In this volume.

Romaine, Suzanne. 1984. 'On the Problem of Syntactic Variation and Pragmatic Meaning in Sociolinguistic Theory'. *Folia Linguistica* XVIII/3-4.409-432.

Rydén, Mats. 1979. *An Introduction to the Historical Study of English Syntax* (= *Stockholm Studies in English*, LI.) Stockholm: Almqvist & Wiksell.

Samuels, Michael, 1972. *Linguistic Evolution, With Special Reference to English*. Cambridge: Cambridge University Press.

Tannen, Deborah. 1982. 'Oral and Literate Strategies in Spoken and Written Narratives'. *Language* 58.1-21.
Tannen, Deborah, ed. 1984. *Coherence in Spoken and Written Discourse* (=*Advances in Discourse Processes*, XII.) Norwood, New Jersey: Ablex.
Thompson, Edward Maunde, ed. 1878. *Correspondence of the Family of Hatton* (= *Publications of the Camden Society*, 22.) London: Nichols and Sons.
Traugott, Elizabeth Closs. 1981. 'The Sociostylistics of Minority Dialect in Literary Prose'. *Proceedings of the 7th Annual Meeting of The Berkeley Linguistics Society*, 308-316. Berkeley, California: The Berkeley Linguistics Society.
Udall, Nicholas. 1939. *Nicholas Udall's Roister Doister* ed. by G. Scheurweghs (= *Materials for the Study of Old English Drama*, 16.) Louvain: Librairie Universitaire, Ch. Uystpruyst.
Visser, F.Th. 1973. *An Historical Syntax of the English Language*. Part 3, Second Half: *Syntactical Units with Two and with More Verbs*. Leiden: E.J. Brill.
Webber, Joan. 1968. *The Eloquent "I", Style and Self in Seventeenth-Century Prose*. Madison, Milwaukee & London: The University of Wisconsin Press.

REMARKS ON COMPLEMENTATION IN OLD ENGLISH

RUTA NAGUCKA
The Jagiellonian University of Cracow

In this paper I shall be mainly concerned with the methodology suggested by Anthony Warner (1982) in his recent monograph on complementation in Middle English. This book deals with the analysis and interpretation of complex syntactic structures, i.e. verbal complements, in the Wyclifite Sermons. The book is important not only for the linguistic subject discussed there, but also for its methodological significance for the theory of historical research, some aspects of which I intend to check against OE material. Warner very aptly shows that data-based analyses are fundamental for historical interpretation and that all types of information are indispensible and "mutually supporting factors" in this research (Warner 1982: 5). The following would play a supportive role in the analysis: frequency and distribution of occurrences, statistical tests of significance, translation of the text, the grammarian's knowledge of general linguistics, comparison with other languages, etc.

All these seem methodologically justifiable, although the reliability of some of them does not receive sufficient and convincing evidence. For instance, saying that there is a "roughly similar situation in PE (= Present-day English)" (p. 5), or a "partial parallel with PE" (p. 87) does not seem to be obviously warranted, especially as Warner claims to build his "interpretation of the ME situation on the data from ME and PE in the light of general theory" (p. 5).

However, this is not the point which seems controversial and even dubious to me. More disturbing is placing too much reliance on Latin sources. According to Warner,

> the sermons were produced in a milieu ... in which English was much under the influence of Latin (p. 17)

> English is beginning to discharge functions previously the
> province of Latin (or French) and is therefore tending to adopt
> Latin vocabulary and constructions ... We can interpret the
> grammatical parameters controlling infinitival constructions
> as a series of 'minimal alterations' of English structure
> designed to accommodate it to Latin (granted the salience of
> accusative and infinitive constructions with verbs of knowing,
> thinking and declaring) and resulting in a series of increasing-
> ly Latin-related registers reaching out from English, ... (p. 148)
>
> It seems reasonable to suggest ... that lME infinitive clauses
> with verbs of knowing, thinking and declaring show accommodation
> to Latin accusative and infinitive structures which have been
> adopted as a target (p. 151),

etc.

In order to test the validity of the methodology which Warner used to support the plausibility of his claim that the accusative and infinitive construction was dependent on Latin, I wish to examine the same type of complementation in Ælfric's English. I have selected a sample of his prose, i.e. the *Colloquy* and *De Temporibus Anni*, because for both texts Latin sources can be fairly easily attested: the Latin *Colloquy* is furnished with an OE interlinear gloss (added probably somewhat later) which is not confined to the meaning of particular Latin words, but gives the sense of the sentence as a whole. For the English of *De Temporibus Anni* there are a few known texts in Latin which Ælfric might have used. It is not a direct and consecutive translation, "there are considerable variations in the closeness of (text) correspondences. Some gave Ælfric his material only, others gave him the words as well" (*De Temp. Anni*, Henel 1970: lvi). Thus, the situation is similar to that described by Warner; there is no doubt about the closeness of Latin-English correspondences, and one may hypothesize that the influence of Latin syntax upon its English counterpart was significant in the domain of the accusative and infinitive with the verbs of "knowing, thinking and declaring". This is the hypothesis which I am trying to test and finally consider questionable.

Following Warner's cautiousness, I have accepted a 'surface-based approach' (Warner 1982: 8); I have not here attempted a more abstract syntactic analysis. I have assumed that the English which was used in the texts under analysis can be regarded as a sample of grammatically correct and acceptable every-day speech, easily understandable for those for whom the books were intended, i.e. for those who did not know Latin.

The decay in knowledge of Latin was emphasized on various occasions: Ælfric himself said that he rendered Latin into "usitatam Anglicam sermocinationem" 'ordinary English speech' (*Lives of Saints*, Skeat 1966: 2), or that he "awende þas boc of ledenum bocum to engliscum gereorde þam mannum to rædenne þe þæt leden ne cunnon" 'translated the book from the Latin into the English language for these (men) to read who do not know Latin' (*Catholic Homilies*, Godden 1979: 1). Consider also what Alfred said earlier in his Preface to his translation of the *Cura Pastoralis*. Thus it follows that I am taking the "hearer's" (user's) standpoint rather than that of the "speaker" (writer) who, in most cases, was bilingual and did not need any English translation or rendering of Latin material.

In view of the frequency requirements, I have collected all instances of the accusative and infinitive construction in both versions, and have arrived at the following results: (1) in the *Colloquy* there are only two examples of the accusative and infinitive which have parallel structures in the Latin counterpart. There is one example of *secgan* which does not occur with the accusative and infinitive, and the same is observed in the Latin source sentence in which *dicere* is followed by *quod*. In this way we have an ideal one-to-one correspondence. The verbs in question are *afandian* 'prove', *witan* 'know' and *secgan* 'say'. (2) in *De Temporibus Anni* the situation is less clear as we do not have an exact rendering of Latin into English. However, the closest sources given by the editor show that in four cases the Latin source has accusative and infinitive after such verbs as: *dicere*, *argumentari*, *admonere*, *credere* (verbs of saying and verbs of mental perception and affection, using Visser's classification), while in the English parallel cases there appears only *secgan* for all these verbs followed by a *þæt* clause and not an accusative and infinitive. It is true that in classical Latin all these verbs are followed by the accusative and infinitive, and that OE *secgan* only just tolerates this construction, and seems to be rather resistant to Latin influence (cf. Visser 1973: 2333). Compared to the *Colloquy* the proportion is the reverse: no identical or corresponding structures are discerned in the English and Latin of the *De Temporibus Anni* texts.

As I have said above, I wish to test the hypothesis that in Ælfric's English, supposedly influenced by Latin, the accusative and infinitive is used more often than in texts in which Latin influence is hardly noticed in the domain of syntax. For this purpose I have chosen *Beowulf*,

which has very few traces of Latin, and, if at all,
only in the use of certain appositive participles and,
likewise, in the predilection for passive construction
(although the editor adds that he is not quite sure that
these constructions are indeed influenced by Latin)
(*Beowulf*, Klaeber 1950: xciv). *Beowulf* provides more
examples of complementation with the verbs used by Ælfric,
i.e. *witan* and *secgan*: there are as many as thirteen
instances with these verbs altogether, but none of them
is followed by the accusative and infinitive construction;
they all occur with a *þæt* clause. Since the verb *afandian*,
which is used in the *Colloquy* with an accusative and
infinitive complement, does not occur in *Beowulf*, I have
added to the *Beowulf* corpus the verb *gefrignan* 'learn by
inquiry', which according to Visser belongs to the same
group as *afandian*, i.e. verbs of mental perception and
affection (Warner's verbs of knowing and thinking).[1]
Gefrignan is extensively used with an accusative and
infinitive (five times) and once with a *þæt* clause. In
order to be as fair and objective as possible, I have
considered two sets of data: one set contains the uses of
two verbs only, *witan* and *secgan* (seven occurrences in
Ælfric's texts and thirteen occurrences in *Beowulf*), and
the other set contains the uses of four verbs, *witan*,
secgan, *afandian* and *gefrignan* (eight occurrences in
Ælfric's prose and nineteen occurrences in *Beowulf*).
Before proceeding with my observations and argumentation,
I should like to make a few comments on the verb *secgan*.
As I have already mentioned, the sentence in Ælfric,

   Ic secʒe þæt behefe ic eom ʒe kinʒce[2]
   'I say that I am useful to the king' (*Ælfr. Coll.*: 150)

is an exact translation of the Latin,

   Ego dico quod utilis sum et regi

The English and the Latin sentences express the same syntactic relations; both are generated by the same grammatical operations which result in the same surface structures. However, according to Lakoff (1968: 82, 76-7), the Latin sentence would be ungrammatical. She states that "verbs of saying, in classical Latin, may only occur with accusative-infinitive"; otherwise they must be treated as Vulgar Latin. Whether Vulgar Latin or not, the Latin construction *dico quod* must have been considered grammatical by the author of the *Colloquy* if he decided to use it in a Latin manual. Nydam (1976: 93), who wrote about two types of verb complements in Old Saxon, states that the accusative and infinitive "constructions did not occur after *verba dicendi* in Old Saxon", for which she finds some corroboration in Callaway (1913).[3] The same is observed in the English version of the *De temporibus Anni*, in which there are only *þæt* clauses after *secgan* although Latin sources have the accusative and infinitive construction.

Now let me repeat briefly the main claim made by Warner about the English of the Wyclifite Sermons. What he maintains is that the accusative and infinitive constructions with verbs of knowing, thinking and declaring (i.e. according to Visser verbs of mental perception and affection as well as verbs of saying and declaring) are modelled after Latin. I have also hypothesized, though tentatively, that Ælfric's English shows strong relatedness to Latin. The details of the hypothesis may be open to question but let us assume for the sake of the argument that it is essentially correct.

In the following I will evaluate the relevant OE data according to the same procedures and computations as those applied by Warner, i.e. the chi squared test (X^2). The incidence of Latin-relatedness, i.e. Latin-influenced English (Ælfric's prose by the initial hypothesis), and Latin-free English (*Beowulf*) with accusative and infinitive complements and *þæt* clauses is presented by two contingency tables:

Table 1: the following verbs have been considered:
witan and *secgan* in Ælfric's prose and *witan* and *secgan* in *Beowulf*

Complements	Ælfric Latin-related	*Beowulf* Latin-free	Total
Accusative and infinitive	1	0	1
þæt clause	6	13	19
Total	7	13	20

X^2 (with a correction factor) = 0.104   d.f. = 1 $p < 0.05$

Table 2: the following verbs have been considered:
witan, secgan and *afandian* in Ælfric's prose and
witan, secgan and *gefrignan* in *Beowulf*

Complements	Ælfric Latin-related	*Beowulf* Latin-free	Total
Accusative and infinitive	2	5	7
þæt clause	6	14	20
Total	8	19	27

x^2 (with a correction factor) = 0.304   d.f. = 1
p is very small

Below follow some examples from Ælfric's prose (1) and (2), and from *Beowulf* (3) and (4), where (1) and (3) are instances of the accusative and infinitive and (2) and (4) of *þæt*-clauses.

(1) a. Ac   we witun þe   bilewitne wesan
       (Sed scimus   te   mansuetum esse)
       But   we know   thee   kind   be
       'but we know you to be kind'
                                              (*Ælfr. Coll.*, 9)

   b. ic hæbbe afandod þe   habban ʒode ʒeferan
       (probaui   te   habere bonos socios)
       I have found   thee have   good companions
       'I have found that you have good companions'
                                              (*Ælfr. Coll.*, 203)

(2) a. Ic   secʒe þæt   behefe ic eom ʒe cinʒce
       (Ego dico   quod utilis sum   et regi)
       I   say   that useful I am   to the king
       'I say that I am of use to the king'
                                              (*Ælfr. Coll.*, 150)

   b. Woruldlice uðwitan   sædon þæt   seo sceadu astihð up
       Natural   philosophers said that   the shadow rises up
       oð þæt heo becymð   to þære lyfte ufweardan
       until it reaches the upper part of the sky
       (... quam uidelicet umbram noctis (Acc.) ad aeris usque
       et aetheris confinium philosphi dicunt exaltari (INF))
                                              (*De Temp. Anni*, III, 6)

(3) Ne gefrægen ic þa mægþe (Acc.) maran   weorode
    Not heard   I the kinsmen   (in) bigger troop
       ymb   hyra sincgyfan   sel   gebæran (INF)
    around their treasure-giver better (to) behave
    'I have never heard of a greater bond of kinsmen behave
    with such dignity around their lord'
                                           (Beow. 1011)

(4) a.   wisse he gearwe,
                             knew he well
       þæt he dæghwila   gedrogen hæfde,
       that he life-period performed had
       eorðan wynn(e)
       of earth the joy
       'He knew well that he had ended his days, his joy
       on earth'   (Beow. 2725)
    b. secgað sæliðend, þæt þæs sele stande,
       say   seafarers that this hall stands
       reced   selesta rinca   gehwylcum
       building the best of warriors for each
       idel ond unnyt
       empty and profitless
       'Seafarers say that this hall, the noblest building,
       stands unpeopled and profitless to all warriors'
                                           (Beow. 411)
    c. ac hie hæfdon gefrunen, þæt hie ær   to fela micles
       but they had   heard   that them before far too many
       in þæm winsele   wældeað   fornam,
       in the wine-hall murderous death took away
       Denigea leode
       of the Danish people
       'but they had heard that in the past murderous death had
       carried off far too many of Danish people in the wine-
       hall'   (Beow. 694)

The figures in Table 1 and 2 present OE complements classified by dependence on Latin and type of complements (accusative and infinitive and þæt clause). Since X^2 does not exceed the value for the significance level that I have chosen (i.e. 0.05), one has to accept the null hypothesis, which means that there is no difference between Latin-relatedness and Latin-non-relatedness, or better, Latin-dependent and Latin-free complements. It turns out that the results obtained by means of the same statistical measures as those applied by Warner do not corroborate his assumption about the relation between Latin influence and Latin non-influence in the domain of the accusative and infinitive construction. However, it would be a gross

oversimplification to suggest that Warner's observations
are meaningless. They may be significant for Wyclifite
Sermons and may show tendencies of the development of
this type of complement within a limited corpus of data.
Nevertheless there are several questions which must be
asked in relation to this methodology. (1) Is the
statistical method really significant for the whole
language if the hypothesis under consideration is tested
in only one type of text in this language? The fact that
Warner additionally uses a collection of instances from
the Wyclifite Bible and from Chaucer (Warner 1982: 138)
is not a counterargument because the contacts with Latin
in all these cases are obvious. I wonder whether Warner
would have obtained the same results if he had considered
texts which are not modelled upon Latin sources (directly
or indirectly), for example, alliterative poems such as
Piers Plowman. (2) Can we ignore observations about the
same construction in earlier stages of the language, say
Old English, in order to make reasonable comparisons?
(Warner compares Middle English with Present-day English,
and only occasionally refers to Old English.) Such observations would support and strengthen our appreciation
of and confidence in the interpretation of the results.
For instance, it is generally accepted that the accusative
and infinitive existed in Germanic languages after some
verbs and is of native origin. However, it seldom appears
after *secgan*. What happens is this: in Ælfric's *Colloquy*
Latin *dico* appears with *quod*, which is not classical Latin,
yet it is parallel to OE *secge þæt*. The reverse is not
true; when the accusative and infinitive occurs in Latin
sources of *De Temporibus Anni* it is not rendered by the
same structure in Old English.[4] (3) Would it not be better
to assume that the syntactic rules generating the accusative
and infinitive construction, which are already part of
the grammar of the language, are applied to newly borrowed
verbs (a great number of them of French-Latin origin)
which belong to the same semantic field (i.e. verbs of
knowing, thinking, declaring, or verbs of mental perception
and affection, and verbs of saying and declaring)? Why
should we take it as the influence of Latin syntactic
form upon English rather than simple lexical borrowing of
the verb, which is assimilated and treated in the same way
as native verbs of the same semantic affiliation? All the
more so since English and Latin go back to a common ancestor.

The answers seem difficult if not impossible without
many detailed corpus-based studies of various text-types.
I do not wish to ignore the fact that languages do exercise

influence upon one another when they are in contact, but I am convinced that "... the effect of the borrowing on the grammar of the recipient language [is] largely confined to the phonology and the morphology, the syntax remaining relatively untouched" (Bynon 1977: 239).

To conclude, in this paper I have tried to argue that there are systematically significant parallelisms between English and Latin accusative and infinitive constructions. It is therefore doubtful that English modelled its accusative and infinitive structure on Latin. I have also attempted to show that the claim about the importance of statistics is open to attack because the characteristics which seem significant do not always match the mathematical model used to draw valid inferences about these observations.

NOTES

1. In this group there are very few OE examples, most verbs given by Visser are of French-Latin origin, borrowed much later.
2. For typological reasons Garmonsway's wynn is here represented as <w>.
3. Cf. what Visser (1973: 2333) says about *say* and the accusative and infinitive construction.
4. See also Nydam (1976) and other papers on complementation in Germanic langauges published in Volume 1 of the same journal.

SOURCES

Ælfric's Catholic Homilies. The second series. Text edited by Malcolm Godden (E.E.T.S. S.S. 5) 1979.
Ælfric's Colloquy, edited by G.N. Garmonsway (University of Exeter) 1978 (reprint).
Ælfric's De Temporibus Anni, edited by Heinrich Henel (E.E.T.S. O.S. 213) 1970.
Ælfric's Lives of Saints, edited by Walter W. Skeat. Vol. I (E.E.T.S. O.S. 76 and 82) 1966.
Beowulf and the Fight at Finnsburg, edited by Fr. Klaeber. 3rd edition (Boston: Heath) 1950.

REFERENCES

Bynon, Theodora. 1977. *Historical Linguistics*. Cambridge: Cambridge University Press.
Callaway, Morgan. 1913. *The Infinitive in Anglo-Saxon*. Washington: Carnegie Institution.
Lakoff, Robin. 1968. *Abstract Syntax and Latin Complementation*. Cambridge, Mass.: The M.I.T. Press.

Nydam, Linda. 1976. 'On Two Types of Verb Complements in Old Saxon'.
    The Journal of the Linguistic Association of the Southwest 1. 82-93.
Visser, F.Th. 1973. *An Historical Syntax of the English Language*. Part
    Three. Second Half. Syntactical Units with Two and with More Verbs.
    Leiden: E.J. Brill.
Warner, Anthony. 1982. *Complementation in Middle English and the
    Methodology of Historical Syntax*. A Study of the Wyclifite
    Sermons. London & Canberra: Croom Helm.

THE INTERPRETATION AND DEVELOPMENT OF FORM ALTERNATIONS CONDITIONED ACROSS WORD BOUNDARIES. THE CASE OF *WIFE'S*, *WIVES*, AND *WIVES'*

FRANS PLANK
Universität Konstanz

Much attention has recently been paid to a supposedly general constraint on morphological structures disallowing the conditioning of allomorphy and similar alternations at a distance. While there is considerable empirical support for the assumption that such conditioning relationships can only hold between formatives which are adjacent in terms of linear and/or operational sequence, it also faces some empirical and theoretical problems. These are not at issue in this paper, however. Here I propose to consider the implications of tightening up the locality requirement on the conditioning of allomorphy by adding (1) to the adjacency constraint.

(1) Allomorphy cannot be conditioned across (grammatical) word boundaries.

This word-internality constraint, which is more general than alternative constraints with similar aims, including in particular the 'Insensitivity Claim' of Carstairs (1981:4ff.), may seem attractive because it appears to prohibit conditioning relationships not disallowed by the adjacency constraint alone. What is at issue here is whether the implications of (1) indeed are empirical or rather conceptual. This question bears upon the partial demise of an allomorphic alternation in the history of English, which will be argued to have been inevitable in view of a universal constraint on the conditioning of form alternations - a constraint, however, which pertains to syntactic rather than morphological structures.

That a word-internality constraint such as (1) should have empirical implications would seem fairly obvious: after all, it is not difficult to adduce actual instances of conditioning relations which should not exist if (1) were valid cross-linguistically. For example, the singular and plural masculine definite articles in Italian have allomorphs (*il/lo* Sg., *i/gli* Pl.) the choice among which depends on the initial segment(s) of the following word, *lo/gli* appearing before 'impure *s*' /ts/, /dz/, and /ʃ/, and *il* (prevocalically*l*')/ *i* elsewhere (cf. 2).

   (2) *il libro* 'the book' - *lo zio* 'the uncle'

If (1) is intended as a universal constraint, it is evidently falsified by examples of this familiar kind. On the other hand, note that the conditioning factors in this and numerous similar examples are purely phonological and do not involve any morphosyntactic or lexical categories. The selection of the Italian masculine definite article allomorphs is uninfluenced, for instance, by factors such as the word-class membership of the following word: *lo/gli* or *il/i* are chosen in the appropriate phonological environments no matter what category of word hosts the conditioning initial segments (compare 2 with 3).

   (3) *lo stesso libro* 'the very book' - *il caro zio* 'the dear uncle'

The exceptions to (1), if they were exclusively of this kind, would be principled rather than random: one could still maintain that (1) is generally valid except for sandhi-type conditioning, as we might call the conditioning of allomorphy by purely phonological properties of adjacent words, preferably within phonological words or phrases.

   What would be required, then, to falsify this more liberal version of the word-internality constraint are actual instances of allomorphy conditioned across grammatical word boundaries with morphosyntactic or lexical categories acting as conditioners. But would such empirical discoveries really enforce the abandonment or at least some further liberalization of this constraint on morphological structures? Not necessarily, because under certain circumstances form alternations thus conditioned need not count as instances of allomorphy in the first place. Some hypothetical examples should help us to gauge the scope of (1).

   Consider a language that is like Italian except that the initial segments of nouns alone determine the choice among the masculine definite article variants *lo/gli* and *il/i*; instead of the article variants in (3), we would thus get those in (3'):

   (3') *il stesso libro* - *lo caro zio*

Would *lo* and *il*, and *gli* and *i*, still be recognized as allomorphs?

Consider a language that is like English in that it has person/number agreement between subjects and finite verbs, but, unlike English, has alternative agreement markers with 3rd person singular subjects depending on the gender or sex of the subject:

(4) *He come-s - She come-t - It come-th*

Would *-s, -t,* and *-th* be recognized as allomorphs of the 3rd person singular agreement marker?

Consider a language that is like English except that its personal pronouns appear in different forms depending on the verbs whose objects the pronouns represent, as illustrated in (5).

(5) *Smith helps/trusts/follows him - Smith supports/watches/ pursues hin*

Would *him* and *hin* be recognized as allomorphs of the 3rd person singular masculine (direct) object pronoun?

Consider, finally, a language resembling English but having at its disposal four postpositional markers of 'genitive' noun phrases of which one, *is*, appears after singular common nouns or strong verbs at the end of genitive noun phrases (6a), another, *id*, after singular proper names or weak verbs (6b), the third, *ib*, after prepositions (6c), and the fourth, *im*, after plural nouns (6d).

(6) a. *the king/the king of this country/ the king we slew is successor*

b. *King Kong/ the king of England/the king we killed id successor*

c. *the girl you live with ib parents*

d. *the kings/the king of these countries/our children im friends*

Would *is, id, ib* and *im* be recognized as allomorphs of one attributive postposition?

If such form variants were regarded as allomorphic variants, their totally or partly morphosyntactic or lexical conditioning would be across grammatical word boundaries, contrary to the prohibition of the liberalized version of (1).

As is well known, there is no single notion of allomorphy on which morphologists unanimously agree, and it is only wise, therefore, not to be too specific in one's pronouncements on questions like those posed after the hypothetical examples above. Nevertheless, there would seem to be some basic consensus among standard conceptions of allomorphy concerning the extreme limits of this notion. Roughly, allomorphy is to do with the selection of forms alternatively realizing particular lexemes or morphosyntactic categories; different forms realizing different lexemes or different morphosyntactic categories are not usually regarded as allomorphs but as different morphemes. We may refer to Bazell (1949/1966) as one of the authorities to have codified this standard assumption:

> For morphemic unity it is necessary in the first place, that the limit between one expressive variant and another should not answer to the limit between one semantic variant and another, i.e. that no variation in the expression should be accompanied by a variation in content ... The mutual indifference of expressive and semantic variants is a necessary, but not of course a sufficient, criterion of the unity of a morpheme. (1966: 220)

Bazell goes on to comment on the conditioning of allomorphic ("expressive") and morphemic ("semantic") alternants, effectively postulating a word-internality constraint like (1) as well as suggesting an explanation of the different syntagmatic domains of conditioning:

> The expressive alternants are usually determined by the other morphemes within the same word, whereas the semantic alternants are usually determined by morphemes outside the word in which the semantic alternant of the morpheme is found. Typical examples are the variants of 'case-form' in different declensions, and the variations of 'case-value' with different verbal or prepositional rection. This is a consequence of the fact that the expressions of morphemes combine in an expressive unit, the word, whereas their meanings combine in a unit of meaning, which is not the word. (1966: 22)

Whatever value Bazell's explanation may have (for my part, I am not convinced that it is not circular), it is evidently the absence of a syntactic relationship between conditioned and conditioning formatives (e.g. between the variants of a particular case/number category and the host nouns belonging to various declension classes in languages such as Latin) which licenses the allomorphic interpretation of the conditioned form alternation even if it answers to a paradigmatic contrast involving the conditioner (between lexical classes of nouns in the declension-class example). That is, any word-internally conditioned form alternation may in principle count as allomorphic, whereas word-externally conditioned form alternations must meet additional requirements to be recognized as allomorphic rather than morphemic, specifically that of not answering to paradigmatic contrasts.

On this basis we can practically rule out an allomorphic interpretation of the *-s/-t/-th* and the *him/hin* alternations in our first two quasi-English examples. In (4) as well as in (5) the conditioning is word-external, and the (grammatical) words showing formal variation and the words conditioning this variation (or maybe rather the phrases containing these words) are linked by asymmetric syntactic relationships: the subject-verb and the verb-object relationships respectively, which could perhaps be identified at some more general level as a uniform relationship of dependency. If the form variations of one partner in such relationships, then, correspond precisely to morphosyntactic or lexical, i.e. any non-phonological paradigmatic distinctions pertaining to the other partner, one is entitled to assume that different morphosyntactic categories are being expressed by the formal variants, instead of having to take the alternative conditioned forms for alternative realizations of single morphosyntactic categories. These different morphosyntactic categories established by this reasoning can be assigned the function of expressing the syntactic relationship holding between the elements in the conditioning relation: in particular, they express these syntactic relationships in so far as they signal syntagmatic relatedness by means of answering to paradigmatic contrasts, i.e. agree with or are governed by contrasting elements elsewhere in syntagms. The alternants in these quasi-English examples would thus be interpreted as different morphemes rather than as allomorphs of one morpheme: *-s, -t,* and *-th* in (4) as forms for the different gender (or sex) categories of 3rd person singular agreeing with the corresponding subclassification of the subject; *him* and *hin* in (5), or maybe only their contrasting constituent parts *-m* and *-n,* as forms for different subcategories of (direct) objects of personal pronouns governed by different classes of verbal lexical items. A word-internality requirement such as (1) does not apply to such conditioned form variations simply because they are no instances of allomorphy.

It should be mentioned that what has been presented as the consensus view of the limits of allomorphy is not universally agreed on either. Among the dissenters one

even finds so prominent a theoretician as J. Kuryłowicz
(1949/1973, 1964), who calls the ablative and genitive
inflections of objects governed, or at any rate admitted,
by certain verbs in Latin (cf. 7) allomorphs of the more
usual accusative inflection of direct objects, 'des
variantes combinatoires de la désinence de l'accusatif
du régime direct, variantes conditionnées par les groupes
sémantiques des verbes qui régissent les cas en question'
(1973:138).

(7) *urb-e potiri - urb-is potiri - urb-em capere*
    'to take possession of the town (Abl./Gen./Acc.)'

This 'syntactified' notion of allomorphy strikes me as
decidedly non-standard, as do certain unusually wide
characterizations of this notion temporarily entertained
by one or the other of the early American structuralists.

The quasi-Italian example above is different from
the quasi-English patterns (4) and (5). The words showing
formal variation, viz. the singular and plural definite
articles, and the words conditioning this variation, viz.
exclusively the head nouns, are also linked by an asymmetric syntactic relation, which might be called determination. Here the form variations of the articles, however,
do not correspond to any morphosyntactic or lexical
distinction pertaining to the head nouns nor to any other
paradigmatic contrast elsewhere in the whole syntagm, but
to a purely phonological distinction. It is due to the purely phonological nature of the crucial distinctive property, even if this property is one of a morphosyntactically identified class of words, that prevents an interpretation of the form alternation as manifesting a distinction of morphosyntactic or lexical categories. Since such
variants, thus, count as allomorphic according to the
standard view, despite their partly morphosyntactic word-external conditioning, their conditioning falls within the
jurisdiction of a word-internality constraint such as (1),
and is not licensed by the provisions its liberalized
version makes for sandhi-type conditioning. The same would
hold, for example, for form alternations whose conditioning
involves word-order rather than phonological distinctions.
If in a language similar to English, masculine singular
personal pronouns were found to take different forms
depending on whether the subject precedes or follows the
finite element, as illustrated in (8),

(8) *She admires him - Does she admire hin?/Not for a second has
    she admired hin*

it would seem difficult to associate a categorial distinction with the formal alternation between *him* and *hin* - unless of course the word-order alternation itself has some primary categorial significance.

The quasi-English pattern (6) is different again. This is a typical sandhi-pattern in so far as the word which happens to precede the postposition causes the form alternation. There is an asymmetric syntactic relation of dependency between noun phrases as a whole and the formally variable postposition governing them; but it is not the dependent noun phrase or its internal head noun which conditions the postpositional form variation: all words which may occur phrase-finally act as conditioners. This hypothetical pattern is entirely unlike sandhi-style conditioning, however, in so far as the conditioning properties of adjacent words are clearly morphosyntactic rather than phonological. Presumably such form alternations answering to paradigmatic contrasts of adjacent words with no, or no unique, syntactic relation to the words showing the form alternation should be regarded as allomorphic, and should be accepted as another pattern on which the liberalized constraint (1) has some bearing.

The overall conclusion so far is that the empirical scope of the word-internality constraint (1) is more limited than it might have seemed at first sight. Conditioning of allomorphy by purely phonological factors cannot, on empirical grounds, be prohibited from taking place across grammatical word boundaries. If the conditioning factors are morphosyntactic or lexical, the conditioning across word boundaries cannot, under the particular circumstances set out above, be prohibited by a constraint on morphological structures either, because under the relevant circumstances formal alternations fall outside the domain of morphology and within that of syntax. There is, however, a residue of patterns of word-external, not purely phonological or entirely non-phonological conditioning, exemplified by quasi-Italian article alternations (2/3') and quasi-English postposition alternations (6), where (1) appears to have empirical implications - provided such conditioning patterns cannot be ruled out on different grounds (e.g. by purely phonological constraints on the linear segmental distance between phonological conditioning factors and conditioned alternations). The empirical question, then, is whether patterns resembling in their essential features the hypothetical quasi-Italian and quasi-English ones are really unattested, as predicted by (1). (The alternation of singular definite articles *la* and *el* with feminine nouns in Spanish, discussed in

Plank 1984a, does not instantiate the conditioning pattern
(2/3'), because this alternation is conditioned by the
initial segment of feminine nouns only if these are adjacent to the article, and, moreover, is not allomorphic but
a manifestation of syntactic disagreement. The alternation
of segmental nominative markers in Somali, which, as outlined in Banti 1984, is determined by various morphosyntactic properties of all kinds of words at the end of
nominative-marked noun phrases, seems comparable to
pattern (6), except that from Banti's account it is not
clear that the Somali nominative marker really is separated from the preceding word by a grammatical word
boundary.)

But rather than to embark on a cross-linguistic search for
examples that would help decide this empirical question, I
shall devote the remainder of this paper essentially to
the examination of a single pattern of formal alternation
in English, viz. the alternation of stem-final voiceless
and voiced fricatives in nouns such as *wife - wives* [f - v],
mouth - mouths [θ - ð], *house - houses* [s - z]. In particular,
I shall argue that general considerations about the limits
of allomorphy and constraints on the conditioning of formal
alternations are able to illuminate the evolution of this
pattern. Attention will also be paid to variations of the
marking of 'genitives', i.e. of the category that is of
primary diachronic importance for voice alternation.

To begin with, it is not self-evident how best to
describe the voice-alternation pattern in Modern English.
The observational basis includes the following facts:
(a) A set of nouns with stem-final voiceless labiodental,
dental, or alveolar fricative have the corresponding
voiced fricative when accompanied by a regular plural
suffix; (b) this alternation is most productive with labiodental, less productive with dental, and least productive (in fact restricted to a single noun: *house*) with
alveolar fricatives; (c) among the partial regularities
which help to specify which nouns will show this alternation is the phonological one designating noun stems with
long vowels or diphthongs, and with short vowel plus /l/
in the case of final /f/ (cf. *elf, shelf, self*), as the most
likely candidates; (d) a further regularity excludes non-
Germanic nouns (such as *chief, paragraph;* partial exception:
beef) and nouns whose spelling indicates that their final
/f/ has developed relatively late from /x/ (such as *cough,
laugh*) from this alternation; (e) a number of nouns vacillate between voiced and voiceless fricative in the plural
(e.g. *hoof, oaf, self, scarf, beef, youth, truth, oath,* in American
English also *house*), reflecting an overall diachronic tendency towards the levelling of voice alternation; (f) no

noun shows voice alternation when followed by the genitive marker, whose alternants /s - z - ɪz/ are formally identical to the regular plural alternants (cf. *my wife's knives* etc.), (g) nor when followed by reduced enclitic forms of the verbs *is* and *has,* whose alternants are the same as those of the regular plural and the genitive (cf. *My wife's here too, My wife's been told that...*). For present purposes we may ignore to what extent this voice alternation applies to non-nominal stems: it is categorically excluded with verbal inflections of the same form as the regular plural marker (cf. *he knifes/*knives*), and it is sporadic in certain derivational patterns (cf. *thief - to thieve - thievish*, but *leaf - to leaf - leafy*).

One possibility to account for these observations - the one that seems to me preferable and has recently been defended against alternatives by Lieber (1982) - is to assume two equally basic stem allomorphs of the nouns which exhibit voice alternation (i.e. /waɪf - waɪv/, /mauθ - mauð/, /haus - hauz/etc.), and to make the selection of the voiced alternant of these stems contingent on the presence of a following plural marker. The strongest motivation for this purely allomorphic solution that involves no general morphonological rules but at best a set of lexical correspondence statements comes from the essential unpredictability of the individual nouns which partake in voice alternation. It does not account very well for the partial regularities noted above (b, c, d), nor for the fact that the relevant stem alternants do not really differ radically from one another (as do stem allomorphs such as *go - wen(t)*) but only in one phonological feature of their final fricative. The purely allomorphic description further fails to acknowledge the at least partly phonological rationale of voice alternation: in the absence of a rule of voice assimilation, it looks like an accident that the regular exponents of the morphological category, plural, which conditions the stem allomorphy, turn out to agree in voicedness with the final segment of the stem allomorphs they co-occur with. Nevertheless, it is obvious that the conditioning does involve the morphological category of plural and is not purely phonological. The conditioning, moreover, is strictly local: it does not take place at a distance nor across a word boundary.

An alternative descriptive solution would be to take one variant of the relevant noun stems as basic, and to derive the other by morphonological rule - by a rule of fricative devoicing if, somewhat implausibly (despite Householder 1971:111ff.), voiced variants are assumed as basic, or by a rule of fricative voicing if, more plausibly, voiced variants, the citation forms, are assumed as basic. A further alternative (suggested by Harris 1942/1966) would be to take neither of the actual stem variants as basic, but rather to derive, by morphonological rules, both variants from a common base form whose final fricative is unspecified as to the feature of voicing. (See Lightner 1968: 58-60 and Zwicky 1975: 149-152 for brief discussions of these alternatives.) As they involve rules rather than only individually listed stem alternants, these solutions are obviously better equipped to deal with the partial regularities of voice alternation. Another advantage claimed by Strauss (1984) for the fricative-voicing solution is that basic forms such as /wæɪv/ would violate a putative morpheme structure condition requiring retracted [ɑɪ] before [v] (cf. with [ɑɪ] *hive, dive, drive* etc.) but [æɪ] before [f] (as in the pronunciations of both *wife* and *wives*); hence forms such as [wæɪvz] can only be non-basic, derived by a morphonological rule of fricative voicing triggered by plural marking. Irrespective of the merits of this particular argument, it should be noted that the rule solutions share essential features with the allomorphy solution: the conditioning involves a morphological category, viz. plural (in fact, in the case of the implausible final-devoicing solution, devoicing would occur *unless* nouns are in the plural); and the formal variation conditioned by plural must be limited to a phonological no doubt partly arbitrary set of nouns. In this last respect the impression of regularity created by rule statements is thus to some extent illusory.

The following discussion is in terms of conditioned allomorphy. If we had adopted one of the alternative descriptive solutions, the constraints we are primarily interested in here would be ones pertaining to the morphological conditioning of morphonological rules - which may after all not be an entirely different issue from that concerning the conditioning of allomorphy.

Of particular diachronic interest are observations (a), (f), and also (g) above. As is well documented in the handbooks (e.g. Jespersen 1942: 258-266), the voiced allomorphs conditioned by the regular plural in present-day English, if with slowly decreasing frequency, once also occurred before the segmentally identical genitive markers. Needless to emphasize, the historical period referred to here is not the one where stem-final voiceless fricatives (as in Middle English *wif*) were voiced intervocalically (as in *wives* Plural/Genitive Sg.) by a regular phonological rule, but a later one where this voice alternation of stems had become morphologically conditioned.

Such a voice alternation between basic noun forms and genitives was widespread in late Middle English once the alveolar fricative formatives had been generalized as the common genitive marker, had (between the 14th and the 16th century) become voiced like /s/ everywhere else in unaccented syllables, and had lost their unaccented vowel except after a sibilant, requiring the assimilation of /z/ to a preceding voiceless segment. It was still the norm in certain editions of Shakespeare at least with stem-final labiodental fricative (cf. e.g. *for my wiues sake, my liues counsell, at the staues end*), but was levelled entirely in later Modern English, with things apparently coming to a head in Elizabethan times and with only a few nouns retaining occasional voiced stem allomorphs until the end of the 18th century, especially in fixed compounds (such as *calves-head, knives-point*). During the period where genitive and plural markers both conditioned this voice alternation of certain noun stems the verbs *is* and *has* could take the same phonological forms as these markers, but were usually enclitic to pronouns (or vice versa: *'Tis* instead of *It's*) rather than to nouns. So far as I was able to determine, there are no instances of nouns with final voiced fricative conditioned by reduced enclitic forms of these verbs.

Thus, what demands an explanation is, firstly, why the voice alternation was given up with the genitive but was by and large retained with the plural, after it had been equally characteristic of these two categories in late Middle and early Modern English, and, secondly, why it was given up with the genitive at a particular time, viz. essentially in the Elizabethan period. And, thirdly, one is also entitled to wonder about a non-event: the apparent failure of voice alternation ever to be extended to nouns followed by reduced enclitic forms of *is* and *has*. Of course, what has and has not happened may have been historical accidents, in which case the search for explanations would be in vain. On the whole, however, it seems intellectually more satisfying to start from the assumption that patterns of language behaviour are or are not modified for particular reasons, and that some modifications may even be historically inevitable given the right circumstances.

In the case at hand, I am not the first to ask for reasons why the history of later Modern English has taken the direction it took. Jespersen offered this explanation for the levelling of voice alternations with the genitive but not with the plural:

the power of analogy, which was here [with the
genitive - FP] stronger [than with the plural]
because the genitive ending was felt to be a
looser addition than the pl[ural] ending ...,
has now introduced the voiceless sound with
scarcely any exception (1942: 264)

If the *s* of the genitive is more loosely connected
with the word it belongs to than is the *s* (or other
suffix) of the plural, that is the reason why it
tolerates no change in the body of the word
(1918/1960: 332)

This explanation, he assumes, also accounts for the selective levelling of allography of nouns spelled with final *y*: cf. *lady* - *ladies* (Pl.) - *lady's* (Gen.), which used to be spelled *ladies* in earlier Modern English as well (1960:332). In fact, Jespersen is fairly specific about what he means by 'looseness of an addition/connection'. From the next chapter (ch. XVII) of the same volume of his *Modern English grammar* it becomes obvious that 'genitive ending' in our first quote cannot have been intended as a technical term in the sense of 'case morpheme bound to nominal stems' (i.e. 'case suffix'), because there Jespersen takes great care to show that the genitive marker has developed into a rather unaffixlike type of marker which he calls 'interposition', on account of its occurrence at the end of whole attributive phrases and before their heads. In his *Chapters on English* he also uses the term 'interposition' ('partly a suffix as of old, partly a prefix', 1960:331f.), but in addition draws typological comparisons: the uniform genitive marker *s* (with alternants /ɪz - z - s/), having ousted all other original genitive suffixes of the various Old English declension classes, reminds him of 'those endings in agglutinating languages like Magyar, which cause no change in the words they are added to, and which need only be put once at the end of groups of words' or of 'the so-called empty words of Chinese grammar' rather than of a typical inseparable inflectional suffix of flexional languages (1960:335).

The general law Jespersen apparently had in mind here is that 'endings' are the unlikelier to condition stem allomorphy (and allography) the more independent they are of stems - which is reminiscent of our word-internality constraint (1). If Jespersen's observation about the different conditioning capacities of 'endings' in flexional and in agglutinating languages should prove valid (as it may well do), this need not perforce invalidate our version of the constraint: agglutinative 'endings', unlike flexional ones, may turn out to be separated by grammatical word boundaries from the elements they phonologically lean on. But regardless of whether the constraint on the conditioning of allomorphy is stated in terms of word boundaries or, more generally, in terms of some other notion of relative independence, it is not entirely above suspicion, as was argued in the first part of this paper. Hence its explanatory value should not be taken on trust, despite the appeal it had for Jespersen. One must agree with Jespersen, though, that the changing conditioning behaviour of the genitive 'ending' is somehow a consequence of a change in its formal and functional status; and it is therefore appropriate briefly to recapitulate the metamorphoses of this relational marker.

At stage 1, which is actually a complex sequence of stages spanning Old and most of Middle English, -(e)s was a genitive singular morpheme bound to certain masculine and neuter noun stems and later generalized to all noun stems, i.e. an impeccable inflectional suffix cumulatively expressing case and number, whose evolving formal variants /ɪz - z - s/ were regular phonological alternants, as were voicing variations of stem-final fricatives. In fact, in the later phases of this stage, with the generalization of -(e)s also to the genitive plural of nouns that utilized umlaut rather than a suffix to encode plural (cf. e.g. Middle English *man* Sg. - *mannes* Gen. Sg. - *men* Pl. - *mennes* Gen. Pl.), the cumulative character of this marker began to be eroded. Due to its presence also with a particular type of plural nouns, -(e)s began to be interpretable as a pure genitive marker, with a zero alternant appearing in the plural whenever a noun formed its plural by suffixation rather than umlaut (cf. e.g. Middle English *book - bokes* Gen.Sg./Pl./Gen.Pl., *oxe* Sg. - *oxes* Gen.Sg. - *oxen* Pl./Gen.Pl., morphologically *bok-es-∅, ox-en-∅* Stem-Pl.-Gen. vs. *menn-es* Stem (Pl.)-Gen.).

At stage 2, spanning late Middle and early Modern English, with its first symptoms appearing in the 13th century and with its full bloom coming in the 15th, 16th, and 17th centuries, we have a marker of the attributive syntactic relation that is no longer bound to the stem of the internal head nouns of attributive phrases but occurs at the end of entire attributive phrases preposed *in toto* to their heads. The clearest evidence for the conversion of the word-marker -(e)s into a phrase-marker is the appearance of 'group genitives' (9a), and also of spellings such as (*h*)*is,* (*h*)*ys,* '*s,* resembling those of the 3rd person singular masculine possessive pronoun (9b).

(9) a. *for your bothes peynes, of the quene his modres owne brestis, your worship & the childis auaille, my wife and childrens ghosts*

b. *the quene ys modyr, her Grace is requeste, at þare ditch his grunde, Winchestre his toun*

One causal factor in this reanalysis of an inflectional suffix (i.e. a morphological marker) as a phrase-final (i.e. a syntactic) marker, in the course of a word-order change gradually outlawing the extraposition of parts of an attributive phrase after the head (as in *the wyues loue of Bathe*), indeed was the homophony with the 3rd person singular masculine possessive pronoun (*h*)*is*, which had acquired the same phonologically conditioned *h*-less alternants as the genitive marker (as reflected in Shakespearian spellings such as *Put off's cap, kiss his hand*), and also the functional similarity to this possessive pronoun, which could link possessor and possession phrases in anacoluthon (cf. *euery man that eateth the sowre grape, his teeth shall be set on edge*) and in ditransitive constructions (cf. *þet tu wult... reauen God his strencðe*). As a result of this reanalysis, two formerly distinct elements, a possessive pronoun and a genitive marker, became virtually indistinguishable in attributive constructions. (See Jespersen 1960:336-345 for a detailed account of this development, and more recently also Janda 1980, who seems to believe he is the first to appreciate the significance of this conversion of a morphological into a syntactic marker. Further, in my opinion inconclusive, discussion of the present status of 'genitive' *'s* may be found in Hansen 1970:273ff.) Notice, however, that the attributive marker at this stage is invariably /ɪz - z - s - ∅/, i.e. does not vary with the gender, person, and number of the possessor in the manner of a possessive pronoun. As to the alternants of the attributive marker, note that zero at this stage is further limited to nouns taking the regular plural suffix (cf. e.g. *oxens*, morphologically *ox-en-s* Stem-Pl.-Gen., instead of *ox-en-∅* as at stage 1), which reinforces the impression that this marker is no longer cumulatively encoding a syntactic relation and number, but has purely relational function, even though it remains partly, on account of the distribution of its zero alternant, sensitive to the expression of number.

At stage 3, which partly coincides with stage 2 and is gradually phased out in the 18th and early 19th centuries, the attributive relation is encoded more indirectly by a cross-reference marker that is syntactically associated with head phrases and varies with the gender, person, and number of the possessor:

(10) a. *the daulphin of France his power, Harlesdon ys name*
b. *Juno hir bedde, the Queenes Majestie her request*
(illustrating two kinds of attributive marking)
c. *Me (poore man) my Librarie*
d. *Canterbury and Chillingworth their books, Estrangers their ships*

In so far as it could be seen as continuing a traditional habit (cf. e.g. *Asia & Europe hiera landgemircu togædre licgað* Ælfred, Oros.), this cross-referential attributive construction is no genuine early Modern English innovation out of the blue. On the other hand, its usage seems to become much more popular in this period, somewhat later than the merger of the original genitive marker and the 3rd person singular masculine possessive pronoun at the zenith of stage 2. It is only at this stage 3 that the marker continuing the original genitive singular suffix -(e)s entirely loses its sensitivity to plural, because forms expressing a different morphosyntactic category, viz. plural, rather than number-sensitive alternants expressing a single category, are chosen with plural possessors (cf. 9d).

At stage 4, continuing without any clear-cut boundary stage 2 since the 18th century, the attributive marker again forsakes agreement variation. The essential difference to stage 2 lies in the reassertion of the distinction between an attributive marker and the 3rd person singular masculine possessive pronoun, also reflected by changes in the alternants of the possessive pronoun, which dropped its non-syllabic variants. Jespersen claimed justification for his characterization of this marker as an interposition from its resistance to occur phrase-finally if there was no head immediately following the attributive phrase, as in examples of his such as *The entire turmoil had been on Lem's account and nobody's else* or *There shall nothing die of all that is the childrens of Israel* (1942:298). Since this resistance has certainly lost much of its vigour and 's now occurs relatively freely in phrase-final position without a following head phrase, this attributive marker is presumably best categorized as a postposition of attributive phrases, to the last element of which it is enclitically attached. Nida's (1949:104f.) attempt to defend the suffixal rather than enclitic categorization of this 's strikes me as misguided: not only must Nida himself admit that 's combines with all kinds of classes of forms rather than only with nouns and pronouns; his insistence that the external distribution class memberships of clitic combinations be numerous, moreover, seems exaggerated, because only very few forms that can be considered clitics on other grounds appear to meet this criterion. (See also Carstairs 1981:3ff. for a defence of the clitic interpretation of *'s* .)

The fact of crucial relevance for present purposes is the transformation of the genitive marker from a word-level, i.e. morphological, to a phrase-level, i.e. syntactic, marker, which the erstwhile suffix -(e)s underwent at stage 2 and which has not been reversed at any of the subsequent stages. Since the end of the 18th century this fact has been orthographically acknowledged through the use of an apostrophe, but Jespersen recommends a more radical recognition when he suggests that 'there would be no great harm done if the twentieth century were to go the whole length and write, e.g., *my father s house, the Queen of England s power, somebody else s hat,* etc.' (1960:335f.). Clearly, occasional occurrences of plural markers on the last element of more or less fixed word-groups (as with *lady friends, postmaster-generals, whisky-and-sodas, grown-ups, son-in-laws,* etc. - see Jespersen 1942:298-300) do not suffice to demonstrate that plural marking too now operates at the phrase level: plural markers in English remain fairly typical suffixes bound to noun stems, even though they have ceased to be cumulative exponents of number and case. It is the transformation of the genitive marker which provides the perspective for the interpretation of the development of voice and other form alternations.

Evidently, if the attributive marker is separated by a grammatical (though not by a phonological) word boundary from the internal head noun or any other final word of attributive phrases, the conditioned alternations of its own form must be seen as being conditioned across a grammatical word boundary. As far as the alternation between the three forms with an alveolar fricative, /ɪz - z - s/, is concerned, regardless of whether it is handled allomorphically or phonologically (see Zwicky 1975 for a thorough survey of alternative analyses), its conditioning is of the straightforward sandhi variety, hence does not offend against any universal constraints. The same applies to the identical form alternations of the verbs *is* and *has*, when these are enclitic, their encliticization being subject to further non-phonological conditions. It seems fairly unobjectionable on general grounds for the same form alternation to be phonologically conditioned across as well as within grammatical word boundaries, especially if these do not correspond to phonological word boundaries. Thus, there is nothing unusual in the parallel alternation behaviour of the regular plural suffix, the attributive marker, and the enclitic auxiliaries in Modern English. (The evolving boundary differences, incidentally, are again reflected more faithfully in spelling; notice the absence of allographic alternants of the attributive marker after sibilants: *bus's* Gen. vs. *buses* Pl.)

What really seems rather unusual is the conditioning of the zero alternant of the attributive marker. The least worrisome alternation is the optional one between forms with alveolar fricative and zero with singular attributes, where zero may appear after and/or before words with final/initial alveolar fricative (cf. *Jesus'(s) parents, for fashion('s) sake*). Even though its conditioning may involve several factors not all of which are phonological, a (mor)phonological rule of haplology seems the best solution here. Complications begin with singular internal head nouns of complex attributive phrases whose final noun is in the plural:

(11) a. *a mother of five children's chance to re-marry, an owner of five geese's chance to sell them all*

b. *a mother of five girls' chance to re-marry, the compiler of indices' first rule of thumb*

If this final plural is irregular, the attributive marker appears in its regular forms (11a), but if it is regular, at least in so far as the plural suffix resembles the regular one (cf. *indic-es*, with /iz/ rather than /ɪz/), the attributive marker is obligatorily, rather than optionally, zero (11b). (Jespersen 1942:287 quotes a single example with non-zero attributive marking, *after a couple of miles's riding*, but this sounds decidedly odd.) Regardless of whether one prefers to handle this pattern in terms of a rule of haplology or in terms of allomorphy, the conditioning here is crucially morphological: to account for the distribution of zero, reference must be made to the category of regular plural rather than to the phonological environment of a preceding alveolar fricative, because an alveolar fricative, if not the last segment of a regular plural suffix, at best conditions optional haplology (cf. *the mother of Jesus'(s) chance to re-marry, the reader of theses'(s) first rule of thumb*). Things are getting even more intricate when the internal head nouns of attributive phrases are in the plural:

(12) a. *our children's friends, the addenda's main purpose, both sheep's owner, women's liberation*

b. **both geese's/geese' owner*, *two teeth's/teeth' loss*, *these theses's/theses' common denominator*

c. *the queens' mutual dislike, your wives' common denominator, these indices' main purpose*

d. **the Queens of England's common denominator*, *the queens of these countries' mutual dislike*, *the children of these women's/countries' education*

With irregular plurals we again encounter the regular forms of the attributive marker (12a), unless such plurals, while differing from their singulars, end in an obstruent, in which case, strangely enough, the postpositional attributive construction as such is prohibited, no matter which form the attributive postposition would take (12b). As before, the attributive marker is obligatorily zero after regular or semi-regular plurals (12c). (In dialects, a regular plural need not exclude the non-zero form of the attributive marker; cf. *the færmers's kye, other boyses head* etc. (Jespersen 1942:272).) Regardless of the regularity or irregularity of the plural of the internal head nouns of attributive phrases, and also of their final nouns, group genitives with plural heads, where plural and attributive markings are not associated with the same word (to use one of Zwicky's 1975:166 formulations of this constraint), are generally avoided (12d). Their prohibition is probably not quite categorical: when such marginal plural group genitives occur, as in the example quoted by Jespersen (1942:287), *three-quarters of an hour's journey*, it is the phrase-final noun rather than the internal head which determines the form of the attributive marker. The avoidance of plural group genitives, nevertheless, appears to argue against the assumption once popular among grammarians (such as Bullokar, Wallis, and Lane - cf. Jespersen 1942:272) that all that is needed here is a phonological or rather morphophonological rule of haplology ('duo s in unum coincidunt', as Wallis put it in 1653): examples like those in (12d), where the plural and attributive markers are not adjacent, with the latter hence being no possible victims of haplology, ought to be unobjectionable if this were the correct analysis.

Unlike the Old English genitive plural suffix *-a*, which presumably is its formal ancestor ($-a > -e > \emptyset$), the zero alternant of the Modern English attributive marker, whether or not it is analysed as a genuine allomorph of /ɪz - z - s/, thus is conditioned across grammatical word boundaries. Even though, on account of the causal involvement of the morphological category of plural, its conditioning is not of the pure sandhi type, which would exempt it from the word-internality constraint, it bears some resemblance to this type, much as the hypothetical pattern (6) above did. Firstly, it is hardly entirely coincidental that zero appears only after *regular* plural suffixes: after /ɪz - z - s/ (or /ɪz/) it makes more phonological sense to avoid another alveolar fricative than after other phonological segments. Secondly, even if this is partly covered up by the general aversion to plural group genitives (12d), it is the plural marking of the noun that happens to precede the attributive marker, rather than that of the internal head noun of complex attributive phrases, which conditions the choice of zero. That is, the morphological conditioning factor is associated with a word that by itself bears no syntactic relation, except that of linear precedence, to the word showing the conditioned alternation. Thirdly, differing from the hypothetical pattern (6), it is no categorial paradigmatic distinction as such which conditions the choice between zero and alveolar fricative forms of the attributive marker, but rather the distinction between alternative formal expressions of one morphological category, plural. In this last respect the alternations of the Modern English attributive postposition, thus, differ, for example, from the (non-allomorphic) alternation between the directional prepositions *in* and *nach* in German, which is conditioned by the categorial morphosyntactic distinction between place names with and without definite articles (cf. *in die* Sowjetunion - *nach* Russland 'to the Soviet Union/Russia'), resulting in a pattern of alternation that is cross-linguistically rather uncharacteristic of adpositions. The second and the third feature of the Modern English conditioning pattern certainly preclude an interpretation of the variants of the attributive postposition as syntactic agreement forms corresponding in number to the internal head noun of attributive phrases - which would be a cross-linguistically uncommon, if not unique pattern (if adpositions agree, they do so in person *and* number). This set of three properties, then, would seem to define the somewhat unusual circumstances where conditioning of allomorphy or similar form alternations must be admitted to take place across grammatical word boundaries, in violation of constraint (1) as liberalized above.

Given this further liberalization that is inevitable on empirical grounds, it could seem as if the present version of our word-internality constraint would also license the retention of voice alternation with genitive markers after their separation from noun stems by a word boundary (from stage 2 onwards), as well as the extension of this stem alternation to relevant nouns in subject phrases when followed by enclitic *is* and *has*. Here is the pattern that could accordingly be expected to have evolved from the original state of affairs:

(13) a. *my wive's tale, My wive's here too*

b. *the Wife of Bath's tale, The Wife of Bath's here too*

c. *the knife of my wive's blade, The knife of my wive's been found*

Note that in this hypothetical pattern it would always be the last noun of attributive or subject phrases, rather than only their internal head noun, which shows stem allomorphy when followed by the attributive marker or enclitic *is/has,* in the manner that is typical of sandhi-style conditioning. This is reminiscent of the conditioning of the zero alternant of the attributive marker dealt with above; but the two other factors that were also involved there have no parallels here. In so far as the conditioned stem-final fricative and the adjacent alveolar fricative of the conditioning attributive marker or enclitic *is/has* agree in voicedness, the conditioning does make phonological sense. It is, however, the voicing or devoicing of the attributive marker or enclitic *is/has* themselves that can be understood as being due to phonological assimilation to the stem-final segment rather than vice versa: that is, the phonological form of the morphologically conditioning elements depends on the phonological form of the morphologically conditioned element. And the conditioning factors here indeed would be morphological or morphosyntactic categories as such, viz. the presence of a particular attributive postposition or of 3rd person singular indicative present forms of enclitic *be/have,* rather than distinctions between alternative formal expressions of particular categories, as above. In the case of the attributive marker it seems legitimate to attribute the conditioning force to this marker as such rather than only to its non-zero alternants, because its zero alternant in fact never occurs adjacent to stem-final fricatives, hence is positionally prevented from manifesting its potential conditioning capabilities. Thus, contrary to initial appearances, the development of a pattern like that in (13) turns out not to be sanctioned by the liberalized version of the word-internality constraint to which we currently subscribe.

Consider now another hypothetical pattern which differs from (13) in that only the internal head nouns of attributive or subject phrases show voice alternation, but which *a priori* would seem an equally imaginable result of historical developments.

(14) a. *my wive's tale, My wive's here too*

b. *the Wive of Bath's tale, The Wive of Bath's here too*

c. *the knive of my wife's blade, The knive of my wife's been found*

Also imaginable would have been the evolution of a pattern differing from that in (14) in that internal head nouns show voice alternation only when immediately followed by the attributive marker or enclitic *is/has:*

(15) a. *my wive's tale, My wive's here too*

b. *the Wife of Bath's tale, The Wife of Bath's here too*

c. *the knife of my wife's blade, The knife of my wife's been found*

What is peculiar about (14) is that conditioning words cause the same effect whether they are adjacent to or distant from the stems showing the conditioned alternation. What is peculiar about (15) is that words capable of conditioning form alternations of head nouns sometimes do (when adjacent), but sometimes don't (when distant) cause this effect. In these respects they are different from plural markers, which are always adjacent to the noun stems (such as *wife, mouth, house*) whose allomorphy they condition and which, therefore, always cause this effect. Obviously, these differences relate to the fact that plural in Modern English is word-level marking, whereas the attributive postposition is a phrase-level marker and, like enclitic *is/has*, separated by a grammatical word boundary from the preceding word. Which brings us back to the question whether some constraint against the word-external conditioning of allomorphy is to be held responsible for the levelling of voice alternation with the attributive marker (as seems to have been Jespersen's opinion) and for its non-extension to enclitic *is/has.*

This may well be the correct explanation in the case of the non-extension. The words which would, always (14) or only in phrase-final position (15), show formal variation, viz. the relevant internal head nouns of subject phrases, and the words conditioning this variation, viz. the 3rd person singular indicative present forms of enclitic *is* and *has,* would be linked by an asymmetric syntactic relation, that of subject, which is also encoded by the finite verbs themselves, which agree with subjects in person and number. Despite this clearly word-external morphosyntactic conditioning, the form variation of head nouns would presumably still count as allomorphic, rather than, say, as syntactic agreement of subjects with finite verbs, because it is arguably the phonological realization of certain 3rd person singular indicative present enclitic verbs (viz. of *be* and *have*), rather than any non-phonological paradigmatic contrast pertaining to finite verb forms, to which the formal distinction of subject head nouns corresponds. In our discussion of patterns like the quasi-Italian one (3') above, we concluded that the word-external conditioning by phonological properties of morphosyntactically identified classes of words falls within the jurisdiction of the word-internality constraint. Therefore, the refusal of Modern English to endow enclitic *is* and *has* with the capacity of conditioning stem-final voicing of subject head nouns, as hypothetically illustrated in (14) and (15), is in accordance with this universal constraint.

The explanation of the levelling of voice alternation with attributive markers, however, seems to me to be outside the scope of this morphological constraint. Supposing the voiced stem allomorphs of internal head nouns had been retained with the enclitic attributive postposition, always (14) or only in phrase-final position (15), how would the resulting form variations between (singular) internal head nouns of attributive phrases and other nouns have been interpreted? According to our previous reasoning, they could not be interpreted allomorphically because it is a morphosyntactic distinction, viz. presence vs. absence of an attributive postposition, rather than a purely phonological distinction, which is reflected, across word boundaries, by the form variation concerned. Moreover, since the conditioning word, the attributive marker, syntactically governs the nouns (or rather the entire noun phrases headed by them) which would exhibit the formal variation vis-à-vis their occurrences in other syntactic environments, the conclusion would have to be that this is no instance of the selection of alternative forms realizing certain nominal lexemes (i.e. stem allomorphy) but rather an instance of the selection of different morphosyntactic categories associated with these lexemes. What is expressed by these morphosyntactic categories associated with nouns are the grammatical relations of these nouns, or the phrases headed by them, to other elements they are in construction with - and morphological markers with that function fit the usual criteria of the category of case. Thus, retained stem-form alternations conditioned by what used to be a genitive inflectional suffix but had turned into an attributive postposition would have become interpretable as an incipient system of case marking, amounting to the innovation of a 'postpositional' case syntactically governed by the attributive postposition and in paradigmatic opposition with what might be called the 'general' case, serving all other syntactic functions. This would be the most straightforward interpretation in particular of pattern (14). With pattern (15) one might have been slightly irritated by the lack of case marking on internal head nouns which do not occur at the end of attributive phrases. No major irritation should have been caused, however, by the limitation of this postpositional case marking to singular nouns, the relevant nouns appearing always with the voiced stem-final fricative in the plural: neutralizations of case distinctions with the marked member of the number opposition after all are nothing extraordinary.

Thus, since the patterns that would have resulted if voice alternation had not been selectively abandoned in later Modern English would not have been of the allomorphic type, the actual development cannot be explained by a general constraint on the conditioning of allomorphy. We must look elsewhere for an explanation of the levelling of voice alternation with the attributive marker. If it is to be accounted for in general terms, the constraint(s) needed must pertain to case systems. And there indeed are some such constraints that may be brought to bear on the development at issue.

The forms case marking can possibly take are no doubt subject to certain limitations. Note that the postpositional case in Modern English which would have been innovated if voice alternation had not been levelled with the attributive postposition, would have been expressed by segmental modification, viz. the voicing of stem-final fricatives, rather than by the addition of segments, i.e. by affixation (specifically suffixation), which is the most familiar method of encoding case distinctions. Still, segmental modification is cross-linguistically attested in this function, even though it is not nearly as widespread as affixal case marking, whose potential of encoding paradigmatic distinctions is inherently much greater. The skewed cross-linguistic distribution of segment-modifica-

tional and affixal case marking, nevertheless, suggests
an implicational universal:

> (16) In any language, case marking by means of
> segmental modification implies that affixes
> are also utilized in this paradigmatic domain.

In explaining this tentative descriptive generalization,
the greater distinctive potential and systematicity of
affixes appear to be key factors. In view of languages
such as Irish, where relation-coding heavily, though not
exclusively (cf. the 2nd declension feminine Gen. Sg. in
-e, the obsolescent Dat. Pl. in -(a)ibh), relies on initial
mutations, stem-vowel and final-consonant alterations,
the empirical validity of (16) perhaps should not be taken
for granted; the vast majority of case languages, however,
clearly confirm constraint (16). (See Plank 1984b for a
survey of the phenomenology of relation-coding.) The
retention of voice alternation in Modern English would
have created a pattern blatantly violating this constraint:
the only paradigmatic case distinction, between the general
and the postpositional case, would have been encoded by
segmental modification rather than affixation.

Another disadvantage of the incipient case system
might have been the limitation of the new postpositional
case to an arbitrary set of nouns, one that was definable
neither in morphological nor in phonological terms (not
all nouns ending in a voiceless fricative were taking part
in voice alternation even within word boundaries). On the
other hand, if this limitation was so undesirable, it
should have been possible in principle to extend the scope
of postpositional case marking by generalizing the formal
alternation to all nouns with final voiceless fricatives
or even to all nouns with final voiceless segments. No
such extensions are on the historical record, though.
Moreover, it would probably be rash to exclude as a matter
of universal principle case marking variation that is
sensitive to phonological properties or also to arbitrary
lexical distinctions of case-marked nouns. Admittedly,
however, limitations like those defined by the original
incidence of voice alternation in early Modern English
would be rather unusual for genuine and stable case systems.

As far as pattern (15) is concerned, which Modern
English could have ended up with but managed to steer
clear of, the prevention of case marking when internal
head nouns do not occur at the end of their phrases is
cross-linguistically uncommon. To be sure, patterns are
attested where internal head nouns are or are not case-
marked depending on their phrase-final or phrase-internal

position. In such patterns, however, it is always the
phrase-final word, head noun or other, which carries the
appropriate case marker, whereas in the hypothetical
pattern (15) noun phrases would remain without postpositional case marking altogether whenever their internal
heads happen not to be phrase-final. Thus, by assuming
a universal constraint on case-marking languages along
the lines of (17),

(17) The non-phrase-final position of internal head
nouns may (in particular with agglutinative
rather than cumulative case morphology) prevent
the case marking of these head nouns themselves,
but not that of the entire noun phrases containing such non-final heads.

we are able to rule out on principled grounds at least one
turn the history of Modern English might have potentially
taken.

A potent factor, finally, may have been a constraint
that sets limits to the categorial infrastructure of case
paradigms. If voice alternation had not been levelled
with the attributive marker, the incipient case system
would have included a single marked case governed by a
single attributive postposition, in paradigmatic opposition to the unmarked general case, taking the form of
basic noun stems and encoding all other grammatical
relations of noun phrases in construction with verbs and
adpositions. A case system of this kind appears to be
cross-linguistically highly unusual, possibly even unique.
Surveying the attested minimal, i.e. two-term, case
paradigms, one tends to encounter instances where one
general, or 'direct', case is either opposed to one
grammatical case encoding the core relations of object or,
more rarely, subject (and maybe subject/object complement),
or to one local or, more rarely, non-local adverbial case.
In either case, the noun phrases receiving the single
non-basic marked case tend to be in construction with
verbs and perhaps other lexical relational expressions
(such as nouns and adjectives), or also with both lexical
and grammatical (in particular adpositional) relational
expressions, but not exclusively with adpositions. The
prevailing paradigm infrastructures, thus, could seem to
justify this universal constraint:

(18) It is impossible for minimal case systems to
include, in addition to the basic general case,
only a single further case exclusively marking
noun phrases in construction with (adverbial/
grammatical) adpositions.

An adpositional case, accordingly, would imply the presence of a second grammatical or of an adverbial case marking noun phrases in construction with verbs or other lexical relational expressions. However, constraint (18) may turn out to be untenable in its present strict form: there in fact are languages, especially among the modern Indo-Aryan ones, where a single 'oblique' case coexists with a basic 'direct' case and predominantly marks noun phrases in construction with postpositions. To be more precise, the relevant languages (such as Hindi, Urdu, Marathi) usually boast a vocative as a third case, hence do not really have *minimal* case paradigms, and usually retain a few uses, if marginal ones, of the oblique case without a postposition, i.e. in construction with verbs. But regardless of whether or not the empirical evidence available suffices to overthrow (18), the oblique case in the languages potentially threatening to undermine the strict version of this constraint is employed with all postpositions, and is above all employed with the postpositions occurring at clause level rather than only with a single phrase-level attributive adposition. And a diachronic aspect of these somewhat unusual case systems also deserves to be mentioned: they are old rather than new, i.e. are the remnants of earlier richer case paradigms rather than innovations *ex* (morphological) *nihilo*.

Presupposing that a constraint such as (18) can be maintained in perhaps slightly modified form, it follows that a case governed by a single attributive postposition cannot be the first non-basic, marked case in the rise of a case system in any language. If later Modern English nouns had retained the *wife/wive*- type voice alternation with the attributive marker as well as with the plural, English would have innovated the very kind of minimal case system disallowed by this universal constraint. This innovation in English would have come about, not by the creation of some new formal device, but by the retention of a previously existing form alternation of noun stems. Given a constraint such as (18), it is understandable that this voice alternation was selectively levelled in the Elizabethan period: it was at this time that the word-marking genitive suffix had been re-analysed as a postpositional marker of attributive phrases that was no longer bound to noun stems. (Within the context of this paper it is instructive to see that Kelkar 1959:138, in his careful attempt to separate genuine cases from other kinds of relation coding in Marathi, wonders whether it might not be preferable to analyse oblique noun forms as grammatically conditioned allomorphs of direct noun forms rather than as proper case forms syntactically governed by postpositions. This (in my opinion questionable) move would eliminate potential counterexamples to the minimal-case-system constraint (18) while saddling the word-internality constraint on the conditioning of allomorphy with new problems.)

   A constraint such as (18) is no more than a descriptive generalization with (ideally) universal scope. As such, it serves the purpose of explaining, in some sense, why particular languages have the minimal case systems they have rather than any others, and of course also why they cannot innovate such conceivable alternative case systems. Ultimately one would wish to be able to explain such descriptive generalizations themselves. To indicate at least where to head for, this higher-level explanation of (18) presumably would have to focus on the functional basis underlying the formal distinction of casual and adpositional relation coding. Typically, adpositions are less systematically grammaticalized than cases, and have more specific relational content of their own compared to cases. Consequently, adpositions are predestined to encode the semantically more specific and more diversified relations of noun phrases outside the valency of verbs and other lexical relational expressions, whereas cases, while not excluded from the same domain, preferably encode the semantically less specific and less diversified valency-bound syntactic relations whose specific semantic content is supplied by verbs and other elements from the lexical fund. Adpositions may encode the valency-bound syntactic core relations of subject and object and perhaps attribute only if languages dispense with morphological case marking altogether; but if cases and adpositions coexist in a language, it is cases rather than adpositions which are employed with the core relations. If noun phrases take case marking when occurring in core relations governed by verbs and other lexical expressions, they will also do so when in construction with adpositions in syntactically more peripheral relations, even if this dual grammatical relation coding on single noun phrases would seem redundant (unless several adpositional cases may contrast). These two relation-coding devices may be employed redundantly as long as at least one of them has uses where it is not redundant. But to create and preserve a grammatical coding device that cannot be employed but redundantly - such as a morphological case marker co-occurring exclusively and non-contrastively with adpositional relation markers -, would seem to be too uneconomical a step to take under normal linguistic circumstances.

The pattern that was primarily at issue in this paper, the alternation of stem-final voiceless and voiced fricatives of English nouns, admittedly is a minor and rather peripheral one, situated at the margins rather than the core of English grammar. But it is this marginality which renders it so instructive from the point of view adopted here, which aims to bring cross-linguistic generalizations to bear on structural regularities of particular languages. Usually only the *major* patterns of particular languages - for instance, general word order patterns, the overall morphological make-up, relational organization - are foregrounded within this comparative perspective. What I hope to have demonstrated with the present case study is that *minor* patterns of individual languages, and very marginal ones indeed, may likewise be determined by general, typological or universal, principles. However minor and peculiarly Modern English the pattern primarily discussed here and its development may seem, they can only be understood, or explained, in terms of universal constraints on morphological or rather syntactic structures - that is, by looking beyond English.

REFERENCES

Banti, G. 1984. 'The morphology of the nominative case in Somali'. *Fifth International Phonology Meeting, discussion papers* ed. by W.U. Dressler, O.E. Pfeiffer & J.R. Rennison, 27-31. Wien: Wiener Linguistische Gazette, Beiheft 3.

Bazell, C.E. 1949. 'On the problem of the morpheme'. *Archivum Linguisticum* 1.1-15. (Reprinted in *Readings in Linguistics II* ed. by E.P. Hamp, F.W. Householder & R. Austerlitz, 216-226. Chicago: University of Chicago Press, 1966.)

Carstairs, A. 1981. 'Notes on affixes, clitics and paradigms'. Bloomington: Indiana University Linguistics Club.

Hansen, K. 1970. 'Zur Kategorie des Kasus im modernen Englisch'. *Zeitschrift für Anglistik und Amerikanistik* 18.262-282.

Harris, Z.S. 1942. 'Morpheme alternants in linguistic analysis'. *Language* 18.169-180. (Reprinted in *Readings in Linguistics I* ed. by M. Joos, 109-115. Chicago: University of Chicago Press, 1966, 4th edn.)

Householder, F.W. 1971. *Linguistic Speculations*. Cambridge: Cambridge University Press.

Janda, R.D. 1980. 'On the decline of declensional systems: The overall loss of OE nominal case inflections and the ME reanalysis of *-es* as *his*'. *Papers from the 4th International Conference on Historical Linguistics* ed. by E.C. Traugott, R. Labrum & S. Shepherd, 243-252. Amsterdam: Benjamins.

Jespersen, O. 1918. 'Chapters on English'. Reprinted in *Selected Writings of Otto Jespersen*, 153-345. London: Allen & Unwin/Tokyo: Senjo, 1960.
Jespersen, O. 1942. *A Modern English Grammar on Historical Principles. Part VI: Morphology*. London: Allen & Unwin/Copenhagen: Munksgaard.
Kelkar, A.R. 1959. 'The category of case in Marathi. A study in method'. *Indian Linguistics* 19. 131-139.
Kuryłowicz, J. 1949. 'Le problème du classement des cas'. *Biuletyn Polskiego Towarystwa Jezykoznawczego* 9. (Reprinted in his *Esquisses Linguistiques 1*, 131-150. München: Fink, 1973, 2nd edn.)
Kuryłowicz, J. 1964. *The Inflectional Categories of Indo-European*. Heidelberg: Winter.
Lieber, R. 1982. 'Allomorphy'. *Linguistic Analysis* 10.27-52.
Lightner, T.M. 1968. 'Review of *Readings in Linguistics I* ed. by M. Joos (1966)'. *General Linguistics* 1.44-61.
Nida, E.A. 1949. *Morphology. The Descriptive Analysis of Words*. Ann Arbor: University of Michigan Press, 2nd edn.
Plank, F. 1984a. 'Romance disagreements: Phonology interfering with syntax'. *Journal of Linguistics* 20.329-349.
Plank, F. 1984b. 'Identifying case'. Unpublished manuscript.
Strauss, S.L. 1984. 'The morphological conditioning of phonological rules'. *Fifth International Phonology Meeting, discussion papers* ed. by W.U. Dressler, O.E. Pfeiffer & J.R. Rennison, 245-248. Wien: Wiener Linguistische Gazette, Beiheft 3.
Zwicky, A.M. 1975. 'Settling on an underlying form: The English inflectional endings'. *Testing Linguistic Hypotheses* ed. by D. Cohen & J.R. Wirth, 129-185. New York: Wiley.

A NOTE ON THE VOICING OF INITIAL FRICATIVES IN MIDDLE ENGLISH

PATRICIA POUSSA
University of Helsinki

In his paper on the voicing of ME initial fricatives in *SAP* 1984, Fisiak argues that the voicing of /f-/ to /v-/, /s-/ to /z-/, /θ-/ to /ð-/ and /ʃ-/ to /ʒ-/, which were found together in the same south western districts in Modern English by the *Survey of English Dialects*, is to be regarded as a unitary phonetic process of weakening (lenition). Though the spelling system of ME gives us no evidence for the lenition of initial /θ-/ and /ʃ-/, he concludes that all these fricatives would have been subject to the same process in the OE and ME period also. /ʃ-/, which developed out of earlier OE /sk-/ (the change being complete by about the 10th century), is regarded as the last fricative to fall in with the process, which began in the south in the early OE period, and continued to spread northwards into ME times. The precise dating of these changes has not yet been firmly established. They are of course obscured by the standardized spelling of OE literary texts.

In his paper Fisiak summarizes the evidence of recent investigations, notably McIntosh and Samuels for the 15th century, and Kristensson for the 14th century, and concludes that the medieval border of the voicing of /f-/ and /s-/ (and by implication the other initial fricatives) must be placed much more to the north than has so far been accepted. (See Maps 1 and 2.)* The isoglosses based on Kristensson's previously unpublished onomastic evidence from the Lay Subsidy Rolls for the West Midlands between 1290 and 1350 give the most northerly boundary ever attested for this process. (Kristensson is still working on the East Midland counties.) McIntosh and Samuels' isographs, based on 15th century texts, suggest that the isophones were in the process of moving southwards again in the late ME period. Since writing is more conservative than speech, it is likely that the isophones had already

Map 1

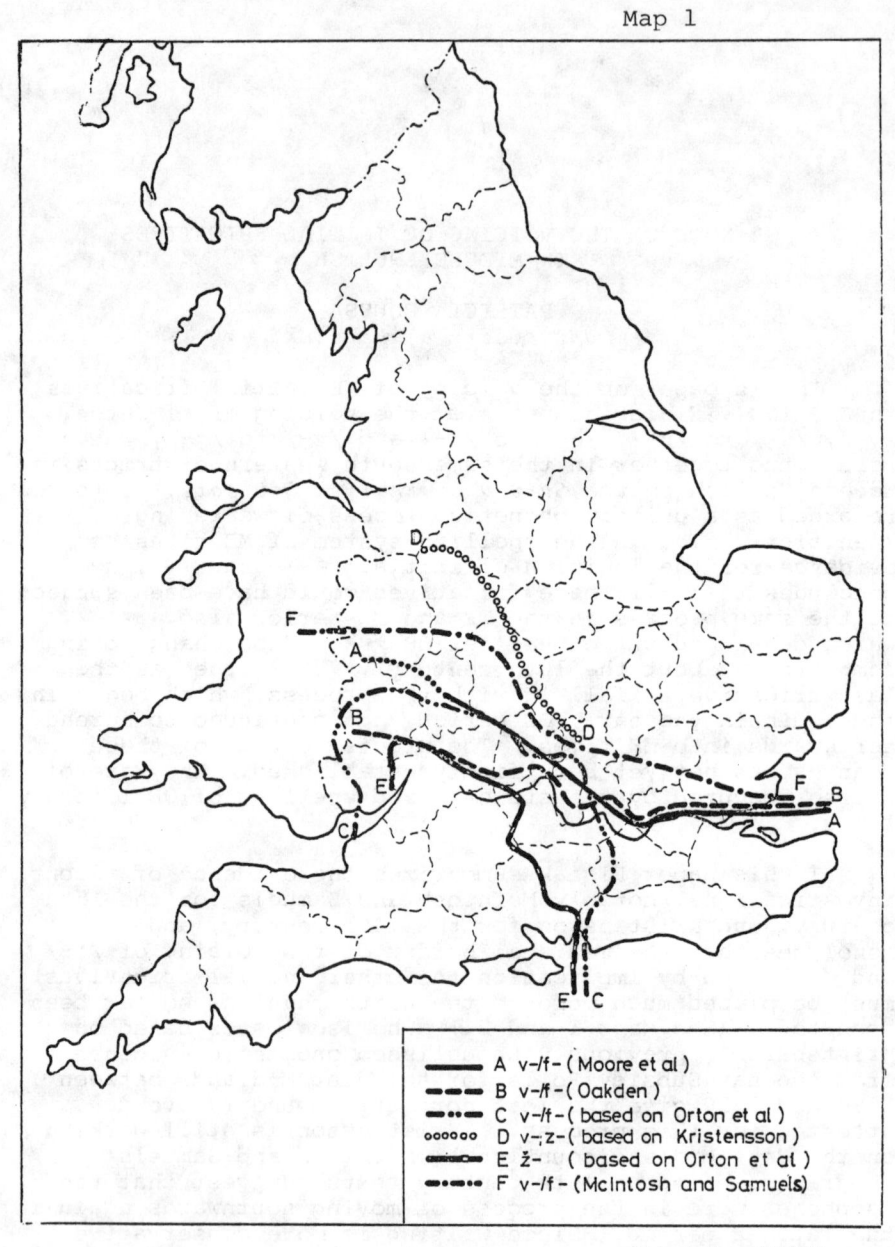

A v-/f- (Moore et al)
B v-/f- (Oakden)
C v-/f- (based on Orton et al)
D v-;z- (based on Kristensson)
E ž- (based on Orton et al)
F v-/f- (McIntosh and Samuels)

(Fisiak: 1984)

Map 2

MIDDLE ENGLISH
(XIV / XV c - McIntosh / Samuels)

● v-
○ z-

0   25 miles
0   50 kms

(Fisiak:1984)

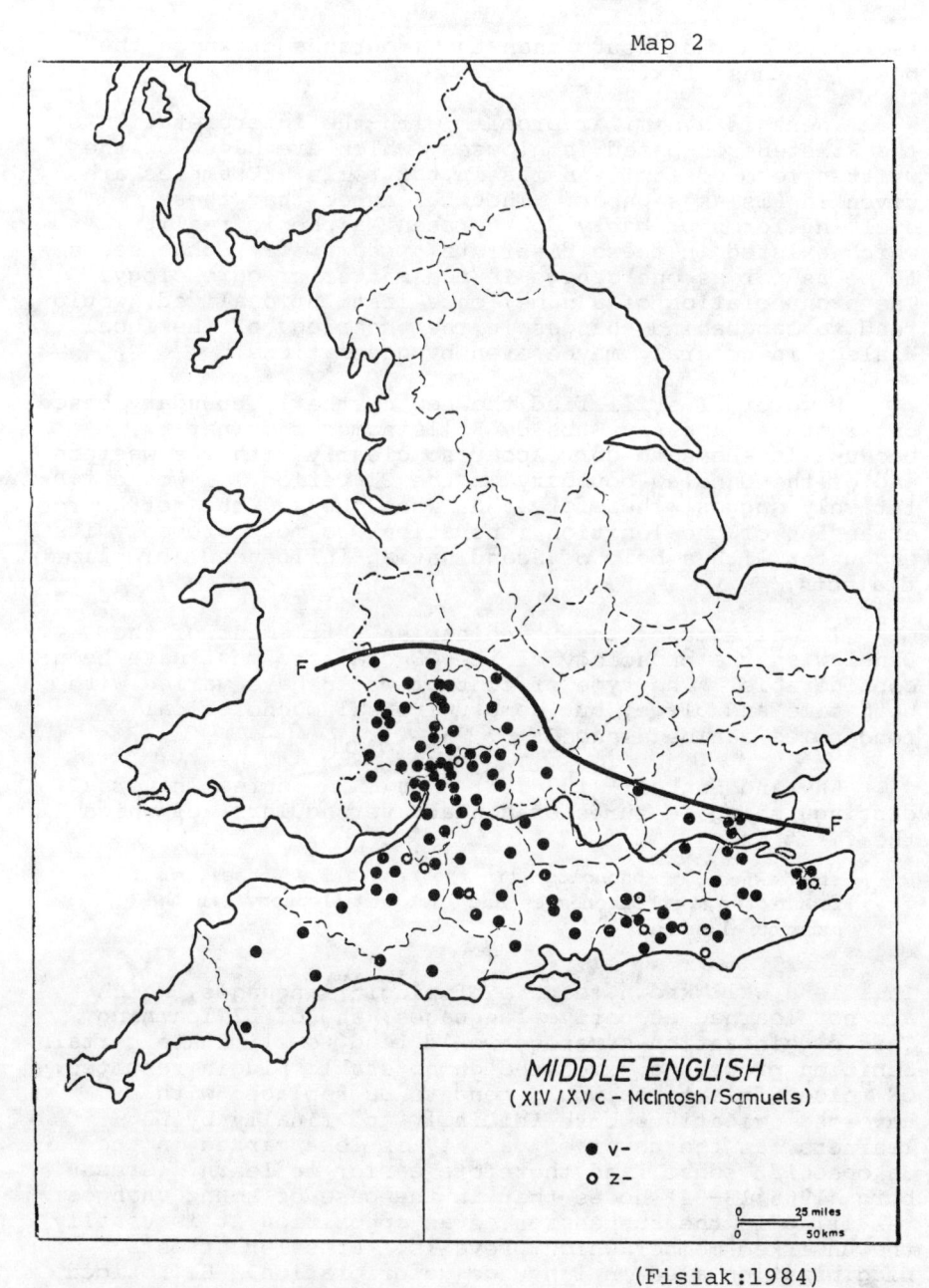

retreated further south than the isographs drawn on the basis of these texts.

There is a similar problem with the interpretation of the Kristensson-based isoglosses, which are based on the written form of family names in tax rolls. Examples are given in Fisiak's paper. Though I agree that these spelling forms probably do represent a phonic reality, which existed in these districts *at some time*, that seems to be as far as one can go in the matter of chronology. The pronunciation of a name, once institutionalized, would tend to lag behind changes in the phonology of the local dialect in general, maybe even by generations.

However, I still find the new northerly boundary based on Kristensson's Lay Subsidy Rolls names fascinating, because it seems to correspond so clearly with the western end of the Danelaw boundary in the OE period. I would tentatively suggest therefore that what checked the northward expansion of the lenition innovation was most probably its encounter with a belt of Scandinavian-influenced (creolized) dialects.[1]

The effects of the Scandinavian settlement of the Danelaw on the phonology of the OE dialects must have been considerable. The type of contact would have varied with both time and place, but some universal phonological tendencies can be assumed.

Kay and Sankoff (1974:61) enumerate three universal distinguishing features of contact vernaculars, of which the first is:

> shallowness of phonology (in the generative sense), or restricted morphophonemics and lack of allophony (in the structural sense)

This is a well known feature of pidgin languages, which are not learned as native languages, and of L2 learning. This pidginization strategy would tend to eliminate certain lenition processes, even though no stable pidgin resulted. OE voiced fricatives would tend to be replaced with unvoiced fricatives both initially and finally by L2 learners, as the unvoiced variety is less marked in the Jakobsonian sense, and therefore easier to learn. Greenberg (1966:13-24) notes that in the case of sound changes resulting in the suspension of an opposition it is usually the unmarked member which prevails. Dressler attests pidginization also in language deterioration. He noticed in the Breton of young French-Breton bilinguals a sudden admittance of natural phonological processes which are not permitted by either of the full languages (Dressler 1977: 32). Given input containing rules of this sort, the next generation of children would be likely to adopt this innovation to an increasing degree. As Slobin puts it:

> It seems, given the limited but suggestive evidence, that it is adult speakers who invent new forms, using them with some variability in their speech. Children, exposed to this variability, tend to make these new forms obligatory and regular. (Slobin, 1977:205)

This process would come under the definition of creolization, in my opinion, if it also involved accelerated simplification in different components of the grammar, together with language mixing and language shift, through the agency of children. In the nature of things a creolization situation is always going to be messy, a matter of more or less, but it seems to me that language death is an obligatory element in the situation.[2]

Settlers in densely Scandinavianized parts of England, where bilingualism prevailed, would have had another option open to them in speaking English: to relexify their language to English, while retaining their own phonological system.

Moulton gives the following distributions for the relevant consonants of Old Icelandic and early West Saxon. (This is probably close enough to the languages used by the Scandinavians and English in the Danelaw of the ninth century for our purposes, though Moulton does not include the later OE developments which are unrecognized by the spellings.)

OI:

```
p-   -pp-   -p-   -p      t-   -tt-   -t-   -t      k-   -kk-   -k-   -k
f-   -ff-   -ƀ-   -ƀ      þ-   —      -ð-   -ð
b-   -bb-   ↑     ↑       d-   -dd-   ↑     ↑       g-   -gg-   -g-   -g
                          s-   -ss-   -s-   -s
m-   -mm-   -m-   -m      n-   -nn-   -n-   -n
                          l-   -ll-   -l-   -l
                          r-   -rr-   -r-   -r
v-   —      —     —       h-   —      —     —       —    —      -j-   —
```

OE:

```
p-  -pp-  -p-  -p    t-  -tt-  -t-  -t    ć-  -ćć-  -ć-  -ć    k-  -kk-  -k-  -k
f-  -ff-  -v-  -f    þ-  -þþ-  -ð-  -þ                         h-  -xx-   —   -x
b-  -bb-   —   -b    d-  -dd-  -d-  -d       -ġġ-   —   -ġ    g-  -gg-  -g-   —
                     s-  -ss-  -z-  -s
m-  -mm-  -m-  -m    n-  -nn-  -n-  -n
                     l-  -ll-  -l-  -l
                     r-  -rr-  -r-  -r
w-   —    -w-  -w                             j-   —   -j-  -j
```

(from Moulton, 1972: 150-153)

The initial fricatives /ð-/ and /ʃ-/ develop in later OE.

A comparison of the systems shows that the voiced/unvoiced distinction in the fricatives is different. In OI, [s] does not weaken to [z] as in WS. OI [f] does have a weak grade [ƀ] intervocalically, but it is unclear whether this is the same sound as WS [v]. [θ] does weaken to [ð] intervocalically in both languages, but the distribution is different. Moulton does not list in his inventory two fricatives which developed in the OE period, /ʃ/ and initial /ʒ/. Brunner, however, is of the opinion that the initial sounds of *the*, *that* and *this* were voiced in the OE period, as they are in Mod E (Brunner, 1960: 376). In Modern Icelandic there is no /ʃ/, and no words with initial /ð-/. In words beginning with /θ-/ in Mod I, it appears that the tongue tip may be slightly retracted from the position in Mod E, where 'the tip and rims of the tongue make a light contact with the *edge* and inner surface of the upper incisors' (Gimson 1970: 183, - my italics).[3]

For Old Danish at the same period, Skautrup gives the following fricative inventory:

```
b       ð                            q
b̥       þ      s (ss)    χ           h
```

The labiodental /f/ was a somewhat later development (Skautrup 1944: 125).

We can thus conclude that the fricative system of English would have caused difficulties to both groups of Scandinavian learners.

The best evidence for the phonology of an early ME Danelaw dialect is to be found in the spellings of the *Orrmulum*. McIntosh and Samuels have placed it in Stamford; Laing and Parkes suggest Crowland and Bourne respectively, both in S. Lincs. Suggested dates have generally been

early 13th century, but Parkes argues for the last quarter
of the 12th (Parkes 1983: 127). Orm's spellings for /θ~ð/
suggest that the phonetic realization is postdental and
unvoiced. Initial þ is regularly written t after a word
ending with d or t, so we have þe~te, þatt~tatt, þu~tu,
þær~tær, þe33~te33, þiss~tiss, etc. This assimilation
pattern would not be possible if þ in these words represented the same sound as Mod E /ð/, but is consistent with
Modern Icelandic initial /θ/. The other fricatives are
invariably spelled with f, s and sh, with no indication of
intervocalic voicing. (The doubled letters indicate a previous short vowel.) Examples of Orm's spelling are given
below. On the right, for comparison, are forms from *The
Thrush and the Nightingale*, a West Midland text (Brown
1932: 101-107).

	ORM	THRUSH & NIGHTINGALE
1.	33, *ferrs* 'verse'	
	39, *lofen*, 40, *lef*	1, *loue*
	73, *lufe off Gode heffne*	
	21, *hafe*, 51, *icc hafe*	79, *haue*, 85, *hauest*
		91, *heuede i-gon*
		96, *Icc habbe leue to*
	44, *wass biginnen*	
	36, *þe deofless walde*	
	61, *æfre* 'ever'	100, *neuere* 'never'
		120. *war* 'whether'

As Orm is so meticulous with his symbols for the different sounds normally represented by þ and 3, we may
suppose that his invariable use of the voiceless symbols
f, s, and sh means that there is no /f~v/, /s~z/, /ʃ~ʒ/
variation in his dialect, or at any rate it has not been
phonemicized, so has no psychological reality for the
speakers of this dialect.

Burchfield (1956: 69) comments:

> By and large a given word was to have one form
> throughout the work, and a given sound was always to be
> represented by the same graph.

Burchfield also remarks in the same passage on the
uniqueness of the *Orrmulum* MS in this respect, compared
to all other existing ME manuscripts:

> ... it had been decided in advance to write a given
> form in one way throughout, where all other contemporary
> English manuscripts display the casualness or indifference

of their compilers (1956:69-70).
Possibly the impetus for the work came from outside England. In Iceland, *The First Grammatical Treatise* had been written about half a century earlier. The same concern to achieve an unambiguous writing system is evidenced by both writers.

In sum, we may say that Orm's transcription of the fricative system of his dialect seems to be trustworthy, and is entirely consistent with what we would expect of a community which spoke English with a Scandinavian-influenced phonology. Even if Orm's manuscript did not exist, we could say that language acquisition universals, intersecting with the Scandinavian substratum, would predict this kind of result.

How much is to be ascribed to substratum effects, how much to language universals, is a debatable point. Recent research in SLA has tended to support the universals thesis. For example, Eckmann (1981) found that both Spanish and Chinese learners of English failed to produce final voiced obstruents. Spanish speakers devoiced, Chinese added a final schwa-like vowel. This was interpreted not as the transfer of a standard phonological rule from the native language, but a universal tendency, based on the physical nature of the speech organs. Gass and Ard (1984: 39) comment:

> This type of universal does have a strong effect on L2 learners and can in fact override facts of native and/or target languages.

Zobl (1978) discusses the interaction between developmental and transference phenomena in learners' interlanguage, and concludes that learners will be slower to abandon an interlanguage structure on their way to mastering the target language, if the interlanguage structure corresponds to a structure in their native language. The same would naturally apply to decreolization, which Andersen (1979) regards as comparable to second language acquisition.

Orm's dialect has, however, adopted /ʃ/, the result of the OE /sk-/ > /ʃ-/ sound-change. This suggests that the dialect described by Orm was already decreolizing. However, there were no doubt much broader lects than this to be heard. Bickerton (1981) warns of the dangers of relying on written texts of creoles, because the speakers are most likely bidialectal, and will adjust towards the superstrate. As creole continua change over time, the whole

system moves up, and the original creole is obscured. The
same general sociolinguistic argument would seem to apply
to the *Orrmulum*: if Orm was writing something fit to be
read in churches, it would not have been the broadest local
dialect. However, in more northerly ME dialects, as we can
see from *sk-* spellings, this /sk-/>/ʃ-/ sound-change was
either not adopted, or then was again supplanted by /sk-/.
In the sound systems of dialects which had /sk-/ but no
/ʃ-/, there would be phonological space for /θ-/ and /s-/
to shift backwards, so that /θ-/ might be realized as a
post-dental fricative, as in Modern Icelandic. This [s]
-like allophone of /θ-/ - might be phonemicized as /s-/ by
a new generation of speakers. Such a process would explain
the spread of the 3rd person *-es* verb inflection at the
expense of *-eþ* in northern ME. This phenomenon was
recorded earliest in 10th century glosses to the Lindisfarne Gospels. This development is not too early to be
ascribed to Scandinavian influence. This explanation is
suggested by Campbell (1959:301). In terms of distinctive
feature theory, the [θ]>[s] change would be a change of
Sonority Feature VIII, *Mellow* to *Strident*, i.e. acous-
tically, a change from lower intensity noise to higher
intensity noise (Jakobson and Halle 1956: 31). Such
a change would have been very noticeable to speakers from
districts which retained the mellow feature. Even in
modern dialects, there seem to be traces left by this sound
change. For instance, the pronunciation of the initial
fricative in the word *the* has remained distinctive in the
areas of heavy Scandinavian settlement up to modern times,
though the boundaries have receded since Orm's day.

Ellis, who gathered his material in 1869-74, considered the pronunciation of the initial fricative of *the* an
important dialect boundary. He based three of his Ten
Transverse Lines across the map of England on this feature.
(Ellis 1890: 6-9 and frontispiece.) Ellis' isoglosses for
the are given in Map 3. I have interpreted Ellis' 'suspended *t*' as an unexploded stop, or as a glottal stop.
Though the accuracy of Ellis' isoglosses is questionable
because of his method of sampling, yet his evidence for the
occurence of *t* and 'suspended *t*' forms within the area of
lines 7 and 4 is valuable. The pronunciation of *the* is
still popularly regarded as an indexival form, as in the
stereotype stage Yorkshireman's 'trouble up at t' mill'.[4]
In this connection we may compare the *LAE* maps for the
initial cluster in the words *three* (Map 4) and *thread*,
which show /dr-/ in the south west, and pockets of /tr-/ in
East Anglia and the north east. They have presumably
developed from /ðr-/ and /θr-/ respectively.

Map 3

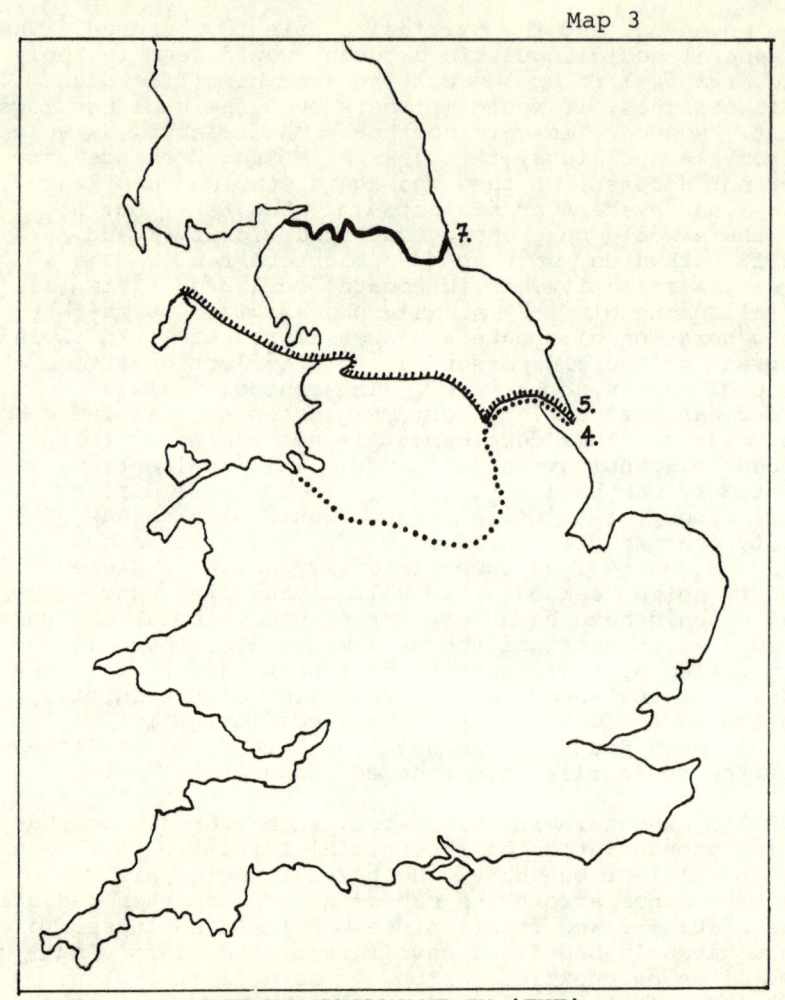

INITIAL CONSONANT IN 'THE'

7. Northern limit of [t]
5. Northern limit (in England) of [ð].
4. Southern limit of [θ] and 'suspended t'
(After Ellis: 1890)

Map 4

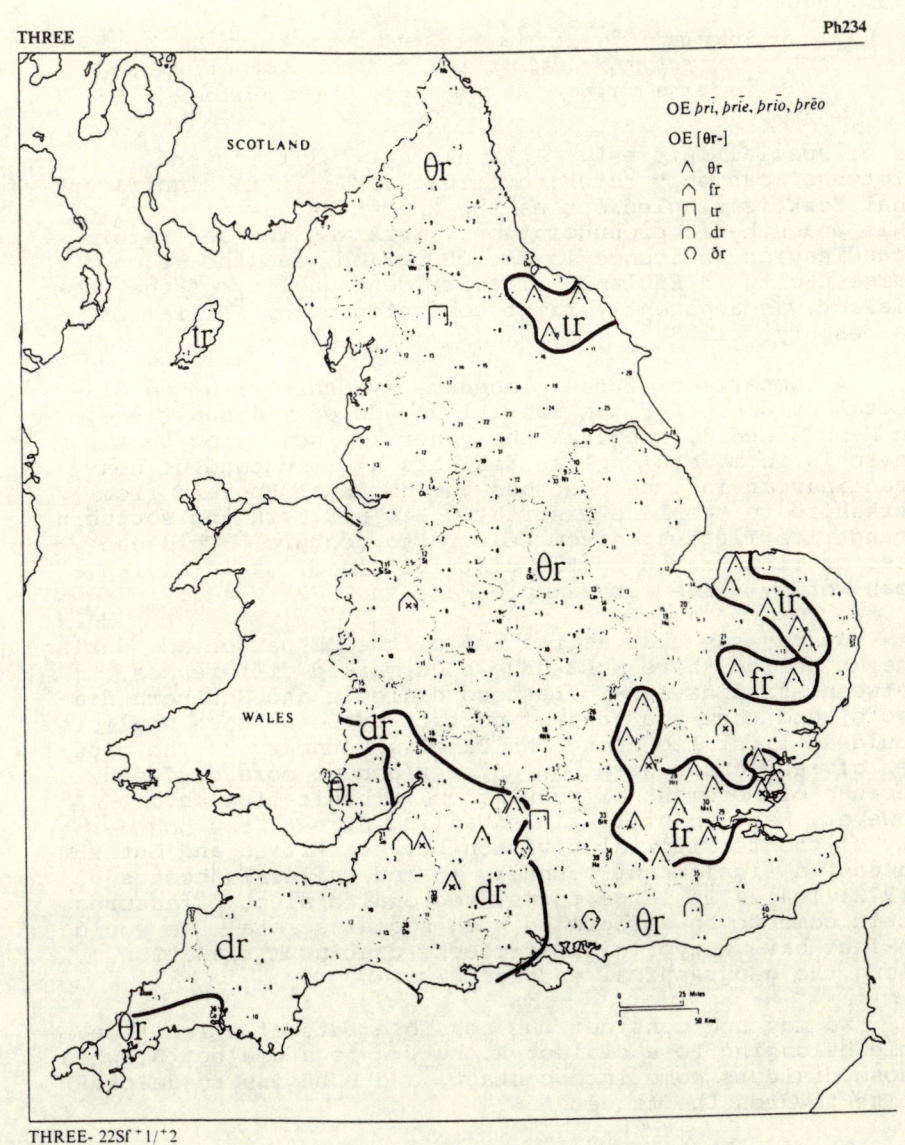

THREE — Ph234

OE *þri, þrie, þrio, þrēo*
OE [θr-]

- ∧ θr
- ∩ fr
- ⊓ tr
- ∩ dr
- ◯ ðr

THREE- 22Sf⁺1/⁺2

(*LAE*:1978).

In the light of the above, Trevisa's often quoted (1387) comment:

> Al þe longage of þe Norþhumbres, and *specialliche at Ʒork, is so scharp, slitting, and frotynge,* and vnschape, þat we souþerne men may þat longage vnneþe vnderstonde,

is of special interest. I think that 'slitting and frotynge' can only refer to fricatives. It is significant that York is singled out as the epicentre, as it were, of this unaesthetic pronunciation. York was the centre of Scandinavian influence in the OE period, and the second largest city in England. The strident quality of the York dialect was apparently first commented on by William of Malmesbury, c1125.[5]

A comparison of the placename evidence with the dialectal evidence for the initial sounds of *the* and *three*, in Maps 3 and 4, supports the generally-held view that there is in modern English dialects a broad band of heavy Scandinavian influence across the north of England from Yorkshire to the Lake District. Its northern and southern boundaries fluctuate from feature to feature. This can also be illustrated by the distribution of Scandinavian loan-words. (See for example Wakelin 1972: 134-5.)

We may say that at the end of the OE period and during the ME period there must have been marked differences between Scandinavian-influenced dialects and Southern dialects, and that the area of contact between these dialects would at first lie along the Danelaw boundary.[6] The cluster of isoglosses here would later become more diffused because of movement of population, urbanization, etc. However, Wakelin still finds Watling Street (the boundary of the territorial division between Alfred and Guthrum in 886) a significant boundary in modern local accents (1972: 104). In large towns, regional dialectal features would come to be associated with social strata. We would in fact have a typical post-creole continuum situation, along the geographical and social axes.

We may now consider the possible fate of a lenition rule belonging to a dialect A, but not to a dialect B, when those dialects come into contact, and B begins to de-creolize towards the target A.

Foreign language teachers know that the L2 learner typically does not acquire all the juncture features, elisions, etc., used by the native speaker. The same applies to acquirers of dialect. Wells comments on adoptive (i.e. non-native, often bidialectal) speakers of RP that:

> One crucial characteristic of most speakers of adoptive RP is their lack of control over the informal and allegro characteristics of RP. Native speakers of RP make extensive use of Elision, Assimilation, Smoothing, and other special-context variants, particularly of course in informal contexts; adoptive RP speakers tend to avoid them. Consciously or unconsciously, they may regard such variants as 'lazy' or 'slipshod' and hence incompatible with their 'best' speech, their adoptive RP. (Wells, 1982:284)

Labov's Radnor, Philadelphia study (1972: 305-307) showed that the older the acquirer of a dialect was, the less likely he was to adopt the sound-system of that dialect regularly across the whole lexis, but he would tend to adopt a new rule only partially, in some items, by lexical diffusion. Younger children transplanted to a new dialect area adopted a new dialect phonology more completely than older children. 'The higher-level rules seem to remain fixed, while the lower-level conditions seem to have shifted to the Philadelphia pattern.' In this connection we may also note Trudgill's incidental finding in his Norwich study, that even a child born and brought up in Norwich may not acquire a fully Norwich system if his caretaker came from elsewhere, in spite of peer influence (forthcoming, 1986). This bears out the example quoted by Labov of Athens-born middle-class teenagers retaining the Istanbul dialect of Greek spoken by their parents and grandparents, in spite of peer pressure. In this case the strength and prestige of Istanbul family ties and the value of Istanbul identification seem to have been great enough to resist peer pressures (Labov 1972:307).

It seems to me that the voicing of initial /f-/, /s-/, /θ-/ and /ʃ-/ in OE and ME, which Fisiak convincingly argues are caused by one and the same lenition process, is precisely the type of rule which is typically jettisoned when a language is pidginized or creolized, and acquired only partially by learners of a new dialect. Furthermore, why should the speaker of a Danelaw dialect of English want to sound like a southerner, whether he lives in his home district, or has been transplanted to London? It would depend on what pronunciation he (or she), consciously or unconsciously, regarded as prestigious.

If this explanation is accepted as the reason why such

an expansive lenition innovation stopped at approximately
the Danelaw boundary during the late OE or early ME period,
then the reason why the area of voicing subsequently
receded southwards is presumably related: migration of
population and the rise in the social prestige of the East
Midland dialect meant that the phonologically simpler
variety became the standard to be imitated.

The position of the isophones as plotted by the *SED*
in the 1950's is shown in Map 1: the area of initial fricative voicing has retreated to the south west, and a small
island of rural Sussex in the south east. It has vanished
completely from Kent, where (according to DeCamp, 1958) it
may have originated in the 7th century. Wakelin, however,
suggests that it may have arisen 'in or near the Devon area,
where it is still most vigorous' (1982: 9). The extirpation
of initial fricative voicing in Kent is probably to be
explained by the proximity of the capital and the prestige
of the spoken standard. Dobson's 16th century examples
of commentators on contemporary speech indicate the
nature of the model for imitation by the upwardly mobile.
Of particular interest is the quotation from Elyot's
Governour (1531), in which he gives advice about the
English to be spoken by nurses and other women who attend
a nobleman's son in infancy. If they cannot speak Latin
to him, they should:

> at the lest way... speke none englisshe but that which is
> cleane, polite, perfectly and articulately pronounced,
> omittinge no lettre or sillable, as folisshe women often-
> times do of a wantonnesse, whereby divers noble men and
> gentilmennes chyldren (as I do at this daye knowe) have
> attained corrupte and foule pronuntiation.
> (Dobson: 1955:27)

This speech of women and nurses, which is held up to
opprobrium here, is presumably the native, informal
allegro speech of southern England, with all its natural
lenition processes. A similar attitude seems to have been
held by the anonymous London schoolmaster writing at the
end of the 17th century who regarded London speech as too
'fine' and 'smooth' compared with that of the Universities
(referred to by Dobson 1955: 30). Later, as Fisiak notes,
the southern voicing of initial fricatives became the index
of the stage country bumpkin in Renaissance and Restoration
drama. The stigmatization of /$ʒ$-/ would seem to suggest
that at this period the feature was probably to be met with
much closer to the capital than is the case today, though
clearly recessive. Such stigmatization would hasten its
demise, first in the towns of the south east with good

communications with London, then in their rural hinterlands.

However, we have retained into Modern Standard English one important group of words showing initial fricative voicing, the class of form words which includes *the, that, this, they, them, their, then, than, there, though, thus,* (*thou, thee, thy*). Regardless of their etymologies (some are originally Scandinavian loans), they have all adopted the voicing feature, while even the commonest lexical words with *th*- spelling are pronounced with /θ-/ in Standard English. I would set this class of words aside from the general argument on the advance and retreat of initial fricative voicing in OE and ME dialects, though reasons of space prevent me from going into this question here.

In sum, I submit that, whereas the original advance of the initial fricative voicing innovation through the OE dialects is a natural and not unusual phonetic process (it has its parallels in other Germanic dialects on the continent), the halting and then the reversing of such an innovation in ME is an unexpected development, requiring explanation. It can only be explained by some kind of intervention in the dialect continuum. The Scandinavian settlement of the north and east Midlands in the late OE period seems to supply the right kind of intervention at the right place and time to explain this remarkable linguistic U-turn.

* Maps are reprinted by permission.

NOTES

1. See Poussa, 1982, for a more general discussion of evidence for OE-Scandinavian creolization.
2. For a review of recent discussions of creolization (which do *not* presuppose development from a stable pidgin as Hall (1966) assumes), see Corne (1983) and Traugott's introduction to Highfield and Valdman (1981). I personally find Bailey and Maroldt's (1977) definition too wide.
3. For information on Modern Icelandic, I am obliged to my colleague Erlingur Sigurdsson.
4. An example from a recent novel (Lodge, 1984:110-111) shows the stereotype associated with geographical region and social class:
    'Hurrying downstairs, he passes his son, Matthew, on his way up. ''Ullo, our Dad,' says Matthew, whose current humour it is to pretend to be a working-class youth from the North of England. 'Shouldn't you be at school?' Philip coldly enquires. 'Trooble at t'pit,' says Matthew. 'Industrial action by the

Association of Schoolmasters.' 'Disgraceful,' says Philip, over his shoulder, University teachers would never strike.' 'Only because no one would notice,' Matthew calls down the stairs.'
The novel is set in a town resembling Birmingham, in the Midlands.
5. As Wakelin points out (1972:34), the passage derives from the prologue of William of Malmesbury's *Gesta Pontificorum Anglorum*, c1125, via Higden's Latin *Polychronicon* (1327-1352):
> Tot lingua Northimborum, maxime in Eboraco, ita strident incondita, quod nos australes eam vix intelligere possumus.

Here too, York is singled out for special mention.
6. Kristensson, at this conference, tells me that his further studies in this area confirm that the dialect boundary follows the border of the Danelaw. In addition to the phonological evidence, he finds morphological differences, e.g. the dative plural forms are north of the Danelaw boundary *-um,-om* and south of it *-on,-en*.

REFERENCES

Andersen, R. 1979. 'Expanding Schumann's pidginization hypothesis'. *Language Learning 29*. 105-1099.
Bailey, C. and K. Maroldt. 1977. 'The French lineage of English'. In Meisel. 21-53.
Bickerton, D. 1981. *The Roots of Language*. Ann Arbor: Karoma Publishers, Incl.
Burchfield, R. 1956. 'The language and orthography of the Ormulum MS'. *Transactions of the Philological Society*. 56-87.
Brown, C. 1932. *English Lyrics of the 13th Century*. Oxford: Clarendon Press.
Brunner, K. 1961-62. *Die englische Sprache*. Tübingen: Niemeyer.
Cambell, A. 1959. *Old English Grammar*. Oxford: Clarendon Press.
Coetsem, F. van-, and Kufner, H. eds. 1972. *Towards a Grammar of Proto-Germanic*. Tübingen: Niemeyer.
Corne, C. 1983. 'Review Article' (on Valdman & Highield, 1980, and Highfield & Valdman, 1981). *Language. 59*. 176-190.
DeCamp, D. 1958. 'The genesis of Old English dialects: a new hypothesis'. *Language 34*. 232-44.
De Camp, D. and I. Hancock, eds. 1974. *Pidgins and Creoles. Current Trends and Projects*. Washington, D.C.: Georgetown University Press.
Dobson, E. 1955. 'Early modern Standard English'. *Transactions of the Philological Society*. 25-53.
Dressler, W. 1977. *Grundfragen der Morphonologie. (Sitzungsberichte der Phil.-hist. Klasse, Bd. 315.)* Vienna: Osterreichischen Akademie der Wissenschaften.
Eckmann, F. 1981. 'On the naturalness of interlanguage phonological rules'. *Language Learning 31*. 195-216.

Ellis, A. 1890. *English Dialects - Their Sounds and Homes*. English Dialect Society 60. London: Kegan Paul, Trench, Trübner. Reprinted 1965. Vaduz: Kraus Reprint.

Fisiak, J. 1984. 'The voicing of initial fricatives in Middle English'. *Studia Anglica Posnaniensia XVII*. (forthcoming)

Gass, S. and J. Ard. 1984. 'The ontology of language universals'. In Rutherford. 33-68.

Gimson, A. 1970. *An Introduction to the Pronunciation of English*. Second edition. London: Arnold.

Greenburg, J. 1966. *Language Universals with Special Reference to Feature Hierarchies*. The Hague: Mouton.

Highfield, A. and A. Valdman. eds. 1981. *Historicity and Variation in Creole Studies*. Ann Arbor: Karoma.

Holt, R. and R. White, eds. 1878. *The Orrmulum*. 2 vols. Oxford: Clarendon Press.

Jakobson, R. and M. Halle. 1956. *Fundamentals of Language*. The Hague: Mouton.

Kay, P. and G. Sankoff. 1974. 'A language-universals approach to pidgins and creoles'. In DeCamp and Hancock. 61-72.

Labov, W. 1972. *Sociolinguistic Patterns*. Philadelphia: University of Pennsylvania Press.

Lodge, D. 1984. *Small World*. London: Secker and Warburg.

McNamara, J. ed. 1977. *Language Learning and Thought*. New York: Academic Press.

Meisel, J. ed. 1977. *Langages en contact: pidgins, créoles/Languages in Contact*. Tübinger Beiträge zur Linguistik 75.

Moulton, W. 1972. 'The Proto-Germanic non-syllabics (consonants)'. In van Coetsem and Kufner. 141-173.

Orton, H. et al. 1962-71. *Survey of English Dialects*. 4 vols. Leeds: Arnold.

Orton, H. et al. 1978. *The Linguistic Atlas of England*. London: Croom Helm.

Parkes, M. 1983. 'On the presumed date and possible origin of the manuscript of the Orrmulum: Oxford, Bodleian Library, MS Junius 1'. In Stanley and Gray. 115-127.

Poussa, P. 1982. 'The evolution of early Standard English: the creolization hypothesis'. *Studia Anglica Posnaniensia XIV*. 69-85.

Rutherford, W. ed. 1984. *Language Universals and Second Language Acquisition (= Typological Studies in Language. Vol. 5)*. Amsterdam & Philadelphia: John Benjamins.

Skautrup, P. 1944. *Det Danske sprogs historie. Vol. I*. Copenhagen: Gyldendal.

Slobin, D. 1977. 'Language change in childhood and history'. In McNamara. 1977. 185-214.

Stanley, E.G. and D. Gray. eds. 1983. *Five Hundred Years of Words and Sounds. A Festschrift for Eric Dobson*. Cambridge: Brewer.

Trudgill, P. 1986 (forthcoming). *Dialects in Contact*. Oxford: Blackwell.

Wakelin, M. 1972. *English Dialects*. London: Athlone Press.
Wakelin, M. 1982. 'Evidence for spoken regional English in the 16th century'. *Revista Canaria de estudios ingleses*. 1-25.
Wells, J.C. 1982. *Accents of English 2. The British Isles.* Cambridge: University Press.
Zobl, H. 1984. 'Uniformity and source-language variation across developmental continua'. In Rutherford. 185-218.

EXPRESSION OF EXCLUSIVENESS IN OLD ENGLISH AND THE DEVELOPMENT OF THE ADVERB *ONLY*

MATTI RISSANEN
University of Helsinki

In this paper, I will discuss the Old English variant expressions of exclusiveness representing the types normally indicated by the adverb *only* in present-day English, as in *God only knows, He ate only three apples*, or *Not only now but also later*. I will exclude from my discussion the closely related expressions of isolation or singleness generally indicated by the complement *alone* and the attributive *only* as in *He was sitting alone in the room*, or *He is my only son*.

The notion of exclusiveness is one of the basic semantic concepts in language. For this reason, it is surprising that the development of the English expressions of exclusiveness has been so little studied, particularly as this development involves an interesting word-class shift, from numeral to adverb, in early historical English. Apart from the general historical surveys of English, there are only a few studies dealing with the rise and development of the exclusive adverbs.[1]

There were three main ways of expressing exclusiveness in Old English, all centering round the numeral *an* 'one'. The first was the numeral in itself, the second was the combination of the demonstrative pronoun *þaet* and *an* ; the third was the prepositional phrase *for an*. I will first give a brief survey of the syntactic characteristics of each of these expressions.

When the numeral *an* in itself was used to express exclusiveness, it was not used adverbially but always as part of a noun phrase, either as a pre-modifying, or more often, as a post-modifying element. The noun or pronoun it modifies forms the focus of exclusiveness. When *an* was a pre-modifier, it was always preceded either by a genitive, a possessive pronoun, or the demonstrative pronoun (or definite article) *se, seo, þaet* (examples 1-2; for further examples, see Rissanen 1967.1: 155-8).[2]

(1) Ac cweþ þin an word & min cnapa biþ gehæled.
(Mt WS 8.8)
'sed tantum dic verbo'

(2) ic geteohhode, þæt ic þa ana wundru asecgan wolde, þe in Suþlangbeardum gewordene wæron
(GD 237)
'sola quae in Italia gesta sunt'

(3) She was turned into a Man, and by that only Means avoided the Danger (Addison, OED s.v. *only* a. 4b)

The ModE usage as exemplified by (3) offers a striking parallel to the OE construction. There are, however, only some thirty examples of this attributive exclusive *an* in the whole OE corpus of texts.

The post-modifying *an* (examples 4-7) is by far the most common way of expressing exclusiveness in OE. There are some 700 instances of this type in the OE corpus of texts, as against the total of c. 150 of the other types. It is significant that there are virtually no instances of the appositive *an* in anteposition to the focused element. In all OE texts, excluding the interlinear glosses, I have only found three examples in which *an* precedes a pronominal head. All the three occur in OE poetry, in the formulaic expression *anum þe* (example 8; the other examples are quoted in Rissanen 1967.1: 151). The word-order is regulated by the demands of metre and probably does not represent a natural OE structure.

(4) Wæs þæt beorhte bold tobrocen swiþe ...
hrof ana genæs ealles ansund (Beo. 998)
'only the roof was left untouched'

(5) Nu ic cyþe mid dædum, ... næs mid wordum anum, þæt ic wiste (BlHom 184)
'Now I shall make known with deeds, ... not only with words'

(6) þæt he hit ne do for þæm anum þæt hine man herige ac ma for Gode (CP 451)
'that he should not do it only to be praised'

(7) He þa wende on þa ane þe him þa getriewe wæron
    (Or 112)
    'he turned only to those that were faithful to him'

(8) Ic to anum þe, middangeardes weard, mod staþolige
    (And 80)
    'Only on you I fix my mind'

Another conspicuous feature in the use of the OE postmodifying exclusive *an* is its concord with the focused part, that is, with the nominal or pronominal head. As is pointed out in standard reference works of OE grammar, *an* has both strong and weak declensions, but the only weak form which seems to be in current use in written Old English is the masculine nominative singular form *ana*, as in example (4) (cf. Rissanen 1967.1:138-42; Mitchell 1985: 212-15). The corresponding weak feminine form *ane*, occurs a few times, but in the oblique cases and in the plural the strong forms prevail almost without exception. The oblique weak form *anan* can be found a couple of times, but mainly in contexts in which it may well be a weakened form of the strong dative *anum*. Thus, Ælfric's gloss in his Latin *Grammar*, dating from about the year 1000, seems to describe the usage accurately:

(9) solus, sola, solum ana and heora ealra solius
    anes; soli anum; et cetera (ÆGram 115)

The weak form *ana* can, however, occasionally be found in contexts in which an oblique form is expected:

(10) ne lufode he woruldlice æhta for his neode
     ana (ÆCHom. II 194)

(11) þuruh þæt gescead ana we synd sælran (ÆLS I 150)

The consistent post-modifying use of *an* and its concord with the head of the NP, clearly indicate that the adverbialization of *an* in the exclusive use had not taken place in Old English. But the spread of *ana* into the feminine and neuter nominative singular, and the few instances of *ana* in the oblique cases, imply that this form was becoming generalized as the word indicating exclusiveness, and the way was thus paved for the development of the adverbial.

The construction *þæt an*[3] occurs mostly in negative expressions, typically in correlative constructions of the type 'not only...but also' (12-13). But as (14) shows, it can also be used in affirmative clauses.

> (12) nales þæt an oþerra leoma ac swylce eac þære
> tungan onstyrenesse biswicade (Bede 290)
> 'non solum membrorum ceterorum sed et linguae
> motu caruit'

> (13) forþon þe þa stanas þæs toglidenan wages nalæs
> þæt an, þæt hi his limu tobræcan, ac swylce eac mid
> ealle his ban gebrysedon (GD C 125)
> 'quia collapsi saxa parietis, non solum ejus
> membra, sed etiam ossa contriverant'

> (14) þa weallode wide dæges & nihtes geond þa muntas
> & þa dena,... & þæt an, þæt heo þær gereste,
> þær hi seo werignes genydde, þæt heo restan
> sceolde (GD C 176)
> 'ibique tantummodo quiescebat, ubi hanc quiescere
> lassitudo coegisset'

The following late OE glosses imply that this construction may have been regarded as a stereotyped equivalent of Latin exclusive adverbials:

> (15) dumtaxat þæt an, tantummodo þæt an (ÆGram 241)

> (16) Non modo na þæt an (AldV 67)

There are two types of construction formed with the demonstrative pronoun and *an*: in one, the phrase is used like an adverbial, preceding the focused element (12); in the other, *þaet an* is followed by a subordinate clause introduced by the conjunction *þaet* (13-14). The focused element can be found in this subordinate clause; the pronoun *þaet* which precedes *an* seems to be an antecedent to this clause.

The type with the subordinate clause is somewhat more common than the phrase without a following clause: roughly eighty examples as against forty in the OE corpus of texts.

The analysis of the *þaet* preceding *an* in this construction is somewhat problematic. It can be taken either as a cataphoric pronoun 'that', or as a weakened form approaching the definite article. The construction with a following subordinate clause would seem to suggest the first interpretation, 'not that (al)one...'; the shorter construction, as in (12), might favour the second: 'not the one...'. It is impossible to give a definite answer to this question, but in view of the very frequent post-modifying use of the exclusive *an*, the common Germanic origin of this construction referred to below, and the latish development of the definite article in Germanic languages, the first alternative seems the more likely one. Furthermore, the construction *þæt an þæt* represents the same basic syntactic pattern as the common OE phrases *for þam anum þe, to þam anum þe, þa ane þe*, etc., which go back to *for þam þe, þa þe*, etc. (examples 6 and 7, above; cf. Rissanen 1967.1:168-77; Mitchell 1985:730-1). It is quite possible, however, that the stress relations of the two elements changed towards the end of the OE period.

The third exclusive expression, *for an*, can be found nine times in eleventh-century texts (examples 17 and 18; for further examples, see Rissanen 1967.1:183-4).

(17) Gaþ and offriaþ eowrum Gode: foran eowre yrfe
sceal beon her (Hept Ex 10.24)
'oves tantum vestrae et armenta remaneant'

(18) he bruce, for an þæt he þæt fæsten oþ æfen
symbellice breme (ThCap 391)
'utatur, tantum ut ieiunium usque ad uesperum celebret'

As these examples show, *for an* can be used as an adverbial to translate the Latin *tantum*; it is also worth pointing out that it seems to have an intensifying force in Old English.

In addition to the three constructions discussed above, there were, of course, periphrastic ways of expressing exclusiveness in Old English. Those ways are, however, negligible; a study of the OE translations of Latin originals shows that the Latin exclusive expressions were normally translated by one or another of the constructions based upon *an*, or the notion of exclusiveness was left untranslated. The expression 'no more than' can, of course, be found, but the word 'but', or the phrase 'nothing but' does not occur as an equivalent of 'only' in Old English.

It seems that the expressions of exclusiveness with the numeral, or with the construction dem. pron. + numeral, are very old and go back to pre-Old English times. In Gothic, in Ulfilas' Bible translation, both types can be found (examples 19 and 20). The same is true of Old Icelandic; in Old High German, the numeral seems to have reached the status of an adverbial at an early date, as can be seen in example (21) (for further examples, see Rissanen 1967.2:421-2). These early uses in the other Germanic languages are of interest in the discussion of the process of adverbialization of the Old English exclusive constructions.

(19) ni bi hlaib ainana libaid manna (Ulfilas Lk 4.4.)
'non de pane solo vivit homo'

(20) jabai þatainei atteka wastjai is, ganisa
(Ulfilas Mt 9.21)
'si tantum attingo vestem eius, sanor'

(21) nieht ein ze suhte, nube ze tode (Boethius, Graff Ahd. Sprachschatz, s.v. *ein*)
'not only to the illness but to the death'

A good starting-point for the discussion of this process of adverbialization is offered by a survey of the translations of the Latin exclusive expressions in the Old English *Bede*. This text contains a higher number of instances of the *þæt an* construction than any other Old English text and thus makes possible a comparison of the contexts in which the different types occur.

Table 1. Translations of the Latin expressions of exclusiveness in the OE *Bede*

	Neg. correl. (not only ... but)		Other context	Total
	Focus NP	Focus V/Cl		
þæt an þæt	4	12	-	16
þæt an	6	1		7
an (post-mod.)	-	1	21	22
others no transl.		- 20		

The figures in Table 1 show a very clear-cut distribution. The *þæt an* constructions are used fairly mechanically to translate the Latin phrases meaning 'not only... but also', *non solum/non tantum...sed etiam*. In all other contexts, the post-modifying *an* is used. There is only one example that deviates from this pattern.[4] There is not a single occurrence of either the attributive exclusive *an* or of the prepositional phrase *for an* in this text. The post-modifying construction is used even in contexts in which the Latin structure might suggest a premodifying one, as in (22) and (23).

> (22) se þe Seaxna gereorde an cuþe (Bede 362)
> 'qui Saxonum tantum linguam nouerat'

> (23) þa studu ane, þe se biscop onhleoniende forþferde, þæt fyr gretan ne meahte (Bede 204)
> 'sola illa destina, cui incumbens obiit'

Seaxna an gereorde and *þa ane studu* would be possible constructions as attested by examples 1 and 2.

The next question which is of interest in the discussion of the development of exclusive adverbials concerns the distribution of the constructions *þaet an* and *þaet an þaet*, as in examples (12) and (13)-(14). It can easily be seen from Table 1 that the choice between the two expressions depends largely on the quality of the focus of exclusion: with a noun phrase focus, the shorter type is preferred, with a verb or sentence focus, the longer one prevails (cf. Mitchell 1985:731-2).

As was pointed out above, the longer type is probably analytic: the first *þaet* seems the antecedent to the conjunctive *þaet* following *an* and introducing a subordinate clause. This kind of structure is easier to create with a verbal or clausal focus than with a nominal one. Artificially constructed present-day English examples may illustrate this matter. Sentence (24a), in which the focus of the exclusion is *eat all the apples*, can be, hypothetically, reproduced as in (24b). But sentence (25a), in which the focus is the noun phrase *all the apples*, is more complicated. The rendering (25b) is stylistically unsatisfactory because it ruins the syntactic symmetry of the original; there are, in fact, only a few examples in OE texts in which this type of rendering of a Latin original can be found. A more common solution is the construction exemplified in (25c), but this requires the creation of a new verb in the second part of the correlative pair. For this reason, the use of the shorter adverbial phrase *þaet an*, in (25d), is preferable.

(24a) He did not only eat all the apples but
       also felled the tree.

(24b) Not   that alone that he ate all the apples but he
      Nales þæt an   þæt (+ clause)   ac

       also felled the tree.
       eac (+ clause)

(25a) He did not only eat all the apples but also
       the bananas.

(25b) Not   that alone that he ate all the apples
      Nales þæt an   þæt (+ clause)

       but also the bananas.
       ac eac (+ NP)

(25c) Not   that alone that he ate all the apples,
      Nales þæt an   þæt (+ clause)

       but he also gobbled the bananas.
       ac   eac (+ clause)

(25d) He ate not *þæt an* all the apples but also
       the bananas.

But these considerations do not answer the question why the translator did not systematically use the shorter form to render the Latin *(non) solum (...sed etiam)* as it was obviously handier and demanded less change in the structure of the original. Why did he, instead, resort to complicated circumscriptions as in (13) and (14)? The most likely explanation is that the shorter type was not immediately acceptable as an adverbial form: at least in the dialect of the translators, it may have sounded 'incorrect' just as 'that alone the apples' would sound strange to our ears. For this reason, the translator may have preferred the longer analytical construction whenever possible.

The translators' or scribes' uneasiness with the shorter form is also implied by a slightly different type of analytic construction, with an anaphoric *þæt* preceding *an*:

(26) gif munuc inne on his heortan eaþmod biþ and
na þæt an, ac swylce utene mid his lichoman
eaþmodnesse eallum ... gebycnige (BenR 7)
'si non solum corde monachus, sed etiam ipso
corpore humilitatem videntibus se semper
indicet ...'

There are a few examples of this type in OE texts (quoted in Rissanen 1967.1:181-2).

It would be tempting to suggest, although impossible to prove, that the shorter *þaet an* construction was current only in the Anglian dialects and that the analytic *þaet an þaet* might be due to the West Saxon translator's or copyist's unfamiliarity with the shorter type. It is significant that the shorter type occurs a dozen times in the OE *Bede* and Waerferth's translation of *Gregory's Dialogues*, while it can be found only once in the other texts originating from Alfred's court.

Thus, the figures in Table 1 do not only show the contextual restriction of the use of the dem. pron. + *an* construction; they also imply that the shorter, non-analytical type was not lexicalized as an adverb. It is possible, however, that towards the end of the OE period, the shorter type was regarded as more acceptable in its adverbial use than in Alfred's time. Judging from examples (15) and (16), *þaet an* was a current expression to translate the Latin exclusive adverbials. Furthermore, the figures in Table 2 show an increase in the popularity of the shorter type in relation to the longer one in late OE prose.[5]

Table 2. The occurrence of *þaet an þaet* in early and late OE texts

	Early (Alfred, etc.)	Late (Ælfric, etc.)	Total
þæt an þæt	52	15	67
þæt an	16	15	31
Total	68	30	98

But even if the proportional increase of the type *þaet an* in comparison to *þaet an þaet* might imply a tendency towards the adverbialization of the shorter form, the most conspicuous feature in the figures in Table 2 is the low frequency of both types. The unmarked expression of exclusiveness was no doubt the appositive *an* throughout the OE period, and *þaet an* never gains a sufficient distributional richness and variability of use to make it a serious competitor. It is worth mentioning that there is only one example of the *þaet an* types in the whole corpus of Old English poetry - and even this is in the *Meters of Boethius*, a text based on a prose translation from Latin. In the *Anglo-Saxon Chronicle* there is not a single instance of *þaet an*. It seems that non-Latin-based writings simply avoided correlative negative expressions of exclusiveness and expressions with a verbal or clausal focus. It is a fair assumption that this was also the case in spoken language and in colloquial styles.

Like *þaet an*, *for an* never developed into a serious competitor of *ana*, *ane*, as a variant expression of exclusiveness. Examples (27) and (28) show that *for an*, and not *þaet an*, is used twice in the *West Saxon Gospels*, in contexts in which the focused part is a verb and the use of the appositive *an* therefore impossible.

(27) Ne ondræd þu þe, gelyf for an (Mk WS 5.36)
'noli timere, tantummodo crede'

(28) For an ic beo hal, gyf ic hys reafes æthrine
(Mt WS 9.21)
'Si tetigero tantum vestimentum ejus, salva ero.'

This phrase cannot be found in early Middle English texts; it emerges again in Caxton's writings, in late Middle English (Mustanoja 1960:292-3). It seems that after the establishment of the adverbial *ane*, *for an* lost its exclusive function but may have survived as an intensifying expression in spoken language. It is possible that this phrase lies behind the modern *I for one*, although this connection is not pointed out by the OED (s.v. *for* 19d).

Thus, at the close of the OE period, the circumstances were favourable for the development of an exclusive adverb. There were three alternative expressions: the receding phrases *þaet an (þaet)* and *for an*, and the prevailing weak form of the numeral, *ana*, *ane*. It is not surprising that it was the last-mentioned form which developed into the adverb. But before this development could take place, the bondage between the numeral and the focused part, the head of the NP, had to be broken. The necessary condition for this development was created by the collapse of the system

of inflectional endings in late OE. The form *ane* was
generalized for most cases and genders, both in the
singular and in the plural. Furthermore, this form was
identical with a large number of OE adverbs derived from
adjectives, such as *softe, mirige, milde*, etc. An OE adverb
derived from the numeral *an* also existed: this was *æne*
'once', which was originally an instrumental form of the
numeral but was obviously adverbialized at an early date.[6]

The earliest text which gives some evidence of the
use of *an(a)* as an adverbial is the *Lindisfarne Gospels* of
the late 10th century. Although, as pointed out in fn. 5,
the value of this text as evidence of syntactic structures
is highly questionable, examples (29) and (30) are worth
quoting as *an* is here used with a clausal focus:

(29) ah an cuoeþ miþ word & gehæled biþ cnæht min
 (Mt Li 8.8)
 'sed tantum dic verbo'

(30) nælle þu þe ondrede gelef ana 7 hal hio biþ
 (Lk Li 8.50)
 'noli timere crede tantum et salua erit'

But in negative correlative constructions *þæt an* is
regularly used in the *Lindisfarne Gospels*.

In early Middle English texts, there is ample evidence
of the rapid adverbialization of *ane*. There are a considerable number of instances in 12th- and early 13th-century
texts which show the use of *ane, one* in negative clauses.
It is used in correlative constructions (32) and in the
phrase 'but only' (33) both with a nominal and a clausal
focus. It also occurs in affirmative clauses, and in
anteposition to a nominal focus (34), (35). (For further
examples, see Rissanen 1967.1:152). Yet the normal
position of this adverb in early Middle English texts is
still in postposition to a nominal or pronominal focus;
it is only much later that the antepositive placement
becomes the favoured one (see Nevalainen forthcoming).

(32) þet is naht one mid worde ne mid tunge, ac eac
 mid worke and mid soþfestnesse (Lambeth Homilies
 125)

(33) vre lauerd þet nauede sunne, buten ane þet he
 ber flesch ilich ure þet is ful of sunne.
 (Ancrene Riwle 133)

(34) Ane þurh þet þu luuest þe God þet is in an
oþer wiþ þe ruininge of þi luue þu makes
wiþ uten oþer swink hire god tin ahne
(Ancrene Riwle 151)

(35) Ant tah ha ful were of alle gode þeawes, ane
of hire meokelec ha seide ant song to Elizabeth
(Hali Meiþhad 22)

After the adverbialization of *ane* was completed, the period of coexistence of the three variant expressions of exclusiveness was probably short. As mentioned above, *for an* is not recorded even once in early ME texts, and only four instances of *þaet an* can be found. Three occur in the *Bodley Homilies*, which were probably copied from OE sources. One can be found in the *Peterborough Interpolations* (Rissanen 1967.2:426).

In view of the preceding survey, what is the origin of the form *only*? All standard works of reference, including the OED and the MED, derive *only* from the OE adjective *anlic, aenlic*, also referring to the OE adverbs *anlice, aenlice*. This development is, however, problematic. The adjectival forms are not common in the sense 'only' in OE or early ME. They were infrequent as such, and their primary meaning was 'unique' or 'solitary' (MED s.v. *only* adj. 2b). The adverbial forms are not recorded in the exclusive sense in OE or early ME; the earliest examples appear round 1300. It seems, indeed, that the rise of the adverbial forms *anliche, onliche > only* must be seen as part of a more general development of ME adverbs. The ending *-liche* (> *-ly*) was added even to adjectives from which an adverb had originally been derived by the ending *-e*.[7] In the same way, the adverb *only* can be derived from the numeral *an* and the adverbial *ane/one*, rather than from the infrequent adjective *anlich/onlich*. Naturally, the adverbial form derived from *onlich* and meaning, roughly, 'in solitude', may have supported the development of the adverb *only*, but I cannot see it as the primary source.

By the addition of the ending *-li(che)*, the adverbialized numeral was given the formal appearance of an adverb. It is worth pointing out that approximately at the same time, in early ME, the combination of *all* and *an/on* gave the forms *allan, allon, alone* - another development which resulted in a distinction between the simple numeral and a form with a more pregnant meaning.

The aim of the present survey has been to show how a new adverb emerges in early English as a result of the extension of meaning and consequent morphological marking.[8] The adverbialization of the numeral was made possible by the levelling and loss of the endings which had earlier linked together the head of a noun phrase and its post-modifying elements. The most important factor favouring the adverbialization process seems to have been the gap which existed in the OE system of focusing adjuncts - a gap that became particularly apparent with the rise of literary language and the need to translate Latin correlative structures. The emergence of the adverb meaning 'only' brings about a balance in the system of additive and exclusive adjuncts. The adverbial *eac* 'also' was well established in OE. But after the development described above we do not only have *also* but we also have *only*.

NOTES

1. See, in particular, Mitchell (1985:210-16; 728-39), and Bloomfield (1930); Rissanen (1967.1, 2); Erickson (1973); Nevalainen (1982, 1983 and forthcoming). Miss Nevalainen's articles will be followed by a doctoral dissertation on the exclusives in the early Modern English period.
2. All OE examples are quoted from the *Microfiche Concordance to Old English*. The Latin renderings of GD are from Migne, vol. 77; those of Bede are from the edition by Colgrave and Mynors. For typographical reasons, ð has been replaced by þ; in italic type, the combination *ae* has been used for the letter æ.
3. See Mitchell's (1985: 728-39) excellent survey of this structure.
4. *Nalas þaet he þaem mynstre anum regollices lifes manunge ... gearwode, ac swelce eac þaet ymbsette folc feor & wide ... to lufan þara heofenlicra gifeana georne gemde to gehwyrfenne* (Bede 362) 'Nec solum ipsi monasterio regularis uitae monita simul et exempla praebebat, sed et uulgus circumpositum ... ad caelestium gaudiorum conuertere curabat amorem'.
5. In Table 2, texts from Alfred's time (Mart, Bede, Or, CP, Bo, GD, BlHom) are compared with Ælfrician and other late OE texts. Two somewhat problematic texts have not been included in the figures presented above. One is the *Lindisfarne Gospels*, an interlinear gloss dating from the end of the tenth century. In this text, only the shorter type is used (six examples), but the gloss hardly gives us a reliable picture of the syntax of the language of the glossator. The other text is the prose life of St. Guthlac, an eleventh-century MS. This is the only late text in which the longer type clearly prevails with eight examples as against one. This deviation from the normal pattern seems to support the suggestion that we are, in fact, dealing with a late MS of a much earlier text.

6. The uses of *ane*, *aene* 'once' are discussed in Rissanen (1967.1: 217-26). This adverb was not homonymous with *ane* 'only' because its initial vowel became *e-* in late OE or early ME, depending on the dialect. But analogy seems to have favoured forms with initial *a-*, *o-* for this adverb in early ME, and the ensuing homonymic clash may have accelerated the development of the forms with a final *-ε* (*enes*, *ones*) for 'once'.
7. E.g. *softe*; the earliest instance of *softlice* is given from the 13th century by the OED.
8. It must be pointed out that the foregoing discussion differs from the definition of the world-class of *only* to be found in the *Middle English Dictionary*. According to the MED, *only* is an adjective, for instance, in the following passages:

> We granten þe sentence and not oonli þe wordis (Wycl. MED s.v. *onli* adj. 1a)

> He3est of alle oþer, saf onelych tweyne (Cleanness, MED s.v. *onli* adj. 1b)

It is not easy to see the basis of this analysis, particularly as the MED defines *onli* as an adverb in the following contexts:

> of non other planets saue only of the mone (EPlanets MED *onli* adv. 1a(d))

> I schal moue not oonly erthe, but also heuene (Wycl. MED *onli* adv. 1b(a)).

REFERENCES

Ancrene Riwle. 1963. Ed. by F.M. Mack. (=EETS, 252.) OUP.
Bloomfield, L. 1930. 'OHG *Eino*, OE *Ana* Solus'. *Curme Volume of Linguistic Studies* ed. by J.T. Hatfield, W. Leopold & A.J.F. Zieglschmidt, 50-9 (=Language Monograph, 7.) Baltimore: Waverly Press.
Colgrave, B. & R.A.B. Mynors, eds. 1969. *Bede's Ecclesiastical History of the English People* (Oxford Medieval Texts.) Oxford: Clarendon.
Erickson, J. 1973. '*An* and *Na þæt an* in Late Old English Prose: Some Theoretical Questions of Derivation'. *Archivum Linguisticum* 4.75-88.
Hali Meiþhad. 1982. Ed. B. Millet. (=EETS 284.) OUP.
Healey, A. diPaolo & R.L. Venezky. 1980. *A Microfiche Concordance to Old English*. University of Toronto Press.
Lambeth Homilies. 1867-8. Ed. by R. Morris (=*Old English Homilies and Homiletic Treatises of the 12th and 13th Centuries*. EETS OS, 29, 34.) OUP.
Middle English Dictionary. 1956-. Ed. by H. Kurath & S.M. Kuhn. Ann Arbor: University of Michigan Press.
Migne, J.P., ed. 1855-64. *Patrologiae Cursus Completus: Patrologia Latina*. Paris
Mitchell, B. 1985. *Old English Syntax*. Oxford: Clarendon.

Nevalainen, T. 1982. 'Determining the Contextual Focus of Exclusive Focusing Adverbials'. *Papers on English Philology Read at the Symposium Arranged by the Modern Language Society at Tvärminne on 26-28 November, 1981* (=*Neuphilologische Mitteilungen,* Extra Issue.)

Nevalainen, T. 1983. 'Corpus of Colloquial Early Modern English for a Lexical-Syntactic Study: Evidence for Consistency and Variation'. *Papers from the Second Scandinavian Symposium on Syntactic Variation* ed.by S. Jacobson (=*Stockholm Studies in English,* 57.) 55-68. Stockholm: Almqvist & Wiksell.

Nevalainen, T. Forthcoming. 'The Development of Preverbal *Only* in Early Modern English'. To appear in *Papers of the 12th NWAVE, Oct. 1983.*

Oxford English Dictionary, The. 1933. Ed. by J.A.H. Murray *et al.* Oxford: Clarendon.

Rissanen, M. 1967.1. *The Uses of 'One' in Old and Early Middle English* (=*Mémoires de la Société Néophilologique de Helsinki,* 31). Helsinki.

Rissanen, M. 1967.2. 'Old English þæt an 'Only'.' *Neuphilologische Mitteilungen* 68.409-28.

Vices and Virtues. 1898. Ed. by F. Holthausen (=EETS OS, 89). Oxford: OUP.

N.B. All references to Old English texts are from the editions used by the *Microfiche Concordance to Old English* (see Healey & Venezky 1980).

THE GREAT SCANDINAVIAN BELT

M.L. SAMUELS
University of Glasgow

I. The purpose of this paper is to discuss the significance of Scandinavian influence in an area of Northern England which appears to show an especially strong form of it: a belt stretching from Cumberland and Westmoreland in the west to the North and East Ridings of Yorkshire in the east, often including part of Lincolnshire but excluding the old kingdom of Bernicia in Durham and Northumberland.

As already pointed out by Kolb (1965), the prominence of this area shows up clearly when one examines the distributions of Scandinavian words in the modern dialects. A schematisation of the distributions given by Orton and Wright (1974) and the *Linguistic Atlas of England* (*LAE*) is shown in Figure 1 (shown overleaf). There, the area in question is represented as double-hatched, and is, essentially, the area shown in the following maps in Orton and Wright: *lake* 'play' (45), *stee* 'ladder' (47), *garth* 'paddock' (63), *ket* 'rubbish' (67), *lait* 'seek, look for' (68), *lea* 'scythe' (69), *brant* 'steep' (79), and *steg* 'gander' (194). To these may be added *I is* 'I am' in *LAE* M5 and M16.

In what follows, this double-hatched area will be referred to as the *focal* area. Naturally, it would be misleading to represent it as paramount or wholly transcending other distributions, but since the arguments presented below to some extent hinge on the relative importance to be attributed to the various configurations of the belt, wider or narrower, the principal remaining wider ones are represented by the addition of single-hatched areas on Fig. 1. Examples of intermediate widths of the belt are Orton and Wright's maps for *stithy* 'anvil' (15), *slape* 'slippery' (25), *addled* 'earned' (42), *gimmer-lamb* 'ewe' (44), *throng* 'busy' (49), and *bairn* 'child' (77, 77A), where ON reinforced the already present OE *bearn*; and some of the widest include S. Lancs. in the west or Norfolk in

Fig. 1

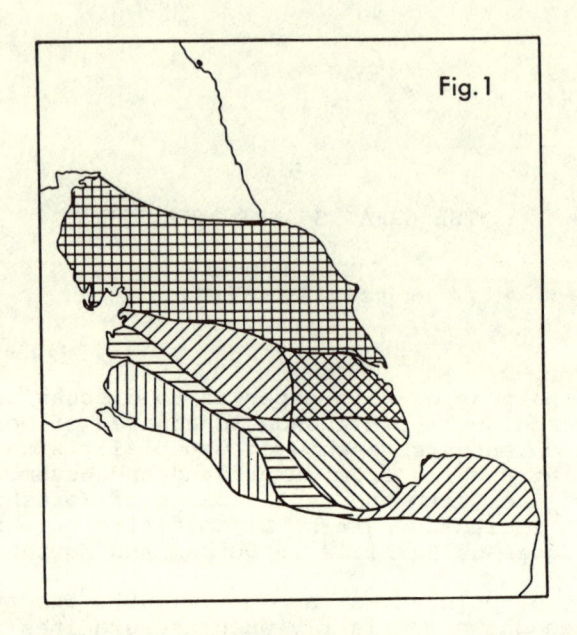

the east, as *clip* 'shear' (43), *sile* 'strain' (46), *teem* 'pour' (48), *gallows* 'braces' (91), *headwark* 'headache' (149), *toothwark* 'toothache' (172: here again, ON *verkr* reinforced OE *wærc*), *clatch* and *laughter* 'brood' (183). Similar but less complete distributions appear for *loup* 'jump' (57), *nieve* 'fist' (59), *kale* 'charlock' (66), *stee* 'stile' (74), *axle-teeth* 'molars' (179); and certain forms appear only in the east and/or west of the area, as *lops* 'fleas' (70), *quey* 'heifer' (72), *stower* 'rung' (76), *skell-boose* 'partition' (191). Finally, words with distributions different from those shown in Fig. 1 are in a minority, and it is noticeable that some of them, like *stack*, are in Standard English and occupy a much wider area, while others, like *nay* 'no', are found in configurations that are clearly relict and recessive.

Some of the words listed above (e.g. *steg*, *nieve*, *gimmer*, *stithy*) were introduced to Scotland by settlers from Northern England. In such cases there will *either* be an enclave in Durham or Northumberland, where the English form survived in a pattern such as that shown in Fig. 2; *or* that enclave, as an area of secondary Scandinavian influence, is submerged, so that there is a simple north-south division, as in Fig. 3. For our present purpose it is a secondary matter whether Scotland is included in the configurations,

Fig. 2

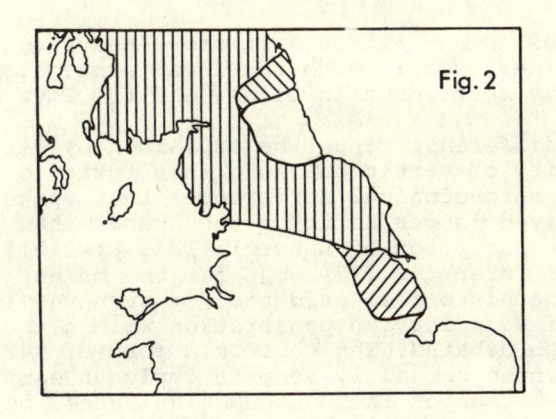

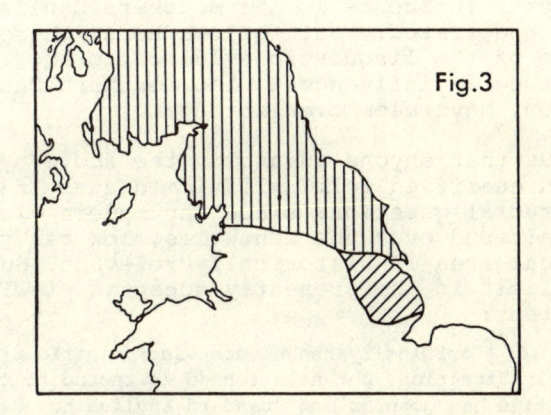

Fig. 3

but the fact that the Bernician enclave could be submerged in this way is, as we shall see later, of some importance for our interpretation of other simple north-south divisions of features not hitherto regarded as due to Scandinavian influence.

If the modern distributions outlined above are compared with what is known about the Scandinavian invasions and settlements, one might postulate, as a working hypothesis, that the two main settlements north of the Humber (i.e. of Danes in the east in 875, and of Norwegians in the west, 900-950) must have been of a kind that was denser, and brought about a deeper linguistic penetration, than the Danish settlements south of the Humber in Lincs. and the Five Boroughs (876) and in East Anglia (879). Such a hypothesis would, however, receive no support from the place-name evidence, which, although it shows heavy settlement which coincides exactly with the focal area, also shows equally heavy settlement in Lincs. and the Five Boroughs.

If the difference cannot be explained by differences in the density of settlement, one then turns to the possibility of a chronological difference: that spoken Scandinavian survived longer north of the Humber than south of it (with the exception of Lincs.). This possibility will be discussed later (p. 277), but for the moment we might note that the historical evidence for such varying strengths of Scandinavian penetration within the Danelaw has been much debated. The Chronicle poem of 942, if taken literally, would certainly seem to imply an earlier cultural assimilation of the Southumbrian Danes, but, as Cecily Clark has recently shown, the strength of surviving Danish cultural influence in the southern Danelaw is by no means to be underrated. What follows here, therefore, is a discussion of the linguistic evidence to suggest that the Dano-Norwegian influences in the Northern Danelaw must, by comparison, have been even stronger.

It is obvious that anyone advancing the above hypothesis, even in such qualified form, will immediately face the following crucial question: since the modern distributions could have altered over the centuries, how can you prove that the focal area is historically relevant? Such a question is implicit in the presently accepted view, as stated by Wakelin thus:

> [These words] originally had a much wider distribution in a southerly direction, but have tended to recede to the north as time has gone on and Standard English has become a more powerful factor. Many of them have apparently receded as far as the Humber-Ribble boundary ... (1972: 137).

Now there is no denying that this explanation is valid for a certain limited number of items. For example, the ME map for 'church' in McIntosh (1973: 56) shows *kirke* extending as far south as Cheshire and Norfolk, whereas today it has receded much further north (Wakelin 1972: 131). But whether it is the whole, or even the main, explanation is more open to doubt. There is a sizable body of evidence to the contrary, showing that the focal area, as an entity, is of long standing. The past work on this question may be summarised as follows.

(i) Dieth, in 1955, showed a connection between two distributions. He pointed out, firstly, that in the modern dialects the focal area is the only one to show the typi-

cally West Norse phonetic change /hj-/ to /ʃ/, as seen in
the map for *hips* (= 'rose-hips', from OE *hēope*), with
shoops, *choops* or similar forms restricted to that area.
He then showed that the restriction of that phonetic change
to the focal area is likely to have been original, because
the same restriction applies to place-names: only in this
area do the native elements *hēap* 'heap' and *hēope* 'hip'
show the change, in the names *Shap* (Westmoreland), *Shaps*
(East Riding), *Shipton* (North and East Riding), whereas
elsewhere they always show the expected native form in *H-*,
as in *Hapton*, *Heapey*, *Hepple*, *Hepworth*. Of especial relevance here is the fact that the early spellings of the
four names in *Sh-* within the focal area leave us in no
doubt as to the precise phonetic process and dating of the
change. They progress from the original *Hep-*, *Hip-*, to
Hyep- and later *Yhep* in the twelfth century, and lastly
to *S(c)hap*, *Schupton* etc. in the thirteenth and fourteenth
centuries. As Dieth rightly pointed out, these spellings
exactly mirror the expected phonetic sequence
[h- > hj- > ç > ʃ]; I return below to the significance of
the dating.

(ii) A further correspondence of the focal area with
historical place-name boundaries was pointed out by Kolb
(1965: 141-2). He showed that, in A.H. Smith's map for the
native place-name element *-worþ* 'enclosure', an area
corresponding exactly to our focal area is the only appreciable one in the whole of England from which this
element is absent, presumably because all the places in
question had been renamed.

(iii) The substitution of Scandinavian /k/ for English
/tʃ/ (as in *Lancaster* compared with *Lanchester*) is a fairly
widespread feature throughout the Danelaw area, and the
parallel phenomenon in which English names containing /tʃ/
were replaced by others of Scandinavian nomenclature (some
of which would naturally contain /k/) is similarly widespread. However, it is significant that in Gevenich (1918)
the focal area stands out as the only one in which she
found no names containing /tʃ/ at all, only those containing
/k/.

(iv) That such place-name distributions are an accurate
reflection of the linguistic situation in the period 1290-
1350 (and therefore confirm the existence of the focal area
in that period) has been demonstrated, in a remarkable way,
by G. Kristensson (1979). By examining the words for
'stream' in the Lay Subsidy Rolls, he shows, firstly, that
the area occupied by *beck* (ON *bekkr*) in that period was the

same as is indicated by the place-name evidence, and secondly, that, within the Northern area researched by him, the area for *beck* corresponded to the focal area plus Lincs. This was, as Kristensson puts it, "the area that was most strongly Scandinavianised".

(v) A more general indication comes from the geographical distribution of the surviving inscriptions written in Scandinavian runes. As recently observed (Hansen 1984: 67), these tell us little about the nature of language contact, but the fact remains that their sites can be plotted on a map, and, when this is done, all except one at London are in the focal area: three in Cumberland, two in N.Lancs., two in N.Yorks and one at Lincoln (Page 1973: 194-9). This provides at least a cultural indication in support of the others.

There is thus strong evidence for the focal area as an entity in medieval times, and it is therefore perhaps surprising that its linguistic and historical significance has not been followed up. It may be that the evidence so far produced has not appeared sufficiently striking to merit attention; that it is indeed striking can now be confirmed by fresh evidence from the Middle English Dialect Survey (McIntosh 1963, Benskin 1977).

In Middle English, before the coming of standardization, there were many more items that conformed to the various patterns shown in Fig. 1. Some of these were of the widest pattern, e.g. the southernmost limit of *stern* 'star' ran from Cheshire to the Wash (McIntosh 1973: 58). But others, even at that time, were restricted to the focal area, and two are of especial interest.

(1) The forms for 'are', plural of the verb *to be*, are given in the handbooks as *ar(e)* for Scots but *ar(e)* and *er(e)*, undifferentiated, for the North and North Midlands of England (Jordan-Crook 1974: 18). The form *ar(e)* is often said to be Scandinavian influenced (Hansen 1984: 71, with reference to Kisbye 1982), and it is possible that its selection in preference to *ben* could have been so influenced; but we have to recognise that *aron*, *earon* are well evidenced in the Old Anglian dialects, and that consequently *er(e)* is the only form that is of proven Scandinavian origin. It must therefore be significant that the distribution is predominantly *er(e)* in the focal area and Lincs. but predominantly *ar(e)* in the areas to the north and south of it; and since this is a Middle English distribution, established before Standard English had had any effect, it

is difficult to believe that *er(e)* had at that time undergone any recession.

(2) The strongest indication against recession in such forms comes from the distribution of the infinitive-markers *at* and *til*. Since *til* is not found with the infinitive in any Scandinavian language, its use thus in English is merely an extension of its use with substantives, on the analogy of *to*. We might therefore expect to find *at* in areas of primary settlement but *til* in any adjoining secondary areas, and that is, in the main, what we do find: *at* predominantly in the focal area and Lincs., but *til* in Lancs. and S.Yorks to the south and in Northumberland and Scots to the north. Here it is significant that for *til* there is some geographical correspondence with the so-called Grimston hybrids, for these provide an exact lexical counterpart to the grammatical hybrid seen in the *til* + infinitive construction.

It is thus possible to prove fairly conclusively that the focal area (with Lincs., to a greater or lesser extent) was, from the period of the actual settlements onwards, an area of deeper Scandinavian linguistic penetration than the rest of the Danelaw.

II. The conclusion reached above could have a number of implications for the study of English dialects. I choose for consideration here two topics, one morphological and the other phonological.

The first - probably the biggest puzzle of Middle English grammar - concerns the conjugation of the present indicative, especially the very different developments of the plural endings. For these, the reflex of OE *-aþ* survived as *-eþ* (*-iþ*, *-uþ*) in the South and South West Midlands only. The rest of the Midland area (especially the south and central portions) shows what we might regard as the natural and normal analogical development, in which *-en*, already firmly based in the preterite-present verbs, the present subjunctive, and both the indicative and subjunctive of the preterite, replaced *-eþ* in the present indicative. Analogical support for this development was also present in Norse, where both infinitive and 3rd present plural ended in *-a*, thus leading the English infinitive *-en* to be equated with the present plural. While it is difficult to assess the proportion of native and Norse pressures in this development, we need presuppose for it no more than an acceleration of the normal processes of change (Bryan 1921). But if so, why the quite different plural in *-es* in the North? The standard view, based on the evidence of the Late Old Northumbrian Lindisfarne Gospels, is that this too was an analogy, though a rather less expected one: the -*es*, original in the 2nd singular, spread first to the 2nd plural, then to the 1st and 3rd plural, and finally to the 3rd singular (Blakeley 1949). Naturally, there is no denying that this was the ordering of the process as it took place in the idiolect of the Lindisfarne glossator; but we have to remember that he worked at Chester le Street in Co. Durham, north of the focal area where the real change must have taken place, and an area for which we have no Old English evidence whatsoever. It seems more likely that in areas of primary Scandinavian influence the 3rd singular would have been the first ending to be affected by the analogy, if only because there was a clear model for it in the Old Norse -*R* which was common to both 2nd and 3rd singular, and which would still have been -*z* at the time of the Scandinavian settlements (Keller 1925: 85). A further reason for according priority to the 3rd singular in -*es* is that it occupied a larger area in Middle English, extending as far south as Norfolk, eventually entering London English and providing a model for the replacement of -*th* by -*s* throughout the present tense paradigm in southern dialects (Wright 1905: 296).

Now, if that analogical replacement of -*th* by -*s* could take place later in the southern dialects, it may be that the Northern Middle English -*es*-plural endings are no more than an earlier instance of the same analogy; and there have, of course, been other explanations of them in the past (Ross 1934, Bazell 1960). However, none of them account for the difference between the Northern and Midland developments, and it is therefore worth considering that difference in relation to the differing strengths of Scandinavian linguistic penetration discussed above.

At first sight this does not seem a promising line of enquiry, for there is nothing in the Old Norse present indicative to suggest a reason for the Northern -*es*-plural endings. If the Old Norse plural endings had provided the model, we would expect the normal Midland -*en*, because the 1st plural had the ending -*om* and the 3rd plural -*a*; while the 2nd plural in -*eþ* would merely have supported OE -*aþ* or its reflex -*eþ*. However, although it is often said that Old Norse and Old English were similar and to some extent mutually intelligible, there is a tendency to overlook one important difference between the Scandinavian and the Ingvaeonic languages: Old Norse preserved the original reflexive *sik*, whereas Ingvaeonic had the innovation *him/ hem*; and the *sik* in Old Norse had been incorporated, in enclitic form (-*zk*, -*sk*), in five of the six personal endings of the specifically Norse innovation - the Medio-Passive. Here, therefore, was a radical difference of conjugation between the two languages, and, in situations which assumed some degree of mutual intelligibility, this feature was bound to be misinterpreted by one side or the other. An obvious source for such misinterpretation would exist where Old English intransitive verbs corresponded to Old Norse reflexives, e.g. OE *hie sittaþ* 'they sit down', ON *þeir setjask*; a probable compromise form would be *hie sittas*, as in late Old Northumbrian.

The different developments of the plural endings in Middle English could thus be taken to reflect the different depths of Scandinavian penetration: the comparatively shallow penetration in the southern Danelaw led to the expected analogy in *-en*, while deeper penetration in the northern Danelaw led to the less expected development of a compromise or blend form in *-es*, which would be supported by its identity in form with the already-established *-es* in the 2nd and 3rd singular.

III. If the above view of the Northern development of the present indicative plural is correct, it must be assumed to have taken place well before its appearance in the tenth-century Lindisfarne Gloss, i.e. quite early in the history of the Scandinavian communities in the north. But that is not the only period or type of contact-phenomenon to be considered. We must also consider the survival of Scandinavian proper, including transmission via bilinguals, which would be greatest among the younger generations during the period of language death. We have already seen that the focal area is the only one in the country to show a typically Scandinavian sound-change in progress in the twelfth century and first appearing completed in thirteenth-century spellings. It therefore seems reasonable to postulate that Scandinavian survived till the twelfth century in comparatively closed communities in that area, and that the ensuing language death could have brought about changes comparable to those observed for other language deaths today.

Above (p.270), the simple north-south pattern of Fig.3 was mentioned as one of those typical for the distribution of Scandinavian lexical items. But this pattern, with some minor variations, corresponds with two of the most important phonological features of the Northern dialect: the fronting of OE $\bar{a}$ to /æ:/, later /e:/, as in *hame*, *stane* compared with *home*, *stone*; and the parallel fronting of ME (close) $\bar{o}$ to /ø:/ or /y:/ as in *gud(e)*, *buk(e)* compared with *go(o)d*, *bo(o)k*. On the modern map the southern limits for these two features correspond with the well-known Lune-Humber line (Kolb 1965: 150); in ME the limit for *gude* etc. was slightly further south, while for OE $\bar{a}$ there was a mixed $\bar{a}/\bar{o}$ area similarly just south of the present line.

This line has traditionally been regarded as of great antiquity, representing 'the ancient boundary between the Anglo-Saxon kingdoms of Northumbria and Mercia' (Wakelin 1972: 102), and the fact that it coincides with the southern boundary of the focal area is regarded as nothing more than coincidence. But why should it be? There is no proof that the two phonological changes in question antedate the Scandinavian invasions: the fronting of $\bar{o}$ is not evidenced before the mid-thirteenth century (Aitken 1956); and the evidence for the early fronting of $\bar{a}$ is only negative, since the change is merely presumed from the absence of $\bar{o}$-spellings (Luick 1914: 359). It is noticeable, too, that both changes are unexpected in their phonetic nature, and run counter to the usual trends in circular vowel-shifts (on $\bar{o}$, cf. Luick 1914: 426, 429).

As an alternative to the usual view, the following sequence might be suggested:
(i) Spoken Scandinavian survived, in closed communities, till the twelfth century in the focal area.
(ii) With the opening up of these communities, Scandinavian tended to become restricted to the older generation, and language death ensued (any far reaching event, like the Civil War of the mid-twelfth century, could have provided the catalyst for this process).
(iii) During the process and to a greater extent than previously, the younger generation would become sensitive to differences between their parents' and monolingual English speakers' realisations of ME $\bar{o}$ and Northern ME $\bar{a}$. In the case of $\bar{o}$, there was in any case considerable etymological correspondence between the English and Norse distributions; in the case of $\bar{a}$ (= Prim. Germanic *ai*), the question is complicated by the ON development to *ei* (as in *heim*, *steinn*), but even so it is natural to assume that bilinguals would in such words replace ON *ei* by $\bar{a}$. It would, therefore, need only a slight difference between the English and Norse realisations to occasion hypercorrection by the younger generation. Since it seems likely, from the modern Scandinavian languages, that it was the Scandinavian $\bar{a}$ and $\bar{o}$ vowels that were more retracted than those of Northern

English, it would be natural for the younger generation to front these vowels in the direction of /æ:/ and /ø:/. (That the Southern English $\bar{a}$ was itself becoming /ɔ:/ in the twelfth and thirteenth centuries is not really relevant here, since the spread of that change northwards was slow.) Though differing in phonetic direction, the process of hypercorrection postulated here is the same as that found by Labov in immigrant families in New York (1972: 171).

(iv) Many of the same younger generations who either initiated or imitated these hyperforms migrated to Scotland, and that accounts for the increased area of these changes. One might even postulate that the hyperforms were first used on arrival in Scotland, as a direct result of migration to a less Scandinavianized milieu, and that would account for the fact that the earliest spellings of u for $\bar{o}$ are Scottish (Aitken, and cf. Kristensson 1967). It is also perhaps worth noting that within the focal area in the ME period, the incidence of both u for ME $\bar{o}$ and of o for Northern ME $\bar{a}$ is somewhat patchy and unpredictable, and this might reflect varying dates and periods for language death, but also a complex sociolinguistic situation in which some speakers favoured the hyperforms /æ:/ and /ø:/, while others preferred the corresponding Southern English sounds /ɔ:/ and /o:/.

IV. Naturally, in considering such alternative solutions, there can be no place for dogma. They are simply further possibilities that are suggested by the geographical evidence, and, as so often in such cases, we are left to weigh the balance of probabilities. And the two cases considered above are by no means the only ones. Another very striking one is the reduction of the definite article to *t'* or *th'* (e.g. *t'man*, *th'mon*), or its complete deletion. This occurs in an area similar to the widest in Fig. 1 but excluding Norfolk (Wright 1905: 238) and Lincs. (*SED* IV.4.1). Why, we may ask, does this happen only to the definite article and not to other proclitics? Surely, this must be because the substratum had (except with adjectives) *nothing* in that position: the ON definite article was a postpositive enclitic (e.g. *maþrenn*, Acc. *mannenn*, Norw. *mannen*), which in English would come to be treated like any deletable inflectional syllable.

This case, like the others, is difficult to prove conclusively on its own. But it is in an area of study where the further one looks the more correspondences one is likely to find. It would not be at all surprising if, when further points have been researched and they are all considered together, they were to point to the same conclusion:

that the greatest single formative influence on the
English dialect map was the Scandinavian invasions.*

* My special thanks are due to Professor Angus McIntosh for permission to use the results of his work on the dialects of Northern Middle English. I have also to thank Professor Michael Benskin, Paul Johnston, Caroline Macafee and Jeremy Smith for helpful discussion, and Cecily Clark, Professor J. Fisiak, and Gillis Kristensson for bibliographical references. However, this acknowledgment of their help should not be taken to imply that they agree with my views.

REFERENCES

Aitken, A.J. 1956. *Specimens of Older Scots*. Edinburgh University (mimeograph).
Bazell, C.E. 1960. 'A Question of Syncretism and Analogy'. *TPS*, 1-12.
Benskin, M. 1977. 'Local Archives and Middle English Dialects'. *Journal of the Society of Archivists*, 5.500-14.
Blakeley, L. 1949. 'The Lindisfarne s/ð problem'. *SN* 22.15-47.
Bryan, W.F. 1921. 'The Midland Present Plural Indicative in -(e)n'. *MP* 18.457-73.
Clark, Cecily. 1983. 'On Dating *The Battle of Maldon*: Certain Evidence Reviewed'. *Nottingham Medieval Studies*, 27.1-22.
Dieth, E. 1955. 'Hips: A geographical Contribution to the 'she' Puzzle.' *ES* 36.208-17.
Gevenich, Olga. 1918. *Die englische Palatalisierung von k > č im Lichte der englischen Ortsnamen*. Studien zur englischen Philologie 57. Halle a.S.: Niemeyer.
Hansen, Bente H. 1984. 'The Historical Implications of the Scandinavian Linguistic Element in English.' *North-Western European Language Evolution*, 4.53-95.
Jordan, R. 1974. (1934). *Handbook of Middle English Grammar*. Translated and revised by E.J. Crook. The Hague: Mouton.
Keller, W. 1925. 'Skandinavischer Einfluss in der englischen Flexion.' In W. Keller, ed. *Probleme der englischen Sprache und Kultur: Festschrift Johannes Hoops*, 80-87. Heidelberg: Winter.
Kisbye, T. 1982. *Vikingerne i England: Sproglige Spor*. Akademisk Forlag.
Kolb, E. 1965. 'Skandinavisches in den nordenglischen Dialekten.' *Anglia* 83.127-53.
Kristensson, G. 1967. *A Survey of Middle English Dialects 1290-1350: The Six Northern Counties and Lincolnshire*. Lund Studies in English 35. Lund: Gleerup.
Kristensson, G. 1979. 'A Piece of Middle English Word Geography.' *ES* 60.254-60.
Labov, W. 1972. *Sociolinguistic Patterns*. Philadelphia: University of Pennsylvania Press.

Linguistic Atlas of England, ed. H. Orton, S. Sanderson and
  J. Widdowson, 1978. London: Croom Helm.
Luick, K. 1914-, reprinted 1964. *Historische Grammatik der englischen Sprache*. Stuttgart: Tauchnitz.
McIntosh, A. 1963. 'A New Approach to Middle English Dialectology.' *ES* 44.1-11.
McIntosh, A. 1973. 'Word Geography in the Lexicography of Medieval English.' *Annals of the New York Academy of Sciences* 211.55-66.
Orton, H. and Wright, N. 1974. *A Word Geography of England*. London: Seminar Press.
Page, R.I. 1973. *An Introduction to English Runes*. London: Methuen.
Ross, A.S.C. 1934. 'The Origin of the *s*-endings of the Present Indicative in English.' *JEGP* 33.68-73.
SED = *Survey of English Dialects*, ed. H. Orton *et al.*, 1962-71. Leeds: Arnold.
Smith, A.H. 1956. *English Place-Name Elements*, Vol. II. *EPNS* 26, Map 3. Cambridge: University Press.
Wakelin, M.F. 1972. *English Dialects: An Introduction*. London: Athlone Press.
Wright, J. 1905. *The English Dialect Grammar*. Oxford: Clarendon Press.

DISCOURSE MARKERS IN EARLY MODERN ENGLISH
DIETER STEIN
Justus-Liebig University of Giessen, W-Germany

1. One of the salient characteristics of EME is its wealth of variant forms on all levels of language. Not surprisingly, one of the preoccupations of many linguists - including myself - has been to look for factors determining the choice of one or the other of these variants. This paper will be concerned with two areas of notorious variability: the choice between the two endings *s* and *th* of the third person sing. pres. ind. and the use of *do* or finite form in declarative sentences, such as in example 1:

(1) he sings - he singeth   he sings - he doth sing.

An interesting clue where to look for such factors are phenomena like the so-called *mystery particles* (Longacre 1976 b), which refer to the global organisation of discourse, such as story main line, backbone tags, main participants or narrative peak. Surface marking of these functions are typical examples of markers of the *level of the organisation of the utterance* in Praguian terms. Expressions with this type of function have *textual meaning* in the Hallidayan sense.

In English, discourse meaning is marked on the surface by a most diverse array of forms, by a *bag of tricks* (Longacre 1976 a: 217). Given the notorious and apparently intractable and random variability of the morphological and syntactic variable, one might wonder whether they might not also to some extent be part of this *bag of tricks*.

2. The distribution of *s* or *th* has been said to depend primarily on stylistic factors, but rhythmical and phonological factors have also been mentioned (e. g. Samuels 1972: 174 f). Example 2 from Robert Greene's *Art of Conny-Catching*[1] will be used to analyse the distribution of *s* and *th* in detail, at the expense of the discussion of the other examples.[2]

In example 2, consisting of four consecutive pages from one of these pamphlets, in which the relevant forms are underlined, a first obvious phenomenon to be noted is a sudden increase in the use of *th* on the fourth page. This increase appears even *more* marked when we note that, on the first three pages, the only cases of *th* are the auxiliaries *have* and *do*, the verb *say* and verbs with sibilant ending verb-stems, such as *discourseth* on [19]. Now these latter cases - represented as example 3 - are *not* part of the variable, as they appear exclusively with *th*. The variable consists only of *non-sibilant ending main verbs*. This state of affairs characterizes one distinct isolectal stage in the change process from *th* to *s*, as it is reflected in the texts investigated.[3]

In example 2, if we are looking for something to change in line with the endings, the obvious candidate is the content structure of the text, and not micro-linguistic environments. In other words: the formal structure of the *s/th* distinction i.e. the asymmetrical distribution of *s* and *th* over the four pages alone suggests a discourse structure explanation. If we are looking for some parameter in the structure of the discourse the impression is that in the *s* parts the circumstances, the agents and the places are described in more detail. They are more specific, whereas the *th* parts represent the conny-catching technique from a more general or generic point of view. The *s* parts represent a specific occasion: the impression is that a scene is built up before us, with specific persons and places, a specific, if imagined, event is described. In the *th*-part, the focus is less on the specific event in its uniqueness, but on how it is normally, typically, done. When we read: '*The countryman spying the shilling, maketh not daintie, ..., but stoupeth very mannerly and taketh it up: ...*' [21], the impression is that it could be *any* countryman, not a definite one in an imagined scene that has been built up with identified and specific persons, places and circumstances, such as in the *s* passages. We also have the impression that the *s* passages have us look at a scene from outside, a natural consequence of being made to look at an imagined scene, whereas in the *th* stretch we seem to be given more of an inside view of the technique with focus on the technicalities of the tricks.

It is remarkable that the three occurrences of *s* in *th* country on [21] are all cases which stand outside this perspective created in the *th* passages: they take us back to relating what is going on from outside. But *th* reappears when *a further policie* is related: focus is again on the technique.

The *th/s* contrast, then, appears to have a discourse function in the sense of differentiating between two different and alternating modes of narrating or reporting.

(2) from Greene 1591: 18-21.

circumstance which they vse in catching of them. And for because the poore countrie farmer or Yeoman is the marke which they most of all shoote at, who they knowe comes not emptie to the Terme, I will discouer the means they put in practise to bring in some honest, simple & ignorant men to their purpose. The Conny-catchers, apparelled like honest ciuil gentlemen, or good fellows, with a smooth face, as if butter would not melt in their mouthes, after dinner when the clients are come from Westminster hal and are at leasure to walke vp and downe Paules, Fleet-street, Holborne, the sttrond, and such common hanted places, where these cosning companions attend onely to spie out a praie: who as soone as they see a plaine cuntry felow well and cleanly apparelled, either in a coat of home spun russet, or of freeze, as the time requires, and a side pouch at his side, there is a connie, saith one. At that word out flies the Setter, and ouertaking the man, begins to salute him thus: Sir, God saue you, you are welcom to London, how doth all our good friends in the countrie, I hope they will be all in health? The countrie man seeing a man so curteous he knowes not, halfe in a browne studie at this strange salutation, perhaps makes him this aunswere. Sir, all our friends in the countrie are well thankes bee to God, but truly I know you not, you must pardon me. Why sir, saith the setter, gessing by his tong
[18]
what country man hee is, are you not such a cuntry man, if he say yes, then he creeps vpon him closely: if he say no, the straight the setter comes ouer him thus: In good sooth sir, I know you by your face & haue bin in your companie before, I praie you (if without offence) let me craue your name, and the place of your abode. The simple man straight tels him where he dwels his name, and who be his next neighbors, and what Gentlemen dwell about him. After he hath learned al of him, then he comes ouer his fallowes kindly: sir, though I haue bin somwhat bold to be inquisitiue of your name, yet holde me excused, for I tooke you for a friend of mine, but since by mistaking I haue made you slacke your busines, wele drinke a quart of wine, or a pot of Ale together: if the foole be so readie as to go, then the Connie is caught: but if he smack the setter, and smels a rat by his clawing, and will not drinke with him, then away goes the setter, and discourseth to the verser the name of the man, the parish hee dwels in, and what gentlemen are his near neighbours, with that away goes he, & and crossing the man at some turning, meets him ful in the face, and greetes him thus.

What goodman Barton, how fare al our friends about you? you are well met, I haue the wine for you, you are welcome to towne. The poore countryman hearing himselfe named by a man he knows not, maruels, & answers that he knowes him not,
[19]

and craues pardon. Not me goodman
Barton, haue you forgot me? why I
am such a mās kinsman, your neigh-
bor not far off: how doth this or
that good gentleman my friend?
good Lord that I should be out of
your remembrance, I haue béene at
your house diuers times. Indeede,
sir, saith the farmer, are you
such a mans kinsman, surely sir if
you had not chalenged acquaintance
of me, I should neuer haue knowen
you, I haue clean forgot you, but
I know the good gentleman your co-
sin well, he is my very good neigh-
bor: & for his sake saith ye verser, wéel drink afore we part,
haply the man thanks him, and to
the wine or ale they goe, then ere
they part, they make him a cony,
& so feret-claw him at cardes, y^t
they leaue him as bare of mony, as
an ape of a taile: thus haue the
filthie felows their subtle fe-
tches to draw on poor men to fal
into their cosening practises:
thus like consuming moths of the
common welth, they pray vpon the
ignorance of such plain soules,
as measure al by their own hones-
ty, not regarding either con-
science, or the fatal reuenge
thats thretened for such idle &
licentious persons, but do imploy
all their wits to ouerthrow such
as with their handy thrifte sa-
tisfie their harty thirst: they
preferring cosenage before labor,
and chusing an idle practise before any honest form of good liuing. Wel, to ye method again of
taking vp their conies. If the
poore countreyman smoake them
still, and wil not
[20]

stoupe vnto either of their lures:
then one, either the verser, or
the setter, or some of their crue,
for there is a general fraternity
betwixt them, steppeth before the
Cony as he goeth, and letteth
drop twelue pence in the high way,
that of force the cony must see
it. The countreyman spying the
shilling, maketh not daintie, for
quis nisi mentis inops obla-
tum respuit aurum, but stoupeth very mannerlie and taketh it
vp: then one of the cony catchers
behind crieth halfe part, and so
chalengeth halfe of his finding.
The countriman content, offreth
to change the mony. Nay faith
frend, saith the verser, tis ill
luck to kéep founde mony, wele
go spend it in a pottle of wine,
or in a breakefast, dinner or
supper, as the time of day requires: If the conye say he wil
not, then answeres the verser,
spende my part: if stil the cony
refuse, he taketh halfe and away,
if they spy the countriman to be
of a hauing and couetous mind,
then haue they a further policie
to draw him on: another that
knoweth the place of his abode,
méeteth him and saith Sir, wel
met, I haue run hastely to ouer-
take you, I pray you dwel you not
in Darbishire, in such a village?
Yes marry doe I frend saith the
cony, then replies the verser,
truely sir I haue a sute to you,
I am going out of town, & must
send a letter to the parson of
your parish, you shall not refuse
to do a stranger such a fauor as
to cary it him, haply, as men may
in time meet, it may lie in my
[21]

(3) *have*, *do*, *say*, main verbs with verb-stem ending in a
 sibilant: → *th*

This discourse use can also be illustrated with another example, where the Setter, the Verser and the Barnacle, three types of criminals collaborating in a task, are at it again, to relieve the Connie of his money. Again, it will be noted that the first eligible *th* on [26] occurs after a number of *'s* (the occurrences of *say* do not count): *steppeth*, which is again part of the criminals' game: the act of pretending to step back is not genuine – it is part of the criminal practice; its purpose is to mislead the conny into believing that the Verser and the Setter have never before met the newly entering Barnacle. This is announced by the meta-sentence *but now begins the sport*, which marks off another structural part of the discourse, which analyses the technique of conny-catching – how it is typically done – in great detail. It is part of the game with marked cards to let the conny win until he wages all his money, and of course loses it all. In the run-up to this, the Barnacle is deliberately losing and pretends to be angry and swears – again with a *th* (bottom of p. 27). Again, *th* appears in those passages which describe what is typical, rather than individual.

In example 5, *th* appears in the passages where the central part of the criminal practice is described. What is narrated must be called the central part of the narrative:

A pleasant tale howe an honest substantiall Citizen
was made a Connie, and simply entertained a knave
that carried awaie his goods very politickely.

After telling us for nine pages how the Conny-Catcher gets the conny to entertain the knave at his home, *th* occurs in those passages in which the knave carries away the goods very 'politickely' – again, there is an individuated scene built up before us, but again followed by a change of gear: the second part shows what typically happens, as in 6.

The hypothesis that *th* marks those passages which are not individuated in a typically narrative way is also supported by the incidence of *th* in example 7 ('A table of the words of art, used in the effecting these base villanies') [p. 37], which obviously represent the typical, and *not* the individual: the predominant ending is *th*.

If the *th/s* contrast reflects two discourse modes in these pamphlets, this can be related to the position of those pamphlets in the development of prose narratives from allegory to fiction proper. Greene's pamphlets occupy a halfway position on the way to the early novel or narrative proper, for which the illusion of reality with individuated, concrete events as an end in themselves may be said to be constitutive. Now it is a characteristic of Greene's pamphlets that there is a repeated changing of gear between passages of the developmentally more novel kind and passages which analyse the *arts* or *laws* in a more general, unindividuated way. This distinction between the two modes in the pamphlets has long been established in literary analysis of the pamphlets. In the relevant study by Klein (1969), the two categories are labelled (p. 36) *erzählerische Vergegenwärtigung einzelner Betrugsfälle* - the *s* passages, and *analysierender Bericht* - the *th* passages.

It is not surprising that *s* is assigned to the passages with the illusion of a real-life scene: *s* is after all the normal ending in the colloquial and spoken language of the time.

Klein (ibid.) also notes that in the later pamphlets - the *Third and Last Part of Conny Catching*, and *A Disputation between a He-Conny-Catcher and a She-Conny-Catcher*, the number of general and typical descriptions decreases: this has been interpreted as progress in narrative technique. This is also the obvious explanation for the finding that the number of *th's* decreases drastically, but only the members of the variable: non-sibilant ending main verbs. All other phonological environments continue to be realised with *th*. Only the contrast between the members of the variable restricted to this environment is the basis for discourse meanings.

These are not the only contexts where the *th/s* contrast is semioticised; *th* also appears in proverbs, sayings, and in the speech of judges passing sentence, but it is the characteristic one for these texts.

Apart from more literary evidence, there is also independent *linguistic* evidence for the existence of these two narrative modes. In the *s* passages the use of direct speech makes for a more involved and vivid impression of the scene. Also, generally speaking, much more verbal effort is invested in making the scenes individuated in terms of details and circumstances. Another good grammatical diagnostic is the kind of anaphoric forms used: In example 2, in the first three pages reproduced, in the more narrative part, of the 21 times the conny is referred to, there is considerable variation in anaphoric forms. There are 9 personal pronouns plus a range of nominal forms, such as *the plain country fellow*, *the man*, *the country man*, *the simple man*, *the fool*, *the farmer*, *the poor countryman*, whereas of the 9 cases in the *th* passage, there is only one personal pronoun, 4 times *countryman* and 5 times *the conny*. So it can be said that the *s* parts contain much more descriptive, circumstantial, detailed individuating verbal effort, while the *th* parts are distinctly more technical. They contain more terminology; they are like an instruction manual for the *laws* or *arts*.

(4) from Greene 1591: 26-27

saith the verser, Ile do it for thanks, and therfore marke me where you haue taken out the four knaues, lay two together aboue, and draw vp one of them that it may be seene, then prick the other in the midst, & the third in the bottome, so when any cuts, cut he neuer so warily, three knaues must of force come together, for the bottom knaue is cut to lie vpon the vpper knaues. I marrie, saith the setter, but then the 3. knaues you shewed come not together. Truth saith the verser, but one among a thousand marke not y^t, it requires a quick eie, a sharp wit, and a reaching head to spy at the first. Now gramercie sir for this trick, saith the connie, Ile dominere with this amongst my neibors. Thus doth the verser and the setter feine friendship to the conie, offering him no shew of cosnage, nor once to draw him in for a pint of wine, ye more to shadow their vilany, but now begins the sporte: as thus they sit tipling, comes the Barnacle and thrusts open the doore, looking into the roome where they are, and as one bashfull steppeth back againe, and saith, I crie you mercie gentlemen, I thoght a friend of mine had bin here, pardon my boldnes. No harme saith the Verser, I praie you drinke a cup of wine with vs and welcome: so in comes the Barnacle, and taking the cup drinkes to the Connie, and then saith, what at cards gentlemen? were it not I should be offensiue to the company I would play for a pint till my friend
[26]

come that I looke for. Why sir, saith the Verser, if you will sit downe you shalbe taken vp for a quart of wine. With all my heart, saith the Barnackle, what will you play at, at Primero, Primo visto, Sant, one and thirtie, new cut, or what shall be the game? Sir, saith the Verser, I am but an ignorant man at cards, & I see you haue them at your fingers end, I will play with you at a game wherein can be no deceit, it is called mum-chance at cardes, and it is thus: you shall shuffle the cards, and I will cut, you shal cal one, and this honest countrie yoman shal call a card for me, and which of our cards comes first shal win: here you see is no deceit, and this Ile play. No truly, saith the Connie, me thinkes there can be no great craft in this: well saith the barnacle, for a pint of wine haue at you: so they play as before, fiue vp, and the verser wins. This is hard luck, sayth the Barnacle, and I beleeue the honest man spies some carde in the bottom, and therefore Ile make this, alwais to prick the bottom card: content saith the verser, and the Connie to cloak the matter, saith: sir, you offer me iniury to think that I can call a card, when I neither touch them, shuffle, cut, nor draw them: Ah sir, saith the barnacle, giue loosers leaue to speak: wel, to it they go againe, and then the barnacle knowing the game best, by chopping a card winnes two of the fiue, but lets the verser win the set, then in a chafe he sweareth tis but his ill
[27]

(5) from Greene 1592: 20

dead time of the night, when sound sleep makes ye eare vnapt to heare the verie least noyse, he forsaketh his bed, & hauing gotten all the plate bound vp togither in his cloke, goeth downe into the shop, where well remembring both the place and percels, maketh vp his pack with some twenty pounds-worth of goods more. Then setling to his engin, he getteth the doore off the hindges, and being foorth, lifteth close to againe, and so departes, meeting within a dozen paces, three or foure of his companions that lurked therabouts for the purpose. Their word for knowing ech other, as is said, was *Quest*, and this villaines comfortable newes to them, was *Twag*, signifying he had sped: ech takes a fleece for easier carriage, and so away to *Bell brow*, which, as I haue heard is as they interpret it, the house of a theefe receiuer, without which they can do nothing, and this house with an apt porter to it, stands redie for them all houres of the night: too many such are there in London, the maisters whereof beare countenance of honest substantiall men, but all their liuing is gotten in this order, the end of such (though they scape awhile) will be sayling westward in a Cart to Tiborn. Imagine these villaines there in their iollitie, the one reporting point by point his cunning deceipt, and the other (fitting his humour) extolling the deede with no meane commendations. But returning to the honest Citizen, who
[20]

(6) from Greene 1591: 10

the time with strange recreations and pastimes, beguyling hunger with the delight of the new sports, and eating but euery third day, and playing two, so their frugal sparing of victuals kept them from famine, the Cittie from sacking, and raysed the foe from a mortall siedge. Thus was the use of Cards and Dice first inuented, and since amongst Princes highly esteemed, and allowed in all common-wealths, as a necessarie recreation for the mind: But as in time and malice of mans nature hatcheth abuse, so good things by ill wits are wrested to the worse, and so in Cardes: for from an honest recreation, it is grown to a preiudiciall practise, and most high degree of coosenage, as shalbe discouered in my Art of Cuny-catching, for not onely simple swaines, whose wits is in their hands, but yoong Gentlemen, and Marchants, are all caught like Cunnies in the hay, and so led like lambs to their confusion.

The poore man that commeth to the Tearme to trie his right, and layeth his land to morgadge to gette some Crownes in his purse to see his Lawyer, is drawn in by these diuelish Cunny-catchers, that at one cut at Cardes looseth all his money, by which meanes, he, his wife and children, is brought to vtter ruine and miserie. The poore Prentice, whose honest minde aymeth only at his Maisters profites, by these pestilent vipers of the commonwealth, is smoothly intised to the hazard of this game at Cardes, and robd of his Maisters money, which forceth him oft times eyther to

(7) from Greene 1591: 37 ff.

A table of the words of art, vsed in the effecting
       these base villanies.
*Wherein is discouered the nature of euery terme, being
    proper to none but to the professors thereof.*

1	High law	*robbing by the highway side.*
2	Sacking law	*lecherie.*
3	Cheting law	*play at false dice.*
4	Cros-biting law	*cosenage by whores.*
5	Conycatching law	*cosenage by cards.*
6	Versing law	*cosenage by false gold.*
7	Figging law	*cutting of purses, & picking of pockets.*
8	Barnards law	*a drunken cosenage by cards.*

These are the eight lawes of villanie, leading the
        high waie to infamie.

In high Lawe.
   The Theefe is called a High lawier.
   He that setteth the Watch, a Scrippet.
   He that standeth the watch, an Oake
   He that is robd the Martin
   When he yeeldeth, stouping.

In sacking Law.
   The Bawd if it be a woman, a Pander
   The Bawd, if a man, an Apple squire
   The whoore, a Commoditie
   The whoore house, a Trugging place.

In cheating law.
   Pardon me Gentlemen for although no man could better then my self discouer this lawe and his tearmes, and the name of their Cheats, Barddice, Flats, Forgers, Langrets, Gourds, Demies, and many other, with their nature, & the crosses and contraries to them vpon aduantage, yet for some speciall reasons, herein I will be silent.

In Cros-biting lawe
   The whore, the Traffique
   The man that is brought in, the Simpler.
   The villaines that take them, the Cros-biters.

In Coni-catching law.
   The partie that taketh vp the Connie, the Setter.
   He that plaieth the game, the Verser
   He that is coosned the Connie,
   He that comes in to them, the Barnackle
   The monie that is wonne, Purchase

In Versing law.	He that bringeth him in, the Verser The poore Countrie man, the Coosin And the dronkard that comes in, the Suffier
In Figging law.	The Cutpurse, a Nip He that is halfe with him, the Snap The knife, the Cuttle boung The picke pocket, a Foin He that faceth the man, the Stale Taking the purse, Drawing Spying of him, Smoaking The purse, the Bong The monie, the Shels The Act doing, striking
In Barnards lawe.	He that fetcheth the man, the Taker He that is taken, the Coosin The landed man the Verser The dronken man the Barnard And he that makes the fray, the Rutter.

Cum multis aliis quæ nunc præ scribere longum est.

(8) from Latimer 1549: 173

Amonge the other there was one wyser then the rest, and he commes me to the Bishop. Whi mi Lord, sayth he, doth your lordship mak so grat matter of the bell, that lacketh hys clapper?

(9) from Latimer 1549: 163

Factum est autem. (Sayth the text) cum turba irrueret in cum.* Sayncte Luke telles the storye, and it came to passe, when the people presed vpon him, so that he was in peril to be cast into the pond they rushed so faste vpon hym and made such throng to him.

(10) from Latimer 1549: 196

He resortes to hys frendes, seking some comfort at theyr handes seynge he hade none at hys fathers hande, he comes to hys disciples, and fyndes them a slepe, he spake vnto Peter, and saied. Ah Peter arte thou a slepe, Peter before had bragged stoutly, as thoughe he woulde haue kylled, God haue mercye vpon hys foule.

(11) from Latimer 1549: 166

When Sayncte Augustyne came to Myllane, (he telles the storye hymselfe in the ende of his boke of confessions) he was very desirous to here S. Ambrose.

(12) from Latimer 1549: 153

I can tell where one man flew an other, in a tounshyp, and was attached
vpon the same. xii. men were impaneled, the man hadde frendes, the
Shryue laboured the bench, the. xii. men stacke at it and fayed, excepte
he woulde disburse. xii crownes they woulde fynde hym gyltye.
 Meanes were found that the xii. crownes was payed. The quest comm<u>es</u>
in and say<u>es</u> not giltye.
 Here was a not gyltye for xii. crownes. This is bearyng. And some of
the bench were hanged, thei were wel serued.

(13) from Nashe 1592-1599: 267, 339

but the tragedy followeth,here beginneth my purgatory

(14) from Nashe 1529-1599: 335 ff.

He grasped her by the ivory throat and shook her as a mastiff would
shake a young bear, swearing and staring he would tear out her weasand
if she refused. Not content with that savage constraint, he slipped his
sacrilegious hand from her lily lawn-skinned neck and enscarfed it in
her long silver locks which with struggling were unrolled. Backward he
dragged her, even as a man backward would pluck a tree down by the twigs,
and then, like a traitor that is drawn to execution on a hurdle, he
trail<u>eth</u> her up and down the chamber by those tender untwisted braids,

 In Bishop Latimer's sermons from 1549, the change from
th to *s* can also be shown to be related to discourse structure. In this text, the *s* forms are the exception, there
are 90 *s* forms compared to over 500 *th* forms. So what has
to be *explained* is uses of *s* forms. The linguistic or
isolectal basis is the same as with Greene: the variable is
again confined to non-sibilant ending main verbs. A very
characteristic use of *s* is in introducing direct speech or
stories with which the sermons are interspersed for illus-
trative and rhetorical purposes. *s* appears typically in
passages such as in example 8, where *s* occurs in a kind of
orientational overture to the story proper in direct speech.
s may be said here to belong to or to signal a different
level of discourse. Similarly in 9, where *s* occurs in the
announcing of the story, as in example 10, which is
also similar to 8 in introducing a story in direct speech.
The assumption that the decisive factor is the marking of
a change in discourse level is also supported by the fact
that a change of tense is often involved between preterite
and present: at these points of changes in discourse level,
it is *s* that appears and not the predominant or normal *th*.
In example 11, *s* appears in parenthesis. What appears in
the brackets is clearly on a meta-level of discourse in
comparison to the surrounding discourse. In the final

example 12, *s* appears in what must be called the peak of the story at that particular point of the sermon. The effect of *s* is certainly to make that passage felt as more vivid and dramatic.

If a change of tense from preterite to the historical present has the effect of making a passage more vivid, making us re-live a scene (Schiffrin 1981: 57-61), again it is only natural that *s*, the ending of spoken language, should appear.

Similar textual functions of *th/s* contrast can of course be observed in other texts of the same period such as in Nashe's *Unfortunate Traveller*, where the exceptional *th* appears in structure-demarcating meta-sentences such as in example 13, or in example 14, where the use of *th* coincides with the peak of the episode, also demarcated by a change in tense. As a last typical case of structure-demarcating one may mention the use of *th* in direct speech, but *s* in the other parts in Deloney's novels, as well as in Nashe.

When we sum up this section by saying that the *th/s* variable has a textual function, we mean that this contrast is functionalised as a broad denominator for a broad range of heterogeneous functions, depending on the specific type of content of that text type or genre.

Following a usage by Quirk (1971: 70 ff.) in his discussion of the pronominal contrast between *you* and *thou*, where the latter is the marked choice with additional meaning, one would have to posit *s* as the marked form for the earliest texts studied and *th* for the later texts studied. The fact that, in the printed text, *s* eventually follows the colloquial spoken language is reflected in the markedness formulation by a markedness reversal: in the later texts - Deloney and Nashe - it is *th* which carries the extra-textual-information besides designating person, tense and mood.

There is, of course, the obvious possibility of printers' and editors' tampering, particularly with the inflectional endings. But the pattern of usage described here[4] is too systematical and too far away from randomness to have been caused by factors of textual history.

3. The general statements on the *th/s* contrast also hold true for the contrast *do/finite* form in declarative sentences. Here too, the current literature states that there is no difference in meaning between the finite form and *do*:

(15) It is certain that at this time it did not in general
convey any special shade of meaning. It was completely
synonymous with the simple verb form.
(Ellegård 1953: 209)

...ohne daß ein Bedeutungsunterschied solcher Um-
schreibungen gegenüber den nicht mit do verbundenen
Verben deutlich wäre ('pleonastische Umschreibungen').
(Brunner 1962: 323-324)

Here again, if the problem is approached from a semantic point of view, it is possible to show that there are distinctly recognisable factors of meaning. Painter's *Palace of Pleasure* (1560) is a collection of translations of Italian novellas or short novels by Bocaccio and Bandello into English. In many of these stories there is an orientation phase which gives the setting for the ensuing complication. At the juncture of these two structural parts there is often a clearly recognisable point which marks the beginning of the complication, and this is where *do* typically appears, such as in examples 16 and 17. In 16 the complication is a consequence of what the duke says; in 17 it is the fact that this duke kept the fifth key which ultimately causes all the problems.

(16) And in this state stood this passionate lover a long
time, tormented with the exceeding hot love and
feeltie that he bore her. And many times making his
reverent complaints to love, did say: ...
(Painter 1560, Vol. II: 4)

(17) When this Palace and Treasure house was done, he caused
all furnitures of silkes...(a long list of valuables
follows)...to be carried thither, which he called La
Torpea del Doge and was kept under five keys: whereof
four were delivered four of the chief citizens,...,
and the fifth key the Duke himself did keep,...
(Painter 1560, Vol. I: 9)

Do seems to be related to what is the high point of the content, the essential parts. This is also suggested by a look at the distribution of *do* over longer stories: *do* is distributed extremely unevenly over the whole story and shows distinct clusterings in certain places which represent events that are pivotal for the complication. Obviously, the explanation cannot be a correlation with syntactic or grammatical features, but must make reference to content structure.

Andrew Boorde's *Introduction to Knowledge* (1545) is a description of the ways of life and customs of various nations and countries, a type of literature very popular at the time. The descriptions of the individual countries are introduced by geographical facts, followed by the description of customs of the particular region. It is in this second part that *do* appears in larger numbers, such as in ex. 18 and 19. Here too, *do* seems to be related to what in that genre must be considered the gist or the peak of the content.

(18) from Boorde 1545: 172 ff.

Constantinople is one of the greatyst cytes of the world: the cyte is built lyke a triangle; two partes <u>stondeth</u> and <u>abutteth</u> to the watter, and the other parte hath a respect of the londe: the cyte is well walled, and there <u>commeth</u> to it an arme of the See, called Saynct Georges arme or Hellysponte, or the myghte of Constantinople: saynt Luke and saynt Iohan Erisemon <u>lyeth</u> there: and <u>they say</u> ...

⋮

the Greciens do erre & swere in mani articles concerning our fayth, The whyche I do thinke better to obmyt, and to leue vnwryten, than to wryte it.

(19) from Boorde 1545: 160

Hyghe Almayne, or hyghe Dochelond, begynneth at Mens, and some say it begynneth at Wormes, & contayneth Swauerlond or Swechlond, and Barslond, and the hylles or mountayns of the most part of Alpes, stretching in length to a town called Trent by-yonde the mountayns: half the towne is Doche, & the other halfe is Lombardy. There is a greate dyfference betwyxt Hyghe Almayne and Base Almayne, not only in theyr speche and maners, but also in theyr lodgynge, in theyr fare, and in theyr apparell. The people of Hygh Almayne, they be rude and rustycall, and very boystous in theyr speche, and humbly in their apparell; yet yf some of them can get a fox tale or two, or thre fox tayles, standyng vp ryght vpon theyr cappe, set vp with styckes, or that he maye haue a capons feder, or a goose feder, or any long feder on his cap, than he is called a *yonker*. they <u>do fede</u> grosly, and they wyll eate magots as fast as we wyll eate comfets. They haue a way to brede them in chese. Maydens there in certayne places shall <u>drynke no other drynke</u> but water, vnto the tyme she be maryed; yf she <u>do</u>, <u>she is taken for</u> a comyn woman. Saruants also <u>do</u> drynke water to theyr meat.

This use of *do* to mark discourse semantic prominence makes it seem a plausible assumption that the famous *do*'s in the Diary of Pepys also have to be interpreted in a parallel way: they make sense if they are read as indicating what seems to be the most significant point for the author.

(20) from Pepys 1660-1669, Vol, I, p. 87 ff.

Early, packing up my things and sending them to my Lord's lodgings to
be sent by cart with the rest of my Lord's. So to Wills, where I took
leave of some of my friends. Here I met with Ad: Chard and Tom Alcock,
one that went to school with me at Huntington, but I have not seen him
this sexteen years. So in the Hall paid and made even with Mrs. /and/
Mr. Michel. Afterwards met with old Beale, and at the Axe paid him
this Quarter to Lady-day next. In the afternoon Dick Mathews comes to
town and I went and drank with him at Harpers. So into London by water;
and in Fish-street my wife and I bought a bit of salmon of 8d. and
went to the Sun tavern and eat it, where I did promise to give her all
that I have in the world but my books, in case I should die at sea.
From thence homewards; in the way, my wife bought linen for three
smocks and other things. I went to my Lord's and spoke with him; so
home with Mrs. Jem by coach and then home to my own house. From thence
to the Fox in King-streete to supper at a brave turkey of Mr. Hawlys,
with some friends of his there, Will Bowyer, &C: after supper I went
to Westminster-hall and the Parliament sat till 10 at night, thinking
and being expected to dissolve themselfs today; but they did not.
Great talk tonight that the discontented officers did think this night
to make a stir; but prevented. To the Fox again; home with my wife and
to bed, extraordinary sleepy.

(21) from Pepys 1660-1669, Vol. I, p. 89 ff.

This morning bade Adieu in bed to the company of my wife. We rose and I
gave my wife some money to serve her for a time, and what papers of
consequence I had. Then I left her to get her ready and went to my
Lord's with my boy Eliezer to my Lord's lodging at Mr. Crews. Here I
had much business with my Lord; and papers, great store, given me by
my Lord to dispose of as of the rest. After that, with Mr. Moore home
to my house and took my wife by coach to the Chequer in Holborne;
where after we had drunk &C., she took coach and so farewell. I
stayed behind with Tom Alcock and Mr. Anderson my old chamber fellow
at Cambrige his brother, and drank with them there, who were come to
me thither about one that would have a place at sea. Thence with Mr.
Hawly to dinner at Mr. Crews. After dinner, to my own house, where all
things were put up into the dining-room and locked up, and my wife
took the key along with her. This day, in the presence of Mr. Moore
(who made it) and Mr. Hawly, I did (before I went out with my wife)
seal my will to her, whereby I did give her all that I have in the
world but my books, which I gave to my Brother John, excepting only
French books, which my wife is to have.

In examples 20 and 21 *do* occurs when he talks about his
will to his wife. Despite the implications of the passages
in his Lingua Franca the will to his lawful wife must have
been an item of great personal concern for him. Therefore
one takes the use of *do* as indicative of the significance

of this topic for Pepys personally. The occurrence of *did* at the end of example 20 belongs to a frequent type in reported speech. There also seems to be a case of peak-*do* in example 2 from Greene, page 20, eleventh line from the bottom: *do imploy*. To end this section, the peak-marking uses of *do* discussed here tie in with three notorious findings which are repeatedly cited as examples of the randomness of the appearance of *do*. In the *Polychronicon* (1450), a universal history (see Ellegård 1953: 167), there are 816 instances of *do*, 243 of which (nearly one third) occur with the verb *slay*; *slay* never occurs in the finite form. In such a work it is certainly very important who killed whom, in other words, discourse semantic prominence seems to be a major determinant of *do* use in this text. Another major use of *do*, which has also been frequently noted is with the verb *eat*, *did eat*. This use seems to go back to the episode reported in the Bible which obviously was of major significance. Finally, in the diary of Henry Machyn (1550-1563), out of the *370* occurrences of *do*, *216*, nearly two thirds, occur with *preach*, *did preach*. The particular significance of who preached becomes clear if we bear in mind that Machyn was by profession funeral director - a mortician. These uses are bound to appear quite idiosyncratic if looked at in isolation. But they start making sense when they are interpreted as a variant of marking semantic prominence.

As in the morphological case, there are other uses of *do*, which cannot be discussed here, but it should be pointed out that these uses and the one described here are not unrelated. It does seem possible to see them all within the broad scope of a common *Grundbedeutung* such as Marchand's *Modus emphaticus* (Marchand 1938-39, esp. 236). But such a *Grundbedeutung* becomes visible only if occurrences are analysed in semantic, not only syntactic terms. We have to remember that these meanings have to be to a very large extent contextually inferred. We could even avail ourselves of pragmatic terminology and call them conventional implicatures. From this perspective it is highly improbable that the inferencing process is not guided or constrained by a common basic meaning in order to be understood correctly.

4. From the onomasiological point of view, it is a well-known fact that the type of meaning discussed here, textual or discourse meaning, seems to be a kind of marginal or peripheral type of meaning, such as Sapir and Saussure seem to have had in mind, compared to referential, grammatical or syntactic meaning: textual meaning does not

appear to have a standard grammatical class of expressions fixed to it. Rather, these meanings seem to have to depend for their surface realisations on what happens to be left over by the structural make-up of a language at a given evolutionary stage. On a general level, it has been pointed out (Dressler 1981) that the surface syntactic forms of discourse markers are dependent on the typological make-up of the language. Also, their surface marking is not as obligatory as with the other types of meaning. It is always possible to find environments in which the expected form does not occur, although these environments are to all intents extremely similar to cases where there *is* surface marking. What we can formulate in the way of a regularity is that, given a certain constellation in the content of that particular text, a particular discourse marker such as *do* is likely to occur - but not categorically. This is a finding that has been recapitulated by all modern studies of parallel uses of variant forms, including code-switching, a fact that has also made it hard to identify these uses. For that very reason it is a very important methodological requirement that the existence of these meanings should be established independently in a number of texts, although space limitations forbid doing this to a larger extent in a congress paper. In fact, in their recent book on discourse analysis, Brown and Yule (1983: 106) state that

> ...although we can regularly identify such structural markers, their appearance in discourse should not be treated in any way as 'rule-governed'. They represent optional *cues* which writers and speakers may use in organising what they want to communicate.

Looked at from the semasiological side, these rather loose form-function associations or very weak degrees of grammaticalisation are also reflected in the fact that these forms also have other, although not unrelated meanings. This of course is also true of the discourse markers of modern English, such as expressions like *well*, which has quite a wide range of syntactic functions besides acting as discourse marker for, for example, pitch prominence.

To add one more parallel example from Historical English Linguistics, Zimmermann (1973) has shown that besides the usual tense and aspect functions, in *Sir Gawain* the perfect has clearly identifiable discourse functions such as structural boundary marking or announcing the change to another structural part. Also, the variable is restricted to certain structural-linguistic contexts, just as are the morphological (non-sibilant main verbs) and the syntactic variables (declaratives).

Another aspect is of course the historically ephemeral character of these discourse meanings: they are typical of change situations in a transitional period in which a type of conditioning may become operative, which Lüdtke (1980: 245 f, also 206) has called *Sonderbedingungen* or *Nebenbedingungen*. Being of a peripheral type of meaning in the sense indicated, the discourse meanings of *s/th* and *do* have to be considered as instances of such ephemeral and transitional functionalisations of syntactic and morphological contrasts.

Another such factor was rhythm and, in the case of *do*, the phonotactics of the cluster arising in the suffixation with the second person ending in cases such as *thou sing'st*. A tendency to syntactically bypass such affixed structures can statistically be shown for declarative sentences (Stein forthcoming a, ch. II and III). We have therefore to posit quite a range of factors (semantic, syntactic, phonological, discourse content) determining the appearance of *do* or finite form: this seems to be typical of the type of transitional and variable situation that is characteristic of EME and that results in the very loose form-function association, but which is nevertheless systematic over a number of texts. So the degrees of freedom for these variables to function as discourse markers or, generally speaking, the linguistic basis for the semiotic mechanism, is constrained both by how long such a variable state persists in a particular compartment of the grammar and also by the effect of other factors determining the appearance of a particular form. In a paper (Stein forthcoming b) to the third ICEHL conference at Sheffield the present author has shown that questions were nearly four times as sensitive to this phonotactic factor as declaratives, and consequently *do*-periphrasis was to that extent more frequent in questions. It was argued that this was the trigger for a catastrophic development that ultimately led to the firm grammaticisation of *do* in questions.

The reason why the discourse function of these forms as a short episode in the historical development has been overlooked is a consequence of the concentration on cognitive and grammatical meaning and the history of their realisation, which has persisted longer in historical English linguistics than in synchronic studies of variation. Another factor was the neglect of spoken language, which is where these markers are needed and occur most frequently. Also, research on the historical development of *do* has been on the look-out for pure syntactic explanations and has consequently tended to analyse and classify occurrences in formal syntactic, not semantic terms. After all, historical linguistics is in a way also - or has tended to behave as - an applied discipline, in that it applies the descriptive categories of synchronic linguistics. Finally, traditional studies, without the benefit of modern variation studies and discourse analysis, tended to overlook such patterns and to relegate too hastily to the compositor's practice waste paper basket what could, by the nature of its patterning, not possibly be produced by the pragmatics of textual history.

NOTES

1. For a recent appraisal of the nature of the pamphlets from a wider perspective cf. Grabes 1984.
2. As the formal distribution of the forms over consecutive pages is used as an argument, the examples from Greene reproduce exactly the content of the pages in the edition used and - against otherwise current practice - are not adjusted for syntactic context.
3. For a more detailed analysis of the isolectal stages involved and the semiotic possibilities opened up, including also a consideration of the methodological problems in connection with the compositor's practice cf. Stein forthcoming c.
4. This view is above all supported by the regularity of the linguistic constraints on the occurrence of *s* and *th*. Cf. note 2.

TEXTS

Boorde, Andrew. 1545. *The First Book of the Introduction of Knowledge*. EETS, Extra Series X. Ed. F.J. Furnivall. 1870.
Greene, Robert. 1591-1592. *A Notable Discovery of Coosnage. The Second Part of Conny-Catching*. Elizabethan and Jacobean Quartos. Ed. G.B. Harrison. New York: Barnes & Noble. 1966.
Greene, Robert. 1592. *The Third and Last Part of Conny-Catching. A Disputation between a He-Conny-Catcher and a She-Conny-Catcher*. Elizabethan and Jacobean Quartos. Ed. G.B. Harrison. New York: Barnes & Noble. 1966.
Latimer, Hugh. 1549. *Seven Sermons before Edward VI*. English Reprints. Ed. E. Arber. Westminster: Constable. 1895.
Nashe, Thomas. 1592-1599. *The Unfortunate Traveller and Other Works*. Penguin English Library. Ed. J.B. Steane. Harmondsworth: Penguin. 1972.
Painter, William. 1560. *The Palace of Pleasure*. Ed. J. Jacobs. Hildesheim: Olms. 1968.
Pepys, Samuel. 1660-1669. *The Diary of Samuel Pepys*. Eds. R. Latham and W. Matthews. Berkeley: University of California Press. 1970.

REFERENCES

Brown, Gillian and George Yule. 1983. *Discourse Analysis*. Cambridge: Cambridge University Press.
Brunner, Karl. 1962. *Die englische Sprache. Ihre geschichtliche Entwicklung*. Zweiter Band. Tübingen: Max Niemeyer.
Dressler, Wolfgang. 1981. 'Notes on Textual Typology'. *Wiener Linguistische Gazette* 25.3-11.
Ellegård, Alvar. 1953. *The Auxiliary do; The Establishment and Regulation of Its Use in English*. Stockholm: Almqvist and Wiksell.
Grabes, Herbert. 1984. 'The Rhetoric of Slander'. *Anglistentag 1982 Zürich. Vorträge* ed. by Udo Fries and Jörg Hasler, 107-122.
Klein, Karl L. 1969. *Vorformen des Romans in der englischen erzählenden Prosa des 16. Jahrhunderts*. Heidelberg: Carl Winter.
Longacre, Robert E. 1976a. *An Anatomy of Speech Notions*. Lisse: De Ridder.
Longacre, Robert E. 1976b. ' "Mystery" Particles and Affixes.' *Papers from the Twelfth Regional Meeting of the Chicago Linguistic Society* ed. by Salikoko, S. Mufwene, Carol A. Walker & Sanford B. Steever, 468-475. Chicago Linguistic Society.
Lüdtke, Helmut. 1980. 'Auf dem Weg zu einer Theorie des Sprachwandels'. *Kommunikationstheoretische Grundlagen des Sprachwandels* ed. by Helmut Lüdtke, 182-252. Berlin: de Gruyter.
Marchand, Hans. 1938-39. 'Syntaktische Homonymie. Das umschreibende do'. *Englische Studien* 73.227-252.
Quirk, Randolph. 1971. 'Shakespeare and the English Language'. *A New Companion to Shakespeare Studies* ed. by Kenneth Muir and S. Schoenbaum, 67-82. Cambridge: Cambridge University Press.
Samuels, M.L. 1972. *Linguistic Evolution*. Cambridge: Cambridge University Press.
Schiffrin, Deborah. 1981. 'Tense Variation in Narrative'. *Language* 57:1.45-62.
Stein, Dieter. Forthcoming a. 'Syntactic Variation and Change. The Spread of Syntactic Innovation through Variably Realised Linguistic Space: The Case of *do* in Questions'. To appear in *Folia Linguistica Historica*.
Stein, Dieter. Forthcoming b. *Natürlicher syntaktischer Sprachwandel*. To appear München: TU Druck- und Verlagsunion.
Stein, Dieter. Forthcoming c. 'The Mechanism and Semiotics of Morphological Change: The Case of *s/th*'. To appear in *English Studies*.
Zimmermann, Rüdiger. 1973. 'Verbal Syntax and Style in *Sir Gawain and the Green Knight*'. *English Studies* 54.533-543.

ASSESSMENT OF ALTERNATIVE EXPLANATIONS OF THE MIDDLE ENGLISH PHENOMENON OF HIGH VOWEL LOWERING WHEN LENGTHENED IN THE OPEN SYLLABLE

ROBERT P. STOCKWELL
University of California, Los Angeles

Though the problem has been familiar since at least the end of the 19th century, the challenge of providing an explanation for the lowering of high vowels when impacted by lengthening in some dialects of Middle English seems to have lost none of its fascination. A new phonological theory of course always calls forth renewed efforts to find answers to old problems, if only to demonstrate the power of the new theory. The size of the problem does not matter if the problem, though small, is linguistically interesting. What makes a problem interesting is whether a solution to it tells us anything fundamental about human language, in particular (from the viewpoint of historians) about the nature of language change.

In my attempt to assess what progress has been made in our understanding of this problem, I shall refer by last name to the work of these scholars: Lieber (1979), Malsch and Fulcher (1975), Anderson (1974), Dobson (1963), Stockwell (1952, 1961), Vachek (1959), Trnka (1959), Orton (1952), and Luick (1899, 1914-21). This of course does not exhaust the list of scholars who have had something of interest to say about this phenomenon, but it includes, so far as I have been able to determine, all of the substantively different interpretations.

I feel somewhat apologetic about reentering this particular area of dispute because I have only some minor observations that are new concerning what I believe to be the correct solution to the problem: if the truth be known, I would like to think that for the most part I solved it correctly some 25 years ago. However, it keeps coming up as though my proposed solution did not exist. For instance, Lieber asserts that it has always been maintained that $\bar{\iota}$- and $\bar{u}$- were lowered to $\bar{\text{e}}$ and $\bar{\text{o}}$ when lengthened in the open syllable.(1) Malsch and Fulcher were aware of my non-lowering alternative interpretation, though they misunderstood it so totally that now, ten years after the publication of their paper, there is some justification for an attempt being made to restate in clear English what I once thought I *had* stated in clear English.(2) Apparently Lieber was no more aware of Malsch and Fulcher's work than she was of mine, since Malsch and Fulcher claimed that lengthening caused lowering in all except the low vowels of Middle English, an idea which they acknowledge having gotten from Lass (1969), though in fact it is much older (going back at least to Luick). The claim that *all* vowels were lowered when lengthened requires consideration by Lieber as an alternative hypothesis as much as my claim, long prior to hers, that *none* were lowered. Either interpretation is radically different from the traditional position which she takes as the only one given by all scholarship prior to her own. Lieber's paper has as its starting point Anderson's discussion of disjunctive ordering. His discussion assumes only the traditional interpretation, found in the standard texts, namely a conjunction of lowering with lengthening of the high vowels. Anderson, like Lieber, apparently was unaware of alternative hypotheses. He was, however, only using the putative facts to make a theoretical point: there is no reason to believe he cared about enriching our understanding of the history of English. If the facts of English were otherwise, it was, at least in principle, simply one example fewer in a battery of examples arguing a theoretical claim. Lieber, on the other hand, was adding a chapter to the history of English, as were Malsch and Fulcher.

So it seems that the bibliographical history of this problem is a tangled web. I am not so much concerned to map it in detail as I am to compare the substance of the alternatives and try to determine what evidence and arguments might provide a rational basis for choosing among them. There are only five logically possible alternatives:

1. All short vowels (except the lowest ones) were lowered when lengthened, and later rules such as the Vowel Shift acted upon this system to produce the MnE vowel system. (Malsch and Fulcher).

2. All short vowels (except the lowest ones) were lowered prior to lengthening, independently of the lengthening process. (Luick, Vachek; Dobson takes this view to its ultimate conclusion, perceiving,

as Luick did not, that the antecedent lowering
might have been substantially further in the North
where the phenomenon was most general -- an insight
that may be important to explain the later Northern
development of $\bar{\iota}$- and $\bar{u}$- to [ei] and [ou] whereas
the inherited long open mid vowels developed to
[ɪə] and [ʊə].

3. No short vowels, not even the high ones, were lowered when lengthened; lengthening does not result in qualitative changes directly, though a lengthened vowel always has an independent history which may include qualitative changes after it has been lengthened. The merger with inherited long close vowels, in those dialects where the merger occurred, must therefore have a different explanation. (Stockwell).

4. No short vowels, not even the mid ones, were lowered prior to lengthening; the short vowels remain essentially unchanged from OE to MnE; and the correlations with the long vowels which suggest lowering of short vowels has some other explanation. (Stockwell, Lieber 'Analysis C')

5. Only the high vowels were lowered, and only when lengthened. (Lieber makes no claims about non-high vowels, but this assumption is implicit in the rest of her analysis; her claim about lowering the high vowels requires the dissociation of the features "length" and "tenseness"; all other accounts, except my own, treat length and tenseness as concomitant features.)

Each logically possible alternative has consequences elsewhere in the system, consequences which must be given considerable weight in choosing among them. The consequence which most concerned Lieber was the effect on rule ordering. Briefly, if lengthening + lowering preceded trisyllabic shortening, the output would be vowels of the right quantity but wrong quality; and if in the other order, the output would be vowels that were wrong in both respects, as summarized below:

1.		$ivele s$	$ivel$	$sumeres$	$sumer$
2.	LENGTH	$\bar{e}veles$	$\bar{e}vel$	$s\bar{o}meres$	$s\bar{o}mer$
3.	TRI	$*\breve{e}veles$	----	$*s\breve{o}meres$	----
2.	TRI	$\breve{\iota}veles$	----	$s\breve{u}meres$	----
3.	LENGTH	$*\bar{e}veles$	$\bar{e}vel$	$*s\bar{o}meres$	$s\bar{o}mer$

To avoid this unacceptable consequence, Anderson had proposed that these two rules must be disjunctively ordered (i.e., if one applied, the other could not, with the shorter form being the first checked for applicability --lengthening would be applicable to *ivel* but not to *iveles*). Lieber showed that Anderson's conditions for choosing which form to apply either rule to, in a disjunctively ordered set, could not be met, and that therefore another solution had to be sought (to which we return below).

The consequence elsewhere in the system which most concerned Malsch and Fulcher was to line up the ME vowels in such a way that the Vowel Shift, as they formulated it, would apply uniformly. Since ŏ- falls in with ǭ when lengthened (OE *hopa* > MnE *hope*, not *hoop*), they conclude that 'it necessarily follows that the original back mid vowel must have been lowered when tensed', and correspondingly the original front mid vowel. This conclusion is preceded by the surprising claim that the possibility that non-high vowels lowered as well as high vowels, has apparently been missed by all scholars except Lass. Quite the contrary is true: e.g., Vachek claimed that 'there was the early 13th century lowering of short *e* and *o*, which qualitatively differentiated them from ē̦ and ǭ, their former counterparts'. He refers to Luick's note on the subject (HG #378), where the identical claim is made, and this was not even the first time Luick had made the claim (it appears in his earlier articles). But the conclusion -- whether on the part of Luick, Vachek, Dobson, Lass, or Malsch and Fulcher -- that there must have been a lowering rule applying to the short vowels, whether when lengthened or not, is not a necessary one. All that is necessary is to provide some basis to account for the correlation of the short mid vowels with the corresponding long open vowels, rather than with the corresponding long close vowels. In any case, the observation about the vowel spelled <o> and assigned to the /ŏ/ slot in the system certainly was not 'missed' by anyone: virtually everyone who has written on the subject assumes that the ME ŏ was phonetically [ɔ], just as they assume that ME ĕ was [ɛ], from which assumption it automatically follows that these vowels should merge with ǭ and ē̦ when lengthened (but they don't in the North Midlands, to which we return below). My own assumption is the same as the traditional one with respect to the phonetics of the open mid vowels, both short and long, except that I do not think 'lowering' is necessary to explain the correlation, even in the North Midlands. I differ substantively mainly in the interpretation of the *long close* mid vowels. I return to that difference below.

The consequences elsewhere in the system which most concerned me were two:

1. To show that just as in OE there was a one-to-one match between original long vowels and lengthened short vowels, there was an identical one-to-one match in ME (i.e., if you lengthen any short vowel, in general you should get a long vowel which merges with the corresponding preexisting long vowel if there is one; this is nothing more than the default case in lengthening. Luick also assumed, it is clear, that this is indeed the default case, since if it were not, there would be nothing to explain concerning ĭ- and ŭ-. However, his *only* evidence for this putative change is the correspondence to the long close vowels, which means indeed that there is still really only one issue: how best to account for that correspondence.) A subsidiary consequence of my claim is that the short stressed vowels of OE (except the one written ⟨a⟩) remain phonetically unchanged from OE through ME, and even after that only the back vowels undergo further change to MnE.

2. To show that the sporadic shortenings (with what appears to be concomitant raising) of the long close vowels in words like *sick* (EME sḕk), *must* (mǭste) require no special explanation: their explanation falls out automatically from the correct interpretation of the 'lengthening and lowering' phenomenon in the high vowels. Though his phonetic interpretation was different from mine, Trnka had the same view of their importance and of the necessity to explain them by whatever account is given of the corresponding instances of lengthening.(3)

Since hers is the most stimulating, relatively traditional new formulation of these phenomena (meaning, essentially, not couched in surprising symbols like the Trager-Smith ones which put people off, for reasons that quite mystify me), Lieber's two proposals provide a reasonable starting point for more deliberate discussion. Her first proposal, which she favors over the second one, is that there was a lengthening rule which was independent of tenseness, followed by a lowering rule, followed by a tensing rule. Rather than her label ('Analysis B'), I will call this the 'length-only' analysis. It easily handles the rule-ordering problem posed by Anderson:

EME	iveles	ivel	sumeres	sumer
LENGTH	īveles	īvel	sūmeres	sūmer
TRI	ĭveles	----	sŭmeres	----
LOWER	----	ēvel	----	sōmer
TENSE	----	ę̄vel	----	sǭmer

There are several problems with this analysis. (a) There is no reason to believe that open syllable lengthening ever applied to forms that were subject to trisyllabic shortening. As Minkova (1982) has shown, convincingly to my mind, lengthening is overwhelmingly correlated with loss of schwa in the next (final) syllable -- though *evil* is one of the problematic counterexamples. No matter: to show lengthening on the forms *iveles* and *sumeres* is merely a consequence of the rule-ordering formalism and of the incorrectly stipulated environment for open syllable lengthening. That is not Lieber's fault: she (and Anderson) took as given the familiar formulation that does not include schwa-loss as a condition. (b) More serious, Lindau (1978) has shown -- also, to my mind, convincingly -- that "tenseness" simply cannot be a phonetic feature, unless (conceivably) used as a cover term for some cluster of other features. Phonetically, what has been called tenseness correlates with peripherality in the articulatory and acoustic vowel space. In most languages, length also correlates with peripherality, but not universally.(4) It is not possible, however, simply to replace the feature ⟨TENSE⟩ with the feature ⟨PERIPH⟩ and thereby succeed in having the above rule sequence give correct results. Peripheral vowels in English are now, and as far as we have any evidence, always have been out-gliding, i.e., [-y] and [-w]. But ę̄ cannot have been outgliding because it would have merged with the inherited [ey] in words like the ancestors of MnE *they*, *day*, *way*. It must have been simply long, or more probably ingliding. This argument deletes the bottom line of the length-only analysis. (c) The remaining bottom line, created by an ad hoc rule of lowering, has no motivation whatever: all the evidence about long non-high non-peripheral vowels of English argues that they go up, not down. They started doing it at least by the time of the conquest and were well on their way into the vowel shift by the time of open syllable lengthening (for evidence, consider the sources of ME ę̄ and ǭ; and the same process continues unabated in MnE -- witness the New York City facts, well documented since early in this century, showing the development of low ingliding vowels to mid and high ingliding vowels in words like *ask*, *coffee*). This argument deletes the remaining bottom line. The top three lines are defensible: but they claim, as may indeed be correct, that ę̄ was a type of ī, though in contrast

with the inherited ī. The problem then is to determine
what the difference between them was (I believe it was the
difference between long lax and long tense, if we can live
with the feature ⟨TENSE⟩; or between ingliding ⟨-PERIPH⟩
and outgliding ⟨+PERIPH⟩); and it remains to explain the
spelling.

One way out of these problems would be to claim that
the rules of lowering and tensing were purely synchronic
rules of ME, not intended to reflect historical processes.
That, to me at least, would be an uninteresting cop-out,
since the arguments about open syllable lengthening, vowel
shift, trisyllabic shortening, etc. all concern themselves
with historical processes. One might claim that some synchronic rules have historical reflexes (lengthening, and
trisyllabic shortening, among the four in the length-only
analysis) and others don't (lowering and tensing, in this
case). But such a view allows one to construct any ad hoc
rule whatever to make things come out right in a synchronic grammar of the earlier stages of a language. That
might not bother theoretical phonologists, but it is hardly likely to sit well with historians.

Before turning to Lieber's other analysis, it is
necessary to comment on a dialect argument which she be-
lieves supports her claim for historical validity of the
independence of the features ⟨LONG⟩ and ⟨TENSE⟩. She
quotes from the Wrights' *Elementary Middle English Grammar*
the claim based on Joseph Wright's *English Dialect Grammar*
that the new ĕ- and ŏ- were certainly different in quality
from the inherited ę̄ and ǭ in the North and North Midlands
because they continue different to this day, the new ones
as [ei] and [ou], the old ones as [ɪə] and [ʊə]. Two
things are surprising: (1) that she referred only to
Wright, when the matter has been exhaustively studied by
Orton, whose evidence is much more detailed and doubtless
more reliable; and (2) given the phonetic development,
that she would have inferred that ĕ- was mid-lax-long
while ę̄ was low-tense-long. Surely the inference should be
the reverse, since the modern reflexes of the lengthened
vowels are clearly (tense) peripheral out-gliding diphthongs, and the reflexes of the inherited long open vowels
are the closest thing we have in any dialects today to
what she seems to have meant by long lax diphthongs. Orton
concludes, I believe correctly, that the lengthened vowels
must have been lower than the inherited vowels, and indeed
this evidence is the strongest we have that the short
vowels had lowered substantially before lengthening took
place, at least in these dialects. Dobson (136) finds this
evidence, if not bewildering, certainly irrelevant to the

developments in MnStE: 'I dismiss the North Midland dialects as constituting a problem on their own, unrelated then as they are unrelated now to the general development of the language in this respect.' In that conclusion I think Dobson was wrong, though not in his careful assessment of the bits and pieces of evidence which suggest that these two types of long open vowels did not merge even in the South of England. He emphatically asserts (147) that they did merge, and I believe he is right: 'Certainly there is no sign, in the later history of London English, of a form of speech in which ĕ-and ŏ- were kept distinct [from the inherited long open vowels].' But these dialects are enormously important to a broader perspective on the kinds of changes that the long vowels underwent in English, because they preserve the full range of possibilities for the development of a vocalic structure that I believe is characteristic of English and other Germanic languages. Indeed, if North Midland had somehow become the standard that is the focus of our study, rather than London, nobody would find the Trager-Smith kinds of complex nuclei difficult to credit, either in the modern standard or in its history. In the London melting pot of the later Middle Ages, a great many distinctions and lines of development were merged, leading to an oversimplification of the history of English vocalic structure on the part of nearly all scholars who have studied the vowel shift and the rise of the Standard.

   I turn now to Lieber's other scenario ('Analysis C'), which I will call the 'early vowel shift' analysis. In the end she rejects this analysis, but it has a lot going for it. It assumes (1) that inherited ī and ū had already diphthongized and gone through the first stage of the vowel shift, prior to open syllable lengthening; (2) that ẹ̄ and ọ̄ had already been raised to ī and ū by the vowel shift; (3) that the long open mid vowels had been raised to ę̄ and ǭ; and (4) that i and u when lengthened will necessarily fall in with (2), and e and o when lengthened will necessarily fall in with (3), by the basic principle of default lengthening. Except for notation, this is identical with my own claim (1952, 1961, 1973, 1978) that by Chaucer's time ī was [iy], [ɪy], or even [ɨy] and ū was [uw], [ʊw], or even [ɨw], that ẹ̄ and ọ̄ were [ɪə] and [ʊə], that ę̄ and ǭ were [ɛə] and [ɔə] or [oə], and that the lengthenings and shortenings behaved correctly by default -- if [ɪ] is lengthened it yields [ɪə] = ẹ̄, and so on. An obvious drawback of the early vowel shift analysis is the spellings, but, like me, Lieber has no trouble accepting the view that since ⟨i⟩ was already identified with something else --an outgliding diphthong that she writes [ey] in agreement with the Chomsky-Halle vowel shift switching rule --, then ⟨e⟩ or ⟨ee⟩ is a reasonable way to continue writing the long close *e*. She does not touch on the problem that bothers most historians of English about this radical proposal, namely why did they write the two kinds of long *ee*'s alike (except, of course, for Orrm), especially if one was really a type of *i*? Somehow our colleagues find it easier to accept the writing of long close and long open vowels identically if they are assumed still to be phonetically somewhere in the range of cardinals 2 and 3 rather than 1, and correspondingly in the back, until the spelling was fixed by the printers. The answer, mere speculation, is that spelling was already more fixed and tradition bound than has been commonly assumed.

But Lieber is persuaded to reject the early vowel shift analysis by the same argument that caused Luick to reject it. The problem is the original *ū* in some northern dialects, which fails to vowel shift. If *ǭ* had already gone up to *ū*, and *ŭ-* merged with it when lengthened, how can we explain the fact that only *ǭ* and *ŭ-* underwent fronting to [*ü*:]? Though she did not see it, it seems to me that there is an answer that was readily available to Lieber, given that she is willing to dissociate the features ⟨TENSE⟩ and ⟨LONG⟩: it is in fact my answer, based on the difference between ingliding diphthongs and outgliding diphthongs. First, in her terms, the answer consists in suggesting that it was the *long lax high* vowels, *ǭ* and *ŭ-*, which were fronted. The *long tense ū* would thereby not have been intersected. In my terms, [uə] (from either source) was fronted, but [uw] remained unshifted. This suggestion also provides a more reasonable phonetic basis for a simple fronting rule that results in [*ü*:], probably through the intermediate stages [*ü*ə] and [*ü*y]. Getting there from some kind of [o], as Luick tried to do, requires extraordinary and unnecessary, not to say implausible, phonetic ingenuity. It seems to me that this argument which caused Lieber and Luick to reject the early vowel shift analysis is, on the contrary, another piece of the puzzle that falls neatly into a natural slot and thereby supports the early vowel shift analysis, given either dissociation of the features ⟨TENSE⟩ and ⟨LONG⟩, or the reinterpretation of length as glides.

Let us see now whether there is also a natural interpretation, in these terms, of Wright and Orton's North Midland dialect evidence, which was put aside too lightly by Dobson and misinterpreted by Lieber (i.e., she reversed the phonetically plausible identifications). Orton's summary, with some irrelevant details omitted, appears below.

Recall that these are the only dialects which provably did
not merge ĕ- with ę̄.

	OE		ME	LME/EMnE		EMnE		MnE
Angl	ē							
OE	ē	>	[e:] >	[i:]	>	[i:] >		[i:]
OE	ēo							
OE	ēa	>	[ɛ:] >	[e:]	>	[eə] >		[iə]
OE	ǣ							
OE	ĕ-	>	[ɛ:] > (lowered)	[ɛ:]	>	[ɛɪ] >		[ɛɪ]
OE	æ,a-							
OSc	a-	>	[a:] >	[æ:]	>	[æə]/[ɛə]		[eə]
OFr	a-							
OE	æg,eg							
Sc	ei,eg	>	[aɪ]/[æɪ]>[æ:]		>	[æə]/[ɛə]	>	[eə]

The problem in this analysis is the parenthesized word
'lowered' in the third derivation. What is the real distinction between the ME assignments on the second and
third lines? It seems to me that the correct assignment
has to be [æ:], within Orton's frame of reference, and
since that conflicts with nothing else in the ME column,
and provides a natural basis for the next column, I have
no idea why Orton failed to assign it so. On the other
hand, for me it poses a real problem, within my frame of
reference, since I assume there was only one low vowel in
ME (the one written <a>, which I believe was never actually centralized from OE æ except in some retracting contexts). The chart at the top of the next page shows the
problem. In the OE column, I have asssigned values within
my own frame of reference, omitting irrelevant details
concerning the merged sets. In the second column third row
I have had to assume a fourth short front vowel for this
dialect, i.e., /i e ɛ æ/. The alternative would be what I
suggested above for Orton, which requires the assumption,
even more objectionable, of non-default lengthening: /e-/
> /æə/, which forces the assumption of two low vowels in
this dialect, /æ/ and /a/. The former seems more plausible. Either way, there appears to be no solution to the
North Midlands distinction between ĕ- and ę̄ without assuming an additional short vowel that shows up (as far as I
know at this time) only in the context of lengthening.

LOE	ME	LME/EMnE	EMnE	MnE	Examples
/eə/	/iə/	/iy/	/iy/	/iy/	feet, keep, teeth
/æə/	/eə/	/iə/	/iə/	/iə/	beam, beat, great
/e-/	/ɛə/	/ey/	/ey/	/ey/	eat, speak, steal
/æ-/	/æə/	/ɛə/	/eə/	/eə/	tale, water, father
/ey/	/ey/	/ey/	/eə/	/eə/	nail, tail, way

We are now in a position to recapitulate the five logically possible interpretations and compare them.

1. All non-low vowels lowered when lengthened.

2. All non-low vowels lowered between OE and ME, prior to lengthening and irrespective of lengthening.

3. Lowering was not correlated with lengthening, in general, and in particular it is not necessary to assume it in the cases of the lengthened non-low vowels of ME.

4. There was no lowering of short vowels between OE and ME at least in the South; a new lower mid front vowel may have come into being in the North and North Midlands, but it is in addition to the previously existing three, contrasting, in its lengthened version, with them.

5. Only the high vowels lowered, and only when lengthened.

The first of these can be rejected in favor of the second: there is no motivation to assume lowering just in the lengthening context, since we get the right results by the second assumption, and since lengthening almost universally is associated with raising, not with lowering. A special lowering rule applied only to lengthened vowels is in principle a very costly rule, highly marked and to be avoided if there is an alternative explanation. In trying to explain historical change we always look for the most natural explanation, and the minimum change, possible; we allow ourselves any rules at all, and especially we allow highly marked rules, only if all else fails. Even a lowering rule for lax vowels costs something: it also is to be avoided if there is a reasonable alternative. Rule five is the most costly of all, because it is the narrowest and

most exceptional. It is certainly to be rejected in favor
of two. Three is a special case of four. The real alternatives are therefore two and four. Four, either in Lieber's
terms or in mine, is the simplest alternative because it
makes no ad hoc assumptions about the existence of rules
that are not needed anyway to account for the vowel shift.

The difference between two and four comes down to one
claim on the part of the adherents of two: that the short
vowels of OE were higher than the short vowels of ME.
Their only evidence is inferential: namely that $\bar{\imath}$ and $\bar{u}$
matched $\bar{\imath}$ and $\bar{u}$ in OE (*wilde, wilderness*; *wīs, wisdom*;
grund, hūs), but they matched $\bar{\underset{\sim}{e}}$ and $\bar{\underset{\sim}{o}}$ in ME (OE *wicu*, ME
weeke; OE *wudu*, ME *woode*). But of course if ME $\bar{\underset{\sim}{e}}$ and $\bar{\underset{\sim}{o}}$ are
by ME times of the height that $\bar{\imath}$ and $\bar{u}$ were in OE, and
those OE vowels are something else by ME times, then the
correspondence is just as good as it ever was, and we are
being befuddled only by orthography. To me it seems reasonable to suppose that the OE short front vowels were as
stable in every way as they appear to have been: I think
that words like OE *sincan, þing, fisc, bedd, meltan, nett,
egg, sæt, æppel* and probably the short orthographic diphthongs in *miolc, siolfor, seofon, eorþe, earm* are practically the only words that would sound familiar, indeed
pretty much like Modern English, if we could resurrect
some OE speakers and listen to their conversations.

A recapitulation in chart form of the two most reasonable alternatives, along the lines of Orton's admirable
summary of his interpretation of the North Midlands data,
appears on the next page. I have confined the chart to the
front vowels, but the analogous assignments can be assumed
for the back vowels (except, of course, that the chart
does not tell the whole story of the vowel shift: the
front and back vowels in the shift are not symmetrical). A
blank means unchanged from the entry to the left of the
blank: in this way one can spot the changes, the relevant
claims, more readily. Some of the phonetic assignments
attributed to 4-Lieber are inferential on my part, but I
doubt that they are far wrong, given the content of the
rest of her paper (if they are, of course I apologize and
attribute them instead to a reasonable theory that someone
else might well have suggested).

THE MIDDLE ENGLISH HIGH VOWEL LOWERING

Theory	OE		ME	EMnE	MnStE
4-Stockwell, 4-Lieber	ĭ	[ɪ]	---	---	---
2-Luick et al		[i]	[ɪ]? [e]?(5)	---	---
4-S, 4-L	ĕ	[ɛ]	---	---	---
2-Lu		[e]	[ɛ]		
4-S	ī-	[ɪ]	[ɪə]	[iy]	---
4-L		[ɪ]	[ɪ:]	[i:]	[iy]
2-Lu		[i]	[e:]	[i:]	---
4-S	ē-	[ɛ]	[ɛə]	[ɪə]	[iy]
4-L		[ɛ]	[ɛ:]	[ɪ:]/[i:]	[iy]
2-Lu		[e]	[ɛ:]	[i:]	---
4-S	ī	[ɪə]/[iy]	[iy]/[ɪy]	[əy]	[ay]
4-L		[i:]	[i:]/[ey]	[ey]/[əy]	[ay]
2-Lu		[i:]	---	[əi]	[ai]
4-S	ē	[ɛə]	[ɪə]	[iy]	---
4-L		[e:]	[ɪ:]	[i:]	[iy]
2-Lu		[e:]	[e:]	[i:]	---
4-S	ēa	[æə]	[ɛə]	[ɪə]	[iy]
4-L		[ǣə]	[ɛ:]	[ɪ:]/[i:]	[iy]
2-Lu		[ǣə]	[ɛ:]	[i:]	---

NOTES

1. On pages 7 and 20. One can only assume that her emphasis on the failures of her predecessors is intended to lay claim to being the first to see that there is a viable alternative explanation that does not assume lowering along with lengthening. Since I pointed out this alternative in my 1952 dissertation and in various articles from 1961 onwards, including one that was reprinted in two standard collections of work on the history of English, I must protest the 'firstness' that is implicit in her paper. Also she failed to see that this alternative analysis has much wider ramifications, in particular for the explanation of *shortening* phenomena that are at least as peculiar and interesting as the lengthening ones.
2. While they acknowledge that my analysis 'has the advantage of accounting at the same time for the sporadic shortening of /ē/ (Stockwell's /ih/) to /i/ and of /ō/ (Stockwell's /uh/) to /u/...'(Fn.1), they conclude that this is not worth the trouble

and make no attempt to analyze such ME shortenings: 'We note only that they are indeed sporadic and relatively rare.' But Dobson (1963:131) points out that 'the shortening seems to be a general ME process, not limited geographically, whereas the lengthening is so limited.' In terms of pure numbers, at least in the dialect areas from which MnStE derives, neither the lengthened nor the shortened set is of much interest. One's interest in them is stimulated entirely by the fact that they are superficially highly irregular and may be crucial to understanding other more general aspects of the history of English phonology.

They reprimand me for using the Trager-Smith notation for English vowels, in the form of a quotation from Chomsky saying that the Trager-Smith system 'fails to achieve descriptive adequacy'. But in fact the surface output of the Chomsky-Halle rules for MnStE is exactly the Trager-Smith surface phonemic analysis of MnStE! Chomsky is absolutely right about the massive failure of Trager-Smith and other pregenerative structuralists to deal adequately with the *morphophonemic* (read *systematic phonemic*) regularities in English phonology, but that is a different story. Malsch and Fulcher provide no information at all about ME morphophonemics, nor is the question of open syllable lengthening in general, nor the question of lengthening or shortening of the ME high vowels in particular, primarily a morphophonemic question. It is primarily a question of sound change, which operates variously between the phonetic and the surface phonemic levels. There may be instances where sound change operates more abstractly at the systematic phonemic level: I am not prepared to deny that possibility. On the whole I am persuaded that sound change is not very abstract, though some of the motivations for it are certainly not superficial. But the Trager-Smith notation is still good enough for surface phonemic representations, good enough, for example, to serve Labov and his colleagues well in their brilliant studies of sound change in progress (1972). However, nothing in my analysis depends on specifics of the Trager-Smith analysis, as will become clear in this paper.

Had they read somewhat more of my work, they would not have accused me of assuming that lengthening sometimes adds /-w/, sometimes /-y/ to the vocalic nucleus. Except in the case of palatal consonants (e.g., OE *niht*, LME /niyxt/), which may by assimilation directly create a front glide transition from the vowel to the palatal consonant (a conditioned change); and except in the case of labio-velar consonants (e.g., OE *bōga*, MnE *bough*) which either assimilate to the preceding glide as /w/ or possibly in some instances create a back glide transition -- except in these two instances, I have consistently argued that 'lengthening' begins as the creation of a central glide between the short vowel and the following consonant, which Trager-Smith wrote /-h/ and which I am quite happy to write with schwa, either on the line or superscripted, with or without a diacritic under it to mark non-syllabicity. Nothing, absolutely nothing, hinges on the notation. After the

glide development (= lengthening), the central glide, by normal
sound change, may become a front or a back glide, or even a pure
long vowel: most commonly in English, it is assimilated to a front
glide after front vowels, and a back glide after back vowels, but
this is by no means the only possible development: we will see
quite a different development in the North Midland dialects discussed below.

The vowel shift formulation that results from this analysis
is anything but 'chaotic': indeed, the first step is precisely the
change from /ih/ and /uh/ to /iy/ and /uw/, given impetus, I believe, by the merger with inherited -ig and ug. But this is another story. It is true that the story is not fully compatible
with either the Chomsky-Halle version of the vowel shift or the
Malsch and Fulcher version inherited from Sloat and Hoard, but it
is far from chaotic and is quite compatible, e.g., with the views
of Trnka, Vachek, Jespersen, Labov, and Dobson, among others. Even
with the Chomsky-Halle version, the differences are rather trivial
(see Stockwell 1973)

3. 'Another confirmation of this phonemic shift [the correlation of $\bar{\imath}$
with $\bar{\bar{e}}$ and of $\bar{u}$ with $\bar{\bar{o}}$] is the fact that the result of the sporadic shortening of $\bar{\bar{e}}$ and $\bar{\bar{o}}$ in ME is not e and o, but i and u,
respectively...the reverse process of the lengthening of i and
u....'(441).
4. Both the use of the term 'peripheral' in this phonetic sense, and
the claim that the term should replace 'tense' altogether, are
originally mine, I believe, first at the Texas Conference of 1968
which resulted in the publication of Stockwell 1973.
5. The perfect match for $\bar{\bar{e}}$ presumably is [e], but it is hard to believe that by 'lowering' Luick could have meant that. The perfect
match for [ɪ], however, is [ɪ:] or [ɪə], i.e. long lax or long
ingliding. This is a fundamental vagueness in the 'lowering' theory, as traditionally stipulated. One can argue, given what happened to Latin short i, that tense [e] matches the height of lax
[ɪ], but the world is full of languages in which [e:] matches [e]
or even [ɛ], including close relatives of English such as German
and Dutch. Any way one looks at it, there is something strange
about the ME long close mid vowels, a strangeness that disappears
only if we consider them to have been some kind of high vowels.
6. To make certain generalizations more apparent, I am using surface-
phonemic diagonals rather than square brackets. It should be understood that the ingliding diphthongs in a three-height vowel
system start phonetically from the nonperipheral allophone: i.e.,
/iə/ really means [ɪə], /eə/ means [ɛə]; outgliding diphthongs
start phonetically from the peripheral allophone: i.e., /iy/ means
[ii] in which by convention the second vowel is understood to be
nonsyllabic; similarly /ey/ means [ei]. And of course the symbols
/i/ and /e/, as short monophthongs, mean [ɪ] and [ɛ], at all
dates. I see no reason whatever, except in the North Midland problem discussed here, to believe that OE, ME, or MnE /i/ and /e/
were ever anything else; and since the only arguments ever pre-

sented to the effect that they were higher in OE than in ME and MnE have to do with the correspondences between long and short sets, the arguments are quite circular, since they have an equally natural alternative interpretation.

REFERENCES

Anderson, Stephen R. 1974. *The Organization of Phonology*. New York: Academic Press.
Dobson, E.J. 1963. 'Middle English Lengthening in Open Syllables'. *Transactions of the Philological Society* 1962.
Labov, William, Malcah Yaeger and Richard Steiner. 1972. *A Quantitative Study of Sound Change in Progress*. The U.S. Regional Survey, Philadelphia, Pa.
Lass, Roger. 1969. 'On the Derivative Status of Phonological Rules: The Function of Metarules in Sound Change'. Bloomington: IU Linguistics Club.
Lieber, Rochelle. 1979. 'On Middle English Lengthening in Open Syllables', *Linguistic Analysis* 5.1.1-27.
Lindau, Mona. 1978. 'Vowel Features'. *Language* 54.541-63.
Luick, Karl. 1899. 'Ueber die Entwicklung von ae. ŭ-, ĭ- und die Dehnung in offener Silbe überhaupt'. *Archiv für das Studium der neueren Sprachen*, 102:43-84, 103:55-90.
----------. 1914-21. *Historische Grammatik der englische Sprache*. Oxford: Basil Blackwell.
Malsch, Derry L. and Roseanne Fulcher. 1975. 'Tensing and Syllabification in Middle English', *Language* 51.2.303-14.
Minkova, Donka. 1982. 'The Environment for Middle English Open Syllable Lengthening'. *Folia Linguistica Historica* 3.29-58.
Orton, Harold. 1952. 'The Isolative Treatment in Living North-Midland Dialects of OE ĕ Lengthened in Open Syllables in Middle English'. *Leeds Studies in English and Kindred Languages*, #7-8.
Stockwell, Robert P. 1952. *Chaucerian Graphemics and Phonemics: A Study in Historical Methodology*. Unpublished dissertation.
----------. 1961. 'The Middle English "Long Close" and "Long Open" Mid Vowels'. The University of Texas *Studies in Literature and Language* 2.4.529-38.
----------. 1973. 'Problems in the Interpretation of the Great English Vowel Shift'. *Studies in Linguistics in Honor of George L. Trager*, ed. M. Estellie Smith. The Hague: Mouton.
----------. 1978. 'Perseverance in the English Vowel Shift'. *Recent Developments in Historical Phonology*, ed. Jacek Fisiak. The Hague: Mouton.
Trnka, Bohumil. 1959. 'A Phonemic Aspect of the Great Vowel Shift'. *Mélanges de linguistique et de philologie, Fernand Mossé in Memoriam*. Paris: Didier.
Vachek, Josef. 1959. 'Notes on the Quantitative Correlation of Vowels in the Phonematic Development of English'. *Mélanges Mossé*.

PRELIMINARIES TO THE LINGUISTIC ANALYSIS OF OLD ENGLISH GLOSSES AND GLOSSARIES

THOMAS E. TOON
University of Michigan

Some of the oldest attestations of written English are found in occasional glosses in early Latin manuscripts or in the first glossaries (apparently compiled from collections of such glosses). This paper is a preliminary re-examination of the methods employed and the problems encountered in dealing with this particularly difficult source of data for the study of Old English and the Anglo-Saxon period. Fortunately, excellent scholars have blazed the way, and a good place to begin is acknowledgment of some debts. A.S. Napier (1900) established the base corpus with his meticulously accurate *Old English Glosses*. Napier noticed some dry point annotations, but made no attempt to read them systematically:

> In some of the MSS. containing glosses written in ink we find other glosses merely scratched with the stylus without any colouring matter. These scratched glosses are sometimes perfectly plain and easy to read, whilst in other cases they are only visible in a good light, and when the MS. is held at a certain angle. Sometimes they are so faint that it is impossible to decipher them at all. (1900: xxxiii)

Herbert Dean Meritt (1945) printed many of the few inked glossed which escaped Napier's attention and pioneered the extraordinarily difficult work of hunting out and then reading scratched glosses. R.I. Page has elaborated our knowledge of scratched glosses (1973, 1979, 1981) and has fruitfully initiated the review of methods in dealing with scratched glosses (1982). N.R. Ker (1957) set new standards with his *Catalogue of Manuscripts Containing Anglo-Saxon*, ever a source of fresh insight. Rene Derolez (1957), followed by Louis Goossens (1974), filled the last major gap in the corpus with their work on the Aldhelm glosses in *Brussels Royal 1630*, while Michael Lapidge and Michael Herren (1979) have made Aldhelm's torturous Latin accessible to wider audiences through their careful translations. While a review of nearly a century of work will almost necessarily be critical of some aspects of prior scholarship, that scholarship provides us with the solid base necessary to advance the study.

It was, then, in the context of a well developed field of enquiry that I devoted recent trips to the British Library and to the Apostolic Library to a further test of R.I. Page's suggestions that considerable amounts of Old English material continue to remain undiscovered and unprinted and especially 'that the various Anglo-Saxon libraries contain many more of these [scratched] glosses as yet unfound.' (1981: 105) Because the British Library manuscripts are probably the most extensively studied remnants of the Anglo-Saxon period, they seemed a particularly good test case. I went in search of new material, that is new glosses, and I am happy to be able to report success. The following will give some idea of the sort of things still to be uncovered, before we consider just how such discoveries might be useful to historical linguists.

Cotton Tiberius C.ii: Meritt mentioned that there were a number of glosses here that he could not read. There are, indeed, a number that I am able to read, including some which Meritt read apparently without undue difficulty. On the other hand, this manuscript (and a number of the other manuscripts I am about to mention) has glosses which I can read quite easily, but must have given Meritt trouble, as he does not mention them. I sometimes transcribe what is for me an "easy" scratched gloss only to discover that Meritt missed it, while I might as well have to hunt carefully even to find glosses which Meritt has read with confidence, but I am hardly able to see. I offer these facts not as criticism of Meritt's work, but as invitation to others who will no doubt see glosses both of us have missed.

As further complication, the scratches in this manuscript have apparently been put there by several different scribes, working in very different styles and possibly at different times. Although one rarely feels confident about distinguishing between the contributions of different scribes, this case presents glosses scratched in two quite easily identified styles. One set of glosses was added mostly in the top and bottom margins in a large rough and roundish hand; another group are interlinear and written in a small, careful and pointed hand. They might have been written by the same scribe, but they are different enough

in character that readers of the printed edition should
have the difference indicated for them. That is especially
true as preliminary readings also hint at tantalizingly
different language varieties in the same text, for example,
in their approach to the rounding and raising of Germanic
*a before nasals and the loss of h in initial clusters.
Sifting out these different strands will help us approach
such questions as whether these language differences are
to be considered part of the range of differences among
contemporaries in the same community or to be attributed
to different eras and locales.

Cotton Tiberius A.xiv: While this very important early
manuscript of Bede's history was damaged in the fire, it
is understudied, and I expect has secrets to yield. I saw
the hints of scratches in several places, but I was unable
to read them as I reserved work on bright and sunny days
to more obvious glosses.

Royal 13.A.xv (*Vita Guþlaci*), Add. 40000 (Gospel),
Cotton Vespasian D.xiv (Isidore's *Synonyma*): I continue
to make discoveries in these texts. The Isidore manuscript
is a particularly rich source of unread scratches. Meritt
read some twenty of these, and Page (1981) added another
thirteen. I estimate that there are about a hundred more
to be read, but it won't be easy. Very difficult glosses
remain in *Harley 3826* and *Cotton Vitellius A.xix*. Few of
these glosses would be obvious to a casual observer since
they are often very faint and require focusing one's eyes
on the surface behind the inked glosses. I encourage
others to hunt for what we have failed to see or had
trouble seeing.

In a sampling of Lorsch manuscripts in the Vatican,
especially of those with clear orthographic or textual
Anglo-Saxon connections, I found new glosses in a wide
range of Germanic varieties (insular and continental).
This year one hundred or so of these manuscripts will
visit Heidelberg, their earlier home, and we can expect
a number of fresh discoveries. While perusing *Reg. Lat.
338*, I noticed a runic alphabet. Ker mentions it but does
not note that there are Old English names for the runes
although it is extremely well edited and explained in
Derolez's undercited, *Runica Manuscrita* (1954). Texts like
this have been largely ignored for some very informative
reasons. Principally they suffer from being lexically uninteresting; after all, how many attestations do we need
of the very standard and regular Anglo-Saxon names for
the runes? These texts can however be highly informative.

The presence of an Anglian fossil in a manuscript with late Old English additions is an important bit of data, especially to historical linguists, when the scribe preserves ancient features through unfamiliarity with Old English or by making highly instructive mistakes: reading *monn* as *moun*, reinterpreting the double vowel of *oos* in *cos* -- both easy orthographic confusions to a scribe ignorant of Old English.

Beginning this way helps emphasize that I began these re-examinations of early manuscripts because I was hunting for as yet unprinted materials, and in particular unattested words. In the process however, I began to consider other discoveries to be just as important. For example, I was again impressed with the striking differences between studying a text in a manuscript and studying the text in the printed sources that record the manuscript's contents. It is that impression which I wish to explore in greater detail in this report of work in progress and prospective review of the study of what Cameron termed "Occasional Glosses". His *A Plan for the Dictionary of Old English* (1973) records around one hundred individual sources for these glosses. Although authors like Bede, Isidore, and Prudentius were rather frequently glossed, Napier's original observation still holds: 'A glance...will show how largely the glosses taken from the works of Aldhelm preponderate.' (1900: xi) Indeed, since 3/4 of the manuscripts of Aldhelm's *De Laudibus Virginitatis* are glossed, that work is well suited to serve as a model of Anglo-Saxon practice in glossing and of the ways those glosses are presented in modern editions. By looking at the manuscript source of a set of glosses, we can re-examine the frames through which we view glosses and consider what class of "text" they have become for us. In the process we can evaluate the extent to which the "text" as received accounts for or fails to account for the data.

De Laudibus Virginitatis was a very popular text and survives in an extraordinary number of manuscripts (over 20) for a text dismissed by moderns as quaint and peculiar. This is some justice for that dismissal: the torturous interleafing of the Latin so typical of Aldhelm's prose, his self-conscious and arcane diction, his verbal games (like alliterating on the letter *p* for longer than modern decency allows). The extant manuscripts were all copied hundreds of years after Aldhelm wrote the text; clearly it was a perennial "best seller", probably as a school text. The manuscript tradition even includes the lure of a missing glossed text. Brenner mentions an unedited text in Hannover; Bouterwek (1853) even quotes some of the glosses. Holthausen and others (now including me) have hunted in vain for it, unless it's a garbled reference to one of the continental texts containing Old High German glosses.

The treatise was written to known historical persons, Hildelith the abbess at Barking and her companions. This sample (from the passage we will be examining) gives clues to why it might have been so frequently glossed:

> I had scanned [your letters] with the keen gaze of (my) eyes and had thought them over with a certain natural curiosity about hidden things--as, it is said, is innate in me--and had very much admired the extremely rich verbal eloquence and the innocent expression of sophistication, then, I say, the governor of lofty Olympus and the ruler of heaven rejoices with an inexpressible exultation on seeing, thus, the catholic maidservants of Christ--or rather adoptive daughters of regenerative grace brought forth from the fecund womb of ecclesiatical conception through the seed of the spiritual Word--growing learned in divine doctrine through (the Church's) maternal care, and like talented athletes under some experienced instructor training in the gymnasium through wrestling routines and gymnastic exercises, who eagerly win the crown of laborious contest and the prize of the Olympic struggle by the strenuous energies of their own exertions... (Lapidge and Herren: 59-60)

There are no inked glosses on the relevant folio, but Meritt prints three scratched glosses (with notes) from *Royal 5.E.xi* in the glossarial style initiated by Napier:

```
9v.   insitum        set
      curiositate    fyr  (for fyrwite)
      exerceri       bega (for began)
```

As an example first of how much more scratched material is legible, figure one presents the full page and [Meritt's reading] in context. Figure two places the scratches in *Royal 5.E.xi* in the further context of glosses from other manuscripts, keyed by letter and numeral[1]. In the collation, some of the seemingly arbitrary scratches begin to take on meaning, as the reader will notice. As the data presented are entirely fragmentary, I will leave fuller examples and detailed explication to another occasion.

The scribe who made scratches in *Royal 5.E.xi* may or may not have had eventual glossary-making in mind. He/she might have been looking at an exemplar which had written (or even scratched) glosses in it. Some of the markings suggest that the scribe was looking at more than one

British Library Ms. Royal 5.E.xi, 9^v
Scratched Glosses
[Meritt's Readings]

```
             8: þærg
scripturar(um . sagacissima     sermonu(m serie
   8:o                8:æ
patuer(unt; C(um)q(ue    singulos    epistolar(um text(us
recitans p(er)nicib(us pupillar(um optutib(us spe
cularer atq(ue naturali quada(m, ut m(ihi in
8:[set]                              8:[fyr]
situ(m fert(ur, latentiu(m rer(um curiositate c(on)tem
             8:m
plarer uberrima(m)q(ue uerbor(um facundia(m
8:ac þa
ac virginale(m urbanitatis disertitudine(m
                     8:gerindas       8:u
magnop(er)e admirarer .  en    i(n)qua(m    ineffabili
gratulat(ur tripudio ille sup(er)i rector Oli(m)pi
                              8:þ         8:þi
et reg/na/tor celi . cum talit(er catholicas    uerna
culas (Christ)i immo adoptiuas regeneran
tis gr(ati)e . filias   ex foecundo    eclesiastice
c(on)ceptionis ut(er)o spiritalis uerbi semine
p(ro)genitas . p(er) materna(m uiderit sollicitu
dine(m diuinis dogmatib(us erudiri ; Ac
uelut sagaces gymnosophistas sub p(er)i
tissimo quoda(m agonitheta palestri
cis disciplinis et gymnicis artib(us i(n gym
     8:[bega]
nasio exerceri . qui laboriosi certa
                        /mi
```

Figure One

British Library Ms. Royal 5.E.xi, 9^v
Scratches Collated with Glosses from other Mss.

```
                   7:wraet
                   8:þærg
                 9:on þære glæwestan
scripturar(um . sagacissima sermonu(m serie
                            8:æ
    8:o                B:ænli(p)ie
patuer(unt; C(um)q(ue    singulos    epistolar(um text(us
              9:swiftu(m   9:seona
recitans p(er)nicib(us pupillar(um optutib(us spe
              4:gecyndelic
cularer atq(ue naturali quada(m, ut m(ihi in
B:geset
8:set     4:saed                 8:[fyr]
situ(m   fert(ur, latentiu(m rer(um curiositate c(on)tem
                 8:m
        9:þa g(e)nihtsumestan
plarer uberrima(m)q(ue uerbor(um facundia(m
                                    9:glæwnysse
8:ac þa           9:burhspæce     6:gleawnesse
ac virginale(m    urbanitatis     disertitudine(m
9:þearle         9:efene     8:gerindas      8:u
magnop(er)e admirarer .   en    i(n)qua(m    ineffabili

gratulat(ur tripudio ille sup(er)i rector Oli(m)pi
                                                 8:þi
                                 8:þ         B:þinenne
et reg/na/tor celi . cum talit(er catholicas    uerna
                9:þa g(e)ræddan
culas (Christ)i immo adoptiuas regeneran
                 9:of þa(m tiddriendan
tis gr(ati)e . filias   ex foecundo   eclesiastice

c(on)ceptionis ut(er)o spiritalis uerbi semine...
```

Figure Two

manuscript of the text, or that the finished text was read against another exemplar at a later (?) time. The glossarial format unduly suggests a finished character to what on closer examination appear as jottings in progress while that format also encourages the habit of thinking of these annotations only as fodder for primitive lexicographers. Glosses were often other sorts of notes as well: indications of word class, clues to syntax, word associations rather than meanings, reminders of other contexts within which a difficult word is also known to occur, case markings (not to mention countless genuine mysteries). These various kinds of glosses were confusing to the medievals as well; for example, we find *alnus*, '*alder tree*' glossed as *scip*, modern *ship*, even among a clear list of kinds of trees.

Some scratches of the sort exemplified were apparently read by those who compiled the sources for the early glossaries, which may themselves have contained scratched glosses (other sorts of scratched annotations are common in the *Corpus Glossary*). The *Erfurt Glossary* has a number of highly suggestive mistakes. In one case we find a garbled *fiindi* where we would expect *gearnwinde*. From series of scratched or inked minims in say *uind-*, a scribe might change the *u* to an *f* if the gloss were unfamiliar to him. In a similar fashion, the *Erfurt* divergence of *foetribarn* from the parallel reading of *fosturbearn* in *Epinal* is easily explainable as stemming from a scratch which contained only the consonants, *ftrbrn*, as scratches often do. Spurious Latin words were often created out of unfamiliar Old English lemma; while in some cases the Old English (or the *s* which denotes it's Saxon origin) gets entertainingly incorporated into the Latin lemma. One wonders how much Old English material might be mined out of ghost words in the Latin Glossaries.

The printed page further obscures some major differences from the text in manuscript. All printed texts have the uniform format we expect of books; texts in modern editions tend to appear much more alike than they were in manuscripts. *Cleopatra* glossary, in edition, looks a lot like *Epinal* or *Corpus*. *Corpus* especially was a deluxe full folio production (perhaps a royal book) while *Cleopatra* was a very plain quarto. If one worked only with printed editions, one wouldn't know that the early glossary tradition was dramatically different from the crabbed practice so typical of later glossaries. Printed texts largely ignore or obscure the facts of ornamentation like the rich initials of *Corpus* or drawings common in Aldhelm and Prudentius manuscripts. Such difference as between economical and uneconomical manuscript formats is not easily conveyed in printed books and may be indicative of respect or potential use. *Royal 5.E.xi* looks like it was made with the intention of containing glosses, as were some of the early biblical texts.

Perhaps more importantly, the glossary view of glosses limits us from a full view of the role of the writer of inked and scratched glosses. The evidence cited above strongly suggests that glossators were not always only mere copyists. The work of annotation shows them to be users of texts as well as producers of texts. Careful examination of their notes can lead to speculation about what manuscript resources were available in a medieval library and even the uses to which those libraries were put. Glossators were perhaps collectors, perhaps teachers, in some cases clearly naive readers, maybe students. All of this leads away from a single framed vision of their work to raise questions of how these scribes worked, under what conditions, to what ends. In other words, the study of "occasional glosses" and related items can be approached from so many different perspectives that we must express surprise at how fully the lexicographical perspective has dominated, even obscured, our approach to this material. Through frequent and exclusive usage, the glossary becomes the single frame of perspective into which we slip all too easily. Our focus is unnecessarily limited to individual words in the context only of other individual words.

Editions make a series of claims well worth reconsidering. The printed text of scratches allows us to forget how different scratches are from an inked gloss. Inked glosses are more clearly a public record, while scratches might more reasonably have been a private note. The printed edition of the Latin text is one thing (and so edited); the inked (and perhaps scratched) glosses are then treated as a separate subject, ignoring potentials of intertextuality. In a curious way the Old English text is parasitic -- of interest only because it can be anchored from point to point by direct lexical contact to the Latin. In the manuscripts, glosses occur in the context of sentences and discourses, not single words. The fragmentation of the text leads to a simpleminded sense of completeness; having lined up glosses what more is there to do besides record them in our dictionaries.

A final example will demonstrate the kind of help these studies might be to historical linguists. The analysis of the linguistically heterogeneous data of the early glosses and glossaries is a multiply vexed issue. The interpretation of some of those difficult issues can be informed by establishing close ties between batches of glosses and individual aspects of the very complicated transmission of glossary materials. The heavy influence of Aldhelmian material in *Epinal-Erfurt* has been taken to suggest that Aldhelm might have compiled (or at least used) an archetype of that glossary. I am among those scholars who have argued that many of the features of the language of *Epinal* can be explained when viewed as a very early variety of Mercian Old English. Since the provenance of *Epinal* is uncertain, we need circumstantial secondary evidence of connections between *Epinal* and Mercia -- or active intellectual centers during the period of Mercian political and cultural domination (see Toon 1983). Mercia in fact dominated Kent just during the period in which there must have been active transmission of Aldhlem's works there. Vivien Law, in her insightful analysis of the glosses to the *ars Tatuini*, makes a solid connection between those glosses -- Latin, Old English, and Old English retranslated into Latin -- and the continental *Leiden* and *Erfurt Glossaries*. She carefully demonstrates how archaic linguistic forms were fossilized as scribes became less and less familiar with the Old English words which they were copying. The grammatical text, she establishes was written by the Mercian Tatwine before he received the pallium at Canterbury in his old age. It was glossed by students in his native Breedon or in Canterbury. Such explicit connections between a Mercian text and continental Glossaries which exhibit Mercian features are very important elements in our understanding of the linguistic complexities of this period and its texts.

NOTES

1. B = *Brussels Royal 1650*, 2 = *BL Royal 6.B.vii*, 4 = *CCCC 326*, 6 = *Bodley 97*, 7 = *BL Royal 6.A.vi*, 8 = *BL Royal 5.E.xi*, 9 = *Royal 5.F.iii*.

REFERENCES

Bouterwek, C.W. 1853. 'Angelsächsische Glossen.' *Zeitschrift für deutsches Altertum* 9. 401-530.
Derolez, R. 1957. 'Zu den Brüsseler Aldhelmglossen.' *Anglia* 74. 153-180.
Frank, Roberta & A. Cameron, eds. 1973. *A Plan for the Dictionary of Old English*. Toronto: University of Toronto Press.
Goossens, Louis. 1974. *The Old English Glosses of MS. Brussels, Royal Library, 1650*. Brussels.

Ker, Neil R. 1957. *Catalogue of Manuscripts Containing Anglo-Saxon*. Oxford: Oxford University Press.
Lapidge, Michael & M. Herron, translators. 1979. *Aldhelm: The Prose Works*. Cambridge: D.S. Brewer, Ltd.
Law, Vivien. 1977. 'The Latin and Old English Glosses in the *ars Tatuini*.' *Anglo-Saxon England* 6. 77-90.
Meritt, Herbert Dean 1945. *Old English Glosses*. New York: Modern Language Association of America.
Napier, Arthur S. 1900. *Old English Glosses*. Oxford: Oxford University Press.
Page, R.I. 1973. 'Anglo-Saxon Scratched Glosses in a Corpus Christi College, Cambridge, Manuscript.' In F. Sandgren, ed. *Otium et Negotium*. Stockholm.
Page, R.I. 1979. 'More Old English Scratched Glosses.' *Anglia* 97. 27-45.
Page, R.I. 1981. 'New Work on Old English Scratched Glosses.' *Occasional Papers in Linguistics and Language Teaching* 7.105-115.
Page, R.I. 1982. 'The Study of Latin Texts in Late Anglo-Saxon England [2]: The Evidence of the Glosses.' In Nicholas Brooks, ed. *Latin and the Vernacular Languages in Early Medieval Britain*. Leicester: University Press.
Toon, Thomas E. 1983. *The Politics of Early Old English Sound Change*. New York: Academic Press.

THE ROLE OF INFL IN WORD ORDER CHANGE

LISA DEMENA TRAVIS
McGill University

The goal of this paper is to give an account of the word order change from Old English to Modern English (Stockwell 1977) within the theoretical framework outlined in Chomsky (1981) and recent treatments of word order (Koopman 1984, Travis 1984). This is done with the aim of finding a syntactic explanation for why these word order changes took the form that they did. The claim made is that the INFL node is in a position where several contradictory demands are placed on it. Because no word order may satisfy all of these demands, a tension exists in any D-structure and it is this tension which allows for the reanalysis of certain S-structure variations of word order. The position of INFL also makes predictions concerning possible triggers for reanalysis.

This paper is in two parts: the first gives the necessary theoretical background and some current views on word order. The second part of the paper applies these theoretical notions to Stockwell's account of English word order change.

1.0 *Theoretical background*. Government Binding Theory of Chomsky (1981) represents a shift in transformational grammar from a system of rules to a system of principles and parameters. Principles encode language universals and parameters encode language variations.

1.1 *Movement rules*. In the transformational component which maps D-structure onto S-structure, there is only one maximally general movement rule of Move-α which moves anything anywhere. Overgeneration is restricted by other modules of the theory such as Government, Binding, Case Theory, etc. One example of a principle is Subjacency which states that movement may cross no more than one bounding node. The bounding nodes, however, are determined by language specific parametric values: S and NP are bounding nodes in English, S' and NP are bounding nodes in Italian (Rizzi 1982). Another principle restricts the movement of heads (Head Movement Constraint, Travis 1984) by stating that a head X may only move if it moves into the head Y which properly governs it (see 1.2 below for a definition of proper government). Languages, however, use head-movement for different purposes and to different extents. We will see in the second part of this paper that languages with verb-second effects (V2) move V to INFL and INFL to COMP to identify the heads of maximal projections.

1.2 *Phrase Structure Rules*. This new view of grammar is relevant to the problem of word order in that the shift away from rules implies a shift away from Phrase Structure Rules where both dominance and precedence relations were previously encoded. Parallel to Move-α, we will assume a maximally general rule of Generate-α which will again be restricted by principles and parameters.

Dominance relations. I will make the strong assumption that dominance relations are universal (see Hale 1982 for an opposing view) and are determined by two principles; X'-theory and the Principle of Full Interpretation, as they are stated below.

(1) X' (or XP) $\longrightarrow$ ... X ...

(2) The Principle of Full Interpretation (PFI):
Every element of a string must be licensed.
Licensing may take either of two forms:
(i) complementation
(ii) predication

X'-theory ensures that every maximal projection has a head while the PFI restricts the generation of maximal projections. Other parts of the theory, such as θ-theory which allows the assignment of θ-roles (thematic roles) only under government, will ensure that complements are in the government domain of the head.

With some additional assumptions, we can see how X'-theory and the PFI will provide us with the dominance relations of a full syntactic tree (with order still irrelevant at this point of the discussion). These additional assumptions are given below without further argument (for more discussion see Stowell 1981).

(3) a. S' is COMP'
    b. S is INFL'
    c. INFL' is the complement of COMP
    d. VP is the complement of INFL

For the embedded sentence 'that Mary will eat the carrots raw' (found within 'I believe that Mary will eat the carrots raw') we construct the following tree.

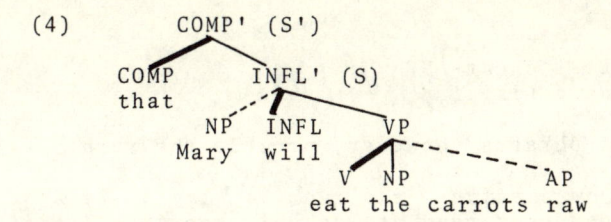

(4)
```
          COMP' (S')
         /        \
      COMP      INFL' (S)
      that     /    \
              NP    INFL    VP
             Mary   will   / | \
                          V  NP  AP
                         eat the carrots raw
```

The three ways of generating a node are encoded in the tree above by heavy lines (X'-theory), light solid lines (complementation - PFI), and dotted lines (predication - PFI). Relations set up by the PFI are used within other components of the grammar as well. We will see in the following section how relations between constituents are important for word order. Also, if we assume that proper government is the relation that holds between a head X, and both the YP complement of X and the head Y of the YP complement, we can describe restrictions on movement through the Empty Category Principle (see Chomsky 1981) and the Head Movement Constraint (see above).

Precedence Relations. The traditional way of accounting for the order of elements within a maximal projection was by a notion of headedness; languages where the verb preceded the direct object being head-initial, and those where the verb followed the direct object, head-final. It appears, however, that finer distinctions are necessary to account for languages that are neither head-initial nor head-final (see Koopman 1984, Travis 1984). Smaller domains within a VP can be described by the relationships of Case assignment and θ-role assignment. Within a VP, these domains are as given below.

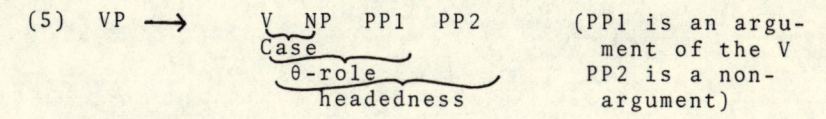

(5) VP ⟶   V NP PP1 PP2   (PP1 is an argu-
              ⎵Case⎵   ment of the V
              ⎵_θ-role_⎵   PP2 is a non-
              ⎵__headedness__⎵   argument)

An example of a language that makes use of such domains is Mandarin Chinese as described by Huang (1982). In Chinese, the object may either precede or follow the verb. When it precedes the verb, it appears with the object marker *ba*, and when it follows the verb, it appears alone.

(6) *ta pian-le Lisi*
    he cheat-ASP Lisi
    'He cheated Lisi.'

(7) *ta ba Lisi pian-le*
    he BA Lisi cheat-ASP
    'He cheated Lisi.'

All prepositional phrases, however, precede the verb.

(8) *Zhang-san zuotian   zai xuexiao kanjian-le Lisi*
    Zhang-san yesterday at school   see-ASP   Lisi
    'Zhang-san saw Lisi at school yesterday.'

This word order may be accounted for by stating that in Chinese, Case is assigned to the right, but otherwise the VP is head-final. In this view of word order, headedness is a default parameter which accounts for the position of elements that do not fall under more specific domains.

(9) Chinese VP: PP2 PP1 V NP
                             ‾‾‾‾‾
                              Case
                   ‾‾‾‾‾‾‾‾‾‾
                   headedness

Not only can we account for word order in this way, if we assume the Case Filter (all NPs must be assigned (abstract) Case), we can also explain why objects that precede the verb must appear with the object marker *ba*. Presumably, *ba* is needed to assign Case to the object NP since the NP is not in a position to be assigned Case by the V.

1.3 *The role of INFL.* Relations within the VP are clear. The verb is the head, it takes complements, and it assigns Case and θ-roles to these complements. The constituents that comprise INFL' do not form such uni-directional relations. Rather, there is a crisscrossing of dependencies as shown in (10) below.

(10) INFL'
         /   \
      NP   INFL   VP

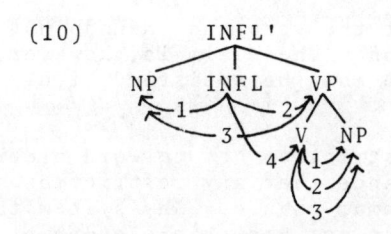

1 - Case
2 - complementation
3 - θ-roles
4 - morphology

While the V takes the NP as its complement and assigns it both Case and θ-role, INFL takes the VP as its complement, assigns Case to the subject NP, and the subject NP is assigned its θ-role by the VP through predication. Also, there is often a morphological dependency between INFL and the V.

I claim that it is this complex tangle of dependencies that allows surface word order variations to be reanalyzed as underlying word orders. More specifically, I claim that there are three contradictory demands on INFL which create a tension and promote reanalysis. These demands are given below:

A: *Adjacency to V.* For reasons of morphology, INFL is in an unmarked construction if it appears adjacent to the V. This is due to the possibility of morphological merger (Pranka 1983) in the case of two adjacent constituents which obviates the otherwise necessary head-movement of V into INFL.

B: *Adjacency to subject.* The effect of adjacency on Case assignment has been noted (e.g. Stowell) and accounts for why, in English, an NP argument which is assigned abstract Case by the V is closer to the verb than is a PP argument.

(11) *Mary put on the table books.

This may be extended to the Case relationship of the subject and INFL.

C: *Uniformity of Case direction.* In the unmarked situation Case will be assigned in the same direction by all categories. If the direct object follows the verb, the subject will follow INFL.

What is important to notice here is that it is impossible to satisfy all three demands at once. For example, in Modern English, where the order is S-INFL-V-O (Subject-INFL-Verb-Object), INFL is adjacent to the verb (A) and adjacent to the subject (B), but the verb and INFL do not assign Case in the same direction. The claim is, however, that as many demands as possible must be satisfied, i.e. two.

The relevance that this restriction has to word order change is the same as the relevance that any restriction on synchronic grammars has for grammar change. Any system that is not a possible grammar is also not a possible endpoint of a change. Chomsky's model of grammar which I am assuming is given below.

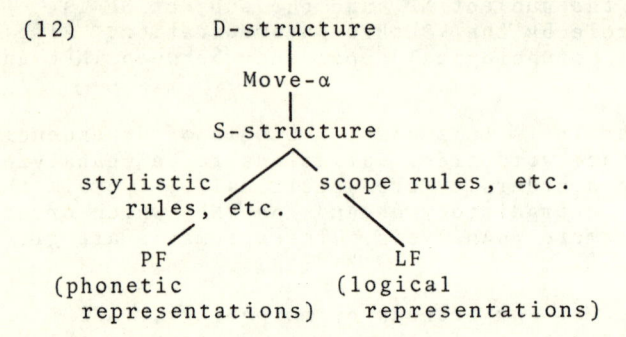

(12)
```
                    D-structure
                        |
                      Move-α
                        |
                    S-structure
                   /           \
       stylistic               scope rules, etc.
       rules, etc.
           |                       |
          PF                      LF
       (phonetic              (logical
    representations)       representations)
```

D-structure represents the underlying word order while S-structure represents surface variations on that order created by Move-α. What is important in the study of word order change is which S-structure variations are viable candidates for reanalysis. The trigger for the change will come from S-structure and it will affect the D-structure representation. Lightfoot (1979) predicts through his Transparency Principle that this reanalysis will have the effect of shortening the derivation of the string. In this case, when a prevalent S-structure is reanalyzed as a D-structure, Move-α is no longer a part of the derivation. However, only those S-structures that do not violate conditions on D-structure representations will be able to trigger a reanalysis. Possible grammar changes, then, are restricted in the same way possible grammars are restricted.

2.0 *Word order changes.* To account for the word order changes described by Stockwell, I will make use of the notion of Move-α to explain S-structure variations and the role of INFL to explain the reanalysis of certain variations as innovative D-structures.

The stages to be accounted for, taken from Stockwell's article, are given below. In the article, v and V are used to indicate inflected and uninflected verbs respectively. Within the context of this paper, I assume that the inflected verb in root clauses has undergone head-movement from the V position to INFL in order to identify the head of INFL'. The inflected verb, therefore, indicates the position of the INFL node. For this reason, each stage has been translated into a form that makes use of INFL.

(13) a. S-O-V-v   S-O-V-I   Stage I
      b. v-S-O-V   I-S-O-V   Stage II
      c. X-v-S-O-V   X-I-S-O-V   Stage III
      d. S-v-O-V   S-I-O-V   Stage IV
      e. S-v-V-O   S-I-V-O   Stage V

Stage I (S-O-V-I): Proto-Germanic appears to be strictly head-final in root as well as embedded clauses. I extend this to INFL' and propose the following structure for Stage I.

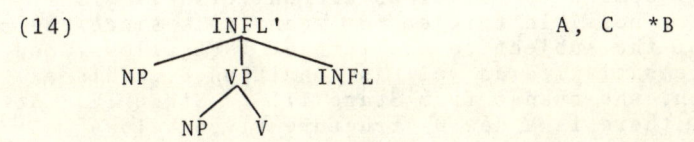

(14)   INFL'   A, C   *B
         ╱   │   ╲
        NP   VP   INFL
              ╱ ╲
             NP V

INFL, in sentence final position, satisfies Condition A and Condition C but not B since it is not adjacent to the subject.

Stage II (I-S-O-V): Stockwell argues that at this stage of the language, there is a rule of Comment Focusing which, in my account, has the effect of fronting the INFL node. Since this is an optional rule used to encode 'vividness of action', I am assuming that it involves a stylistic rule, i.e. a movement rule which appears in the component of the grammar mapping S-structure onto PF (see Rochemont 1978). As such it is not subject to the constraints on Move-α. Also, the structure produced is not a possible D-structure (it satisfies only Condition B) and therefore cannot be reanalyzed as an underlying word order.

Stage III (X-I-S-O-V): The stylistic movement of Stage II, however, does represent a possible syntactic rule of head-movement of INFL into COMP. Reanalysis of Comment Focusing as a syntactic rule predicts certain consequences. Stockwell describes the next change as occurring in two parts. First, 'linking words' such as 'then' and 'there' appeared before the sentence initial verb. Then other elements of the sentence appeared in sentence initial position. At the point where INFL fronting was a stylistic rule, sentence connectives could be analyzed, as in Modern English, as being adjoined to S (INFL'). Once INFL fronting was reanalyzed as head-movement into COMP, 'then' could be analyzed as being in the operator (wh-position) in COMP. As this happened, other maximal projections could move from a sentence internal position to COMP as long as there was head-movement of INFL to identify the head position of COMP. This gave rise to the surface word order variations below.[1]

(15) a. S-I-O-V
b. O-I-S-V
c. PP-I-S-O-V

Stage IV (S-I-O-V): The S-structure variations created in Stage III again raise the question of which variations are possible triggers for reanalysis. (15b) and (15c) violate the restriction that all languages have VPs (assuming, as I do, that all dominance relations are universal). (15a), however, is a possible trigger for reanalysis since the positioning of the subject to the left of INFL allows Condition C to be satisfied as well as Condition B. This explains, then, the change from Stage III to Stage IV. At this point, there is a new D-structure given below.[2]

(16)

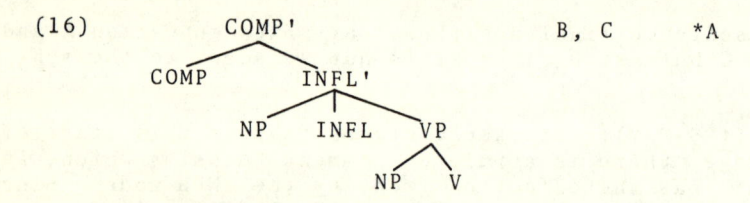

```
         COMP'                    B, C    *A
        /    \
     COMP    INFL'
            / |  \
          NP INFL VP
                  / \
                 NP  V
```

Stage V (S-I-V-O): Stockwell argues that the change from Stage IV to Stage V was caused by a process of exbraciation. Elements from within the VP were moved to the right of the verb. In the case of movement of the object, this would give the surface word order of S-I-V-O. Since this order satisfies both Condition A and Condition B, it is a possible trigger for reanalysis. A further trigger can be found in sentences which contain only one verb. In such a sentence, the verb will move to INFL and there will be no indication of a sentence final verb position. Both of these triggers are given below.

(17) a. S INFL t_i V O_i (exbraciation)
b. S V_i O t_i (single verb sentence)

Again, a new D-structure has been introduced.[3]

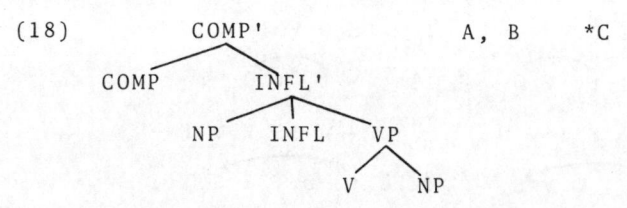

(18)
```
           COMP'              A, B    *C
        /       \
     COMP      INFL'
            /    |   \
          NP   INFL   VP
                     /  \
                    V    NP
```

In summary, only Stages I, IV, and V are possible D-structure word orders as dictated by principles of the theory and the demands on INFL. While Move-α may produce a range of S-structure variations (subject to restrictions on Move-α), only certain of those are possible triggers for reanalysis.

3.0 *Predictions*. The system described in this paper makes clear predictions. It has been suggested in the literature that there is a 'drift' to S-V-O word orders and that this is confirmed by word order changes such as the ones leading to Modern English. I have claimed here that these changes have nothing to do with drift but rather have purely syntactic explanations which are linked to the position of INFL. The reason why subject is reanalyzed as being in sentence initial position is because INFL is sentence initial. The prediction is that a language with a D-structure word order of SOVI will not be able to reanalyze as SVO through a process of exbraciation since SVOI is not a possible D-structure.

The word order changes suggested by the Carib languages as described by Derbyshire (1981) provide support for this prediction. Derbyshire claims that there is a word order change in the Carib languages from SOV to OVS which is puzzling in the face of the presumed drift to SVO. As there appears to be no systematic movement of the verb out of final position, I assume that the more conservative stage of the Carib word order change was, like Proto-Germanic, strictly head-final, i.e. SOVI. Given this, we can understand both why a change to SVO is not possible and why a rule which postposes subjects has triggered reanalysis. The relevant changes are given below.

(19)   ENGLISH   CARIB

　　　I.   S I O V   I.   S O V I

　　　IIa. S I t$_i$ V O$_i$ IIa. S t$_i$ V O$_i$ I

　　　　→ S I V O   → *S V O I

　　　IIb. t$_i$ I O V S$_i$ IIb. t$_i$ O V I S$_i$

　　　　→ *I O V S   → O V I S

When INFL is sentence initial, 'drift' of the subject to the first position is expected. However, as in the case of the Carib languages, where INFL is sentence final, just the opposite direction of drift has occurred. This distinction is predicted in a view of word order change which places importance on the position of INFL in the reanalysis of S-structure variations.

4.0 *Conclusion.* The narrow goal of this paper has been to investigate word order changes in the history of English in light of some speculations concerning the role of INFL in a syntactic structure. I have claimed that INFL, being unable to meet all of the demands placed on it, is a point of tension and thereby a pivotal position in word order change. Although many surface orders are created through both syntactic and stylistic movement rules, only a small number of those can cause a shift in the underlying word order. Reanalysis is both licensed and restricted by these demands on INFL; licensed because INFL can appear in different unmarked constructions, and restricted because a grammar must exhibit two of these constructions at any given point.

The broader goal of this paper is to call into question psychological notions such as drift which are often used as explanations in the study of syntactic change. The idea of drift implies goals and endpoints of change. This makes it difficult to understand why languages continually change, why they are not becoming more similar, and why some languages perversely change in a direction opposing the drift. By searching for syntactic explanations for change that take as triggers and motivations, elements which exist in the particular grammar, we may be closer to answering such questions.

NOTES

1. In this account, V2 effects in Germanic languages have a syntactic explanation. XPs may move to a position in COMP as long as the head of COMP is identified by head-movement of INFL into this position. This has the effect of placing the inflected verb after the topicalized constituent. In an embedded clause, the head of COMP is identified by a lexical complementizer.
2. Note should be taken here that, although Stage II is not a possible D-structure, this is not because INFL is sentence initial. Languages like Welsh and Irish are I-S-V-O (see Sproat 1985). This underlying word order is allowed precisely because of the ordering of the V and the O. In this case, both Condition B and Condition C are satisfied.
3. The same word order change is documented in Yiddish in Hall (1979). At the stage that she describes, Yiddish is underlyingly O-V, but there is productive extraposition of elements to the right of the verb. In Weinreich's grammar, Yiddish has made the change to V-O.

REFERENCES

Chomsky, N. 1981. *Lectures on Government and Binding*. Dordrecht: Foris Publications.
Derbyshire, D.C. 1981. 'A Diachronic Explanation for the Origin of OVS in some Carib Languages'. *Journal of Linguistics*. 17.209-219.
Hale, K. 1982. 'Preliminary Remarks on Configurationality'. *Proceedings from NELS 12*. GLSA, Amherst, MA.
Hall, B. 1979. 'Accounting for Yiddish Word Order'. *Current Issues in Linguistic Theory: Linear Order and Generative Theory*. ed. by J.M. Meisel & M.D. Pam, 253-287. Amsterdam: John Benjamins.
Huang, J. 1982. *Logical Relations in Chinese and the Theory of Grammar*. PhD. Dissertation, MIT.
Koopman, H. 1984. *The Syntax of Verbs: From Verb Movement in the Kru Languages to Universal Grammar*. Dordrecht: Foris Publications.
Lightfoot, D. 1979. *Principles of Diachronic Syntax*. Cambridge: Cambridge University Press.
Pranka, P. 1983. *Syntax and Word Formation*. PhD. Dissertation, MIT.
Rizzi, L. 1982. *Issues in Italian Syntax*. Dordrecht: Foris Publications.
Rochemont, M. 1978. *A Theory of Stylistic Rules in English*. PhD. Dissertation, UMass.
Sproat, R. 1985. 'Welsh Syntax and VSO Structure'. *Natural Language and Linguistic Theory* 3.2.
Stockwell, R. 1977. 'Motivations for Exbraciation in Old English'. *Mechanisms of Syntactic Change* ed. by C. Li. Austin: University of Texas.
Stowell, T. 1981. *Origins of Phrase Structure*. PhD. Dissertation, MIT.
Travis, L. 1984. *Parameters and Effects of Word Order Variation*. PhD. Dissertation, MIT.
Weinrich U. 1979. *College Yiddish*. New York: YIVO Institute for Jewish Research.

In the CURRENT ISSUES IN LINGUISTIC THEORY (CILT) series the following volumes have been published thus far, and will be published during 1985/86:

1. KOERNER, E.F. Konrad (ed.): *THE TRANSFORMATIONAL-GENERATIVE PARADIGM AND MODERN LINGUISTIC THEORY.* Amsterdam, 1975.
2. WEIDERT, Alfons: *Componential Analysis of Lushai Phonology.* Amsterdam, 1975.
3. MAHER, J. Peter: *Papers on Language Theory and History I: Creation and Tradition in Language.* Foreword by Raimo Anttila. Amsterdam, 1977.
4. HOPPER, Paul J. (ed.): *STUDIES IN DESCRIPTIVE AND HISTORICAL LINGUISTICS: Festschrift for Winfred P. Lehmann.* Amsterdam, 1977. Temporarily out of print.
5. ITKONEN, Esa: *Grammatical Theory and Metascience: A critical investigation into the methodological and philosophical foundations of 'autonomous' linguistics.* Amsterdam, 1978.
6. SLAGLE, Uhlan V. & Raimo ANTTILA: taken from the program.
7. MEISEL, Jürgen M. & Martin D. PAM (eds.): *LINEAR ORDER AND GENERATIVE THEORY.* Amsterdam, 1979.
8. WILBUR, Terence H.: *Prolegomena to a Grammar of Basque.* Amsterdam, 1979.
9. HOLLIEN, Harry & Patricia (eds.): *CURRENT ISSUES IN THE PHONETIC SCIENCES, Proceedings of the IPS-77 Congress, Miami Beach, Fla., 17-19 December 1977.* Amsterdam, 1979. 2 vols.
10. PRIDEAUX, Gary (ed.): *PERSPECTIVES IN EXPERIMENTAL LINGUISTICS. Papers from the University of Alberta Conference on Experimental Linguistics, Edmonton, 13-14 Oct. 1978.* Amsterdam, 1979.
11. BROGYANYI, Bela (ed.): *STUDIES IN DIACHRONIC, SYNCHRONIC, AND TYPOLOGICAL LINGUISTICS: Festschrift for Oswald Szemerényi on the Occasion of his 65th Birthday.* Amsterdam, 1980.
12. FISIAK, Jacek (ed.): *THEORETICAL ISSUES IN CONTRASTIVE LINGUISTICS.* Amsterdam, 1980.
13. MAHER, J. Peter with coll. of Allan R. Bomhard & E.F. Konrad Koerner (ed.): *PAPERS FROM THE THIRD INTERNATIONAL CONFERENCE ON HISTORICAL LINGUISTICS, Hamburg, August 22-26, 1977.* Amsterdam, 1982.
14. TRAUGOTT, Elizabeth C., Rebecca LaBRUM, Susan SHEPHERD (eds.): *PAPERS FROM THE FOURTH INTERNATIONAL CONFERENCE ON HISTORICAL LINGUISTICS, Stanford, March 26-30, 1980.* Amsterdam, 1980.
15. ANDERSON, John (ed.): *LANGUAGE FORM AND LINGUISTIC VARIATION. Papers dedicated to Angus McIntosh.* Amsterdam, 1982.
16. ARBEITMAN, Yoël & Allan R. BOMHARD (eds.): *BONO HOMINI DONUM: Essays in Historical Linguistics, in Memory of J. Alexander Kerns.* Amsterdam, 1981.
17. LIEB, Hans-Heinrich: *Integrational Linguistics.* 6 volumes. Amsterdam, 1984-1986. Vol. I available; Vol. 2-6 n.y.p.
18. IZZO, Herbert J. (ed.): *ITALIC AND ROMANCE. Linguistic Studies in Honor of Ernst Pulgram.* Amsterdam, 1980.
19. RAMAT, Paolo et al. (ed.): *LINGUISTIC RECONSTRUCTION AND INDO-EUROPEAN SYNTAX. Proceedings of the Coll. of the 'Indogermanische Gesellschaft' Univ. of Pavia, 6-7 Sept. 1979.* Amsterdam, 1980.
20. NORRICK, Neal R.: *Semiotic Principles in Semantic Theory.* Amsterdam, 1981.
21. AHLQVIST, Anders (ed.): *PAPERS FROM THE FIFTH INTERNATIONAL CONFERENCE ON HISTORICAL LINGUISTICS, Galway, April 6-10, 1981.* Amsterdam, 1982.

22. UNTERMANN, Jürgen & Bela BROGYANYI (eds.): *DAS GERMANISCHE UND DIE REKONSTRUKTION DER INDOGERMANISCHE GRUNDSPRACHE.* Akten, Proceedings from the Colloquium of the Indogermanische Gesellschaft, Freiburg, 26-27 February 1981. Amsterdam, 1984.
23. DANIELSEN, Niels: *Papers in Theoretical Linguistics.* Amsterdam, 1986. n.y.p.
24. LEHMANN, Winfred P. & Yakov MALKIEL (eds.): *PERSPECTIVES ON HISTORICAL LINGUISTICS. Papers from a conference held at the meeting of the Language Theory Division, Modern Language Ass., San Francisco, 27-30 December 1979.* Amsterdam, 1982.
25. ANDERSEN, Paul Kent: *Word Order Typology and Comparative Constructions.* Amsterdam, 1983.
26. BALDI, Philip (ed.) *PAPERS FROM THE XIIth LINGUISTIC SYMPOSIUM ON ROMANCE LANGUAGES, University Park, April 1-3, 1982.* Amsterdam, 1984.
27. BOMHARD, Alan: *Toward Proto-Nostratic.* Amsterdam, 1984.
28. BYNON, James: *CURRENT PROGRESS IN AFROASIATIC LINGUISTICS: Papers of the Third International Hamito-Semitic Congress, London, 1978.* Amsterdam, 1984.
29. PAPROTTÉ, Wolf & René DIRVEN (eds.): *THE UBIQUITY OF METAPHOR: Metaphor in Language and Thought.* Amsterdam, 1985.
30. HALL, Robert A., Jr.: *Proto-Romance Morphology.* Amsterdam, 1984.
31. GUILLAUME, Gustave: *Foundations for a Science of Language.* Translated and with an introd. by Walter Hirtle and John Hewson. Amsterdam, 1984.
32. COPELAND, James E. (ed.): *NEW DIRECTIONS IN LINGUISTICS AND SEMIOTICS.* Houston/Amsterdam, 1984. No rights for US/Can. *Customers from USA and Canada: please order from Rice University.*
33. VERSTEEGH, Kees: *Pidginization and Creolization: The Case of Arabic.* Amsterdam, 1984.
34. FISIAK, Jacek (ed.): *PAPERS FROM THE VIth INTERNATIONAL CONFERENCE ON HISTORICAL LINGUISTICS, Poznan, 22-26 August 1983.* Amsterdam, 1985. n.y.p.
35. COLLINGE, N.E.: *The Laws of Indo-European.* Amsterdam, 1985.
36. KING, Larry D. & Catherine A. MALEY (eds.): *SELECTED PAPERS FROM THE XIIIth LINGUISTICS SYMPOSIUM ON ROMANCE LANGUAGES.* Amsterdam, 1985.
37. GRIFFEN, T.D.: *Aspects of Dynamic Phonology.* Amsterdam, 1985. n.y.p.
38. BROGYANYI, Bela & Thomas KRÖMMELBEIN (eds.): *GERMANIC DIALECTS: LINGUISTIC AND PHILOLOGICAL INVESTIGATIONS.* Amsterdam, 1986. n.y.p.
39. GREAVES, William S., Michael J. CUMMINGS & James D. BENSON (eds.): *LINGUISTICS IN A SYSTEMIC PERSPECTIVE.* Amsterdam, 1986. n.y.p.
40. FRIES, Peter Howard and Nancy (eds.): *TOWARD AN UNDERSTANDING OF LANGUAGE: CHARLES C. FRIES IN PERSPECTIVE.* Amsterdam, 1985.
41. EATON, Roger, et al. (eds.): *PAPERS FROM THE 4th INTERNATIONAL CONFERENCE ON ENGLISH HISTORICAL LINGUISTICS.* Amsterdam, 1985.
42. MAKKAI, Adam & Alan K. MELBY (eds.): *LINGUISTICS AND PHILOSOPHY. Essays in honor of Rulon S. Wells.* Amsterdam, 1985.
43. AKAMATSU, Tsutomu: *The Theory of Neutralization and the Archiphoneme in Functional Phonology.* Amsterdam, 1986. n.y.p.